TABLE OF CONTENTS

IRISH EDUCATIONAL DOCUMENTS, VOLUME 2.

1922 - 1991

INTRODUCTION xii

I GENERAL

I.1 The Constitution of the Irish Free State (Saorstát Éireann), 1922 1
I.2 The Ministers and Secretaries Act 1924 3
I.3 School Attendance Act, 1926 6
I.4 Report of the Inter-Departmental Committee on the Raising of the School-Leaving Age, 1935 11
I.5 Bunreacht na hÉireann (Constitution of Ireland) 1937 13
I.6 School Attendance Bill, 1942 15
I.7 Report of the Departmental Committee on Educational Provision, June 1947 (Unpublished) 18
I.8 Setting up of the Council of Education, 1950 23
I.9 Report of the Commission on Youth Unemployment, 1951 27
I.10 Investment in Education, inaugural speech, October 1962 29
I.11 Second Programme for Economic Expansion, 1963 35
I.12 Third Programme for Economic and Social Development, 1969-1972 40
I.13 Ár nDaltaí Uile — All Our Children 1969 45
I.14 School Attendance Act, 1926 (Extension of Application) Order, 1972 47
I.15 Programme for National Development, 1978-1981 48
I.16 White Paper on Educational Development, 1980 50
I.17 Report of the Pupil Transfer Committee, 1981 53
I.18 The Way Forward — National Economic Plan, 1983-87 59
I.19 Programme for Government, December 1982 61
I.20 Building on Reality, 1985-1987 63
I.21 Programme for Action in Education, 1984-1987 66
I.22 Ages for Learning — Decisions of Government, May 1985 68

I.23 Report of the Committee on Discipline in Schools,1985 71
I.24 Programme for National Recovery, October 1987.......... 75
I.25 Programme for Economic and Social Progress, January 1991.......... 76
I.26 O.E.C.D. Review of National Policies — Ireland, 1991 81

II National Education

II.1 First National Programme of Primary Instruction, 1922 86
II.2 Circular to Inspectors, November 1922.......... 97
II.3 Second National Programme Conference, 1925-1926..... 99
II.4 Report of the Committee on Inspection of Primary Schools, 1927.......... 106
II.5 The Primary Certificate Examination, 1929 - 1967.......... 109
II.6 Circular to Managers, Teachers and Inspectors on Teaching through the medium of Irish; July 1931.......... 111
II.7 Revised Programme of Primary Instruction, 1934.......... 113
II.8 The Infant School - An Naí-Scoil - Notes for Teachers, 1951.......... 115
II.9 Report of the Council of Education on the Function and the Curriculum of the Primary School, 1954.......... 119
II.10 Primary Education Proposed Changes, December 1956. (Response of the Minister for Education to the Report of the Council of Education).......... 126
II.11 Removal of the requirement to teach through the medium of Irish, Circular 11/60 to Managers and Teachers, January 1960.......... 130
II.12 Investment in Education, 1965 (Primary Education)....... 131
II.13 Rules for National Schools under the Department of Education — 1965.......... 134
II.14 Abolition of the Primary Certificate Examination and introduction of the School Record Card System, March 1968.......... 137
II.15 Primary School Curriculum, Teachers' Handbook, 1971 141
II.16 Boards of Management of National Schools, 1975, 1980 and 1986.......... 150
II.17 The White Paper on Educational Development, 1980...... 154
II.18 Programme for Action in Education , 1984 - 1987.......... 157
II.19 Primary Education — a Curriculum and Examinations Board Discussion Paper, September1985.......... 159

Irish Educational Documents

Volume II

A selection of extracts from docu[illegible]
relating to the history of educa[illegible]
from 1922 to 199[illegible]
in the Irish Free [illegible]
and the Republic [illegible]

EDITED By ÁINE HYLAND [illegible]

C.I.C.E.

We are grateful to Ms. Imogen Stuart for permission to use a photograph of her sculpture in Tyrrellspass, Co. Westmeath, as part of the cover design.

ISBN 0 9509289 2 5

Text set in 10 and 11 pt Times.

Printed from camera-ready copy in the Republic of Ireland by the Leinster Leader, Naas, Co. Kildare.

Published by the Church of Ireland College of Education, Rathmines, Dublin 6, Ireland.

II.20 Report of the Review Body on the Primary Curriculum, 1990 163
II.21 Report of the Primary Education Review Body, 1990..... 169

III Post-Primary Education

Secondary

III.1 Dáil Éireann — Commission on Secondary Education; September 1921 - December 1922 178
III.2 Intermediate Education (Amendment) Act, 1924 182
III.3 The Report of the Department of Education for the School Year 1924/25 and the financial and administrative years 1924/5/6. Changes in Secondary Education 184
III.4 The introduction of Irish as an essential subject for the Intermediate and Leaving Certificate Examinations, 1928 and 1934 189
III.5 Changes in the Secondary Schools Programme 1939/40. 192
III.6 Report of the Council of Education on the Curriculum of the Secondary School, 1962 198

Vocational / Technical

III.7 Commission on Technical Education, 1927 206
III.8 Speech by the Minister for Education, John Marcus O'Sullivan, at the Second Stage of the Vocational Education Bill, 14 May 1930 209
III.9 The Vocational Education Act, 1930 214
III.10 Letter from the Minister for Education, John Marcus O'Sullivan, to Most Rev. D. Keane, Bishop of Limerick, dated 31st October, 1930 219
III.11 Apprenticeship Act, 1931 222
III.12 Memorandum V.40; Organisation of Whole-time Continuation Courses in Borough, Urban and County Areas, 1942 224
III.13 Report of the Commission on Vocational Organisation, 1944 233
III.14 Introduction of the Day Group Certificate Examination, 1947 235
III.15 Apprenticeship Act, 1959 238
III.16 Vocational Education (Amendment) Act, 1970 240

III.17 Establishment of Boards of Management of Vocational Schools — Circular Letter 73/74 — July 1974................ 242

Post-Primary

III.18(a) Tuarascáil Shealadach ón Choiste a Chuireadh i mbun Scrúdú a Dhéanamh ar Oideachas Iarbhunscoile, 1962 555
III.18 Statement by the Minister for Education, Dr. P.J. Hillery, in regard to Post-Primary Education, 20 May 1963........ 247
III.19 Investment in Education — 1966.................................... 252
III.20 Letter from George Colley, T.D., Minister for Education, to the Authorities of Secondary and Vocational Schools, January 1966.. 259
III.21 Speech made by Donogh O'Malley, T.D., Minister for Education, on 10th September 1966 announcing the introduction of free post-primary education..................... 263
III.22 Department of Education — Community School Document — October 1970.. 267
III.23 Report on the Intermediate Certificate Examination, 1975 273
III.24 White Paper on Educational Development, 1980............. 276
III.25 Community Colleges, 1980.. 277
III.26 Programme for Action in Education, 1984 - 1987............ 282
III.27 Vocational Preparation and Training Programmes, 1984 284
III.28 Partners in Education — Serving Community Needs. A Green Paper (November 1985).................................... 287
III.29 Curriculum and Examinations Board Publications
(a) Issues and Structures in Education September 1984
(b) In Our Schools, March 1986....................................... 291
III.30 Transition Year Programmes — guidelines for schools, January 1986.. 305
III.31 (a) The National Council for Curriculum and Assessment — A Guide to the Junior Certificate, 1989...................... 307
III.31 (b) N.C.C.A. The Junior Certificate Examination — Recommendations to the Minister for Education, 1990... 313
III.31 (c) N.C.C.A. The Curriculum at Junior Cycle — Curriculum Framework and Junior Certificate Requirements —a Position Paper, June 1991.................. 316
III.31 (d) N.C.C.A. The Curriculum at Senior Cycle: Structure, Format and Programmes — a Position Paper, June 1991 320
III.32 The National Council for Vocational Awards, 1991......... 322

IV TEACHERS — Education, Conditions of Service and Salaries, 1922-1991

IV.1 Teacher Training Colleges in Saorstát Éireann, (the Irish Free State) — Report of the Department of Education for the School Year 1923/24 326
IV.2 The National Programme of Primary Instruction, 1922; recommendations with regard to the training of teachers 328
IV.3 Setting up of the Preparatory Colleges — Dáil Debates, 24th February, 1926 329
IV.4 New Programme for the Training Colleges, 1932 331
IV.5 Report of Committee on Teachers' Salaries, 1949 335
IV.6 Conciliation and Arbitration Scheme, 1951 338
IV.7 Revocation of Rule 72(1) of Department's Rule (i.e. the revocation of the ban on married women teachers) January 1958 340
IV.8 Teachers' Salaries Committee, 1960 343
IV.9 Untrained Teachers — Transfer to Trained Scale, proposal of 22 November 1965 345
IV.10 Report of the Commission on Higher Education, 1967.... 347
IV.11 Ryan Tribunal on Teachers' Salaries, 1968 349
IV.12 H.E.A. Report on Teacher Education, 1970 352
IV.13 Setting up of Teachers' Centres, 1972 356
IV.14 Report of the Planning Committee on the Establishment of An Chomhairle Mhúinteoireachta, 1974 358
IV.15 Announcement of University Degrees for Primary Teachers, 1973 361
IV.16 Thomond College of Education, Limerick, Act, 1980...... 362
IV.17 Review Body on Teachers' Pay — Interim Report, 1980 365
IV.18 White Paper on Educational Development, 1980 368
IV.19 Report of Committee on Inservice Education, 1984 370
IV.20 Programme for Action in Education, 1984 - 1987 373
IV.21 Announcement of the closure of Carysfort College, February 1986 376
IV.22 Report of the Primary Education Review Body, 1990...... 379
IV.23 University of Limerick (Dissolution of Thomond College) Act, October, 1991 381
IV.24 O.E.C.D. Review of National Policies for Education in Ireland 383

IV.25 Memorandum of Understanding between Mary Immaculate College and the University of Limerick, November 1991 ... 388

V HIGHER EDUCATION

V.1 University Education (Agriculture and Dairy Science) Act, 1926 ... 391
V.2 University College Galway, Act, 1929 ... 394
V.3 Bunreacht na hÉireann, 1937 ... 397
V.4 Institute for Advanced Studies Act, 1940 ... 397
V.5 Report of Commission on Accommodation Needs of the N.U.I. Colleges, 1959 ... 401
V.6 Report of the Board of Visitors on U.C.D. 1960 ... 404
V.7 Report of the Commission on Higher Education, 1967 ... 406
V.8 Report of the Steering Committee on Technical Education, 1967 ... 415
V.9 Minister O'Malley's University Merger Proposals, 1967 418
V.10 Minister Lenihan's Statement of Government Policy on Higher Education, 1968 ... 421
V.11 The Higher Education Authority Act, 1971 ... 424
V.12 Some Higher Education Authority Reports ... 427
V.13 National College of Art and Design Act, December 1971 432
V.14 The National Council for Educational Awards ... 434
V.15 Coalition Government Plans for a "Comprehensive" Higher-Level Sector, 1974 ... 438
V.16 Co-operative Agreement between the University of Dublin (T.C.D.) and the City of Dublin Vocational Education Committee (CDVEC), 1976 ... 440
V.17 Reorganisation of the C.D.V.E.C's third level colleges into the Dublin Institute of Technology (DIT), 1978 ... 441
V.18 Legislation for NIHEL and NIHED ... 443
V.19 The White Paper on Educational Development, 1980 ... 446
V.20 Programme for Action in Education, 1984-87 ... 448
V.21 Partners in Education — Green Paper, 1985 ... 450
V.22 Report of the International Study Group on Technological Education, 1987 ... 452
V.23 University of Limerick and City of Dublin University Act, 1989 ... 454

VI Special Issues

Special Education

VI.1 Report of the Commission of Inquiry on Mental Handicap, 1965 458
VI.2 Special Education in Ireland - an article by T.A. ÓCuilleanáin, Assistant Chief Inspector, in Oideas, Autumn1968 466
VI.3 Report of a Committee set up to consider the Provision of Educational Facilities for the Children of Itinerants, 1970 469
VI.4 Report of the Committee on the Education of Children who are Handicapped by Impaired Hearing, February 1972 473
VI.5 Report of the Committee on the Education of Physically Handicapped Children, 1981 476
VI.6 The White Paper on Educational Development, 1980 (Special Provision) 479
VI.7 Report of a Working Party on the Education and Training of Severely and Profoundly Mentally Handicapped Children in Ireland, January 1983 482
VI.8 Programme for Action in Education, 1984 -87 485
VI.9 Guidelines on Remedial Education, 1987 488
VI.10 Educational Provision for the Children of Travelling Families, 1989 490
VI.11 Report of the Primary Education Review Body, 1990 493
VI.12 Needs and Abilities — a policy for the intellectually disabled. Report of the Review Group on Mental Handicap Services, July 1990 496

Reformatory Schools

VI.13 Report of the Commission of Inquiry into the Reformatory and Industrial School System, 1934-1936... 499
VI.14 Report of the Committee on Reformatory and Industrial Schools, 1970 503

Adult Education

VI.15 Report of the Committee on Adult Education in Ireland 1973 509

VI.16 Lifelong Learning - Report of the Commission on Adult Education, 1983 512

Broadcasting

VI.17 Report of the Educational Broadcasting Committee, October 1982 517

General Equality

VI.18 Action Handbook — how to implement gender equality, 1985 521

The Arts

VI.19 The Place of the Arts in Irish Education — Report of the Arts Council's Working Party on the Arts in Education 1979 (by Ciarán Benson) 523
VI.20 The Arts in Education — a Curriculum and Examinations Board Discussion Paper, 1985 526
VI.21 Access and opportunity — a White Paper on the Arts, 1987 529
VI.22 The Arts Council and Education 1979-1989 531

The Irish Language

VI.23 Report of the Commission on the Restoration of the Irish Language — Summary of the Final Report, 1963 534
VI.24 White Paper on the Restoration of the Irish Language, 1965 538
VI.25 Comhairle na Gaeilge — Irish in Education, 1974 540
VI.26 The White Paper on Educational Development, 1980 544
VI.27 Action Plan for Irish, 1983-1986 547
VI.28 Programme for Action in Education, 1984-1987 551
VI.29 Tuarascáil an Chomhchoiste um Oideachas sa Ghaeltacht, 1985 553

APPENDIX I 561

APPENDIX 2 563

Acknowledgements

In 1984, the Church of Ireland College of Education celebrated its centenary. To mark the centenary, an exhibition of educational documents and materials was mounted by the college and a number of educational historians from University Education Departments and Colleges of Education came together to prepare a catalogue of the exhibition. In the course of that work it was agreed that it would be useful to publish extracts from some key educational documents and a committee was formed to carry out the task. Volume I of Irish Educational Documents which was published in 1987 contained a selection of extracts from documents relating to the history of Irish education from the earliest times to 1922. The current volume, which contains extracts from documents relating to the history of education in the Irish Free State and the Republic of Ireland from 1922 to 1991 is the second volume of the series. A third volume, relating to education in Northern Ireland from 1922 to 1991 is also in the course of preparation.

The members of the committee who worked on volumes I and II consisted of Kenneth Milne and Sydney Blain, former and present principals of the Church of Ireland College of Education; Kieran Byrne, Mary Immaculate College of Education, Limerick; John Coolahan, Education Department St. Patrick's College, Maynooth; Harold Hislop, Whitechurch N.S., Rathfarnham; Áine Hyland, Education Department University College, Dublin; Elizabeth MacArthur O'Kelly, Dublin; and Susan Parkes, School of Education, Trinity College, Dublin. All members of the committee contributed in various ways to the preparation and production of this volume. Sections I, II and VI as well as the secondary and post-primary sub-sections of section III were written by Áine Hyland. Kieran Byrne contributed the section on Vocational/Technical Education (documents III.7 to III.17). Susan Parkes was responsible for Section IV and John Coolahan contributed Section V. The cover design is the work of Elizabeth MacArthur O'Kelly, with help and advice from Harold Hislop. Risteárd Giltrap of Coláiste Móibhí, Rathmines, helped to prepare the section on the Irish language (documents VI.23 to VI.28) and the related section in the Introduction. The editors are very grateful for the work of these contributors as well as for the advice and support of the other members of the committee.

We would like to record our deep appreciation of the help and financial support given towards the publication of this book by the Research Committee of the Department of Education, Marlborough Street, Dublin 1; by the Church of Ireland College of Education and by the Faculty of Arts Revenue Committee, University College, Dublin.

We are grateful to the staff of the library of University College, Dublin, particularly Tony Ekloff of the Government Publications section; to the staffs of the libraries of Trinity College, the Church of Ireland College, Mary Immaculate College and St. Patrick's College, Maynooth. We are also indebted to Oliver Marshall, librarian in the Department of Education, Marlborough Street for his help. We are grateful to Tomás Ó Domhnalláin, former Divisional Inspector of Schools, for access to his extensive collection of Department of Education circulars dating from the 1930s.

We would like to pay a special tribute to Monica Dowdall who typed the complete manuscript, often from poor quality originals and who patiently retyped some sections when the authors and editors introduced additions and amendments. She was also responsible for lay-out and for the preparation of the camera-ready copy of the entire volume. She was committed to the project throughout and it was a pleasure to work with her.

For permission to reproduce extracts from reports, acts of the Oireachtas, etc., our thanks are due to the following:

The Controller of the Stationery Office, Dublin, for all reports, documents and papers published by the Stationery Office; Albert Ó Ceallaigh, Chief Executive of the National Council for Curriculum and Assessment for reports and discussion documents published by the Curriculum and Examinations Board and the National Council for Curriculum and Assessment; the National Council for Educational Awards and the Higher Education Authority for documents relating to higher education.

ÁINE HYLAND AND KENNETH MILNE

INTRODUCTION

Volume I of *Irish Educational Documents,* which contained extracts from documents relating to Irish education from the earliest times to 1922, was published in 1987. It was our intention to publish a second volume containing documents on education in Ireland, north and south, from 1922 to the present day. The task proved to be much more demanding than we originally anticipated and the number of documents which we identified as worthy of consideration was considerably greater than we expected. Difficult decisions had to be taken and eventually we decided to confine our attention to "official" documents, which we define as those which were published by the Stationery Office, or issued by the Minister or the Department of Education or by commissions or committees set up by the Minister or statutory bodies dealing with education or education-related issues. Even with this we found that it was not possible to include material relating to Ireland, north and south, in one volume and we decided that two further volumes would be required — volume 2 (the present volume) relating to education in the south and volume 3 (on which work is in progress) relating to education in the north.

Some of the documents contained in this volume, particularly more recent publications, are readily available. Others are not as easily accessible and were found by us only after much searching. We tried to include as many key documents as we could and we believe that by bringing together in one volume extracts from so many and such varied documents, research into Irish education since the foundation of the Irish Free State will be made easier.

This volume is very long. It runs to almost 600 pages even though we have excluded many documents which we would have liked to include. For example, we did not include publications from the teacher unions, such as the *Plan for Education* published by the Irish National Teachers' Organisation in 1947 or that organisation's more recent and impressive series of discussion documents on various aspects of primary education. Policy and discussion documents of the Association of Secondary Teachers of Ireland; the Teachers' Union of Ireland and the Irish Federation of University Teachers are not included. Significant statements from the main Churches, often in response to government policy, had to be excluded as also had key documents from management bodies such as the Catholic Primary School Managers Association, the General Synod, Board of Education of the Church of Ireland, the Joint Managerial Body and the Conference of Major Religious Superiors. Reports and documents of influence and significance in education from relatively new agencies such as the Educational Research Centre, the Economic and Social Research Institute, the National Economic and Social Council and Institiúid Teangeolaíochta na hÉireann have also been excluded. We considered including extracts from statements affecting education issued by the Council of Ministers of the European Community since 1975 as many of these statements influenced policy decisions here in Ireland. However, we reluctantly had to exclude these documents because of lack of space. Similarly, some interesting documents relating to training, particularly some issued by ANCO and its successor organisation, FÁS, have not been included.

Another difficult decision related to what extract or extracts should be chosen from the various documents. Many of the extracts are very short — some readers may well consider some of them too short to provide a satisfactory overview of the content of the report or statement in question. However, in as many cases as possible, we have provided a reference to the source of the document at the end of the volume and if the extract is unsatisfactory for the readers' purpose, they may wish to refer to the full text of the document.

In this volume we tried to adopt the same format as we adopted for the period 1800 to 1922 in Volume 1 where we distinguished between national, intermediate, technical and university education and provided a separate section for each level. This was relatively straightforward in relation to the 19th century when education was clearly compartmentalised and there was little or no overlap between the different levels of education. In the 20th century the situation is less clearcut. One of the first actions of the new Free State government in 1924 was to set up of a single Department of

Education with a Minister responsible for all levels of education (I.2). During the first forty years of independence, many government decisions related to education generally but official documents tended to relate specifically to either national, secondary, vocational/technical, or third level education. From the 1960s onwards, documents relating to education tended to be more inclusive and statements on post-primary education referred to both secondary and vocational education as the distinction between secondary and vocational education became less defined. Moreover, many key educational documents referred to education at all levels and extracts from such documents are included in more than one section.

While our decision to end the collection at the end of 1991 was a pragmatic one, 1991 may well prove to be the end of an era in Irish education. The publication of the historic Green Paper — *Education for a Changing World* — by Séamus Brennan, T.D., Minister for Education in 1992 has been regarded by some educational commentators as heralding the beginning of a new age in Irish education and will undoubtedly be one of the most significant educational documents of the twentieth century.

Section I is a general section and includes documents which provided an important basis for educational policy and decision-making. Extracts from the limited legislation which underpins Irish education are included in this section — the *Ministers and Secretaries Act, 1924* (I.2), the *School Attendance Act, 1926* (I.3), the *School Attendance Amendment Act 1972* (I.14) as well as the *Constitution of the Irish Free State 1922* (I.1) and the *Constitution of Ireland (1937)* (I.5). We also include an extract from the Supreme Court ruling on the ill-fated *School Attendance Bill, 1942* (I.6) since it highlights the difficulty of drafting educational legislation which would not be in conflict with the provisions of the Constitution of Ireland. This section also refers to the setting up of inquiries on education — the Council of Education in 1950 (I.8) and *Investment in Education in 1962* (I.10) — which produced major reports, extracts from which appear in later sections of the volume. Some general reports which impinge on more than one level of education are included in this section — the *Report of the Commission on Youth Unemployment*

1951 (I.9), the *Report of the Pupil Transfer Committee 1982* (I.17), *Ages for Learning — Decisions of Government 1985* (I.22), *Report of the Committee on Discipline1985* and the *O.E.C.D. Review of National Educational Policies—Ireland 1991* (I.26).

A new era of economic expansion from the late 1950s onwards had a beneficial effect on Irish education. Economic documents such as the *Second Programme for Economic Expansion 1963* (I.11) and the *Third Programme for Economic and Social Development 1969-72* (I.12) contain important sections on education as well as the *Programme for National Development 1978-81* (I.15), *The Way Forward — National Economic Plan 1983-87* (I.18), *Programme for Government, December 1982* (I.19), *Building on Reality 1985-87* (I.20), *Programme for National Recovery 1987* (I.24) and the *Programme for Economic and Social Progress 1991* (I.25). We are aware that some policy documents prepared by political parties in opposition during these years contained significant sections on education. However, we reluctantly decided not to include extracts from these documents although we are aware that some of them contributed to educational policy when those parties subsequently came to power.

Section II contains extracts from documents relating to national education. During the first decades of independence, education policy — particularly at primary school level — concentrated almost exclusively on the revival of the Irish language, history, music and culture. This is reflected in documents II.1, II.2, II.3, II.6 and II.7 — all of which concentrate on the language policy and its implementation. (This issue is referred to again later in the volume in documents VI.23 to VI.28). The *Report of the Committee on Inspection 1927* (II.4) raised the issue of a national examination at primary level and the short extract in II.5 attempts to capture the tone of the debate in relation to the introduction of a compulsory Primary Certificate examination. The abolition of the Primary Certificate Examination in 1967 and its replacement by a school record card system is referred to in II.14. *The Infant School — Notes for Teachers 1951* (II.8) presaged the beginning of a shift away from the emphasis on language revival and the re-emergence of a concern with the individual child which had been educational policy in 1900 (see Volume I - III.8). A circular in 1960 which removed the requirement to teach through the medium of Irish (II.11) is included in full as some commentators have argued that this policy decision played a significant part in the alleged subsequent fall in standards in the language at primary level.

The *Report of the Council of Education on the Function and Curriculum of the Primary School* which was published in 1954 was an important and comprehensive document and extracts from it are included in II.9. Extracts from the response of the Minister for Education, General R. Mulcahy, to this report are provided in document II.12 and as far as we are aware, this is the first time that the response of the Inter-Party government to the report of the Council of Education has been published. Many of the policy decisions made by General Mulcahy in 1956 were not formally included in the Rules for National Schools until 1965 and extracts from the 1965 version of the Rules are provided in II.13.

Many people would hold that the most significant document relating to Primary education since the foundation of the state was the *Primary School Curriculum, Teachers' Handbook, 1971* (II.15). The 1970s also saw the setting up of Boards of Management of national schools and extracts from the developing versions of the *Constitution of Boards* are included in II.16. Sections of the *White Paper 1980* and the *Programme for Action in Education 1984-87* which focused on primary education are included in II.17 and II.18. Short extracts from two major reports on primary education in 1990 — the *Report of the Review Body on the Primary Curriculum* (II.20) and the *Report of the Primary Education Review Body* (II.21)— are included to indicate the general flavour of these reports. These reports are readily available and readers who are interested in this period are encouraged to read the full reports.

Section III covers all aspects of post-primary education. We had difficulty in deciding how best to present this section and after some discussion we agreed that we would distinguish between secondary and vocational/technical for the period before 1960 but that we would integrate all sectors of post-primary for the period after 1960. The *Intermediate Education Amendment Act* of 1924, which is a very short document is included in full (III.2). Documents relating to the curriculum of secondary schools include extracts from the report of the *Dáil Commission on Secondary Education 1922* (III.1), from the annual reports of the Department of Education (III.3 and III.4) and a circular of 1939 (III.5). It is appropriate that extracts from the *Report of the Council of Education on the Curriculum of the Secondary School, 1962* (III.6) bring this section to the end as that report marked the end of a conservative era in secondary education.

Documents III.7 to III.17 relate to vocational and technical education during the same period. The first four extracts relate to a key period of change and development in technical education in Ireland. The *Report of the Ingram Commission in 1927* (III.7) was a far-seeing document which led to the *Vocational Education Act* of 1930 (III.9). Documents III.8 and III.9 provide some insights into the educational issues which concerned Church and State around this period. These concerns led to a clarification of the provisions of the act which is contained in *Memorandum V.40* (III.12). Extracts from the *Report of the Commission on Vocational Organisation* are included (III.13) since this report is one of the few reports of the period which commented on vocational education.

Post-primary education underwent a fundamental change in the 1960s. Most educational commentators identify the report *Investment in Education* (III.19) as the catalyst for change, particularly at post-primary level, but we suggest that the impetus for change had begun before then. We publish here for the first time extracts from an unpublished report prepared by a committee of inspectors within the Department of Education in 1962 which recommended major reform of post-primary education in Ireland (III.18[a]). This document came to our attention too late to be included with the other extracts relating to post-primary education and it is included as an Addendum on page 555. Included in the section on post-primary education are extracts from key Ministerial interventions in the 1960s — a statement by Patrick Hillery in May 1963 announcing the decision to build the first comprehensive schools (III.18); a letter from George Colley in January 1966 appealing for co-operation between secondary and vocational schools and Donagh O'Malley's speech in September 1966 announcing the introduction of free post-primary education. Extracts from a Department of Education statement in 1970 clarifying the proposal to set up community schools are also included (III.22). The report of the *Committee on the Intermediate Certificate Examination* in 1975 made proposals for the reform of the Intermediate Certificate examination which are included in II.23 but these proposals were not implemented.

Post-primary developments in the 1980s are covered in extracts III.24 to III.31. Curricular issues predominated during this period and extracts relating to vocational preparation and training programmes (III.27) and the transition year option (III.30) are included as well as extracts from publications of the Curriculum and Examinations Board (III.29), and the National Council for Curriculum and Assessment (III.31). Extracts on post-primary education from the *1980 White Paper* (III.24) and from the *Programme for Action in Education 1984-7* (III.26) are also included as is an extract from *Partners in Education* (III.28) — a Green Paper published in 1985 which proposed the setting up of Local Education Councils. The section ends with an extract from the terms of reference of the National Council for Vocational Awards which was set up at the end of 1991 (III.32).

Section IV relates to teachers — their education, conditions of service and salaries. Document IV.1 provides information on primary teacher training colleges in 1922 and document IV.2 includes the recommendations with regard to the training of teachers of the First National Programme Conference 1922. The setting up of the Preparatory Colleges is the subject of IV.3 and extracts from the new programme for the training colleges introduced in 1932 are given in IV.4. The circular which revoked the ban on the employment of married women teachers in 1958 (IV.7) is one of the few documents in the volume which refers to the discrimination against women in education in Ireland — we failed to locate any document relating to the introduction of the ban in the 1930s. Changes in the delivery of teacher education were recommended in the *Report of the Commission on Higher Education 1967* (IV.10) and in the *H.E.A. Report on Teacher Education 1970* (IV.12). The important decision to set up Teachers' Centres in 1972 is virtually unmarked as far as official documentation is concerned — the most appropriate reference we could find to the event is an extract from the Minister's Estimates speech in the Dáil in 1972 (IV.13). Similarly we had difficulty in identifying a document referring to the introduction of university degrees for primary teachers in 1976 — again we fell back on the Dáil debates for a formal announcement of this very important development (IV.15). We include extracts from the report of the *Planning Committee on the Establishment of an Chomhairle Mhúinteoireachta in 1974* (IV.14) although this report was never published. The issue of teachers' salaries is referred to in IV.5, IV.6, IV.8, IV.11 and IV.17. The setting up by statute of Thomond College, Limerick is the subject of IV.16 and its dissolution in 1991 is covered in IV.23. The implications for primary teacher education of the changing demographic situation is reflected in the closure of Carysfort College (IV.21) and is also referred to in the *Report of the Primary Education Review Body 1990* (IV.22). The recommendations of this Body and the suggestions in the *O.E.C.D. Review of Educational Policy 1991* (IV.23) led to the disassociation of Mary Immaculate College from the National University of Ireland and its linkage with the University of Limerick. The memorandum of agreement between the two colleges in 1991 is reproduced in full (IV.25).

Section V includes extracts from 23 documents relating to higher education, most of which date from 1960. The first four documents are statutory instruments relating to higher education — the *University (Agriculture and Dairy Science Act)1926* (V.1), *University College, Galway, Act 1929* (V.2), *Bunreacht na hÉireann 1937* and the *Institute for Advanced Studies Act 1940.* The 1959 report of the *Commission on Accommodation Needs of the N.U.I. Colleges* (V.5) presages a period of major development of higher education in Ireland. This is followed by the 1960 report of the *Board of Visitors on University College, Dublin* which led to the relocation of U.C.D. on the Belfield campus thereby providing space for an unprecedented growth in student numbers in the 1970s and 1980s. The *Report of the Steering Committee on Technical Education in 1967* recommended the setting up of Regional Technical Colleges — a development which revolutionised higher technical and technological education. The short-lived proposal for a merger of

University College Dublin and Trinity College by Minister O'Malley in 1967 is the subject of V.10 and extracts from the policy statement on higher education announced by Minister Lenihan in 1968 are included in V.10. The setting up of the Higher Education Authority is referred to in V.11 and extracts from some of its early publications are the subject of V.12. Two further pieces of legislation — the *National College of Art and Design Act 1974* and the setting up of the National Council for Educational Awards are covered in V.13 and V.14.

The agreement between Trinity College and the City of Dublin Vocational Education Committee in 1976, which provided for the awarding of degrees by Trinity College for some of the third level courses offered in V.E.C. colleges, is referred to in V.15 and the reorganisation of the V.E.C's third level colleges into the Dublin Institute of Technology is the subject of V.16. Extracts from legislation relating to the setting up of the National Institutes of Higher Education in Limerick and Dublin are included in this section (V.18) as well as extracts relating to higher education from the *1980 White Paper* (V.19), the *Programme for Action in Education 1984-7* (V.20) and *Partners in Education 1985* (V.21). The *Report of the International Study Group on Technological Education 1987* (V.22) recommended that the National Institutes of Higher Education in Limerick and Dublin be given university status and legislation in 1989 (V.23) provided for the implementation of this recommendation.

Section VI includes a selection of extracts from official documents relating to educational issues which do not refer directly to either primary, post-primary or higher education but are limited to a specific educational issue. When we published Volume I we were aware that the format we had adopted tended to preclude consideration of such documents. The first 12 extracts in this section refer to special education, i.e. the education of children with physical or mental handicap. In our search for official documents relating to special education, it became clear that there was little or no official recognition of the educational needs of these children before the 1960s. The *Report of the Commission of Inquiry on Mental Handicap 1965* (VI.1) provides an overview of the history of special education in Ireland as well as making recommendations for its future development. An article in *Oideas* in 1968 provided information on schools for children with special educational needs and document VI.2 includes an extract from this publication. The educational needs of itinerant, deaf and physically handicapped children are referred to in documents VI.3 to VI.5 and the education of severely and profoundly handicapped children is the subject of VI.7. Extracts from the sections on special education in the *1980 White Paper* and the *Programme for Action in Education 1984-7* are provided in VI.6 and VI.8. Document VI.9 contains extracts from *Guidelines on Remedial Education* issued by the Department of Education in 1987 (VI.9) and document VI.10 gives information on the educational provision for the children of travelling families in 1989. An extract relating to special education from the *Report of the Primary Education Review Body 1990* is given in VI.11 and the final document in this section contains extracts from the *Report of the Review Group on Mental Handicap Services 1990.*

Documents VI.13 and VI.14 relate to reformatory and industrial schools and include extracts from two key reports — one in 1934-6 and the other in 1970. The following two documents (VI.15 and VI.16) refer to adult education and VI.17 contains extracts from the *Report of the Educational Broadcasting Committee 1982*. The increasing concern in the 1980s with the question of gender equality in education is reflected in VI.18.

A short section relating to the Arts in Education is included at this point in the volume. We are aware that by including a section on a specific curricular area we might be open to the accusation of selecting one area over another and we accept this as a valid criticism. Why did we choose to include a section on the arts in education but not a section on other aspects such as social and environmental education or mathematics or technology for example? Our decision to include a short section on the arts was taken because of our awareness that there has been consistent criticism of the failure of the Irish education system to make adequate provision for the arts. This concern is articulated in documents VI.19 to VI.22. Had space been available, we would have liked to include examples of other curricular areas but unfortunately this did not prove to be possible.

Baineann na leathanaí deireannaí le cheist na Gaeilge sa chóras oideachais. Ó 1922 i leith is ar réimhse an oideachais go príomha a bhíothas ag brath chun athbheochan na Gaeilge a chur i gcrích. I rith na bhfichidí agus na dtriochaidí bhí an-bhéim ar an nGaeilge sa chóras oideachais idir scoileanna náisiúnta agus mheánscoileanna. Is trí Ghaeilge ar fad a bhí obair na naí-scoileanna. B'éigean an Ghaeilge a mhúineadh ar feadh uair a chloig ar a laghad gach lá do leanaí i rang I ar aghaidh agus bhí sé de dhualgas freisin ábhar nó dhó seachas an Ghaeilge a mhúineadh trí Ghaeilge chomh maith. Bhíothas ag súil go n-úsáidfí níos mó Gaeilge bliain i ndiaidh bliana agus nach fada go mbeadh gach scoil náisiúnta sa tír ina scoil lán-Ghaelach.

Ach bhí deacrachtaí ag baint leis an bpolasai seo ó thús. Ní raibh Gaeilge líofa ag furmhór na múinteoirí i 1922 agus cé gur chaith an rialtas mórán airgid ar chúrsaí in-seirbhíse sa teanga i rith samhraí na mblianta 1922, 1923 agus 1924 bhí suas le 30% den fhoireann mhúinteoireachta fós gan teastas sa Ghaeilge ag deireadh na bhfichidí.

Tháinig feabhas ar an scéal nuair a cuireadh na Coláistí Ullmhucháin ar bun i 1926 (IV.3) agus arís sna triochaidí nuair a neartaíodh stáid na teanga sna Coláistí Oiliúna. Ach, mar sin féin, bhí a lán daoine buartha faoin scéal. I 1941 de réir suirbhé a foilsíodh ag Cumann Múinteoirí Éireann, ní raibh ag eirí leis an bpolasaí i leith na Gaeilge. Bhí ró-bhéim ar fad ar fad ar scríobh na teanga sna ranganna sinsir abhí ag ullmhú do na scrúdaithe teistiméireachta agus gan dóthain béime ar an dteanga labhartha. Ceapadh freisin go raibh meath tagtha ar chaighdeán na n-ábhar eile toisc iad a múineadh tré mheán na Gaeilge. Bhí deachrachtaí ag baint freisin le hobair na naí-scoile toisc an clár iomlán iontu dá mhúineadh trí Ghaeilge. Cheap a lán daoine gur chuir an polasaí seo bac ar fhóras an linbh óig.

I 1951 foilsíodh leabhrán nua maidir le hobair na naí-scoile (II.8) — ón bpointe seo ar aghaidh cuireadh níos mó béime ar dhul chun cinn na leanaí ná ar dhul chun cinn na teanga sa naí-scoil. I 1960 tar éis don Roinn ciorclán a eisiúint (II.11) níor gá a thuilleadh clíodh go docht daingin leis an riail a d'éiligh go múinfí chuile ábhar trí Ghaeilge. De réir a chéile sna seascaidí bhíodh cáineadh á dhéanamh ar chaighdeán na Gaeilge sna scoileanna. Cé gur cuireadh deireadh leis an teastas bunscoile i 1967 (II.14) agus go raibh níos mó béime ar labhairt na teanga ina dhiaidh sin ba é tuairim na coitianachta go raibh an caighdeán ag dul i laige.

Foilsíodh roinnt tuarascálacha tábhachtacha i rith na blianta sin. I 1963 foilsíodh tuarascáil an *Choiste um Athbheochan na Gaeilge* (VI.23) agus bliain ina dhiaidh sin d'eisigh an rialtas *Páipéar Bán* (VI.24) in ar leag siad síos polasaithe maidir le forás na teanga as sin amach laistigh and lasmuigh den chóras oideachais. I 1971 cuireadh Comhairle na Gaeilge ar bun chun comhairle a thabhairt don rialtas faoi pholasaithe éagsúla maidir leis an nGaeilge. Idir 1971 agus 1974 d'fhoilsigh an Chomhairle, ar a laghad, ceithre leabhrán tábhachtacha agus tá gearr-dréacht tógtha againn as *Gaeilge sa Chóras Oideachais* (VI.25). Ar mholadh na Comhairle, cuireadh Bord na Gaeilge ar bun i 1975 agus chuir an Bord go mór le leas na teanga ó shin i leith. Tá tagairt againn do *Plean Gníomhaíochta na Gaeilge 1983-86* (VI.27) mar shampla den saghas cur chuige abhí agus atá ag an mBord.

Níl aon tagairt againn sa leabhar seo don obair thábhachtach abhí agus atá ar siúl ag Institiúid Teangeolaíochta na hÉireann. Níl tagairt, ach an oiread, do thuairiscí tábhachtacha cosúil le *Tuarascáil an Choiste um Thaighde ar Dhearcadh an Phobail* i 1975 nó don taighde a rinne John Harris ar stáid na Gaeilge. D'fhéadfaí leabhar iomlán a líonadh le dréachtaí as tuarascálacha a bhaineann leis an nGaeilge. Níl sa leabhrán seo ach "blas", mar a déarfá, agus táimid ag súil go spreagfaidh na gearr-dréachtaí seo an léitheoir chun tuilleadh taighde a dhéanamh ar an ábhar fíor-tábhachtach seo — an Ghaeilge sa chóras oideachais.

Two appendices are included to help readers in their journey through Irish education since 1922. Appendix 1 provides a list of the Ministers for Education since the foundation of the first Dáil in 1919 to the end of 1991. Appendix 2 gives a source reference for as many of the documents referred to in this volume as possible. Government publications and publications of statutory bodies are referred to by their publication number and the year of publication. Acts of the Oireachtas are also referred to by their number and year of publication. The circular number and year of Department of Education circulars are given, but as far as the authors are aware there is no one collection where all departmental circulars are deposited and accessible. Extracts from a number of unpublished reports are in the possession of the authors but it may otherwise be difficult to obtain access to some of them. Some key speeches and statements made by Ministers for Education were issued at the time by the Government Information Service and were sometimes quoted extensively in contemporary newspaper accounts and newspapers.

ÁINE HYLAND

I

EDUCATION — GENERAL, 1922-1991

I.1. The Constitution of the Irish Free State (Saorstát Éireann) 1922.

With the signing of the Treaty in December 1921, the Irish Free State came into existence. In accordance with Article 17 of the Treaty the Parliament of Southern Ireland assembled on 14 January 1922. This Parliament approved the Treaty, elected a provisional government under the chairmanship of Michael Collins, and then dissolved. On 16 January 1922, the Provisional Government went to Dublin Castle, the seat of British rule in Ireland, and a formal transfer of power took place. The Provisional government assumed responsibility for education affairs on 1st February 1922. The Board of National Education was immediately disbanded and Pádraig Ó Brolcháin was appointed as Chief Executive officer for education. The Intermediate Board remained in control of intermediate education for a further sixteen months until it was disbanded in June 1923 and replaced by two Intermediate Education Commissioners, Seósamh Ó Néill and Proinsias Ó Dubhthaigh. Technical education came under the control of the Department of Agriculture and remained so until 1924.

The first act passed by the new legislature in 1922 was an Act to enact a Constitution for the Irish Free State (Saorstát Éireann). The 1922 Constitution included one significant article on education — Article 10. This article stated that "All citizens of the Irish Free State (Saorstát Éireann) have the right to free elementary education." The following extract from the act includes article 10:

DÁIL ÉIREANN sitting as a Constituent Assembly in this Provisional Parliament, acknowledging that all lawful authority comes from God to the people and in the confidence that the National life and unity of Ireland shall thus be restored, hereby proclaims the establishment of the Irish Free State (otherwise called Saorstát Éireann) and in the exercise of undoubted right, decrees and enacts as follows:

1. The Constitution set forth in the First Schedule hereto annexed shall be the Constitution of the Irish Free State (Saorstát Éireann)

2. The said Constitution shall be construed with reference to the Articles of Agreement for a Treaty between Great Britain and Ireland set forth in the Second Schedule hereto annexed (hereinafter referred to as "the Scheduled Treaty") which are hereby given the force of law, and if any provision of the said Constitution or of any amendment thereof or of any law made thereunder is in any respect repugnant to any of the provisions of the Scheduled Treaty, it shall, to the extent only of such repugnancy, be absolutely void and inoperative and the Parliament and the Executive Council of the Irish Free State (Saorstát Éireann) shall respectively pass such further legislation and do all such other things as may be necessary to implement the Scheduled Treaty.

3. This Act may be cited for all purposes as the Constitution of The Irish Free State (Saorstát Éireann) Act, 1922.

ARTICLE 1.

The Irish Free State (otherwise hereinafter called or sometimes called Saorstát Éireann) is a co-equal member of the Community of Nations forming the British Commonwealth of Nations.

ARTICLE 2.
All powers of government and all authority legislative, executive, and judicial in Ireland, are derived from the people of Ireland and the same shall be exercised in the Irish Free State (Saorstát Éireann) through the organisations established by or under, and in accord with, this Constitution.

ARTICLE 4.
The National language of the Irish Free State (Saorstát Éireann) is the Irish language, but the English language shall be equally recognised as an official language. Nothing in this Article shall prevent special provisions being made by the Parliament of the Irish Free State (otherwise called and herein generally referred to as the "Oireachtas") for districts or areas in which only one language is in general use.

ARTICLE 10.
All citizens of the Irish Free State (Saorstát Éireann) have the right to free elementary education.

I.2 The Ministers and Secretaries Act, 1924

The first Dáil Éireann had not appointed a Minister for Education in 1919 when ministries were being defined and "aireachtai" were being set up. Education was initially the responsibility of Aireacht na Gaeilge (the Ministry for Irish) and it was not until August 1921 that the first Minister for Education, J.J. O'Kelly (An Sceilig) was appointed.

When the Ministers and Secretaries Act was passed in June 1924 a Department of Education was formally established to take responsibility for the following areas of education under a Minister for Education:- primary, secondary, university, vocational and technical training, endowed schools, reformatories and industrial schools. The new department also assumed responsibility for a number of other institutions such as the National Library and the National Gallery of Ireland. The following extracts from the act relate to the setting up of the Department of Education and define the role of the Minister and of the Department. The schedule to the act, Fourth Part, lists the "particular branches of administration" assigned to the new Department:

BE IT THEREFORE ENACTED BY THE OIREACHTAS OF SAORSTÁT ÉIREANN AS FOLLOWS:-

1. There shall be established in Saorstát Éireann the several Departments of State specified and named in the eleven following sub-paragraphs, amongst which the administration and business of the public services in Saorstát Éireann shall be distributed as in the said sub-paragraphs is particularly mentioned, and each of which said Departments and the powers, duties and functions thereof shall be assigned to and administered by the Minister hereinafter named as head thereof, that is to say:-

(ii) The Department of Finance which shall comprise the administration and business generally of the public finance of Saorstát Éireann and all powers, duties and functions connected with the same, including in particular the collection and expenditure of the revenues of Saorstát Éireann from whatever source arising (save as may be otherwise provided by law), and the supervision and control of all purchases made for or on behalf of and all supplies of commodities and goods held by any Department of State and the disposal thereof, and also the business, powers, duties and functions of the branches and officers of the public service specified in the first part of the Schedule to this Act, and of which Department the head shall be, and shall be styled an t-Aire Airgid or (in English) the Minister for Finance.

(v) The Department of Education which shall comprise the administration and business generally of public services in connection with Education, including primary, secondary and university education, vocational and technical training, endowed schools, reformatories, and industrial schools, and all powers, duties and functions connected with the same, and shall include in particular the business, powers, duties and functions of the branches and officers of the public services specified in the Fourth Part of the Schedule to this Act, and of which Department the head shall be, and shall be styled, an tAire Oideachais or (in English) the Minister for Education.

2.(1) Each of the Ministers, heads of the respective Departments of State mentioned in Section 1 of this Act, shall be a corporation sole under his style or name aforesaid (which may be lawfully expressed with equal validity and effect whether in the Irish Language or in its English equivalent as set out in the preceding section), and shall have perpetual succession and an official seal (which shall be officially and judicially noticed), and may sue and (subject to the fiat of the Attorney-General having been in each case first granted) be sued under his style or name aforesaid, and may acquire, hold and dispose of land for the purposes of the functions, powers or duties of the Department of State of which he is head or of any branch thereof.

19. Wherever any statutory board of commissioners or other statutory or public board or body or public authority is by any existing law required to present any annual or other report to the Lord Lieutenant or to Parliament or to any Parliamentary head of any Department of State, every such report shall after the passing of this Act be presented in the first instance to the Minister who is head of the Department of State for the time being concerned with the services or functions of such board,

body, or authority, and if such Minister be for the time being an Executive Minister he shall present the report to the Executive Council, which shall cause the report to be laid before each House of the Oireachtas, but if such Minister be not for the time being an Executive Minister he shall himself cause the report to be laid before each House of the Oireachtas.

20.(1) This Act may be cited for all purposes as the Ministers and Secretaries Act, 1924.

SCHEDULE — FOURTH PART

Particular Branches of Administration assigned to an Roinn Oideachais (The Department of Education).

The Commissioners of National Education in Ireland.
The Intermediate Education Board for Ireland.
The Commissioners of Education in Ireland (Endowed Schools).
The Inspector of Reformatory and Industrial Schools.
The Department of Agriculture and Technical Instruction for Ireland (business and functions relating to Technical Instruction only).
The College of Science.
The Geological Survey in Ireland.
The National Museum of Science and Art.
The National Library of Ireland.
The National Gallery of Ireland.
The Metropolitan School of Art.
Meteorological Services.

I.3 School Attendance Act, 1926

The low level of pupil attendance at national schools in the late nineteenth and early twentieth centuries was a source of concern to educationalists and to government. Efforts to introduce compulsory school attendance at the end of the nineteenth century through the provisions of the Education Act of 1892 met with only limited success. The report of F.H. Dale in 1904 and the report of the Killanin Committee in 1919 referred to the unsatisfactory level of pupil attendance at Irish schools. The 1919 bill had contained a comprehensive school attendance provision but this bill was not enacted. The issue of school attendance was one of the few non-curricular issues which was addressed by the new Free State government after 1922 and the School Attendance Act which became law in October 1926 made school attendance mandatory for those between 6 and 14 years of age. It also empowered the Minister to raise the school leaving age to 16 eventually.

The following extract is taken from a summary containing the principal provisions of the Act:

(1) EXTENT OF ACT
The Act, which is now in force, extends to the entire area of the Saorstát.

(2) ENFORCING AUTHORITY
The Enforcing Authority in every School Attendance Area situated in the County Boroughs of Cork, Dublin, and Waterford, and in the Urban Districts of Blackrock, Dun Laoghaire, Rathmines and Rathgar and Pembroke, is *the School Attendance Committee for that area,* and

The Enforcing Authority in every School Attendance Area not situated in the county boroughs and urban districts named above, is the *Superintendent of the Gárda Síochána, for that area.*

The Superintendent is empowered to exercise all or any of his functions as Enforcing Authority through the members of the Gárda Síochána under his command, and every officer so employed is a School Attendance Officer.

(3) Obligation to attend school

The parent of every child between the ages of 6 and 14 years, and of every other child to whom the Act is applied, is required, unless there is a reasonable excuse for not so doing, to cause the child to attend a national or other suitable school on every day on which such school is open for secular instruction and for such time on every such day as is set forth in Section 2 of Appendix (Order No.79).

A child is deemed to attain any particular age on the last day of the quarter in which the anniversary of his birth occurs.

A "Parent" means the person having legal custody of the child and includes the person with whom the child is living or in whose custody the child is.

(4) Excuses for non-attendance at school

Any of the following will be regarded as a reasonable excuse for non-attendance at school:-

(a) that the child has been prevented from attending school by the sickness of the child;

(b) that the child is receiving suitable elementary education in some manner other than by attending a national or other suitable school;

(c) that there is not a national or other suitable school accessible to the child which the child can attend and to which the parent of the child does not object, on religious grounds, to send the child;

(d) that the child has been prevented from attending school by some other sufficient cause;

(e) until the year 1936, the fact that a child of 12 years of age or over has been prevented from attending school by reason of his having been engaged in light agricultural work for his parent on his parents' land will be regarded as a reasonable excuse for non-attendance at school:

(1) on not more than ten days during the period beginning on the 17th day of March and ending on the 15th day of May following in any year and

(2) on not more than ten days during the period beginning 1st August and ending on 15th October following in any year.

(5) ACCESSIBILITY OF SCHOOLS

A school is regarded as accessible to a child if, either:-

(a) the school is situated, in the case of a child who has not attained the age of ten years, within two miles measured from the child's residence along the shortest way lawfully, and conveniently available for him or, in the case of a child who has attained the age of ten years, within three miles similarly measured; or

(b) there is a suitable means of conveyance to the school available for the child from a point within a reasonable distance from the child's residence.

(6) CERTIFICATION OF SUITABLE SCHOOLS

The Minister may certify any particular school, other than a National School, to be a suitable school for the attendance of children for the purpose of receiving elementary education.

(10) PARENT TO NOTIFY CAUSE OF ABSENCE

Whenever a child is absent from school on any day or days his parent must, as soon as possible, and in any case within three days, communicate in writing, or in person, to the principal teacher of the school the cause of the child's absence.

(11) FAILURE OF PARENT TO COMPLY WITH THE ACT

Whenever a parent fails or neglects to cause his child to attend school and, so far as is known to the Enforcing Authority, there is no reasonable excuse for such failure or neglect, the Enforcing Authority serves on such parent a warning in the approved form requiring him within one week either to cause his child to attend school or to give a reasonable excuse for not so doing, and, if the parent does not comply with that warning, he may be summoned to appear in the District Court and may render himself liable *in the case of a first offence to a fine not exceeding twenty shillings, and, in the case of a second or subsequent offence (whether in relation to the same or another child) to a fine not exceeding forty shillings.*

If the parent in any proceedings against him under the Act satisfies the court that he has used all reasonable efforts to cause the child to attend school, or if he is convicted of a second or subsequent offence in respect of the same child, the court may:-

(a) Order the child to be sent to a certified Industrial school; or

(b) Order the committal of the child to the care of a relative or other fit person named by the Court.

In any prosecution, the burden of proof in any of the following matters lies on the person prosecuted:-

(a) age of child,

(b) that there was a reasonable excuse for non-attendance at school;

(c) that the child is receiving suitable elementary education in some other manner.

(12) RESTRICTION OF EMPLOYMENT OF CHILDREN

The Minister may make regulations prohibiting or restricting the employment of children and any person who employs a child in contravention of such regulations may render himself liable to prosecution and, on conviction, *to a fine not exceeding forty shillings for a first offence and not exceeding five pounds for a second or subsequent offence.*

I.4 Report of the Inter-Departmental Committee on the Raising of the School-Leaving Age, 1935

In 1934 an interdepartmental committee was set up under the chairmanship of John Ingram to report to the Minister on the raising of the school-leaving age. The committee did not recommend this course of action, stating that the lack of adequate facilities for post-primary education in many districts "makes the raising of the school-leaving age impracticable at present." The following is a summary of the conclusions of the committee:

VI — SUMMARY OF CONCLUSIONS

1. The existing requirements of the Saorstát in the matter of compulsory attendance at school are as comprehensive as those of other European countries.
2. Although there has been in many countries in recent years a persistent demand for the general raising of the school-leaving age to 15 and 16 years, scarcely any country has so far yielded to the demand.
3. Large numbers of young persons between the ages of 14 and 16 are employed in agricultural occupations in the Saorstát, but they are the sons and daughters of small-holders, and if the school-leaving age were raised the withdrawal of their labour from the farms would cause considerable hardship to their parents.
4. The withdrawal of juvenile labour in agricultural areas would not result in any material improvement in the employment of additional adult labour.
5. There is not an undue proportion of juvenile to adult workers in non-agricultural occupations and there is no evidence that juveniles are employed to any appreciable extent on industrial work that is suitable only to adult workers.
6. There is no case for the raising of the school-leaving age on the grounds that young people are too immature for employment at the age of 14 years.

7. A large proportion of the employment obtained by juveniles in non-agricultural occupations is blind-alley employment as messengers, etc., but it is difficult to see what better employment could be obtained for such juveniles by keeping them a year of two longer at school.
8. The parents of juveniles who enter blind-alley employment are generally in very poor circumstances and would be unable to keep them longer at school. If the school-leaving age were raised, there would be a very strong demand for maintenance grants for the disemployed juveniles.
9. The withdrawal from the industrial labour market of all boys and girls under the age of 16 years would not lessen adult unemployment to any appreciable extent.
10. There are large numbers of young people between the ages of 14 and 16 who have not obtained employment and do not attend school. There is grave danger in their idleness which tends to make the young people unfit for employment.
11. There is a definite advantage to be gained by keeping unemployed juveniles at school, but if they are to have a reasonable chance of obtaining employment on leaving school they must be kept to 16, and not 15, years of age.
12. Under the conditions that prevail in the Saorstát it would be better that the school-leaving age should be raised to 16 years for unemployed juveniles than it should be raised to 15 years for all juveniles.
13. It is essential to the success of any extension of the period of school life that there should be adequate facilities for post-primary education, and the lack of such facilities in many districts in the Saorstát makes the general raising of the school-leaving age impracticable at present.

14. The provisions of Part V of the Vocational Education Act might be put into operation in two or three carefully-selected areas, all employed juveniles in these areas being required to attend classes for not more than 180 hours per year and all unemployed juveniles in the areas being required to attend whole-time schools.

I.5 Bunreacht na hÉireann (Constitution of Ireland) 1937

Bunreacht na hÉireann (1937) superseded the Constitution of the Irish Free State 1922 and Article 42 of the new constitution enshrined the rights of parents in relation to the education of their children. Article 44 also contained sections which affected educational provision. Both articles are quoted here in full:

ARTICLE 42

1. The State acknowledges that the primary and natural educator of the child is the Family and guarantees to respect the inalienable right and duty of parents to provide, according to their means, for the religious and moral, intellectual, physical and social education of their children.
2. Parents shall be free to provide this education in their homes or in private schools or in schools recognised or established by the State.

3.1. The State shall not oblige parents in violation of their conscience and lawful preference to send their children to schools established by the State, or to any particular type of school designated by the State.

3.2. The State shall, however, as guardian of the common good, require in view of actual conditions that the child receive a certain minimum education, moral, intellectual and social.

4. The State shall provide for free primary education and shall endeavour to supplement and give reasonable aid to private and corporate educational initiative, and,

when the public good requires it, provide other educational facilities or institutions with due regard, however, for the rights of parents, especially in the matter of religious and moral formation.

5. In exceptional cases, where the parents for physical or moral reasons fail in their duty towards their children, the State as guardian of the common good, by appropriate means shall endeavour to supply the place of the parents, but always with due regard for the natural and imprescriptible rights of the child.

ARTICLE 44

1. The State acknowledges that the homage of public worship is due to Almighty God. It shall hold His Name in reverence, and shall respect and honour religion.

2.1. Freedom of conscience and the free profession and practice of religion are, subject to public order and morality, guaranteed to every citizen.

2.2. The State guarantees not to endow any religion.

3. The State shall not impose any disabilities or make any discrimination on the ground of religious profession, belief or status.

4. Legislation providing State aid for schools shall not discriminate between schools under the management of different religious denominations, nor be such as to affect prejudicially the right of any child to attend a school receiving public money without attending religious instruction at that school.

5. Every religious denomination shall have the right to manage its own affairs, own, acquire and administer property, movable and immovable, and maintain institutions for religious or charitable purposes.

6. The property of any religious denomination or any educational institution shall not be diverted save for necessary works of public utility and on payment of compensation.

I.6 School Attendance Bill, 1942

The 1926 School Attendance Act introduced compulsory school attendance for children aged 6 to 14. It required parents to "cause the child to attend a national or other suitable school" or to ensure "that the child is receiving suitable elementary education in some manner other than by attending a national or other suitable school." In 1942 the Minister for Education, Tomás Ó Deirg, introduced a bill in the Dáil which inter alia sought to increase the power of the Minister in relation to the type of education being received by children who were not attending national schools. The bill sought to give power to the Minister to determine what constituted a minimum education. The bill was passed by the Dáil but when referred by the President to the Supreme Court under Article 13.3.1 of the Constitution, it was deemed unconstitutional and was never enacted.

The following extracts from the report of the Supreme Court indicate the basis on which the bill was found repugnant to the Constitution:-

In The Matter of ARTICLE 26 of the Constitution and in the Matter of the SCHOOL ATTENDANCE BILL, 1942 (1).

..........We adopt the principle laid down by this Court in *In the Matter of Article 26 of the Constitution and in the Matter of the Offences against the State (Amendment) Bill,* 1940 (1), that where any particular law is not expressly prohibited and it is sought to establish that it is repugnant to the Constitution by reason of some implied prohibition or repugnancy, such repugnancy must be clearly established (per Sullivan C.J. at p.478), and it therefore becomes necessary to consider whether the provisions of s.4 of the Bill can be said to be clearly repugnant, expressly or impliedly, to any provision of the Constitution.

..........What is referred to as "a certain minimum education" has not been defined by the Constitution and accordingly, we are of opinion that the State, acting in its legislative capacity through the Oireachtas, has power to define it. It should, in our opinion, be defined in such a way as to effectuate the general provisions of the clause without contravening any of the other provisions of the Constitution. Subject to these restrictions, it seems to us that the State is free to act, so long as it does not require more than a "certain minimum education" which expression, in the opinion of this Court, indicates a minimum standard of elementary education of general application.

If the standard contemplated by the section which has been referred to us exceeds these limits we do not think it can be justified under the Constitution.

Sect.4 of the Bill deals with the granting of certificates by the Minister certifying that children are receiving suitable education otherwise than by attending school. We must construe that section as we find it and try to ascertain its meaning and effect. We assume that the powers conferred upon the Minister by the section if passed into law will be exercised in a reasonable, conscientious and temperate manner. But, making this assumption, we are nevertheless of opinion that a Minister, construing the section in a reasonable manner, might require a higher standard of education than could properly be prescribed as a minimum standard under Article 42 (3) (2) of the Constitution. We are further of opinion that the standard contemplated by the section might vary from child to child, and, accordingly, that it is not such a standard of general application as the Constitution contemplates. In these respects we are of opinion that the proposed legislation exceeds the limits permitted by the Constitution and is repugnant to it.

Our attention has been directed to the position of a child who has reached the prescribed age of 6 years and is being educated, and properly educated, at home or in a private school. A certain period of time must necessarily elapse before the Minister can give a certificate under the section. Before giving the certificate, the Minister may require that the child be submitted to such educational test as he may direct. If this test is to be directed, as the section would appear to contemplate, to the efficacy of the education which the child is receiving, a considerable period of time must be allowed to elapse. Eventually, the Minister may be satisfied that the child is being suitably educated and he may thereupon give the necessary certificate. Notwithstanding this, it is clear under the section that the parent would be in default in respect of the period intervening between the time when the child attained the age of six years and the time when the certificate is actually given, and might be subjected in respect of such default to penalties. Under sub-s.1 of s.4, a child shall not be deemed to be receiving suitable education in a manner otherwise than by attending school unless such education *has been* certified by the Minister to be suitable. In this respect also the section seems to us to be repugnant to the Constitution.

We are of the opinion that the section is open to objection from a constitutional point of view in one other respect. Under sub-s.1 not only the education, but also the manner *in which such child is receiving it* must be certified by the Minister. We do not consider that this is warranted by the Constitution. The State is entitled to require that children shall receive a certain minimum education. So long as parents supply this general standard of education we are of opinion that the manner in which it is being given and received is entirely a matter for the parents and is not a matter in respect of which the State under the Constitution is entitled to interfere.

Another point was taken in opposition to the Bill and was argued by counsel on both sides. One of the excuses under s.3 is that there is not a national school, a suitable school or a recognised school accessible to the child which the child can attend and to which the parent of the child does not object on religious grounds to send the child. It is contended that the grounds of objection should not be restricted to religious grounds in view of the provisions of Article 42 (3) (1) of the Constitution that the State shall not oblige parents in violation of their *conscience and lawful preference* to send their children to the schools named therein. As this is an objection arising on s.3 and not strictly on s.4. which alone has been referred to us, we express no opinion upon it.

For these reasons we are of opinion that s.4 of the Bill is repugnant to the Constitution and we shall advise the President accordingly.

I.7 Report of the Departmental Committee on Educational Provision, June 1947 (Unpublished).

Following the Second World War, countries throughout the world were involved in national programmes of reconstruction, and educational reform was high on the agenda of many countries. In England, the Education Act of 1944 introduced major changes in education and similar reforms were introduced in Northern Ireland in 1947. The I.N.T.O. published its comprehensive Plan of Education in 1947 but no major changes in education were introduced by the Dublin government at that time.

Many years were to elapse before it became generally known that detailed proposals for educational change had been put forward by an internal committee of the Department of Education in 1947. This committee, chaired by Labhras Ó Muirthe, afterwards Secretary of the Department, was set up by the Minister for Education, Tomás Ó Deirig, in March 1945. Its terms of reference were:

> To examine the existing educational system, primary, secondary, technical, vocational and the provision available for university education and to make recommendations as to what changes and reforms, if any, are necessary in order to raise the standard of education generally and to provide greater educational facilities for our people.

The Committee recommended radical reforms which, if introduced, would have changed the direction of Irish education. It recommended the raising of the school-leaving age to 16; the provision of second-level education for all pupils and a widening of the curriculum in both primary and second-level schools. Possibly the most significant recommendation was that a new type of school, to be called Senior School, should be provided by the State and that "it would be the duty of the State to provide for free education in these schools for all children." The report made it clear that these schools would be denominational schools, since "children of different religions require different kinds of education."

This report was not published at the time although it is clear that the committee expected that it would. In its introduction to the Report, addressed to the Minister on 27 June 1947, it was stated:

> The establishment of this Committee has been referred to in the course of the debates on the Education Estimates in An Dáil both this year and last year. As therefore it is possible, and even probable, that some publicity must be given to the result of our deliberations, we consider it desirable that our conclusions should be presented in the form of an impersonal Memorandum.

No action was taken by the Minister to implement the proposals of the Committee. This may have been due to the fact that the government fell later in the year and a new Inter-Party government came to power early in 1948 with a new agenda. The following extracts are taken from the report of the Departmental Committee of 1947:

****

20. Obviously nothing could be more calculated to defeat the object of raising the school-leaving age to fifteen or sixteen years than that this should mean merely that the pupil should spend another year or two on the same curriculum, under the same type of teaching, and most undesirable of all, "marooned in the same old school." Even at present many pupils in their last year or so in the National School suffer from a sense of futility and frustration, and count the days till their fourteenth birthday releases them from what they look on as the state of childhood.

21. Apart from these considerations, it would seem to be generally accepted today that one stage of formal education should end, and the next stage begin somewhere between the ages of eleven and thirteen years. Indeed the Hadow Report on "The Education of the Adolescent" lays down categorically that the "break" should occur at eleven plus.

22. Although it has been accepted elsewhere that the "break" should take place at eleven plus, experience goes to show that in this country a transfer at an earlier age than twelve plus would be too early.

* * * * * * * * * *

23. There are, therefore, substantial grounds for the recommendation that the child should, as a rule, be transferred from the existing National School at the age of twelve plus.

* * * * * * * * * *

24. The statistics at present available show that there are some 215,000 children in the country between the ages of twelve and sixteen years. Some two-thirds of these (144,000) are already in whole-time attendance at school, almost one half of them (107,000) being in

National Schools. Reference has been made (par.9 et seq.) to the inadequacy generally of the educational provision made for pupils of this age in the National Schools. What then would be the best way to cater for this age-group as a whole under a system of compulsory attendance up to, ultimately, sixteen years of age?

25. The general educational process is, as stated in paragraph 2, essentially religious, and the new system, however organised, should be subject to ecclesiastical sanction.

26. As to the programme to be followed, it is suggested that there is a type of curriculum which would be suitable and desirable for all children from twelve plus to fifteen or sixteen years of age. Such a curriculum should, of course, provide in the early stages mainly for continuation work in the subjects taught in the Junior School but it should include also Manual Training and General Science (or Rural Science) for boys and Craftwork and Domestic Science for girls, and the emphasis should be laid increasingly on the practical subjects in the later stages of the course. That practical subjects such as those referred to above can be used educatively, i.e. as instruments for the training and formation of the higher human faculties, is generally recognised today. Their use as educational instruments is especially desirable at the adolescent stage when the child is awakening to new interests suggested by the world around him, when he is frequently ill at ease in an atmosphere of books and lessons and when it is most important to turn to advantage his natural impulses towards constructive work.

****

27. This education of the combined literary and practical type will necessarily have to be provided in new schools,

thus involving the erection of new and specially equipped buildings or, in certain cases, the adaptation and equipment of existing buildings. For convenience the new schools will be referred to hereinafter as "Senior Schools," though here again it is not suggested that this description is necessarily the most appropriate one.

28. The principle of separate provision for boys and for girls in Senior Schools should be recognised. The application of the principle should present no difficulty where large numbers of pupils are concerned, but the problem will require further investigation where the number of pupils is small. Separate accommodation for boys and for girls must, of course, be provided for the practical subjects.

31. There are at present 186 Vocational Schools in operation, about one half of that number being situated in rural areas. ....The continuance of the day courses is necessary, as indeed is evident from this account, for the efficient and economic working of the present Vocational Education system. Vocational School buildings under existing control cannot, however, be used as Senior Schools and, even if they could, would provide accommodation for only a fraction of the pupils concerned. It may, therefore, be necessary either to transfer pupils under fifteen or sixteen years of age following whole-time day continuation courses to other buildings, with consequent serious dislocation and increased expense, or to arrange conditions under which the Vocational School buildings may be legitimately used as Senior Schools. It is necessary to observe also that the present continuation courses in the Vocational Schools differ in important respects from the courses of the combined literary and practical type outlined in Appendix II.

****

32. Although the education provided in the Senior School would be suitable for all children from the age of twelve plus, there is an appreciable number of such children for whom the type of education given in the Secondary Schools would be more suitable. This group includes those who have a capacity for dealing with the abstract and who will later fill these positions in life, limited in number, which come generally under the heading of the "professions" in the widest sense of that word. For these children the Department's programme for Secondary Schools may be regarded as generally satisfactory but it is recommended that every Secondary School should include in its curriculum some art or craft either as a formal subject or as an extra-class activity. More attention should also be devoted to Physical Education and to Singing and Music.

It is suggested that in any general reorganisation of the educational system there should be a considerable extension of the facilities for Secondary School education to meet the needs of these children for whom it would be more suitable than education in a Senior School. Since the Secondary Schools are privately owned institutions, such an extension might possibly be effected by an agreed scheme for granting State loans, with repayment on favourable terms, for new buildings or for extensions to existing buildings, and by arranging for a greatly increased number of scholarships of adequate value.

I.8 Setting up of the Council of Education, 1950.

In February 1948, Fianna Fáil failed to secure a majority in a general election after 16 years in government and an inter-party government of Fine Gael, Labour, Clann na Poblachta and Clann na Talmhan came to power. The Minister for Education was Richard Mulcahy, who in April 1950 set up a Council of Education with the following terms of reference: "To advise the Minister, in so far as pertains to powers, duties and functions of the State, upon such matters relating to educational theory and practice as they think fit and upon any educational questions and problems referred to them by him." The Council was to be a permanent body — "a permanent part of the organisation which is the Ministry of Education." All its members were nominated by the Minister for Education and its Chairman was Rev. Canon O'Keeffe. On the death of Canon O'Keeffe in 1952, he was replaced as chairman by Rev. Monsignor Martin Brenan. The term of office of the Chairman was to be three years and of the other members five years, but the Minister could, and did, prolong the term of office of the members.

The first formal task entrusted to the Council was to advise the Minister on: (1) The function of the Primary school and (2) The curriculum to be pursued in the Primary school from the infant school up to 12 years of age. The Council's report on the Primary School was published in 1954. On 12th November of that year, Minister Mulcahy requested the Council to "advise without prejudice to the consideration of the general pattern for primary and post-primary education as to the curriculum which should be followed in recognised secondary schools as a condition for the payment of State grants to these schools." The report of the Council on the Curriculum of the Secondary School was presented to the Minister in 1960 but was not published until 1962.

The recommendations of the Council of Education were, on the whole, conservative, particularly in the area of secondary education. In relation to the primary curriculum, the tone of the report was cautious, but nevertheless it supported a move towards a wider curriculum and recommended the addition of Physical Training, Nature Study and Drawing to the curriculum then in operation. The report also asserted that primary education should end at Standard VI, stating that "At the end of Standard VI, at whatever age that may be, the pupil has completed a course of basic elementary education." "Education to that stage (Standard VI) should be designated primary, and after that stage post-primary, irrespective of its type or the school in which it is given."

The following extracts are taken from Minister Mulcahy's speech in April 1950, when he launched the Council:

Happily the reasons for requiring a Council of Education in this country do not arise out of any problem such as makes education a matter of grave concern from the religious and secular view points in other countries. A main reason is that our people consider that in the complex and exacting world of to-day young people require to be ever better equipped to meet the work of life, economic and social, and that adequate provision for these requirements calls for closer counsel and co-operation between the Minister and Department of Education on the one hand and those acquainted with and interested in our educational problems outside on the other.

* * * * * * * * * *

It is more than appropriate because of the occasion itself and of the times in which we live that I should record that in its relation with the individual, the family and religion, the State approach to education in the Irish republic is one which unreservedly accepts the supernatural conception of man's nature and destiny. It accepts that the proper subject of education is man whole and entire, soul united to body in unity of nature, with all his faculties, natural and supernatural, such as right reason and revelation show him to be. It accepts that the foundation and crown of youth's entire training is religion. It is its desire that its teachers, syllabuses and text books in every branch be informed by the spirit underlying this concept of education, and it is determined to see that such facilities as Ecclesiastical Authorities consider proper shall be provided in the school for the carrying on of the work of religious education.

That the State exists here to-day is due to the fact that there is and down through the centuries there has been an Irish nation.

The State declares the existence of that nation, not so much for the purpose of political nationalism but as a manifestation of the work of God's providence and as bearing on the roots, tendencies and potentialities of our people for themselves and for the world. The roots of that nationality are represented in our language, our literature, our music, our archaeology and our folklore.

To benefit by the past which is enshrined in that heritage, to ensure that our people will follow as closely as possible the line of growth and development that is native and natural to them, our young people must be given the opportunity of becoming acquainted with the thought, the philosophy, the belief and the achievements of their ancestors. Education in this country has a task laid upon it in this connection that is almost unique. There is a breach which it has to fill, and any attempt to ignore that fact or belittle its importance would eventually, I think, be disastrous to the nation's strength and character. We want all our young people to love their country and loving her to serve her loyally and faithfully in whatever walk of life their lot may be cast, but to love her they must first know her not merely as she is to-day or as she was fifty or a hundred years ago, but as she has been at every stage of her long and chequered history.

* * * * * * * * * *

From to-day a Council of Education becomes a permanent part of the organism which is the Ministry of Education. Its personnel will change, its form may develop, but as a vital part of that organism a Council of Education will remain and grow in importance. So far from operating to suppress or to supersede any Bodies hitherto engaged in the work of review or research or consultation in regard to educational matters it is hoped that on the contrary as the work of the Council progresses it will gradually create much wider interest in education generally.

I.9 Report of the Commission on Youth Unemployment, 1951.

In May 1943, Seán Lemass who was then Minister for Industry and Commerce, appointed a commission under the chairmanship of Archbishop John C. McQuaid of Dublin, which was asked *inter alia* "to make recommendations as to the most practicable and desirable measures for promoting the religious, intellectual and physical development of young persons." The commission sat for eight years and its report, which was completed in 1951, made a number of recommendations which had implications for education. The report recommended that the school-leaving age be raised "ultimately to 16 years (and) as a first step .... to 15 years." The following is a summary of the recommendations of the commission on "Young Persons," "Their Education and Training:"

RELIGIOUS AND SPIRITUAL DEVELOPMENT OF YOUNG PERSONS

10. Having regard to the conditions obtaining in this country, we have determined that it is not part of our duty to submit specific recommendations in regard to the religious and spiritual development of young persons.

THE SCHOOLING OF YOUNG PERSONS

Primary Education

11. In view of criticism received by the Commission, we consider there is grave need to examine the content of primary education, more particularly the content of Irish and the treatment of that language.

Continuation Education

12. We recommend that continuation schools be further developed as the need arises.

Secondary Education

13. We strongly advise that the attention of those in charge of secondary schools be directed to the desirability of including in their curricula, courses in Manual Instruction or Domestic Science, as the case may require.

Instruction in Thrift

14. Realising that saving, wise spending and the proper use of money develop self-reliance and a sense of responsibility, the Commission is of opinion that lessons on thrift and, where possible, practical methods of thrift bearing on the daily activities of the pupils, should be given in all schools and in all institutions and courses for the training of teachers.

The School-leaving Age

15. We are convinced of the need for post-primary schooling for all normal young persons.
16. We recommend that the school leaving age be raised ultimately to 16 years. As a first step the school leaving age should be raised to 15 years.
17. We consider that the policy most likely to yield the best results and, at the same time, cause the minimum of inconvenience would be to raise the school leaving age area by area, according as local conditions become favourable.
18. As a step towards raising the school leaving age within a reasonable period of time and without prejudice to the main recommendation, we recommend that arrangements be made to expedite the application of Part V of the Vocational Education Act, 1930, or such other measure as may be considered suitable, to those areas to which it is feasible to do so.
19. The County Borough of Dublin calls for special consideration as it presents an urgent and difficult problem.

We are informed that the Dublin Vocational Schools lack sufficient accommodation to cater for the voluntary demand for full-time day continuation education, and that plans are in operation to remedy this situation.

For the County Borough of Dublin, and such adjoining areas as may be considered desirable, we therefore recommend —

(i) that the plans for meeting the demand for full-time day continuation education be expedited;
(ii) that steps be taken to give effect to the recommendations at 16, 17 and 18 above.

I.10 Investment in Education, inaugural speech, October 1962

In 1962 the government, in cooperation with the Organisation for Economic Cooperation and Development initiated a major survey of the Irish education system. The survey team was led by Patrick Lynch, Professor of Economics in University College, Dublin and the background report which was published in two volumes in 1965 and 1966 was fact-finding and analytical. The 1991 O.E.C.D. Review of Irish National Policy has referred to the report as "a landmark both in the national and international memory" and has stated that it was "remarkable for its comprehensiveness, its studied detachment, its theoretical underpinning, its systematic accumulation of a mass of baseline data, its detailed estimates of quantitative trends, and not least for the originality of the methods that it used to penetrate unexplored territory." The report provided striking evidence of the lack of opportunity for poorer children to proceed to secondary and higher education and exposed the waste of talent which resulted from this lack of opportunity. In the words of Seán O'Connor, who was subsequently Secretary of the Department of Education, the Investment in Education report "signposted the direction of educational reform."

The speech given by the Minister for Education, Dr. Hillery, at the first meeting of the Steering Committee in October 1962 contains one of the first statements of the government's acceptance that education was to be a factor in economic policy. The terms of reference given to the survey team ensured that the report would be "essentially a technical study of trends in Irish education and of the use of human resources and material resources in that system."

Extracts from the Minister's speech are reproduced here as well as the full text of the terms of reference and some extracts from the Introduction to the report:

(1) EXTRACTS FROM THE MINISTER'S SPEECH:

One aspect of education on which, perhaps, there has been inadequate emphasis in the past is the role of education in connection with economic development. This is a subject to which increasing attention is now being given internationally. It was, therefore, with alacrity that the Government responded to a suggestion from the Organisation for Economic Cooperation and Development that a survey should be made in Ireland of long-term educational needs. Such a survey seemed particularly opportune at a time when the Government is preparing its second programme for economic expansion and when the prospects of Ireland's association with the European Economic Community are becoming more immediate. At a recent conference in Rome, at which I was present, the European Ministers for Education, under the aegis of the Council of Europe, adopted a resolution which recognised the importance of education as a key factor in economic growth.

At first sight the terms of reference of the survey team which will be conducting this study of long-term educational needs might seem to be rather specialised and limited. The team will, of course, be naturally obliged to take account of the wider aims of education. In no sense will they be concerned exclusively with the "economic man" — if there be any such species. The study is intended to assess the educational needs of our expanding economy as well as the economic implications of ever increasing demand for education. Economic expansion and the full development of the potential of all our citizens is impossible if at every level the necessary educational resources do not exist to sustain and advance these aims. It would be a mistake to think that there can be a serious conflict between the educational needs of society as a whole and the educational desires of individuals. The needs of society will influence the propensities of individuals; individual choices will naturally be influenced by the prevailing or estimated demand of society as a whole.

Education, therefore, is becoming a factor in economic policy. This is a happy augury. Educationists may have become accustomed to a position in which education appeared to have been regarded as a mere residual in the framing of budgetary policy. Education is now accepted as an investment of national resources. Indeed, from a purely economic view, it is now recognised as a major factor in economic growth. A country that allows its "human capital" to lie fallow will, if I may mix my metaphors, be left behind culturally as well as economically. This is particularly true in such a country as Ireland, which in many respects is probably more fertile in human than in natural resources.

This project looks ahead ten years. The decade will almost certainly see great changes in the occupational structure of our people. New occupations will evolve; old ones will die. Mechanisation and automation will produce shifts from primary to secondary and tertiary activities, if we are to keep pace with these other countries in which our exports, visible and invisible, will be competing. The onset of the computer age leads us to expect increasing leisure for our workers; a test of education will be the manner in which that leisure is spent.

In advanced economies the contemporary trend is from making by hand to making by machines, or automation. Many routine skills are rapidly becoming obsolete. There is, therefore, no future in training people in narrow, limited or rigid skills. The future, we may be sure, will not be like the past. In the future, education must be directed towards a level where men and women will have the basic mental and manipulative equipment to adjust themselves towards re-training on the job to the new conditions of production or economic activity.

There will be immense opportunities for availing ourselves of the technical abilities and skills of those in a position to use them. Our young people will be handicapped unless we give them the foundation in scientific principles which must underly practical application as well as the ability to converse with people speaking other languages.

In conclusion, I should like to ask each member of the Steering Committee to cooperate with the team in the need for continuing public interest in this project which is so essential to our general economic as well as to our educational future.

(2) Terms of Reference

(a) Preparation of inventory of the existing position in relation to skilled manpower. This would involve prior agreement on the definitions which would be applied to the various categories of workers.

(b) Framing of educational targets, including provision for research, in relation to the assessments to be made of overall needs for skilled manpower according to field of study and level of skill, for the next 10-15 years. Alternative estimates, made according to different basic assumptions will take into account trends in economic and demographic factors, and also the experience of other countries.

(c) Assessment (on alternative bases) of future essential demand for educational facilities at different levels based on present trends and international experience and having regard to any other factors likely to influence such demand.

(d) Estimates of future enrolments at different levels of education and by subject of specialisation, according to the alternative assumptions mentioned above.

(e) Interpretations of estimated enrolment figures in terms of the expansion of educational resources, i.e. teachers, buildings, equipment, etc., taking into account possible improvements in the quality of teaching.

(f) Evaluations of the expenditure entailed by the various alternatives for the expansion of educational resources — the evaluations should be expressed in relation to macro-economic data, such as GNP and volume of investment.

(g) Consideration of arrangements necessary to ensure the review of the position at intervals in the light of changing circumstances in the field covered by the study. In this connection to recommend the nature and extent of the additional statistical data concerning current activities which should be collected and the methods and frequency of such collections.

(h) The extent to which the foregoing assessments might be influenced by the provision of educational facilities in Ireland for students from other countries and of educational aid in the form of teachers and other trained personnel for service in the emergent countries.

INTRODUCTION

In this Survey we have tried to keep before our minds at all times the character and purpose of education and that the term "educational system" has little meaning if it is considered apart from the human needs which it is there to serve. Our limited task, however, was the prosaic one of examining those resources which are indispensable to any system of education. This Report, therefore, is essentially a technical study of trends in Irish education and of the use of human and material resources in that system. It estimates the demands that are likely to be made on those resources and considers the extent to which the system seems likely to meet future needs. These needs include satisfactory participation in education by all sections of the community and an adequate supply of qualified persons. Arising out of these investigations an examination is made of the effects of possible changes in the educational system and in its traditional use of resources. The Report is a long one and is essentially fact-finding and analytical in character.

The Report has been drafted with an awareness of the interrelationship between means and ends. In education, as in other areas, decisions on ends are often influenced by considerations of means. A recognition of the resources needed to meet a given set of objectives may lead to changes in objectives or to a different arrangement of priorities.

It is not our function to say what the objectives of the educational system should be or to say what priority or weight should be given to particular objectives. Our role is an ancillary one. To be most effective, decisions and policies require an adequate basis of relevant information: it is our responsibility to supply such information and to recommend how it can continue to be made available. The implications and likely outcome of various courses of action need to be indicated both as regards the attainment of certain objectives and the scale of resources involved.

* * * * * * * * * *

The Report does not claim to be conclusive or exhaustive. Some aspects of our subject are not discussed. Others would have been more thoroughly and, perhaps, more fruitfully discussed but for the time limit, which is necessarily a feature, and, almost certainly a desirable discipline in a pilot survey of this kind. Time for the survey was limited. In addressing ourselves to the terms of reference we were faced with certain difficulties not inherent in such a survey and arising mainly because our task was, in a sense, a pioneering one. There was a dearth of the basic data needed for our analysis of the educational system. The collection of this information and the demographic and manpower forecasts occupied a substantial amount of time, which otherwise might have been differently employed. We see in the Report only a beginning, a foundation on which others may build. There is no finality about it nor could there be, for change is perennial and will not stop this year or next. The process, which the Report initiates, should be regarded as a continuing one if the intention of the Report is to be realised. The two basic problems of making the most effective choices and using means to greatest advantage will always remain. With them will remain the need for adequate information if policy is to be as fully informed as possible.

I.11 Second Programme for Economic Expansion, 1963

When Fianna Fáil returned to power in 1957 for what was to be a second period of fifteen years, a policy of coherent economic and social planning was introduced which eventually encompassed education policy. The accession of Seán Lemass as Taoiseach in 1959 provided the country with a dynamic new leader committed to improving the economy, increasing industrialisation and reducing emigration. The First Programme for Economic Expansion was issued in November 1958 and although there was no specific reference in it to education, it set out a framework for economic expansion within which education would subsequently play an important role.

The Second Programme for Economic Expansion was issued by the Department of Finance in 1963. This report had major significance for education in that it acknowledged that expenditure on education was an investment in the country's primary resource — its people — and that this investment could be expected to yield increasing returns in terms of economic progress. The report stressed the need for balanced expansion of educational facilities as a whole so as to ensure the greatest possible use of talent at all levels of ability. A full chapter of the report was devoted to education and while many of the policies in the Programme had previously been announced by the Minister for Education, Dr. Hillery, in May 1963, the fact that education was seen by the government as meriting a chapter in a

Programme for Economic Expansion was very significant. The following paragraphs are taken from Chapter 8 of the Second Programme for Economic Expansion:

1. A society which rates highly spiritual and moral values, and seeks to develop the mental and physical well-being of its people, will devote a substantial part of its resources to education. There are, in addition, social and economic considerations which reinforce the claim of education to an increasing share of expanding national resources. Improved and extended educational facilities help to equalise opportunities by enabling an increasing proportion of the community to develop their potentialities and raise their personal standards of living. Expenditure on education is an investment in the fuller use of the country's primary resource — its people — which can be expected to yield increasing returns in terms of economic progress. Economic growth is becoming increasingly dependent on the application of the results of scientific research and development to the practical problems of production. This calls for more than the training of the required cadre of technicians and technologists; there must be balanced expansion of educational facilities as a whole to ensure the greatest possible use of talent at all levels of ability.

2. During the first programme, annual Exchequer expenditure on education almost doubled and now amounts to over £30 million a year. In the paragraphs that follow, an account is given of the proposals at present under consideration for the further expansion and improvement of education. These proposals are necessarily incomplete and, in some respects, tentative — pending the completion of three studies at present in progress. These are the Investment in Education Survey, the Scientific Research and Technology Survey

and the investigations of the Commission on Higher Education. The first two are conducted jointly with OECD. The Investment in Education Survey, which will be completed later this year, will determine the needs of an expanding Irish economy in skilled manpower at all levels over the next ten to fifteen years, assess the investment in educational services required and suggest alternative economic ways of meeting these needs; the other survey, which will be completed in 1965, will assess the need for scientific research and technology in relation to economic growth; the Commission on Higher Education, which hopes to report before the end of 1964, is investigating all aspects of higher education.

I. PRIMARY EDUCATION

3. The improvement of the educational services must begin with the primary section, which is the foundation of the entire structure. An improvement in primary education will provide a solid basis for the extension of post-primary education to all children who are capable of profiting from it. Factors that determine the quality of the instruction given in primary schools and in respect of which the State has a special responsibility because of the financial implications are teacher/pupil ratios, teaching training, teaching aids and school buildings.

* * * * * * * * * *

II. SECONDARY EDUCATION

15. One of the fruits of economic progress, and a pre-condition of further progress, will be the raising of the school-leaving age to 15 years before the end of the programme. This requires detailed long-term planning. It necessitates not only the provision of additional school

buildings and about 1,100 more teachers, but also the revision of both the primary and post-primary school programmes. A special study will be made of the detailed measures necessary to give effect to this proposal.

16. The number of pupils attending secondary schools has risen rapidly in post-war years. In the school year 1945/46 there were 41,799 pupils in 385 recognised secondary schools. By 1962/63 the attendance had risen to 84,916 in 557 schools. If, as seems likely, this rate of expansion is maintained until the end of the present decade, the number will then be over 110,000. The aim of Government policy will be to facilitate the enlargement of the secondary school system on this scale and to ensure that its educational content is adapted to the rapidly-changing social and economic needs of the community.

State Aid

17. Since secondary schools are private institutions, the provision of the necessary facilities depends in general on their own initiative. State aid takes a number of forms: (1) a capitation grant (which includes an element of grant towards capital costs) in respect of pupils following an approved course and registering a certain number of attendances, (2) special grants related to the teaching of certain subjects, e.g. science, manual instruction, music, etc., (3) the payment of teachers' incremental salary and (4) the award of scholarships. A new scheme of grants towards the cost of secondary school buildings is being introduced.

****

Comprehensive Schools

20. The State recognises that it has responsibilities to those areas where adequate facilities for post-primary education (secondary or vocational) do not at present exist and where for various reasons, such as small population, these are not likely to be provided through private initiative. The Government propose, accordingly, to establish in these areas — mainly in the west, north-west and south-west — comprehensive post-primary day schools which will provide for the educational needs of children in the age group 12/13 to 15/16 years.

* * * * * * * * * *

III VOCATIONAL EDUCATION

30. Vocational education comprises continuation education, which is designed to meet the needs of children in the age group 14 to 16, and technical education, which caters for the age group 16 to 18. Continuation education supplements education provided in elementary schools; it includes general and practical training for employment. Technical education covers theoretical and practical instruction in industrial, commercial and household skills.

* * * * * * * * * *

Continuation Education

33. The limitation of whole-time day courses in continuation education to two years has retarded the development of vocational education. To remedy this defect the Government propose, in addition to establishing the comprehensive schools described above, to extend from two to three years the present course in vocational schools. Pupils who complete the three-year course will be eligible to sit for the Intermediate Certificate Examination.

Technical Education

34. The changes proposed for continuation education and the establishment of the new comprehensive schools will entail the provision of courses for those over 16 who have obtained the Intermediate Certificate and wish to follow a technical education. The Government have, therefore, decided to introduce within the next year or two a two-year course in technical education that will lead to an examination for a Technical School Leaving Certificate. This certificate will testify to the satisfactory completion of a course of general and technical education that will fit the holder for entrance to certain university faculties or advanced courses in a college of technology.

* * * * * * * * * *

IV UNIVERSITY EDUCATION

40. Detailed decisions regarding future policy on higher education in general and university education in particular must await the report of the Commission on Higher Education. Meanwhile, action is being taken to overcome the shortage of accommodation, which is likely to become more acute with the growth in the number of school-leavers.

I.12 Third Programme for Economic and Social Development 1969-1972

The first and second programmes for economic expansion in 1958 and 1963 respectively have been referred to earlier in this volume I.11. The second programme was scheduled to run from 1964 to 1970 but by 1967 its targets were so far from being achieved that it was abandoned and a third programme was laid before the Houses of the Oireachtas in March 1969. The third programme again highlighted the important role of education in economic and social development and adverted to the increased government investment in education during the terms of the previous programmes. The following extracts are taken from the section on education:

(2) EDUCATION

6. The vital role of education in economic and social development and the need for fundamental changes in this sector have been repeatedly stressed in recent years. This increased emphasis has been reflected in the expansion in State expenditure. During the first programme, Exchequer expenditure on education (excluding agricultural education) increased from less than £16 million in 1958/59 to over £25 million in 1963/64 at current prices. The rate of increase has been even greater during the second programme; Exchequer expenditure in 1968/69 is estimated at £56 million.

7. The shape of development in the next four years will be determined by important changes which have been introduced in recent years, and by the implementation of proposals which have recently been announced; these are described in the following paragraphs.

8. The Report of the Survey Team on Investment in Education, which was published in December, 1965, plays an important part in the framing of official policy on education. A Development Branch has been established within the Department of Education to continue the work that the Survey Team began, and to undertake long-term planning in education.

Primary Education

9. The number of pupils in National Schools is roughly static at about half a million; this is a reflection of the relatively static population. It is expected that, despite the projected increase in population, this number will

fall slightly during the 1970s according as policy is directed towards ensuring that the last three years of compulsory attendance at school will be spent in post-primary schools. The number of schools is decreasing in line with the policy of discontinuing small schools where possible and bringing children to larger schools where better educational facilities can be provided. Over 350 amalgamations have taken place. The number of teachers continues to increase in accordance with the policy of reducing the pupil-teacher ratio; this policy will be continued as circumstances permit until no teacher will have more than 35 pupils. Old and unsuitable schools will continue to be replaced, and major schemes of improvement and enlargement undertaken, at the rate of 26,000 places each year until all pupils are housed in buildings with reasonable standards of hygiene, heating and comfort; this will involve maintenance of the annual target of 100 new schools and 50 major enlargement and improvement schemes.

10. The curriculum is being broadened, and the syllabuses in all subjects are being revised and modernised...... Greater provision will be made for the education and training of the physically and mentally handicapped child. In addition, special assistance will be provided for the retarded or slow-learning child.

Post-Primary Education

11. The growing demand for post-primary education has been accelerated by the introduction in 1967 of free education and transport for post-primary pupils. The number of pupils in post-primary schools increased from about 149,000 in 1966 to 184,500 in 1968. The raising of the school leaving age to 15 years in 1970 will

cause some further increase, though a large proportion of the 14 to 15 age-group is already receiving whole-time education. It is expected that the number will exceed 200,000 before the end of the third programme.

12. The Intermediate Certificate programme has been introduced successfully into vocational schools. By pooling the resources of secondary and vocational schools, every student can be offered, to the greatest extent which resources will allow, a comprehensive education suited to his needs and aptitudes.

13. The Department of Education has already published plans to meet the increased enrolments at junior cycle level and has at present under consideration, in conjunction with the revision and extension of the Leaving Certificate programme, plans to cater for senior cycle requirements.

14. The number of teachers in secondary and vocational schools has been increasing by about 400 per year. The increase in 1968/69 is about 800. An even larger annual increase will be required in future. To meet these needs, there are greatly increased numbers in the relevant faculties in the Universities; courses leading to the Higher Diploma in Education have been introduced in Maynooth, and departmental courses for the training of vocational teachers are being increased.

15. The new system of groupings in the Leaving Certificate course to be introduced in the year 1969/70 will broaden the scope of the programme, particularly in regard to technical and commercial subjects. A third year course and examination, to be known as the Advanced Certificate course, will be introduced in 1972.

State comprehensive schools

16. State comprehensive schools of medium size are already in operation at Cootehill, Carraroe, Shannon and Glenties, and one is planned for Raphoe. It was originally intended that these schools would serve areas where facilities for post-primary education (secondary and vocational) are inadequate and, for various reasons, such as small population, are not likely to be provided through private initiative. To cater for the special needs of the Ballymun area in Dublin two large comprehensive schools are planned, each to accommodate 750 pupils.

Regional technical colleges

17. Five regional technical colleges will be in operation by 1970, and four more shortly after that. The main long-term function of these colleges will be to train pupils for entry into trade and industry, covering a broad spectrum of occupations ranging from craft to higher level, especially in engineering and science but also in commercial, linguistic, catering, art and design and other specialities.

Higher education

21. The Commission on Higher Education presented its report in 1967, and the future structure of higher education is being reviewed in the light of its recommendations. The Minister for Education has announced the Government's intention to constitute a new University of Dublin of which University College Dublin, and Trinity College Dublin, would be complementary colleges. The Government have established a permanent Authority — the Higher Education Authority — to advise on the financial and organisational problems of higher education. The Authority will examine and advise the Minister on

proposals for the co-ordination and development of the higher education system generally. It will also advise on allocation of the public funds made available for higher education between the institutions and maintain a continuous review of the country's needs in higher education.

I.13 Ár ndaltaí uile - All our Children, 1969.

Many changes took place in education in Ireland in the 1960s. With the introduction of free secondary education in 1967 the Primary Certificate Examination was abolished and during the final years of the 1960s a new Primary School Curriculum was piloted in a number of National Schools throughout the country. At post-primary level, the first comprehensive schools were opened; some new subjects were introduced and the syllabi of many of the existing subjects were revised. Regional Technical Colleges were being built in eight towns. Brian Lenihan, T.D., Minister for Education decided to explain these changes and developments to parents and a booklet - All our Children - was produced in 1969 and distributed to all households in the country. It was a colourful and attractively presented booklet, with diagrams and illustrations to explain the various changes that had occurred and were about to happen. It explained both the structures and the curriculum of schools at primary, post-primary and third level. It provided an overview of the proposed new Primary Curriculum; explained why the government had decided to close small schools; discussed the free transport scheme; and explained why report cards for pupils were being introduced. In regard to post-primary level, it included a section on 'the comprehensive idea ' and on comprehensive schools; a section on student guidance and on junior examinations. The booklet made it clear that pupils coming to the end of the junior cycle would have a major decision to make. Would they proceed to the Leaving Certificate after a two year course (choosing one of five 'groups' - Language; Science; Business Studies; Applied Science or Social Studies) and subsequently continue in second level education for a further year and sit for the Advanced Certificate? Or would they proceed after junior cycle to Technician and Trade Courses with a view possibly to attending the new Regional Technical Colleges which were in the process of being built? At the end of second-level education would they opt for Higher Education either in a University, a College of Technology or a Regional Technical College?

While second level education in the 1970s, particularly at senior cycle, did not develop along the lines indicated in the booklet "All our Children", the booklet is a useful indicator of the plan for educational development as perceived by the government in 1969. The following is the text of the Minister's introduction to the booklet:

ALL THE CHILDREN OF THE NATION
This booklet is for parents. Its purpose is to give them, as briefly as possible, the basic facts about the education of their children.

PARENTS want their children to grow up to be good people, healthy in mind and body, skilful and happy in their work. This is what education is for. In its broadest sense, education is a process that begins in infancy and continues right through life; and the most important educators are of course the parents themselves. However, the word "education," as used in this booklet, means the specialised education that is given in schools. Today's children must receive the right kind and the right amount of this education if they are to cope with the very complex world of tomorrow.

EVERYONE is aware that Irish schools are going through a period of rapid change. People have even spoken of an educational revolution. Important developments are taking place *in content* (what we teach) and *in method* (how we teach it). At the same time, there is a vast increase in the number of pupils. This means that a great deal more money is now being spent on increased *facilities* (buildings, equipment, transport, and so on). The nation is investing heavily in its children.

ALL these changes are necessary if we are to attain our most urgent social and educational objective: *equality of opportunity.* Every child, without exception, will receive the best possible education suited to his or her individual talents. We are in a hurry to bring this about. Indeed, in the past few years we have gone a long way towards doing so. Already we can claim that wider educational opportunities are open to more of our children than ever before in our history.

OPPORTUNITY, however, means very little unless people know that it is there and how best to use it. It is essential, therefore, that parents understand the structure of Irish education, and particularly that they know when and how to make those crucial decisions on which, to a great extent, their children's future depends. That is why this booklet has been compiled and is being sent to every household in Ireland.

I.14 School Attendance Act, 1926 (Extension of Application) Order, 1972. (Statutory Instrument No.105 of 1972)

The question of raising the school-leaving age had been discussed at various times in the late 1940s, 1950s and 1960s. It was not until 1972 that the provisions of the 1926 School Attendance Act were extended to make school attendance compulsory for children from 6 to 15 years of age. The following is the full text of the Order of 1972:

SCHOOL ATTENDANCE ACT, 1926
(EXTENSION OF APPLICATION) ORDER, 1972

1. Pádraig Ó Fachtna, Minister for Education, in exercise of the powers conferred on me by section 24 (1) of the School Attendance Act, 1926 (No.17 of 1926), hereby order as follows:
   (i) This Order may be cited as the School Attendance Act, 1926 (Extension of Application) Order, 1972.
   (ii) This Order shall come into operation on the 1st day of July, 1972.

2. The Interpretation Act, 1937 (No.38 of 1937), applies to this Order.

3. The provisions of the School Attendance Act, 1926 (No.17 of 1926), shall extend to children who have attained the age of fourteen years and have not attained the age of fifteen years.

GIVEN under my Official Seal,
this 12th day of April, 1972.
PÁDRAIG Ó FACHTNA,
Minister for Education.

I.15 Programme for National Development, 1978 - 1981.

Following the General Election in 1977, Fianna Fáil came to power with an overall majority. The Taoiseach, Jack Lynch, recognised the need for sustained economic recovery and two Green Papers published in 1978 (National Development 1977- 1980 and Development for Full Employment) projected an optimistic picture of economic growth, improved standards of living and the creation of new jobs. In January 1979, a government White Paper entitled Programme for National Development, 1978 - 1981, was laid before both Houses of the Oireachtas. The White Paper

— reviewed in general terms the economy and its potential for further development;

— indicated how the Government intended to shape national development over the immediate years ahead;

— outlined the Government's policies for economic and social development and the measures proposed to implement them.

The White Paper maintained the optimistic scenario of the earlier Green Papers - a scenario which did not materialise in the following years - but the short section on education provided an early indication of the cutbacks which would become widespread in education during the following decade. The following extract contains the proposals on education:

EDUCATION

6.10 The principal challenge in the educational sector in the period up to 1981 and beyond will be the provision of adequate places and teachers for the increasing numbers of pupils expected at each of the three educational levels. An accelerated programme of school building will be necessary to provide school places, and it will also be necessary to augment the teacher supply. A special effort is required at primary level where the Government's aim is to reduce maximum class sizes to forty in the school year 1981-82. Furthermore, additional measures will be required in order to make better provision for remedial instruction, particularly in primary schools.

6.11 A White Paper on education, as promised in the Government's pre-election Manifesto, is being prepared for publication in 1979.This paper will deal, among other subjects, with the optimum use of resources available for education, including the priority to be given to each level in the allocation of available funds and the relevance of present curricula, particularly at second level, to the needs of present-day students.

6.12 The Green Paper put forward two options relating to this sector:

(i) fees charged by third level institutions might be increased; the grant scheme might be improved as a consequence and a loan scheme be examined, and

(ii) training college students might be charged for board and accommodation.

While the NESC agreed with both sets of suggestions, the Higher Education Authority recommended against any substantial increase in third level fees. The Authority felt that if, nonetheless, fees were to be increased significantly, substantial improvements in the grants scheme would be required. The Authority is carrying out a study of the feasibility of a loan scheme for third level students. The Union of Students in Ireland rejected both options in the Green Paper and called instead for a comprehensive grant scheme for third level and suggested that the options, if implemented, would further limit access to third level education.

6.13 On the first of these options, the Government feel that third level institutions should be moving towards a situation where they would collect a greater proportion of their income in fees and that this movement should be accompanied by an appropriate improvement in the grants scheme for poorer students. On the second option they consider that the subsidy for board and accommodation for student teachers should be reduced, with a view to placing these students more on a par with other third level students.

I.16 White Paper on Educational Development 1980.

In December 1980, a White Paper on Educational Development was issued by John Wilson, T.D., Minister for Education. The Fianna Fáil Manifesto of 1977 had promised that, if elected to government, a White Paper would be produced setting out "the lines for future education development in Ireland". During the previous decade, decisive changes had affected the structure, content and funding of the educational system. These included the introduction of free second-level education and the provision of a countrywide school transport system in 1967; the launching in 1971 of the New Curriculum for primary schools; the expansion of third-level education by the setting up of nine Regional Technical Colleges, two National Institutes of Higher Education and the opening of Thomond College. Structural changes had also occurred — with the setting up of comprehensive and community schools at second level and the establishment of the Higher Education Authority and the National Council for Educational Awards at third level. During the decade, government expenditure on education had increased by 100% in real terms; the increase in money terms was much greater — from £78 million in 1970 to £443 million in 1979. It was in this context that the White Paper offered guidelines "for the development of our educational services over the immediate period ahead." The White Paper was not intended as a definitive document — nor were its proposals intended to be regarded "as rigid or inflexible." It was hoped that the Paper would stimulate and foster constructive discussion. The Foreword to the White Paper is reproduced here in full:

FOREWORD

An educational system serves a dual purpose — to conserve traditional values and to prepare for the future. It provides for the task of interpreting the essential features of a social and cultural heritage and, at the same time, that of preparing the young for life in a society characterised by ever-accelerating change. And, if it is to reflect those needs which, indeed, it helps to create, it follows that the system itself will undergo a continuous process of adaptation and development.

Over the past decade the operation of such a process has brought decisive changes affecting the structure, content and funding of the educational system. The introduction of free second-level education and the provision of a countrywide school transport system in 1967 are rightly regarded as major steps towards equality of educational opportunity. The launching in 1971 of the New Curriculum heralded a far-reaching innovation at primary level. Second-level curricula, too, have been subjected to a continuous process of adaptation to the varied needs and abilities of a greatly expanded student population. This development has been accompanied by significant structural changes, notable among which was the establishment of new comprehensive and community schools.

Since the Commission on Higher Education presented its report in 1967, the provision of third-level education has been expanded in many important ways. Nine Regional Technical Colleges offering many third-level courses have been established. In 1971, the Higher Education Authority was set up by an Act of the Oireachtas to advise the Government on the development of higher education facilities. In existence since 1972, the National Council for Educational Awards has been established on a statutory basis. The duration of the course of education for teachers in primary schools has been extended from two years to three and teachers now qualify on successful completion of their course for the award of a university degree in education. A National Institute for Higher Education has been set up in Limerick which provides degree and diploma courses and a similar Institute has been set up in Dublin. Thomond College, Limerick, offers courses for the education of teachers of specialist subjects. Legislation on the re-organisation of the university system is in course of preparation.

All of these developments and particularly those appertaining to the improvement of pupil-teacher ratios and to the greater accessibility of second and third-level education have led to a very rapid expansion in the cost of education to the State. Between 1970 and 1979 expenditure on education increased by 100 per cent in real terms: the increase in money terms was, of course, much greater — from £78 million in 1970 to £443 million in 1979. One measure of the burden represented by State expenditure on education is that at present such expenditure is the equivalent of £9 per week per head of the working population. The likely financing problem which the educational services as at present constituted will pose for public funds in the future for demographic and other reasons cannot be ignored and must be taken into account in considering the pace at which proposals for further development may be pursued.

Against this general background this White Paper, promised in the Fianna Fáil Manifesto, offers guidelines for the development of our educational services over the immediate period ahead. The statement in the manifesto proposed:

> to set out in a White Paper the lines for future education development in Ireland.

It has been suggested that the issue of a Green Paper would have afforded a wider opportunity for discussion. The Government view was that the document to be produced should not be unduly hesitant about making proposals for future development; that an expression of the views of the Minister for Education would be expected and welcomed: AND THAT SUCH INDICATION OF GOVERNMENT THINKING NEED NOT AT ALL INHIBIT WIDE-RANGING DISCUSSION SINCE IT IS NOWISE INTENDED THAT THE PROPOSALS OF THIS WHITE PAPER BE REGARDED AS RIGID OR INFLEXIBLE.

At a time of change and challenge we must constantly be prepared to take our bearings anew and to adapt, as circumstances demand, to a developing situation. Far from stifling constructive discussion, a pointer to Government intent should stimulate and foster it.

I.17 Report of the Pupil Transfer Committee, 1981

In June 1978, the Minister for Education, John Wilson, T.D. appointed a committee with the following terms of reference: "To report on the problems of transition from child-centred primary to subject-centred post-primary schools and to make recommendations as to changes which may be necessary in primary and post-primary curricula in order to alleviate these problems." An Dr. Tarlach Ó Raifeartaigh, former secretary of the Department of Education, chaired the committee which presented its report to the Minister in May 1981. It was a report of 100 pages covering issues such as the age of transfer; problems of transfer; communications between pupils, parents, schools, teachers, public and private agencies; the alignment of syllabi between primary and post-primary and teacher training. It provided a useful overview of the curricular issues which were seen as significant at that time, but surprisingly, the report concluded that "Most of the primary and post-primary syllabi in the various subjects seem to articulate very well with each other. Where they may not appear to do so, a school may easily, as it sees fit, make the necessary adjustments." Nevertheless the report also stated that "The primary and post-primary syllabi in each of the three subjects, Irish, Mathematics and Geography ... we find to be badly in need of better alignment." It did not recommend any radical change in procedures at the point of transfer between primary and post-primary apart from suggesting that "there should be good communication between all parties concerned." It supported the continued use of the School Record Card which "should be seen as a valuable adjunct to the contact between primary and post-primary teachers." The following extracts are from the summary of the report:

Chapter II makes the point that there is no evidence for other than a gradual intellectual, mental and emotional development between the ages of ten and fourteen or thereabouts. Tradition and circumstances, however, insist on the pupil's transfer from the primary to the post-primary stage at some point within that period. The Committee considers that the most suitable age for such transfer is twelve plus, on the educational grounds that by then the generality of pupils will have satisfactorily completed Sixth Class and so will be equipped with the basic cultural tools which will enable them to benefit fully from the next stage of their education.

The distinctive roles of the primary and post-primary schools are then examined.

Nowadays the primary school's approach is geared to more active participation by the pupils in the learning process than used to be the case. In addition, the primary teacher is now free to integrate the teaching of most subjects of the curriculum to the extent that these will be seen by the pupil as interrelated. In contrast to this, the post-primary school must, in view of the ever-increasing in-depth treatment of the subjects which is called for by the prospect of the public examinations which loom ahead, incline more and more towards the teaching of each subject as a separate entity. In this context the role of the public examination falls to be considered. The Committee sees the fundamental advantage of the Intermediate Certificate Examination as for at least two-thirds of the parents the first entirely independent and objective assessment of their children's scholastic calibre. While therefore it may be open to reform, its abolition should not be contemplated.

Chapter III considers the problems faced by the new pupil at a post-primary school. The feature of immediate impact upon him or her will probably be the fact of a different teacher for each of the various subjects where up to then the same teacher had charge of at least the core subjects. Arising from this will be an increased amount of homework. New subjects, or the accustomed subjects in a new dress, may also prove a hurdle for some. For most, however, the excitement of novelty will counterbalance any jarring effects of the new regime.

There remain, however, perhaps 20% of the total whom the transfer will present with emotional, intellectual, social, physical or other problems demanding special attention. The main categories of these are listed and advice tendered as to the remedial provision to be made for them. The largest group among them, the "slow learners," is treated of at some length, as are the nervous, timid, or otherwise "odd man out" type among the new pupils. The difficulties of the latter, while usually ephemeral, can be none the less agonizing. The case is made for the appointment of an experienced member of the school's full-time staff as Transfer Advisor for such pupils.

Chapter IV deals with communication all round as between parents, school authorities, teachers, pupils, and as between schools at both levels. It makes a strong plea for meeting more than half-way those parents who feel themselves to be inadequate or have difficulty in coping with life. Special stress is laid also on the importance of personal contact and rapport between the primary and the post-primary teacher in relation to transfer pupils.

****

Chapter V sees as a first response to the second part of the remit the desirability of an extension or further extension into the first post-primary year, and even beyond, of the new primary school approach referred to in Chapter II. In this regard the question of a bridging period on the United States, French or German model is considered, but ruled out on the grounds that our experience of the transfer problem is insufficient to warrant such an innovation without much further research into the Irish context.

Another possibility considered is the introduction at second level of a four years' Junior Cycle course for all. The practical objection to the immediate institution of a four years' Junior Cycle is that prior provision, over some years, of the additional specialist teachers and accommodation would be needed. As educationalists, however, the Committee sees a four years' Junior Cycle course as highly desirable and recommends it subject to the provision of adequate accommodation and of the specialist teaching personnel as adumbrated, — *but strictly on condition that in no circumstances should it be introduced save where the pupils concerned will have satisfactorily completed the Class VI primary school programme.* This condition is regarded by the Committee as at the very root of the continuity which it seeks as between the primary and post-primary stage.

Chapter VI addresses itself to the syllabi of the various subjects common to the primary and post-primary curricula. The primary and post-primary programmes in Irish are found to be to a considerable degree out of joint, as are, to a somewhat lesser extent, the Mathematics and the Geography programmes. The unsatisfactory showing of a relatively large proportion of candidates in these subjects at the Intermediate Certificate Examination of 1979 (the most recent year for which these statistics are available) is commented on. Certain changes in the post-primary syllabi for these three subjects, with a view to their better alignment with the work of the primary school, are recommended as urgent. No very significant curricula adjustments would appear to be required in other subjects, but suggestions are made for an approach in the class treatment of some areas which would render smoother the path of transition. At this point also the question of teachers of Music, Art and other specialisms is mooted and a plea made for a more ample supply thereof.

In Chapter VII teacher training, both in-service and professional, is considered. The point most borne in on the Committee in the course of their deliberations is the necessity, alluded to in Chapter IV, of a close understanding and rapport between the primary and post-primary teachers immediately involved with pupils at the transfer stage. In the Committee's opinion the only really effective method of bringing this about generally in a short time is a countrywide in-service seminar for the teachers concerned. A plan of operation for this, with an estimate of the cost, is given in outline.

Such a countrywide seminar would probably have to be repeated at intervals for some time, but if it were not to become a permanent fixture, the professional training courses for primary and post-primary teachers should include specific and adequate treatment of pupil transfer problems.

It is also the view of the Committee that there should be a process of selection, including a view of candidates' suitability, for entry to the course for the Higher Diploma in Education (the post-graduate training course for most post-primary teachers). In majority the Committee believes that this selection process should take place following the degree and immediately prior to the commencement of the Higher Diploma course, that is, within the framework of the present system. A substantial minority, however, take the view that the training of the post-primary teachers concerned should, like that of primary teachers, be a continuous combination of the academic and the pedagogic and so that the selection concerned should precede university entry.

With regard to the present framework for the Higher diploma in Education the Committee considers it to be self-evident that the one year's training course (or, as in some cases, two part-time years) is too brief to permit of an adequate insight into the many problems, including that of pupil transfer, which will confront today's teacher. If therefore the present framework is retained, it is their conviction that the course should be extended to comprise a full year plus a part-time year, pending the introduction of a full two years' course.

It is recommended also that by arrangement between the Minister for Education, the University institutions and the host schools of the Higher Diploma in Education students there be created on a pilot basis a number of posts as Tutor Teacher, to be held (with an Allowance, class-time reduction and certain expenses) by experienced members of the staffs of the host schools in question. The duty of the Tutor Teachers would be to assist and supplement the University Departments of Education in the supervision of the teaching practice of whatever number of Higher Diploma students might be allotted to each.He or she would thus, it is hoped, be a very useful link between the theory and the practice of teaching.

I.18 The Way Forward — National Economic Plan 1983-1987

Following the fall of the Fine Gael/Labour Coalition government in January 1982, a Fianna Fáil government again came to power, and in October of that year a new economic plan, *The Way Forward,* was published. The plan committed the government to the phasing out of the huge deficit by 1986 and contained a brief section on education. However, shortly after the publication of *The Way Forward,* the Fianna Fáil government fell and the plan became an election manifesto for the party. The following extracts are from the section on education in *The Way Forward.*

EDUCATION

Policy Framework

2. Within the limits of the financial resources which it has been possible to provide, very significant progress has been made at first and second level in recent years in meeting the priority capital needs in the provision of new buildings and the replacement of sub-standard accommodation. An increased number of second-level pupils have been taking subjects which are more directly relevant to the world of work than the more traditional academic subjects. The general process of making second-level schooling more relevant to the world of work is being further developed by the pre-employment courses now being offered in many schools and by the School/Industry Link Scheme which was initiated by the Manpower Consultative Committee of the Department of Labour. At third level there has been, in recent times, a new emphasis on science and technology with the completion of a programme for expansion of seven Regional Technical Colleges , the provision of the first phase of building for the new National Institute for Higher education (NIHE) in Dublin, the commencement of the second phase of the NIHE in Limerick and a new College of Education in Limerick to train technical subject teachers for second level schools. A special

manpower programme was also initiated under which facilities were provided in many third-level institutions to meet identified manpower needs in science and technology.

3. It is anticipated that net enrolments in the coming decade at first and second level will increase by about 70,000 and the thrust of capital provision over the Plan period will be to utilize the financial resources available to cope with this expansion in numbers. While this increase in enrolments is considerably lower than in the previous decade, there will also be demand for places arising from population shifts and for the replacement of old and uneconomic buildings. The demand for additional third-level capital facilities is also expected to increase rapidly and it will be necessary to order this demand into clear priorities so that the limited resources which will be available for investment in the public sector generally can be used in the most effective way. In this respect, regard will be had to the fact that while capital and later running costs are very heavy in all parts of the labour-intensive education sector, they are particularly high at third-level.

Policy Approach and Measures

4. The basic approach to public capital investment in education over the Plan period will be to achieve maximum effectiveness in the use of the limited resources available and, accordingly, to implement only those policy measures with the highest benefit to cost ratio in educational terms. The 1983 allocation will be £94m and it is intended that the annual allocations for 1984 to 1987 will be of the same order. Low priority expenditure, e.g. on recreational facilities will have to be contained. At first and second-level particular attention will be devoted to ensuring that in the

distribution of scarce resources increased emphasis will be given to what might be called educationally deprived areas.

5. The possibility of providing school transport facilities other than through State agencies will be further examined.

6. The further reform of the curriculum in second-level schools will be advanced by the setting up of a Curriculum Council as referred to in the White Paper on Educational Development. This Council will be representative of educational, cultural, commercial and agricultural interests and will advise on the direction that reform should take. In particular, it will have regard to the need to relate the curriculum to a greater extent to the employment needs of pupils while maintaining the benefits of a broad-based education. At third-level, consideration will be given, in consultation with the interests involved, to making the most efficient use of existing very valuable facilities including, if necessary, the question of restructuring the academic year.

I.19 Programme for Government, December 1982

In the general election of November 1982, Fianna Fáil failed to achieve an overall majority and a coalition government of Fine Gael and Labour, with Garrett Fitzgerald as Taoiseach, came to power. Their agreed Programme for Government, dated December 1982, contained a short section on education, which formed the basis for educational policy during the life of that government. The following is the text of the section on education.

EDUCATION

The reform and development of our educational system is essential to this country's future progress in the modern.world.

In particular, education must be made relevant to the world of work and the nature of a rapidly changing and complex society.

Our young people must be trained in the skills necessary to obtain, and retain, employment as well as being educated to cope with the demands of modern life.

The Government will give priority to reform of the curriculum and examination system and will establish a curriculum and examinations board. A new course designed to prepare young people for taking their place in the world of work and in society will be instituted at second level. The examination system will be re-structured so as to reduce the pressure on students caused by the present Leaving Certificate system, and the excessive influence of third level entrance requirements upon second level teaching and curriculum will be eliminated.

Administrative structures within the educational system will be reformed so as to make it more decentralised and democratic.

A National Parents' Council, through which parents' views on policy matters can be expressed, will be established.

Scientific and technological education will be developed as will facilities for computer education. A special pilot scheme, for the use of computers in senior classes in primary schools, will be carried out.

Support will be given for the establishment of more all-Irish schools at both primary and post-primary level.

Co-education will be encouraged and further steps taken to ensure that both girls and boys have an equal opportunity of studying all subjects in the curriculum.

The Government will ensure the maximum possible integration of handicapped and other children within the educational system.

Special attention will be paid to areas of disadvantage which will have priority for improvements in pupil-teacher ratios and appointment of remedial teachers.

Consultation will be held with third-level institutions with a view to preparing a four-year plan for their future activities. The concept of the "dual-year" in technological colleges will be introduced. The Higher Education Authority will be re-constituted.

A national scheme for adult and continuing education will be introduced. Distance learning and second-chance education will be encouraged.

Special attention will be paid to reducing the "drop-out" of able pupils at senior cycle level, which seems to be the single biggest obstacle to improving equality of opportunity in our society.

I.20 Building on Reality 1985-1987

Building on Reality was the title of the policy document which laid the basis for economic development during the second half of the term of office of the Fine Gael/Labour coalition government. Many contemporary commentators were critical of the document, comparing it unfavourably with the Programmes for Economic Expansion of the 1960s. The following extracts are from the sections on education.

EDUCATION

5.19 The Government give the highest priority to having a well educated population. A detailed account of education policy and priorities is set out in the *Programme for Action in Education, 1984-1987* published by the Government in January 1984. The major policy objectives of the programme seek to achieve a closer relationship between education and modern society and between education and the world of work. Special emphasis is given to achieving much greater real equality of opportunity in education and to providing special help for the disadvantaged within the system. In addition, many changes in courses, curricula and structures are proposed in order to shape the educational system for the new and different challenges of the coming years.

5.20 Primary education will be a priority for expenditure during the course of the Plan, together with special funding for disadvantaged areas as advocated by the National Planning Board. The measures to be taken will include the appointment of additional teaching posts in areas of particular need. A special fund of £0.5 million each year will allow for increased provision for free books and teaching materials, libraries and other requirements for disadvantaged areas.

5.21 The major thrust of policy at second-level will relate to the areas of curriculum reform in order that curricula would be more relevant to the needs and aspirations of the students; to rationalisation of the provision of educational facilities on a local basis; and to special provision for students who are likely to leave the system before or directly after the end of the compulsory cycle, details of which are given in Paragraph 5.24 below. The Curriculum and Examinations Board is charged with the tasks of reviewing curricula and bringing forward new examination and assessment procedures. There will also be provision at post-primary level for special funding for disadvantaged areas, in particular as regards the allocation of additional remedial and guidance teachers.

5.22 Government policy at third-level is to provide education for as many young people as possible. The level of real resources to be made available at third-level will be increased by almost 5 per cent by 1987. ....The question of rationalisation and effectiveness of the third-level sector in order to cater for as many students as possible in the most cost-effective way, is being pursued with the various interests involved with particular regard to the specific proposals made in the Action Programme.

GREATER PROVISION OF COURSES FUNDED THROUGH ESF

5.24 The Government have gained approval from the European Commission for a number of proposals with regard to the provision, with funding from the European Social Fund, of programmes to provide young people, particularly those without qualifications, with full-time courses involving basic vocational training. The proposals involve expanding existing pre-employment courses and extending them to selected secondary schools adapting existing pre-employment secretarial courses to increase their relevance to modern technological needs and providing one and two-year courses for young people who have completed compulsory education and for whom an academic senior-cycle is seen as unsuitable. In the 1984/85 academic year these courses will cater for 19,000 students — a five-fold increase. A feature of these courses is the payment of an annual allowance of £300 to participants.

5.25 Increased ESF funding has also been obtained for the existing middle-level technician programme in the RTCs and Colleges of Technology. These courses will cater for up to 12,000 young people in 1984/85. The cost of all ESF-funded courses is estimated at £32.6 million in 1984/85.

TEACHER TRAINING

5.26 The main policy proposals in the area of teacher-training relate to a review of the B.Ed. courses for national teachers and of the initial training and induction of post-primary teachers and particularly, the increased provision of in-service training for all teachers. The up-dating and widening of teachers' skills throughout their careers is seen as a most important element in providing a modern and flexible education programme and in improving the quality of education generally.

I.21 Programme for Action in Education 1984 - 1987

In January 1984, Gemma Hussey, T.D., Minister for Education, published a Programme for Action in Education for the period 1984 to 1987. In the Foreword to the Programme, the Minister indicated that she believed that there was a need to develop a definite programme for education and to set out the Government's priorities to be met over the following four years. The Programme for Action which reflected the specific commitments with regard to education made in the Programme for Government, December 1982, was described by the Minister as "a realistic document which would as far as possible take account of the views of all interested parties involved in the educational process — parents, teachers and managers — and at the same time take account of the financial and economic situation of the country." It set out to be "specific and to avoid generalisations" while at the same time it claimed to be "rooted in reality." Like the White Paper of 1980, it was hoped that the Programme for Action "will initiate a constructive debate on the educational system."

The Programme was a short document of less than 50 pages. It included chapters on Primary Education, Special Education, Second-level and Third-Level Education and Teacher Education. During the Ministry of Gemma Hussey, a Progress Report was circulated each year indicating the extent to which the proposals of the Programme had been achieved. The following underlying principles were set out in the Preamble:

1.1 THE FOLLOWING PRINCIPLES UNDERLIE THE PROGRAMME FOR ACTION:

(i) The education system should, as far as possible, enable all citizens to have access to an education which is relevant to their needs and which will assist them in seeking to fulfill the potential of their abilities and talents.

(ii) Education should be continuously updated to make it relevant to the modern world, to developments in technology, to changing employment opportunities and patterns as well as to increased leisure time.

(iii) The education system should seek to make permanent and continuing education available for all citizens and to equalize opportunities for educational advancement between the various socio-economic groups in society and between the sexes.

(iv) Education provision should discriminate positively in favour of the educationally disadvantaged within available resources.

(v) The development of our linguistic and cultural heritage should be at the core of our education system.

(vi) Responsibility and authority should be delegated as far as feasible, subject to necessary controls, with a view to achieving a full partnership between all the interests involved.

****

1.4 The Programme must be realistic and must take into account the financial and economic situation of the country. Wealth must be created before it can be distributed. Effective planning cannot be undertaken without having regard to the availability of resources. The rate of implementation of the proposals in the Programme must, therefore, be governed by the rate of progress in the economy, subject to the priority which the Government accords to education within its programme of public expenditure. The harsh reality of the present Exchequer difficulties must be faced entailing, as they do, a reduction in real terms in total Government expenditure for some years ahead.

****

1.7 In contrast to the general Western European outlook of population stagnation and even decline, this country has a rapidly growing population. By 1987/88 it is projected that, compared with 1982/83, the total number of full-time students will increase by some 54,000 to 989,500. The greatest growth in demand in percentage terms will be at third level which is also the most costly. The rising social demand for education, which has few parallels in the developed world, poses exceptional problems in the face of the deterioration in recent years in the state of the public finances..... At a time when resources are scarce it is all the more imperative that the educational services be cost efficient and cost effective. Wastage, where identified, must be eliminated.

****

1.10 While accepting that education cannot by itself redress the social imbalances in our society, nevertheless there is a further challenge in relation to achieving greater equality of access and of opportunity. If we are to be a caring society, priority in the use of resources available for education must be given to removing barriers to equality of opportunity faced by the educationally, socially and economically deprived.......

I.22 Ages for Learning — Decisions of Government, May 1985.

In June 1984, the Minister for Education, Gemma Hussey, circulated a discussion document entitled 'The Ages for Learning." This document opened up the debate on questions such as the appropriate age at which children should make various transitions within the educational system and the number of years which a child should spend at the different levels of education. The age of entry to primary school and the length of the post-primary course were live issues at that time. When John Boland had been Minister for Education some years earlier he had proposed that the minimum age for entry to national school should be raised to five and this had resulted in considerable controversy. There was also a growing debate on the ideal length of the secondary school course and the introduction of Vocational Preparation and Training Programmes and Transition Year programmes in some schools had added a new dimension to the debate.

Following consideration of submissions which were received in response to the discussion paper, the Government took a number of decisions on these matters and these decisions were published in a short paper entitled "Ages for Learning — Decisions of Government" in May 1985. This document was followed in October 1985 by a circular to the authorities of post-primary schools (Circular M85/85) informing them that new structures would be introduced in all post-primary schools to effect the changes decided by government — specifically that all schools could offer a six year programme, three years junior cycle and three years senior cycle. Within a year however, the deteriorating state of the economy forced the government to withdraw that decision and it was not until 1990 that Mary O'Rourke, Minister for Education announced that all pupils entering post-primary schools in 1991 would have access to a six year programme.

The following extract is from Ages for Learning - Decisions of Government:

The Minister for Education, Gemma Hussey, T.D., wishes to announce that, following consideration of submissions received in response to the document "The Ages for Learning" which was published in June 1984, the Government has now decided as follows:

1. That as from 1st September 1987, no child will normally be admitted to first class in national schools unless it has

attained the age of six years by 1st September of the year in which it is enrolled in that class. However a child may continue to be enrolled in infant classes as from four years of age.

2. That pupils may only transfer to post-primary school when they have completed the primary school course up to and including sixth standard or its equivalent. Following from 1 above this will mean that pupils will normally be twelve years of age by 1st September of the year of entry to post-primary school.
3. That post-primary courses will be developed so as to enable pupils to spend up to six years overall in a post-primary school.
4. That the junior cycle will be of three years duration in all post-primary schools — to be applied with respect to all pupils who first enrol in post-primary school on 1st September 1986 and subsequently.
5. That the Leaving Certificate Course be two years in duration in all schools — be applied with respect to all pupils who transfer to the senior cycle on 1st September, 1986 and subsequently.
6. That subject to the approval of the Minister, and taking account of the need to rationalise course provision in the various school centres, schools will be permitted to develop additional courses from among the following:

    (i) Transition Year immediately following the junior cycle. This course will allow for the development of broad general education, including academic study and elements of career education.

    (ii) (a) One or two-year ESF-funded vocational preparation/training courses.
    (b) Post-Leaving Certificate ESF-funded one-year vocational/training courses.

These vocational preparation/training courses are intended for those who might otherwise leave school inadequately qualified to gain employment. Their continuance is contingent upon the availability of ESF support.

I.23 Report of the Committee on Discipline in Schools, 1985

The Minister for Education, John Boland, T.D., made an announcement on 26th January 1982 to the effect that corporal punishment would be prohibited in schools as and from 1st February 1982. Following representations by teacher organisations and managerial associations to Mr. Boland and his successor, Dr. Martin O'Donoghue, T.D., the Committee on Discipline in Schools was established and met for the first time in October 1982. Its report which was published in 1985 was concise, covering less than 50 pages, and its recommendations were wide-ranging. It highlighted the need for good communication structures between primary and post-primary schools and between home and school; the importance of keeping the needs of disruptive pupils in mind when curriculum change was being introduced; the need to provide both pre-service and in-service education to help teachers to develop skills for coping with discipline-related problems among pupils. It recommended that each school should formulate a code of discipline; that the Department of Education should make provision for the appointment of extra teachers in schools with a high concentration of disruptive pupils; that a school-based psychological service should be extended as a matter of urgency to all schools; and that day-care units should be provided in urban areas to cater for the educational needs of those pupils whose behaviour is so disruptive as to infringe the constitutional rights of others to education. The following extracts are from Chapter 8 of the report:

DISCIPLINE AND SANCTIONS

8.1. *The Code of Discipline*

8.1.1 An adequate code of discipline is vital for the efficient organisation of a school. Effective learning requires a high level of attentiveness and participation on the part of the pupils and a ready acceptance of the rules governing behaviour within the school. The age, range of abilities and level of aspirations of the pupils should be taken into account when rules are being formulated for the school. The number of such rules should be kept to a minimum and should be easy to understand and administer. Pupils and parents should have every opportunity to familiarize themselves with the rules of the school and their views should be taken into account in the adaptation of existing rules and in the formulation of new rules.

8.1.2 The managerial authority has ultimate responsibility for what happens within the school and it is its duty to see that a fair and efficient code of discipline is applied therein. The code of discipline should be formulated by the principal and teaching staff, in consultation with the parents and older pupils, and be approved by the managerial authority. The Committee feels that rules which emerge through consensus have the best chance of being effective and generally accepted.

8.1.3 Whereas it is usual for schools to draw up a general code of rules which apply to all pupils, it is often necessary for individual teachers, particularly those in charge of classrooms, laboratories and specialist rooms, to formulate extra rules regarding safety and the correct use of apparatus, equipment and teaching aids. Such extra rules should have the prior approval of the principal and of the managerial authority, where deemed necessary.

8.1.4 Teachers have responsibility for the maintenance of discipline within the classrooms. They should present their lessons in such a stimulating manner as to minimize disruptive behaviour among their pupils and they should make every effort to avoid situations in which pupils find themselves in confrontation with authority. They should refer pupils to the principal or to the teacher in charge of disciplinary matters only for serious breaches of discipline. They are entitled to expect support and advice from the principal or the teacher in charge of disciplinary matters in dealing with the misbehaviour of disruptive pupils.

8.2 *Sanctions*

8.2.1 Various traditional strategies are being used by teachers for dealing with disruptive behaviour, for example, to move the disruptive pupil to some other location in the classroom and to prescribe additional work or detention during or after school-hours. Parents expect adequate notice of any intention to detain a pupil after normal school hours. Sometimes it is necessary to impose other sanctions such as requiring the disruptive pupil to report at regular intervals to a teacher with special responsibility for dealing with instances of serious misbehaviour. Before resorting to serious sanctions, the normal channels of communication between school and parents/guardians should be fully utilized.

8.3 *The Suspension of Pupils in Primary Schools*

8.3.1 In cases where the normal disciplinary procedures of the school have been exhausted, the sanction of suspension may become necessary. Because of the serious nature of this step, standardized procedures should be followed with regard to its implementation. Those procedures should be seen to be reasonable and scrupulously fair to all parties. Suspension may be deemed necessary for a single instance of gross misbehaviour and for repeated instances of serious misbehaviour.

8.5 *Transfer of Pupils to Special Units*

8.5.1 There is a small number of pupils whose behaviour is such that not only does it interfere with the constitutional rights of others to education but renders it impossible for themselves to benefit from the ordinary class situation. It is recommended that the Minister for Education should, as a matter of urgency, establish special day and residential units as recommended in Chapter 7 so as to cater for the educational needs of such pupils. The transfer of pupils to special units should be considered only when all other disciplinary procedures have been totally exhausted.

****

8.6 *The Expulsion of Pupils*

8.6.1 The Committee advises that expulsion should only be considered when the behaviour of the pupil clearly puts the safety of others at risk or where the behaviour is so disruptive as to interfere substantially with the constitutional right of others to education. It should be imposed only when all other disciplinary procedures have been totally exhausted.

8.6.2 Because expulsion has such serious consequences for a child and for his/her parents/guardians, it is absolutely essential that he/she should get a scrupulously fair hearing before the decision to expel is taken. Accordingly, the Committee recommends that a period of suspension should be imposed while consideration is being given to expulsion and parents/guardians notified by registered post. This period of suspension should be used to afford the parents/guardians and the child an ample opportunity to present his/her case in the presence of the managerial authority of the school or its nominee. It should only be in the context of having provided such an opportunity for a scrupulously fair hearing that any decision to expel should be taken.

I.24 Programme for National Recovery, October 1987.

Following the General Election of February 1987, Fianna Fáil and the Progressive Democrats formed a coalition government. In October 1987, the Government, in conjunction with organisations representing employers and employees, issued a Programme for National Recovery. The programme was drawn up in the context of severe economic and social problems. The National Debt amounted to over £25 billion, the equivalent of more than one and a half times the Gross National Product. The unemployment rate was 18.5% of the workforce — one of the highest rates of unemployment in the European Community. Annual net emigration was estimated at close to 30,000 — the equivalent of the natural increase in population. The Programme contained proposals aimed at overcoming "the serious obstacles which at present exist to impede economic and social development." Section IV of the Programme was entitled "Greater Social Equity" and contained the following section on education:

15. The Government recognise the importance of the educational system in the promotion of equity in society and will ensure, in implementing whatever adjustments are necessary in that sector because of financial considerations, that the burden of adjustment does not fall on the disadvantaged.
16. There is a range of measures in place to assist disadvantaged groups. There is also considerable Exchequer support for travellers and the mentally and physically handicapped. Special attention will be given to identifying those with special needs and to provide measures designed to help these groups achieve their full potential.
17. The Government will continue to encourage and foster the participation of the disadvantaged at all levels of education. A particular area of focus will be to encourage more second-level pupils to complete the senior cycle. It is considered that this will be a key factor in encouraging more working class children to advance to third-level education.

18. For those who do not complete second-level there is considerable State support by way of provision for training (FÁS, CERT, ACOT), Vocational Preparation and Training courses, and employment subsidies and schemes. The Government will focus on devising special measures to attract priority one pupils to VPT courses.
19. It is intended that the programme of community education and adult literacy will continue and will be intensified to the limits that resources permit.

I.25 Programme for Economic and Social Progress, January 1991

In January 1991, the Government issued the Programme for Economic and Social Progress. This programme which was the outcome of "prolonged negotiations between the Government and the social partners" was described as "a strategy to accelerate economic and social progress in the nineties." The strategy was to maintain a low-inflation economy with a stable exchange rate which could compete internationally and provide higher standards of living and improved social services.

In Section IV — Social Reform — the Programme provided for major structural reform to achieve greater social equity. The following extracts are from the section on education:

INTRODUCTION

66. This Programme confirms the importance of the education system for the future well-being of the country as well as its role in the country's economic development. The Programme affords an opportunity of agreeing a broad education policy to the end of the decade. The overall strategy in education may be simply stated: to provide the opportunity for all to develop their educational potential to the full. This will be achieved by:

— providing a broadly-based education for all ability levels during the compulsory cycle of education (6-15 year olds);

- encouraging and facilitating pupils to continue in full-time education during the post-compulsory period (16-18 year olds) by providing a range of education/training programmes suited to their abilities and aptitudes;
- providing post-secondary education for all students interested in pursuing such education and capable of benefitting from it:
- intensifying efforts to address the needs of those with educational difficulties and under-achievers in particular during the compulsory cycle;
- providing second-chance education or training for those leaving the system prematurely, and
- facilitating mature students within the education system in upgrading their education or training levels.

67. Particular attention must be paid to children suffering educational or social disadvantage through early identification of those children allied to positive intervention to support them through the provision of remedial teaching, guidance and counselling and the development of home/school links. Such a programme will in itself increase retention rates in education among disadvantaged groups. For those pupils who have left the system without reaching their full potential the development of specific programmes for second-chance education will be pursued. Such programmes are at present provided through schemes such as Youthreach, the Vocational Training Opportunities Scheme and a number of literacy and community schemes.

68. Resources will be targetted to assist the disadvantaged in availing of the various educational or training services.

Areas for action in Programme

69. Within the foregoing broad general framework, it is proposed to initiate action on a number of specific areas as follows:

(a) At primary level, the overall pupil/teacher ratio will be reduced to 25:1 by September, 1992......

(b) A pupil/teacher ratio of 19:1 for recruitment purposes at second-level will be phased in over 1991 and 1992......

(c) A further 60 posts will be allocated to post-primary schools in disadvantaged areas for the 1991/1992 school year......

(d) A phased programme, starting in 1992/93 and for completion in 1994/95, will be introduced to provide for the recognition on an ex-quota basis of vice-principal teachers in post-primary schools of 500 pupils and over,

(e) A phased programme, starting in 1992/93 and for completion in 1994/95 will be introduced to provide for the recognition on an ex-quota basis of 0.5 of a whole-time post for guidance in secondary and community/comprehensive schools in the 350-499 enrolment category, with a similar provision for vocational schools to be made on a VEC Scheme basis in consultation with management and teacher representatives.

(f) A six-year cycle of post-primary education will be introduced for all pupils commencing their post-primary cycle in 1991.

(g) The Department of Education is at present undertaking a study on the future in-service training needs of teachers at primary and post-primary levels. The findings of this study will be available in the first quarter of 1991. It is proposed to allocate an additional £0.5m. in 1992 and £1m. in 1993 and subsequent years for in-service needs to include developing teachers' skills in the areas of pupil assessment, in dealing with disadvantaged pupils and in the area of the organisation and management of schools.

(h) It is proposed to introduce a phased programme commencing in 1992 to expand the provision for caretaking and clerical services to all national schools with 100 pupils upwards and to second-level schools with 200 pupils upwards......

(i) An allocation of £1m. in 1991, £2m. in 1992 and £3m. in 1993 additional to current provision will be provided to assist in various areas of disadvantage at all levels of the education system....

(j) The number of third-level places will be expanded......

(k) Central services and physical facilities in VEC third-level Colleges will be further strengthened to enable them to cope with increased enrolments......

(l) In the context of the provision of additional places, initiatives for increasing participation in third-level education by mature students through improvements in the Higher Education Grants Scheme are set out in paragraph (m)......

(m) The Higher Education Grants Scheme will be re-examined ......

(n) The Vocational Training Opportunities Scheme (VTOS) for the long-term unemployed will be further developed and expanded as will the Youthreach Scheme for early school leavers and other literacy and community programmes......

(o) Strategies for continuing and adult education will be addressed within available resources by providing end-on skill training for those completing their formal schooling so as to equip them for the world of work; providing second chance education/training including literacy programmes for those who leave the school system prematurely; facilitating mature students within the educational system in upgrading their education or training levels; co-operating with FÁS in relation to its training remit for the workforce......

(p) A programme commencing early in 1992 to upgrade or replace all sub-standard buildings at primary, at second-level and at VEC third-level Colleges by the year 1997 will be implemented......

(q) A Green Paper framed as a strategy paper on Education, will be issued by Summer 1991, and will afford the opportunity to all parties to offer views......

(r) The Programme recognises that, in the light of demographic trends in the education sector, particular attention must be given to ensuing the most effective use of available teaching resources.......

(s) Proposals set out above regarding the provision of ex-quota vice-principal teachers and of clerical and caretaking staff are aimed at strengthening the management structure of schools. In this regard also, it is proposed to hold discussions with interested parties with a view to defining and strengthening the respective roles of Boards of Management, Principals, Vice-Principals and holders of other posts of responsibility in the management and day-to-day running of schools.

****

THE ROLE OF PARENTS

74. Parents in recent years have become increasingly involved with schools in the education of their children. They are formally represented on the Boards of Management of primary and many post-primary schools. These developments are consistent with the role of the family as "the primary and natural educator of the child," acknowledged by the Constitution.

75. In furtherance of this acknowledgement there should be an active parents' association in connection with each individual

school, to promote and develop effective and positive participation by parents in education at the school level. Schools will be informed accordingly.

76. The National Parents' Council provides representation for parents, as partners in education, on various Government-appointed educational bodies. Through its representative function, the Council is making a distinctive and valuable contribution to central planning and policy development in education.

77. Positive parental interest is crucial to a child's educational attainment. It must, therefore, be an essential strategy of educational policy and practice to promote parental involvement in the education of their children. To this end, the Department of Education proposes to support development programmes of the National Parents' Council aimed at increasing the level and quality of involvement by parents in education, particularly in disadvantaged areas. It proposes to pay an annual grant of £25,000 to each of the two tiers of the Council to assist them with such programmes.

78. In addition, it is proposed that the effectiveness of their participation, with particular reference to school management, should be strengthened within the programme of in-service training.

I.26 O.E.C.D.— Review of National Policies — Ireland, 1991

In 1991, a report which reviewed educational policy in Ireland was published by the Organisation for Economic Co-operation and Development. The review, which was one of a series of Reviews of National Policies for Education, was undertaken by three examiners on behalf of the O.E.C.D. and referred especially to teacher supply and training. The examiners took account of the background report prepared by the Department of Education as well as of written submissions and statements from a wide variety of organisations and individuals. The report attempts (i) to identify and discuss in general rather than technical terms the present and emerging issues and problems that appear to be facing Irish education and that have a bearing on the condition of teaching and teachers, and (ii) to analyse in greater detail the specific problems of teacher supply and teacher training.

The following extracts give an indication of the issues and problems addressed by the review and some of the suggested future directions which educational strategy might take:

CHAPTER 3 — Issues and Problems

Expansion and its aftermath

The system of education in Ireland has been under fierce pressure throughout the past thirty years. It has been obliged to find places in the primary and secondary sectors at a speed and on a scale experienced by few other OECD countries. It has had to develop post-school education and training provision almost from scratch. It has had to meet a large demand for places in universities while constructing a non-university post-school sector designed expressly to train young people for the needs of a modernising economy. It has had to invest heavily in new buildings and extra staff at all levels. It has had to manage this quantitative expansion and considerable qualitative improvement while respecting the sensitivities of powerful interest groups and avoiding any root-and-branch reforms of structures or brusque changes of direction. It has also had to make do with fewer resources than many other countries have had the good fortune to command. At the present time, the resource constraints are as tight as they have ever been.

The remarkable thing is that there has been relatively little conflict and there have been few signs of public dissatisfaction, at least until very recently. Morale has remained steady. Has not "Education for the Irish.... always been held in high esteem?" Most Irish people, in and out of the education system, take pride in the conviction that they have one of the best educated younger generations in the world. Everyone speaks of the excellent quality of the teaching force and the respected status of teachers in society. But there are urgent issues and problems that must be confronted and there are policy priorities to be determined. Some issues have already surfaced; others are beginning to emerge; a few are perhaps only appropriate for disinterested outsiders to raise.

FORCES OF CHANGE

Some educators in Ireland are persuaded that there have been sweeping reforms in the education system since the first OECD educational policy review. The truth is that, although there has certainly been the remarkable quantitative expansion and creation of new types of secondary school just described and although there have been several important curricular developments, the system as such has remained largely the same. Like the majority of education systems it is of its nature conservative and slow to change; it has behaved reactively rather than pro-actively. Official and other reports, while acknowledging the achievements of the system despite limited resources, have reiterated the necessity of improving classroom organisation, equipment and materials, teaching methods, and learning outcomes.

Forces are now in operation, however, that are bound to have far-reaching consequences. One such force is the demographic downturn. Another is the inexorable withdrawal of the religious orders from control and management of secondary schools. It is proposed, in this chapter, to discuss these and other forces with a view to explaining the background against which the condition of teaching and teachers, now and in the future, is to be understood.

****

On the interim evidence before them, the examiners would recommend the following directions:

1. Data on the performance and quality of educational practice at the school level are not as comprehensive as they could be and such collections and analyses as are made are either not published at all or are issued years after the event. Monitoring of the school, reviews of its achievements, limitations and needs and the pinpointing of aspects of practice that require attention, would all benefit substantially from having a unit responsible for statistical data gathering and analysis within or closely associated with the Department of Education.
2. Within the policy framework, basic education should be affirmed in organisational terms as continuity throughout the whole period of compulsory schooling.
3. Increased flexibility and variety in the organisation of teaching and learning are needed in order to break down many of the present rigidities affecting the timetable, length of lessons, homework and so forth. The single, homogeneous class and the instructional models associated with it are not conducive to co-operative team work or to innovative approaches to teaching and learning.
4. The constraints, among which by universal consent lack of resources is the most pressing, should be systematically identified through monitoring, evaluation and research.
5. Any reduction in the pupil/teacher ratio at both the primary and secondary level should be conditional on negotiated agreements with teachers' representatives to carry out such reforms as those outlined in the succession of reports since the time of the introduction of the new primary school curriculum.
6. Parental involvement in school decision-making has recently developed but is still at a fairly rudimentary stage. It is desirable to take much further the definition

of, and support for, parental roles in school governance and decision-making. This is both a policy issue and a matter of detailed planning. Parent bodies seem willing to participate.

7. The training of principals and others in positions of senior responsibility, as managers of school organisations which are complex and outward-looking, is essential so that modern management, for example in planning, decision-making, resource management, accountability, interpersonal and community relations, can become more widespread in schools. It is important to develop a stratum of middle management in the larger schools
8. The training and retraining of teachers should emphasize their role as articulators, managers and organisers of learning and not purveyors of facts and coaches for examinations, in order to enable them to cope positively with parent and community involvement in schooling and to acquire more democratic and co-operative values.
9. The organisation of the school day and of individual lessons should provide greater scope for more creative and imaginative problem-solving, skills enhancement, and practice-oriented approaches to learning. Students, as they mature, should be shouldering more responsibility for their own learning and at every stage they should be encouraged to display more initiative and independence of mind.
10. Streaming, setting and assessment by competitive examinations should be modified since, while facilitating a high standard of learning and excellent achievement by the minority, they scarcely benefit the majority of students.
11. More broadly, the organisation and practice of schooling should give greater scope for teachers as well as students to develop and apply a wide repertoire of skills in thinking, problem-solving, creative activity and social interaction.

II

NATIONAL EDUCATION 1922-1991

II.1 First National Programme of Primary Instruction, 1922

During the last decades of the 19th century and the early years of the twentieth century, the influence of cultural nationalism became apparent in many European countries. The founding of the Gaelic League in Ireland in the 1890s and its growth in subsequent years reflected the growing support for cultural nationalism in Ireland. After the Sinn Féin election victory in 1918, feelings of patriotism ran high in Ireland and as the determination to achieve independence grew, so also did the conviction that the new Ireland would be not only free but Gaelic as well. There was considerable public support for the expectation that the Gaelicisation of Ireland should and would be achieved through its education system.

At the Annual Congress of the Irish National Teachers Organization at Easter 1920, the Executive was directed by the delegates to convene a representative conference "to frame a programme or series of programmes, in accordance with Irish ideals and conditions — due regard being given to local needs and views." In order to carry out this directive, invitations were issued by the I.N.T.O. Executive to a wide range of organizations to take part in the proposed conference. A number of organizations and individuals declined the invitation, including various associations of school managers and the Professors of Education in the Universities and University Colleges. The invitation was accepted by Aireacht na Gaeilge (afterwards Aireacht an Oideachais); the General Council of County Councils; the Gaelic League; the National Labour Executive; and the Association of Secondary Teachers. Representatives of these bodies together with representatives from the I.N.T.O. constituted the Conference. When the report was published, it recorded that "Rev. T. Corcoran, Litt.D., Professor of Education in U.C.D., placed the benefit of his advice and experience at the disposal of the Conference".

The Conference met during 1921, and on 28th January 1922 its report was issued. It was a short report of 25 pages, almost all of which related to the primary school programme or curriculum. Additional recommendations related to (a) training of teachers; (b) provision to enable existing teachers to acquire a knowledge of Irish; (c) suggestions for the teaching of Irish in schools where as yet the full programme is impracticable; and (d) school attendance. There was no discussion on issues relating to control and administration of schools.

The new Free State government took over responsibility for the administration of national education on 1st February 1922. On that day, a Public Notice relating to the teaching of Irish was issued. Two months later, in April 1922, a copy of the Programme of Instruction as recommended by the First National Programme Conference was issued to all National Schools with a covering circular signed by Pádraic Ó Brolcháin. The full text of Public Notice No.4 (1 Feb. 1922), the circular dated April, 1922 and extracts from the First National Programme of Primary Instruction follow:

(a) Public Notice No.4

RIALTAS SEALADACH NA hÉIREANN
(Irish Provisional Government)
Ministry of Education.

CONCERNING THE TEACHING OF IRISH LANGUAGE
IN THE NATIONAL SCHOOLS

THE MINISTER FOR EDUCATION by virtue of the powers vested in him HEREBY ORDERS that the following regulations concerning the teaching of the Irish Language in all national schools shall come into force on St. Patrick's Day, the

Seventeenth day of March, 1922, and shall remain in force until further notice:

(1) The Irish Language shall be taught, or used as a medium of instruction, for not less than one full hour each day in all national schools where there is a Teacher competent to teach it:

(2) The hour for the aforesaid instruction shall be divided in the following manner:

- (a) One half-hour not earlier than 10 o'clock in the forenoon; and
- (b) the remaining half-hour not later than 2.30 o'clock in the afternoon;

(3) That should it happen in any schools with more than one Teacher that all the Teachers of the school are not competent to give instruction in the Irish Language, then the division of the work in such school must be so readjusted as to enable such Teacher or Teachers in the school as are competent to give instruction in Irish to comply with the terms of this order, provided however, that in the carrying out of such readjustment, due regard shall be had to the amount of work which can reasonably be allocated to any teacher;

(4) That in a school where the Teacher of a standard, though not certificated, is regarded by the principal teacher of the school and by the National School Inspector in charge of the school, as reasonably competent to give instruction in Irish in that standard, then the Principal Teacher will arrange for such teacher to give the instruction in Irish in that standard;

(5) That all time-tables affected by the provisions of this Order should be revised and altered accordingly, and a copy of each time-table so revised and altered should be submitted without delay to the Inspector in charge of the school;

(6) That in cases where there are any difficulties whatsoever in carrying out the regulations herein set forth, statements should be submitted as soon as possible to the Inspector of Irish Instruction, National Education Office, Dublin.

Given this 1st day of February, 1922.

DIARMUID Ó hÉIGCEARTUIGH,

Secretary to the Provisional Government.

(b) Circular dated April, 1922.

NEW PROGRAMME OF INSTRUCTION IN NATIONAL SCHOOLS

This programme, prepared by the National Programme Conference under the authority of Dáil Éireann, is now issued, by direction of the Ministry of Education, for adoption provisionally in Irish National Schools, from the beginning of the next School Year, 1922-1923. Meanwhile, it will be open to Managers and Teachers to modify the present course of instruction so as to bring them gradually into conformity with the new programme.

The programme represents a new starting point in the history of primary education in Ireland, and, as is desirable at the opening of a new epoch in our educational history, considerable allowance is made for local initiative.

At the outset it is important that everything should be done to render the school life and the school surroundings as pleasant as possible for both teachers and pupils; and it is hoped that it will now be possible, with the assistance of organized local effort, to have rapid progress made in this direction.

The pupils, during their school course, should be encouraged to take part in Irish Games, in Feiseanna and other functions organized by National bodies and to acquire the habit of supporting the products of their own country.

Every school will be expected, as a part of the preparation of the pupils for the duties and responsibilities of citizenship, to include in their reading courses matter showing the damage done by intemperance to health and character, and the resultant loss to the nation as a whole.

Our primary education, as well as being Irish in outlook, should also be such as to turn the minds and efforts of the bulk of the pupils in rural schools towards the land of Ireland and the great agricultural industry on which, for generations to come, the economic life of the nation will be based. In selecting literature for reading in the schools, books which tend to develop the pupils' interest in the land, in the pleasures of country life, in the production of crops, in the rearing of herds, should, where available, be given an important place.

In the case of schools in cities and large towns, the pupils' attention should be directed towards the industries that exist, they should be stimulated by talks relating to Irish craftmanship in the past, by visits to factories, workshops, industrial exhibitions and museums, to take a lively interest in the industrial life around them, and to recognize that this is the life to the building of which the majority of them will naturally be called.

To you, the Managers and Teachers of Ireland, this programme is now forwarded in the sure hope that every effort will be made to have it successfully worked in the schools.

****

(c) *Introduction to and Extracts from the First National Programme of Primary Instruction, 1922*

It must be apparent to any person who gave thought to educational matters in Ireland that for quite a number of years past the Programmes of Instruction in our Schools have been the subject of much criticism and complaint. From time to time various bodies representative of public opinion protested against the unsuitability of these programmes.

The criticism of the existing programme fell generally under two heads: (1) The programme contained altogether too many *obligatory* subjects, it was overloaded and there was practically no freedom of choice of subjects left to the teacher. This overloading had arisen from the desire to see the National School function as a primary, technical and intermediate school. (2) The Irish language, which it was evident the vast majority of the Irish people wished to have taught to their children, was placed in a subordinate position on the programme, and except in a few "bilingual" schools was not classed among the obligatory subjects. In addition the programme, generally speaking, was felt to be out of harmony with national ideals and requirements. As was only natural to expect, the teachers, who were charged with the difficult task of giving practical effect to these programmes, were among the foremost in calling attention to their inherent defects, but for many years their protestations were vain, largely because they had not behind them the force of an enlightened public opinion.

In 1920, however, conditions had changed. A new and awakening interest in educational matters was evident among public representative bodies, and, believing the time to be opportune, the Irish National Teachers' Organization, at their Annual Congress at Easter, 1920, directed their Executive to take steps to convene a representative conference in order "to frame a programme, or series of programmes, in accordance with Irish ideals and conditions — due regard being given to local needs and views."

****

At the first meeting, which was held on January 6th, 1921, the following terms of reference were agreed to:

(1) The adoption of a minimum National Programme
(2) Additional Subjects, and the circumstances under which such additional subjects should be made compulsory.
(3) The consideration of the best means of applying items (1) and (2), including the question of National and Local Administration, Training Facilities, Teaching Staffs, School Premises, Attendance, Provision of Text Books, etc.

In approaching the question of the Primary School curriculum the Conference had as its main idea the remedying of the two outstanding defects in the present programme which have already been referred to.

In the programme here outlined the most notable changes adopted are (1) the elimination of Drawing, Elementary Science, Cookery and Laundry, Needlework (in the lower standards) and Hygiene and Nature Study as formal obligatory subjects, the modification of the programme in History and Geography (which now constitute but one subject), in Singing and in Drill; (2) the raising of the status of the Irish language both as a school subject and as an instrument of instruction.

It was decided at an early stage of the proceedings that in the case of schools where the majority of the parents of the children object to have either Irish or English taught as an obligatory subject, their wishes should be complied with.

No recommendation is made regarding the allotment of time to the various subjects other than to state that in schools where it is as yet impracticable to introduce the programme in its entirely, *each pupil shall receive instruction in Irish for at least one hour per day as an ordinary school subject.* The question of grouping is also left to the discretion of the teacher, but it is to be understood in this connection that where two or more standards are grouped, the lower standard or standards are not expected to cover the course prescribed for the highest standard of the group. It will be noted that programmes for differently staffed schools are not submitted; in regard to this it has been decided that, while all the subjects constituting the minimum programme are to be taught in all schools (subject to reservation in preceding par.) a higher standard will be expected in the better staffed schools than in those not so favourably circumstanced. It is to be remembered also that this being a minimum programme, the course of instruction in any subject may be extended beyond that prescribed here.

Teachers are at liberty to draw up and submit for the approval of the Education Authority special programmes to suit the circumstances of their individual schools, taking into account the number and attainments of the staff, the local needs, etc., but all such programmes must be framed along the lines of the National Programme.

Many Bilingual Schools have already been doing more than is demanded in this Programme in the matter of teaching subjects through Irish. Such schools should, as far as possible, now make Irish the sole medium of instruction, English being taught as an ordinary subject.

****

SOME NOTES ON THE SUBJECTS OF INSTRUCTION

In order to bring the pupils as far as possible into touch with European thought and culture, reading in English in the higher standards should be mainly directed to the works of European authors, ancient and modern, drawn from the many good translations which abound. English authors, as such, should have just the limited place due to English literature among all the European literatures.

In the books selected for the Third and Fourth Standards, lessons on Health and on Nature Study should find a place.

Reading in Irish should be of a wide and varied type, covering all forms of literature, including Poetry and Drama.

In estimating the standard attained in the Irish and English languages, due regard should be given to the language prevailing in the school district.

In Singing, the main idea should be to teach the pupils to sing individually and collectively as large a number of songs as possible.

One of the chief aims of the teaching of history should be to develop the best traits of the national character and to inculcate national pride and self-respect. This will not be attained by the cramming of dates and details but rather by showing that the Irish race has fulfilled a great mission in the advancement of civilization and that, on the whole, the Irish Nation has amply justified its existence.

While accuracy of plain calculation is the essential aim in Arithmetic, the principles underlying the various arithmetical rules should be properly understood. In all cases teachers should give such a local bias to their teaching as will connect the school work of the pupils with their surroundings.

PROGRAMME

PART 1.

Obligatory Subjects

I. — IRISH

- (a) Reading and Spelling
- (b) Writing.
- (c) Composition.
- (d) Grammar.

II. — English
- (a) Reading and Spelling.
- (b) Writing.
- (c) Composition.
- (d) Grammar.

III. — Mathematics
- (a) Arithmetic.
- (b) Algebra.
- (c) Geometry.

IV. — History and Geography

V. — Singing.

VI — Needlework (*Girls in Third and Higher Standards).*

VII. — Drill.

Programme for Infants

Note — The work in the Infant Standards is to be entirely in Irish

Junior Infants

Language

To be taught to speak audibly and distinctly by means of conversation, object and picture lessons, story-telling and recitation.

Drawing

Drawing in sand, and afterwards in mass with chalks on small blackboards, or on other suitable surfaces.

Numbers

To count up to 9 by means of kindergarten gifts and occupations

Kindergarten Gifts and Occupations

Colour sorting, building with bricks, threading large beads, arranging shells or tablets, etc., in twos, threes and higher numbers, fraying, stick-laying. Gifts I., II., III.

Songs and Games

Nursery rhymes and simple songs connected with child's surroundings. Finger-plays. Colour and movement games with Gift I.

PART II

Additional Subjects

1 — Drawing

II — Advanced Algebra

III — Advanced Geometry and Mensuration

IV — French (or other Continental Language)

V — Latin

VI — Nature Study

VII — Book-keeping

VIII — Elementary Science
[where there is a suitably equipped laboratory].

IX — Cookery [where there is a separate suitably-equipped room available).

X — Rural Science and School Gardening
[in properly-equipped schools with gardens attached].

XI — Manual Instruction (Woodwork)
[where special facilities exist and where the services of a special teacher are available.]

XII— Domestic Science

(Where Instruction in Woodwork or Domestic Science is given in the neighbourhood of the school, arrangements may be made whereby Senior pupils would attend the classes — such attendance to count as part of the school day.)

N.B.— *In Schools where Irish or English is dropped at the request of the majority of parents, one additional subject must be taken instead of the language dropped.*
It is recommended that where one or more of these subjects is taught outside school hours as an "Extra Subject," special fees according to the existing scales should be paid.

****

(D) SCHOOL ATTENDANCE

The Conference desires to direct special attention to the question of school attendance. A child who attends school irregularly not only fails to make progress himself: he acts as a clog on the class as a whole and thus hampers the progress of his classmates. No matter how suitable the programme or how efficient or enthusiastic the teacher, the instruction cannot be effective unless the pupils attend regularly. .....the average leaving age is 11 years. This is much too low. The Conference strongly recommends that all children between the ages of 5 and 14 should attend school daily. It further recommends that, as soon as practicable, legislation should be introduced to remedy the present deplorable state of affairs; meantime it appeals with confidence to the various representative bodies, school managers, teachers and others concerned to do everything possible to bring the light of public opinion to bear on this crying evil and to show to those responsible the wrong which they are doing to their children and their country.

II.2 Circular to Inspectors, November 1922.

The difficulties of implementing the First National Programme became apparent early in the school year 1922/23. It had been established in April 1922 that only 1,100 of the 12,000 national teachers had bilingual certificates, i.e. that their proficiency in Irish was such that they could teach the new programme competently. Summer courses in Irish for national teachers during June and July 1922 had helped a number of teachers to develop their Irish language skills, but it was to be many years before the majority of teachers would be in a position to implement fully the new National Programme. A circular issued to inspectors in November 1922 indicated that the Office of National Education in Dublin was aware of the difficulties facing teachers and this circular recognized in particular "that the teaching of the Infants entirely through the medium of Irish will not be feasible in a large number of schools during the current school year". However, in these cases it was expected that "steps will be taken from the outset to introduce for at least one hour per day and gradually to extend the use of Irish as a medium of instruction". The following extracts from the circular indicate the informal modifications which the Office of National Education was prepared to allow:

II — School Programme

(a) Regarding the Note at the head of the Infants' Programme, it is recognized that the teaching of the Infants entirely through the medium of Irish will not be feasible in a large number of schools during the current school year, but even in such schools it is expected that steps will be taken from the outset to introduce for at least one hour per day and gradually to extend the use of Irish as a medium of instruction.

(b) Regarding the note at the head of the Programme in History and Geography, it is not expected that, under present conditions, it will be possible in a large number of schools to give instruction in the History and Geography of Ireland through the medium of Irish in the several standards, but, where possible, a beginning should be made in the teaching of History and Geography through the medium of Irish, and the use of Irish in this teaching should be gradually extended according to the capacity of the teachers in Irish.

(c) In Irish-speaking districts, Irish, where the teachers have sufficient facility in the language, should be used as the medium of instruction and English should be taught as a subject.

Where the teachers have not as yet sufficient facility in the language, and generally in districts other than Irish-speaking districts every effort should be made to introduce gradually instruction in the various subjects through the medium of Irish, in accordance with the new programme.

II.3 Second National Programme Conference — 1925-26

Although the 1922 National Programme had been drawn up by a conference convened by the Irish National Teachers Organization, it was the same organization which in 1924 proposed that a further conference should be convened to review the programme. Teachers generally felt that the programme was idealistic rather than realistic and that it should be revised. The Minister for Education, Eoin Mac Neill convened the Second National Programme Conference in 1925, and the report of this conference was issued a year later. Half of its members were nominated by the Minister and it was chaired by Rev. Lambert McKenna, S.J. The conference received submissions and suggestions from a wide range of individuals and organizations and while these were not published, it was stated in the report that they had been taken into account.

The report endorsed the policy of the First National Programme and did not differ fundamentally in its curricular recommendations. It did however, indicate that a more gradual approach to the realization of the aims of the First Programme should be adopted. It reaffirmed the principle that infants should be taught through the medium of Irish, though it modified the position slightly by allowing English to be used before 10.30 a.m.. A higher and a lower course in Irish and English were proposed for First and higher Classes, the higher course to be taken in the predominant language of the school. The requirements in mathematics, history and geography were reduced to take account of the demands of teaching through the medium of Irish. Rural Science was added as a compulsory subject for boys in certain categories of schools. A significant paragraph regarding Religious Instruction was included in the report, a paragraph which was subsequently adopted as departmental policy in relation to Religious Instruction.

The report was signed by all members of the conference on 5th March 1926, but it was subject to a reservation by the representatives of the INTO who sought to limit the compulsory subjects to Irish, English and Mathematics. The report was accepted by the Minister and its recommendations were implemented from the beginning of the following school year. The following extracts from the report indicate the thinking of the conference:

As regards the National Programme, its character, its contents and the arrangement of its subject-matter, the general opinion of the Conference was one of commendation. It was considered to be a very welcome improvement on preceding programmes, above all in its suitability for attaining the end stated by Pádraig Ó Brolcháin in January, 1922, to be an essential part of the educational aim of the Irish Government, namely, "the strengthening of the national fibre by giving the language, history, music, and tradition of Ireland their natural place in the life of Irish schools."

On the other hand, from the very beginning of the Conference there was general agreement that in one important respect the National Programme was open to serious objection, inasmuch as it had been framed rather to mark an ideal attainable only after lengthened and strenuous efforts on the part of educational authorities and educational bodies than to prescribe a scheme of work immediately applicable over the whole country.That such was the object aimed at in it was stated and conclusively proved (by reference to its framers themselves) in a document sent to us by the Irish National Teachers' Organization and written by Mr. T.J. O'Connell, T.D., who had been Secretary of the First Programme Conference. The framers of the National Programme, it was made clear to us, had not overlooked the danger of impracticability incidental to their programme; but had considered that, in spite of this danger, there was an instant necessity for outlining clearly and strikingly an ideal of primary education which would be worthy of Ireland, and which recent events had given the Irish people an opportunity of realizing. At the same time, the hope was cherished by them that a clear statement of the conditions which they deemed necessary for the working of that ideally national system of education, would stimulate the Government to establish these conditions by appropriate administrative measures.

As regards their main object, the framers of the National Programme have won a most gratifying success; the high ideal which they embodied in it has met with general approval. On the other hand, in their expectation that the conditions necessary for the realization of their aim would be rapidly established, they have — owing to causes the responsibility for which does not concern us here — been to a large extent disappointed.

We believe, however, that at the present time, circumstances are far more propitious for our educational future than they were three years ago. As the aim of the National Programme has gained more general acceptance, and as the qualifications of the teachers for forwarding that aim are now considerably improved, there is more reason for hoping that a successful working of a new programme may be achieved.

We have striven so to frame this new programme that it may set before our schools the same high purpose which the National Programme set before them, and will differ from the National Programme only in so far as it will be transitional, being indicative of gradual steps in a steady progress towards an ideal, and being adjustable to the varying circumstances of our schools. Further, the more peaceful tenor of the times justifies us in hoping that more vigorous efforts will be made to realize the conditions which alone can enable such a programme to produce its best fruits.

****

As time went on, it became more and more evident that, in spite of the assurances given by the Minister, the teachers' apprehensions had not been unintelligent. The working of the Programme was found to be beset with many difficulties, and to involve an undue strain on teachers — whose dissatisfaction was increased when the Department made some changes which the teachers in general considered to be additions to the weight of the Programme, and was believed to be contemplating further additions.

It was in connection with Irish that the chief causes of trouble were found. Some teachers and managers — but not many, we think — understood that the Department's Circular of November, 1922, modifying the application of the Programme rules about Irish, was a tacit renunciation of the Programme ideal as being unattainable: others — the majority — made strenuous efforts to carry out the Programme in its perfection. In the cases of teachers who were sufficiently qualified, those efforts were crowned with gratifying success. Where, however, teachers were not adequately prepared — and most of them were in this condition — their efforts, while entailing a severe strain, sometimes resulted in an impairing of the educational value of their work.

One of the leading characteristics of that Programme is its insistence on the principle of teaching the Infant classes through the medium of Irish. The members of our Conference agreed on the supreme importance of giving effect as far as possible to this principle; and in confirmation of their belief they received authoritative evidence. It was argued with much weight that a "direct" method of teaching Irish, continued during the length of an ordinary school-day for a few years between the ages of 4 and 8, would be quite sufficient — given trained and fluent teachers — to impart to children a vernacular power over the language; while, in the case of older children, it was shown that such a result would be more difficult of attainment. The members of the Conference were, therefore, at one in holding that the true and only method of establishing Irish as a vernacular is the effective teaching of it to the Infants.

With this point in view, we would recommend that the

Department favour — it could not, for many evident reasons, make obligatory — the policy of having the Infants entrusted to the best Irish teacher in each school — even if that teacher be the principal of the school. Having had much evidence before us to the effect that the methods at present being followed in the teaching of infants — and especially in the teaching of language to them — leave much to be desired, we would also suggest that some well-qualified persons — Inspectors or others — should be devoted, partially at least, to the duty of giving lectures, specimen lessons, etc., to such teachers throughout the country as seem to need this help.

Yet, in this matter of teaching Irish to very young children, it was felt by us that the principle of the motto *festina lente* is especially applicable. The Note, which in the National Programme stood at the head of the course for Infants, while in some cases it proved of the greatest utility, in other instances had some harmful results. Its wording, being absolute and making no allowance for difficulties, made a literal obedience to it sometimes impossible, and often inadvisable. Though assurances were given that the Note would not be applied without discretion, it was left standing unchanged. Consequently, it was sometimes treated as a dead letter; sometimes — more often — it resulted in inefficient teaching.

We have, therefore, changed its wording; and we hope that in its new form it may serve as an indication to all teachers of what should be their aim, and at the same time serve as a practical direction and a sympathetic exhortation to those of them who are not as yet fully qualified in Irish.

The same principle guided us with regard to the teaching of Irish in the Standards. We were much impressed by the success which rewarded the generally good spirit of the teachers, and enabled so many of them to impart to their pupils a fluent power of dealing with various subjects in the Irish language. At the same time, we received evidence that, when — as often happened — teachers were insufficiently prepared, the effort to teach History, Geography, or Mathematics through Irish resulted in an indifferent teaching of these subjects, and, consequently, in giving colour to some adverse criticism of the general teaching standard of our schools. Though we believe that some of this criticism was inspired by prejudice or exaggerated by foolish rumour, we are also convinced that some of it was quite well-founded.

Manifestly, no grounds should have been given for such criticism. The subjects of the curriculum should have been efficiently taught, and wherever they could not have been efficiently taught through Irish, English should have been used. We have, therefore, re-written the Note which stood at the head of the History and Geography syllabus in the National Programme. While making it more comprehensive (so as to apply to all subjects except English), we have striven so to word it that it may mark the ideal to be aimed at, and, at the same time, take account of actually existing varieties in school conditions.

The intention of the National Programme was that, wherever the children of a school possessed only one language, English or Irish, as a perfectly easy medium of expression, they should receive their general instruction and training in that language; but that, where they had a fluent command of both languages, their teacher, if capable of doing so, should use Irish as the basic language of his school. To make clearer this intention of the Programme we have drawn up *two* courses in each language, a *Higher Course* to be taken in the predominant language of the school, and a *Lower Course* to be taken in the other language. Thus the teacher will have two alternatives, the *Higher Course* in Irish together with the *Lower Course* in

English, and the *Higher Course* in English with the *Lower Course* in Irish. For some time to come, owing to the state of Irish in the country and the yet imperfect qualifications of many teachers, the former of these alternatives will be possible in only a minority of the schools, but we have every reason for hoping that the number of such schools will rapidly increase. The latter of the above alternatives will be practicable immediately in nearly all the schools of the country, and it is hoped that the teaching of Irish will become by degrees more and more efficient, according as the teachers' qualifications improve, until the stage is reached when the former alternative will be everywhere possible. In the notes placed at the head of these courses, we have made it plain that as high a standard of proficiency in Irish as is practicable — but no higher — will be looked for in each case.

As regards the very small number of schools in which Irish is not being taught owing to the want of teachers qualified to teach it, we would recommend that qualified teachers be temporarily engaged and paid by the Department.

Not merely as regards the teaching of Irish and the teaching through Irish, but as regards the teaching of certain subjects through English, we have received much evidence that insufficient allowance has been made for the difficulties which the introduction of a new vernacular placed upon teachers and pupils.

****

For the reasons already mentioned — and owing also, in the case of a large proportion of schools, to the want of proper teaching power, or of material facilities, or of both together, — we have set down Drawing, Domestic Science, Physical Training and Manual Instruction as Optional Subjects.

****

Religious Instruction

Of all the parts of a school curriculum Religious Instruction is by far the most important, as its subject-matter, God's honour and service, includes the proper use of all man's faculties, and affords the most powerful inducements to their proper use. We assume, therefore, that Religious Instruction is a fundamental part of the school course. Though the time allotted to it as a specific subject is necessarily short, a religious spirit should inform and vivify the whole work of the school. The teacher, — while careful, in presence of children of different religious beliefs, not to touch on matters of controversy, — should constantly inculcate, in connection with secular subjects, the practice of charity, justice, truth, purity, patience, temperance, obedience to lawful authority, and all the other moral virtues. In this way he will fulfill the primary duty of an educator, the moulding to perfect form of his pupils' character, habituating them to observe, in their relations with God and with their neighbour, the laws which God, both directly through the dictates of natural reason and through Revelation, and indirectly through the ordinance of lawful authority, imposes on mankind.

As, however, the prescribing of the subject-matter of Religious Instruction, the examination of it, and the supervision of its teaching are outside the competence of the Department of Education, no syllabuses of it are here set forth.

II.4 Report of the Committee on Inspection of Primary Schools 1927

Following the publication of the report of the Second National Programme Conference in 1926, the Minister for Education set up a committee to report on the inspection of primary schools. The chairman of the committee was Rev. L. McKenna, S.J. who had also chaired the Second National Programme Conference. The report was a comprehensive one and included information on the system of primary school inspection in other European countries. The report identified the main purpose of school inspection as being "the fostering and promotion of a high quality of education." It indicated that the chief defect of the inspection system at that time was that "too little attention was attached to the directive and specifically educational aspect of inspection in comparison with its aspect as a controlling agency." It recommended that the teacher should be encouraged to see the inspector as a "co-operator in the school work" and as an adviser and that the inspector's role as an examiner should be less in evidence. The report contained a number of specific recommendations in relation to inspection. It also recommended that a State Primary School Certificate be introduced and this recommendation was adopted by the Minister almost immediately with the introduction of a Primary Certificate examination in 1929. The following extracts are from the Report of the Committee on Inspection:

GENERAL DEFECT OF PRESENT SYSTEM

Believing, as we do, that the value of any educational system depends, not alone on the training and qualifications of the teachers, their mental breadth and adaptability, their high moral character and willing energy, but likewise on the method by which their work in the schools is supervised and directed, we desire to stress the great value to be set on adequate and efficient inspection. We should, indeed, have ill performed our duty if any recommendations of ours impaired, in the slightest, the efficiency of the control which inspectors exercise on our educational system. In estimating, however, the value of an inspection system, attention should be directed not merely to its controlling function, but also to its function as a guiding and inspiring influence. Both these functions are comprehended in what is everywhere regarded as the main purpose of school-inspection, namely, the fostering and promotion of a high quality of education.

The chief defect in our present system, so far as our investigations have shown, appears to be that too little importance was attached to the directive and specifically educational aspect of inspection in comparison with its aspect as a controlling agency. The inspector, with his wide experience and expert training, is in a special manner fitted to exercise a very great influence in the stimulation of the teacher's work. The teacher should be encouraged to regard him as a co-operator in the school-work, able and willing to give advice and assistance whenever difficulties and problems arise. It appears to us that in the past the great power and influence of the inspector in promoting a higher standard of education have not been utilised to the extent to which they might have been: and that this is due, not to unwillingness or want of proper outlook on the part of the inspection staff, but to the fact that the numerous other functions, which they are called on by the administration to perform, have left them little opportunity to give adequate attention to what should be — and what the inspectors themselves more perhaps than any other body recognise to be — the most important aspect of their work. We believe that, as a natural consequence of the tendency of the present system to stress the disciplinary, assessing and controlling rather than the directive and helpful functions of inspection, the relations between inspectors and teachers are not as close, continuous and helpful as they might be, and that the spirit of co-operation between teachers and inspectors in the great work of education is not developed to the extent to which it might and could be.

****

After mature consideration of the matter, we propose that, by way of remedy for what we consider the faulty tendency of the present system, there should be far more frequent incidental visits and much more thorough general inspections.

PRIMARY SCHOOL CERTIFICATE

We recognise the advantages of a State Primary School Certificate which would testify, with the full authority of the Department, to the creditable completion of a Primary Course, and which would have a standard value all over the country.

II.5 The Primary Certificate Examination, 1929 - 1967.

In 1925, Eoin Mac Neill, Minister for Education, announced that he intended to introduce a certificate examination to be taken by pupils at the end of sixth class in national schools. Two years later, the report on Primary Inspection recommended the introduction of such an examination as also did the report of the Commission on Technical Instruction the same year. In March 1928, the Minister for Education accepted the recommendations of the committees and the Primary Certificate Examination was introduced as an optional examination in June 1929 — the subjects examined being Irish, English, mathematics, history and geography and needlework for girls. Only about 25% of eligible pupils sat the examination at any stage during the 1930s and in the early 1940s Eamon de Valera, Taoiseach and Minister for Education, announced that the examination would become compulsory from 1943 onwards for all pupils in sixth class in a national school who had an attendance record of 100 days or more during the previous year. The INTO did not favour the introduction of a compulsory examination at the end of primary education and attempted to have the examination abolished entirely. They failed in their attempts and it became compulsory in 1943, albeit in a narrower range of subjects (Irish, English and Arithmetic).

The following extracts are from de Valera's speech in the Dáil in 1941 when he outlined the government's reasons for introducing a compulsory Primary Certificate Examination:

It is ridiculous to think that (in the short period of school life) you can go over a whole range of human knowledge, the whole range of the things which, in actual practical life afterwards, may be necessary for the child. You cannot and, therefore, you must at the start make up your mind, ruthlessly almost, to eliminate things which are not fundamental and absolutely necessary.

****

I want no frills, the simple elements of arithmetic are absolutely necessary, and we all know it. Therefore, if a child coming through the national school is not able to perform those simple calculations, that child is not reasonably fitted for the life it has to live. The next thing which everybody will know and admit to be necessary is that we should be able to read, so that we get further knowledge.Therefore, from the point of view of the practical life....children will have to be able to read English....... These, to my mind, are the essentials. They are called the three Rs, and I am old fashioned enough — and I think my belief is based on reason — to believe that if we get from the national schools reading, writing and arithmetic — and when I say "reading" I mean using the two languages — we have done a good job. If I were dictator as regards education here, what I should like at the end of the primary schools would be, to be able to get boys or girls and test whether they could do the simple calculations necessary in life — not the complex ones — which will enable them to deal with the ordinary things which come their way, simple reading so that they may be able to read and understand any material put before them — I do not want anything complex here, either, and I do not speak of literature, poetry, flights of the imagination or anything else but simple straight-forward accounts in books of anything they want to know, so that the road to knowledge may be open to them — and, with regard to writing, able to express themselves in the language in which they want to convey their thoughts.

****

I do not care what teachers are offended by it, I say that it is right that the State should inspect the schools; see what the teacher is doing during the day and how he is teaching. I am less interested in the teacher's method of teaching than I am in the results he achieves, and the test I would apply would be the test of an examination. There should be inspection to see that the courses are being kept, but more important still, a test at the end to see whether the results are being achieved. Notwithstanding the fact that the teachers think otherwise, I am, I believe, representing the community in this matter, and I am for a test at the end of the time. Let us who represent the community say here and now that there will be an examination no matter who may oppose it.

II.6 Circular to Managers, Teachers and Inspectors on Teaching through the medium of Irish; July 1931

By 1931, the Second National Programme had been in effect for five years and it would appear that the Department of Education was concerned that greater efforts should be made to move towards a fuller implementation of its ideals. By this stage, two-thirds of the teachers had obtained the Ordinary Certificate in Irish and 4,000 had advanced to the Bilingual Certificate. In spite of this "the number of schools in which considerable and progressive work through Irish is being done is comparatively small." A circular issued in July 1931 to managers, teachers and inspectors exhorted teachers "to address themselves earnestly and courageously to the accomplishment of this important duty of extending instruction through the medium of Irish." The following extracts from the circular indicate the tone of the circular:

It is clear from the foregoing

(a) that the aim of the programme is to secure the full use of Irish as the teaching medium in all schools as soon as possible;

(b) that the use of Irish as the teaching medium is now obligatory when the teacher is competent to give the instruction and the pupils are able to assimilate the instruction so given;

(c) that teaching through Irish is not obligatory unless the two conditions are fulfilled, i.e., ability of the teacher to give instruction and ability of pupils to receive it;

(d) that transitional stages are suggested at which partial use of teaching through Irish should be introduced, according as the teachers become competent to give such instruction and the pupils can understand and assimilate it.

Such, then, are the requirements of the programme. Of the foregoing items the first three need no elucidation. The intention of the programme is that the schools should do their part in reviving the language as a spoken tongue by giving the pupils such a mastery of Irish as will go a long way towards ensuring that revival. The use of Irish as the medium of instruction will do more than increase the pupils' oral grasp of the language. It will convince them that the Irish language is a living speech capable of adjusting itself to the needs of modern life.

****

The Department, therefore, desires teachers to address themselves earnestly and courageously to the accomplishment of this important duty of extending instruction through the medium of Irish. There are difficulties to be overcome, but good will and intelligent effort will overcome them. The Department looks for success in the schools through that good will and intelligent effort, and expressly stipulates that no undue pressure must be put upon teachers to undertake more than their own powers and the conditions of their schools warrant. The inspectors are, therefore, instructed to be guided in their assessment of the teacher's rating, in respect of the requirement of teaching through the medium of Irish, by consideration of the evidence of his good will and capacity to do what is best in his particular circumstances. Should the teacher's performance, in the opinion of the inspector, fall short of the reasonable possibilities of his school, the inspector will indicate clearly in his report what the shortcomings are, and the teacher will not suffer in his rating until he has definitely failed within a year to make adequate improvements. The Department hopes that such failures will be of rare occurrence and that the teachers, willingly accepting the directions and exhortations of this circular, will respond effectively to its appeal for fuller accomplishment of the Irish aims of the school programme.

II.7 Revised Programme of Primary Instruction, 1934

The first Fianna Fáil government came to power in 1932. The new Minister for Education was Tomás Ó Deirig who shortly after his appointment announced that the major responsibility for the revival of the language rested with the schools. Within two years, he circulated a Revised Programme of Primary instruction which came into effect in all national schools in September 1934. The main changes in this programme were a reversion to an all-Irish day for infants and the adoption of the higher Irish course (as set out in the 1926 programme) for all schools. English was optional for First Class and in other classes the lower course in English was to be taken. Rural Science was dropped as a compulsory subject and the requirements in mathematics were reduced. The 1934 programme remained, with only slight changes, the curriculum for national schools until 1971. The following extracts are from the Revised Programme of 1934:

NOTICE TO MANAGERS AND TEACHERS OF NATIONAL SCHOOLS

The Minister for Education has decided on certain modifications in the programme of instruction for Primary Schools. These come into operation immediately.

Rural Science or Nature Study is optional in all Schools. Special Readers, in English for the present, are to be prepared for the Senior Standards, dealing with the main features of rural life; two such Readers will be prepared, one for Standard V, and one for Standard VI, or to be used in alternate years in Schools where Standards V and VI are grouped.

Algebra and Geometry are optional in one-Teacher Schools, in two-Teacher Schools, in three-Teacher *mixed* Schools, and in all classes taught by women. In three-Teacher Boys' Schools, *either* Algebra *or* Geometry is to be taught.

English: The teaching of English is no longer permitted in Infant Classes where the Teachers are competent to do the work of the class through Irish alone. English is an optional subject in Standard I.

A new programme has been prepared in English, less ambitious in scope than that hitherto in operation.

Irish: A revised programme is provided in Irish, on the lines of the former Higher Course in Irish.

The lightening of the Programme, through the omission of Rural Science (or Nature Study) as a compulsory subject, and of Mathematics in many schools, as well as the less ambitious scope of the Programme in English, will, it is expected, make for more rapid progress and more effective work in the teaching of Irish and in the development of teaching through Irish.

****

II.8 The Infant School, An Naí-Scoil — Notes for Teachers, 1951.

With the introduction of the First National Programme in 1922, the child-centred approach to education had been rejected and the development of the child took second place to the revival of the language. This was particularly evident in the Infant classes where the work had to be entirely through Irish — a policy which remained in place for almost thirty years in spite of calls for change. In 1941, the I.N.T.O.'s Report of the Committee of Inquiry into the use of Irish as a Teaching Medium claimed that the majority of infant teachers believed that teaching through Irish inhibited the child intellectually. In 1947, the I.N.T.O. Plan of Education called for major reform in the curriculum of national schools.

General Richard Mulcahy was appointed Minister for Education in May 1948 and within months of his appointment, he issued a revised programme for infant classes. The new programme allowed infant teachers to teach their pupils through the medium of the home language for half an hour daily. The Prefatory Note to the new infant programme, which reads as follows, heralded a return to the child-centred Programme of 1900, with its Froebellian influences:

> The aim of the Infant School is to provide the atmosphere and background in which the child's whole personality may develop naturally and easily. It should therefore take cognizance of the child's interests, activities and speech needs, and utilize them to the full in aiding and directing such developments.
>
> The present programme positively integrates with this a further aim, that of giving to young children, from English-speaking homes, a vernacular power over Irish at an age when their vocal organs are plastic. Where the teachers are sufficiently qualified the aim should be to reach a stage as early as possible at which Irish can be used as the sole language of the Infant School.

In 1951, a more detailed explanation of the new programme was provided in *The Infant School — Notes for Teachers* which was issued to all schools. The Introduction to the Notes is reproduced here in full:

INTRODUCTION

The purpose of the infant school is to provide for young children the environment, opportunities and activities most favourable to their full development. Infant teaching, if it is to be successful, must be based on the young child's instinctive urge to play, to talk, to imitate, to manipulate materials, to make and do things. The richness of his imagination and his love of make-believe must always be kept in mind.

The atmosphere of the infant classroom should be pleasant and stimulating. A varied and colourful selection of pictures, toys, and play materials should be provided. The children should be made to feel happy in school; brightness and joy are their right; their activities should be so arranged that they may learn almost without realising that they are doing so.

An intelligent use of activity methods should be a central feature of all infant teaching. Repetitive, mechanical learning should be reduced to a minimum. Individual differences should be recognised and catered for; every child should be helped and encouraged to do his best, but no child should be forced beyond his capabilities.

Language teaching is of paramount importance and should be made an integral part of practically all activities. The habit of speaking Irish should be gradually established, care being taken to ensure that the methods adopted do not result in any repression of the young child's natural urge to express himself in speech.

There should be in the infant school curriculum a blend of individual, group and class activities. Individual and group work should predominate; class ensemble work should be confined to such activities as story telling, games, drama and music. With large classes the traditional conversation and number lessons are too often ineffective; such lessons being generally chosen to suit the children of average intelligence in the class, leave the above-average retarded and the below-average uninterested. The obvious remedy is more group teaching, and groups should be reasonably homogeneous as regards general ability. Individual activities should be arranged so that the children who are not receiving direct guidance from the teacher at any particular time are purposefully employed at suitable occupations.

The time-table should not be rigid. Oral work should generally be taken for short periods at frequent intervals; activities such as art, handwork, occupations involving the three Rs and suchlike will require longer working periods at a time. There should be order without constraint; formal discipline will not be necessary if the activities are made interesting and purposeful. Training in good conduct and good manners should inform every aspect of the day's activities; politeness, consideration for others, truthfulness and honesty should be constantly inculcated. Sympathy and understanding on the part of the teacher are all-important; success depends almost entirely on her capacity to direct the children wisely.

The Notes in the following pages aim at eliminating formalism from the infant school and at helping the teacher to carry out the requirements of the Revised Programme for Infants. The suggestions given are neither rigid nor exhaustive; they will admit of modification, adaptation and development according to the needs of the children and the circumstances in which they are taught. The teacher who works on the lines indicated should have no difficulty in making her work interesting and varied.

IRISH CONVERSATION

The Programme aims at making the children fairly fluent Irish speakers by the time they are eight years of age and the *Notes for Teachers : Irish* suggest two lines of approach:

(i) The incidental approach;
(ii) The graded approach.

These will interact on each other at almost every stage and formalism should be avoided as much as possible. For the youngest children the incidental approach should predominate; indeed many teachers get excellent results by using the incidental method almost exclusively throughout the infant class stage, basing the work entirely on the speech needs of the children.

If the results are to be satisfactory the teaching must be made interesting and stimulating. If Irish is made pleasant and attractive the children will want to learn it.They will take pride in being able to use little phrases and will be eager to show off how much they know, not only in school but at home.

ENGLISH

English is an optional subject in the infant school; it may be taught for half an hour a day. The course should include speech-training, stories, informal conversation, rhymes, poems, verse-speaking and drama. The initial steps in the teaching of reading may be taken in an informal way if the teacher so desires and if the children are likely to profit by it.

II.9 Report of the Council of Education on the Function and the Curriculum of the Primary School, 1954.

The setting up of the Council of Education in 1950 has been referred to in an earlier section (1.8). The report of the council on the function and the curriculum of the primary school was published in 1954. It was a long report of over 300 pages which included an outline history of primary education in Ireland from earliest times to 1950. Chapters 2, 3 and 4 discussed the definition, function and different aspects of the primary school. Chapters 5 to 9 provided a detailed debate on the various subjects of the primary school curriculum. The final chapters covered issues such as staffing, control, equipment, homework and the Primary School Certificate. In relation to issues such as function, control and the Irish language, the report was essentially conservative but as regards the curriculum, there was general agreement that the existing curriculum was too narrow and should be broadened to include Physical Training, Nature Study and Drawing.

It is difficult to select representative extracts from this report which discusses a broad range of matters at such length. The summary of principal conclusions and recommendations (182 in all) covers 15 pages and even at that does not provide an adequate flavour of the breadth and depth of the report. Since the sections of the report which were subsequently responded to by the Minister for Education related to function, definition, curriculum and staffing, some extracts from these sections are included here:

DUAL PURPOSE OF THE PRIMARY SCHOOL

128. The function, then, of the primary school is to provide an educational foundation. This may be the child's only school training or he may, as we hope he will, continue his education further but, whether he does or not he will later be forced to learn more in the free school of life. It is for the primary school to ensure that by the time he leaves it, he will be able to assess the value of what he will afterwards learn, to reject what is bad and retain what is good. The primary school therefore serves two purposes; it provides a basic education and it prepares the

child for further education should he receive it. It is not to be expected that the primary school can, within the range in which we have placed it, impart the full minimum education that is to-day regarded as necessary but it can provide such a foundation as will answer the common needs of all.

Religious and Moral Training

129. The school exists to assist and supplement the work of parents in the rearing of their children. Their first duty is to train their children in the fear and love of God. That duty becomes the first purpose of the primary school. It is fulfilled by the school through the religious and moral training of the child, through the teaching of good habits, through his instruction in duties of citizenship and in his obligations to his parents and to the community — in short, through all that tends to the formation of a person of character strong in his desire to fulfill the end of his creation.

130. The child should, therefore, leave the primary school well versed in the knowledge and practice of his faith. He should have a clear conception of his dignity as a creature of God and the duties that he owes to his Creator, of his final destiny and the means at his disposal to attain it, of the duties that he owes to his fellow men.

He must also take his place in human society, as a citizen of the State and as a member of various lesser communities. His training for this is again essentially religious and moral, but it will emphasise certain virtues and certain modes of exercising them which are particularly social. His duties towards his parents, love for his country, obedience to lawful authority, respect for private and public property, belief in the dignity of work and the need for service, good manners, courtesy and a sense of order, regard for all God's creatures, all these must take a prominent place in the training of the primary school.

****

SUMMARY OF FUNCTION — TRAINING

144. We have repeatedly used the word "training" in describing the function of the primary school. Properly understood, the word expresses both the aim and the method of the school. On the one hand, it undertakes a common task for all children, the development of the whole individual, composed of the soul with its two great faculties of mind and will, and the body. Yet these two components, though common to all, are not the same in all, and hence the school must provide for the religious and moral, intellectual, cultural and physical development of each of a number of individuals. The method should not attempt to reform each mind or to build each body to a common pattern. In its use of the instruments of development, the subjects of the curriculum, sufficient allowance must be made for the growth of each individual child.

****

1. THE CURRICULUM IN GENERAL

166. In approaching the question of the curriculum of the primary school, we have been influenced by two aims, the religious and moral, intellectual and physical welfare of each individual Irish boy and girl, which is our chief concern, and the cultural and material well-being of our nation, which, though secondary, is our concern also. These two aims are in fact complementary and we have made every effort to keep both in view, allowing neither to obscure the other.

167. The memoranda of evidence received by the Council, much of the criticism of our educational system expressed over a number of years, and our own individual views concerning it convey an almost unanimous conviction that the present curriculum of the primary school is too narrow. It might, therefore, be expected that we should recommend the adoption of a much wider curriculum. We have had, however, to make our recommendations with full regard for facts and realities.

****

STANDARD CURRICULUM PROPOSED

173. Having regard to the views expressed in the preceding paragraphs (pars.166-172), the Council considered the general aims of the primary school would best be served by a standard curriculum, the subjects of which would be obligatory in all schools, as far as possible, allowance being made for the fact that certain other subjects were already being taught in particular schools. Different opinions were held in the Council as to the claims of particular subjects to a place in such a standard curriculum. It is not unreasonable that the views of individual members should vary according to the aspects of each subject which they considered most important, the aim in teaching it, its value to the child, its value weighed against that of a wider course in a subject considered more important, the feasibility of introducing it in small schools, and especially the part it could play in the function of the primary school. All our members, without exception, would agree that Religious Instruction, some Physical Training, Music, Arithmetic, History, Geography, Needlework for girls, should be included in the curriculum. Not all members would agree, however, that both languages, Irish and English, should be obligatory, one member, at least, holding that Irish should not be obligatory outside the Irish-speaking districts and one member being opposed to English being obligatory in any school. In regard to these two subjects also opinions differed as to the stage at which they should be introduced as obligatory subjects; we refer to this problem later. The inclusion of Nature Study and Drawing, while generally advocated, did not find favour with one or two members, chiefly on the ground that time could not well be provided for them in the average school. Several of our members questioned the practicability of and the need for providing separate obligatory courses in Algebra or Geometry even in the larger schools, but all would agree that through the Arithmetic course all pupils should be introduced to these

subjects and that special emphasis be given, as far as possible, to the study of mensuration. After full consideration of the various objections made and having had regard to suggestions received by way of the statements of evidence, the Council, on the whole, recommends the adoption of the following standard curriculum — Religious Instruction, Irish, English, Arithmetic, History, Music, Physical Training, Nature Study, Geography, Drawing, and Needlework (for girls). It recommends also that the subjects, Algebra and Geometry, be included as obligatory subjects in the curricula of schools to the extend to which they are at present obligatory, subject to the suggestion contained in paragraph 184.

****

INFANT TRAINING

185. While we refer again (pars.209-216) to the aims of the Infant school in relation to language teaching, most of our members consider that the present programme of Infant training is on the whole unsuitable. The majority of the Council recommend, however, that the teaching of English, as a subject, be obligatory for one half-hour daily in Infant classes in schools outside the Irish-speaking districts. In schools in the latter districts we do not desire that any change be made in present practice. As we are aware, however, that there are schools in which the training of Infants and other classes is being given solely through Irish, we also recommend that, where the parents, as represented by the manager of a school, desire that the work of the school be conducted wholly through Irish, the Minister should make provision for such school to be conducted on an all-Irish basis. The place of Irish in the schools and the provisions which should govern the use of Irish as a medium of instruction are discussed more fully in Chapter VII.

****

RELIGIOUS INSTRUCTION

194. In Ireland, happily, there is no disagreement as to the place religion should occupy in the school. Through many centuries our people have striven to secure the freedom to have their children taught in schools conducted in accordance with the parents' religious concept of life. For them religion was not merely one of many subjects to be taught in the school: it was the soul, the foundation and the crown of the whole educational process, giving value and meaning to every subject in the curriculum. The undenominational principle underlying the "system of national education" was obnoxious to our people, though at least that system had the merit of recognising that Religious Instruction was an indispensable constituent of the curriculum.

195. The outcome of that past struggle is that our primary schools to-day are essentially religious and denominational in character. They are owned and managed almost exclusively by religious bodies, and their primary purpose is religious. Though the State makes certain demands of them by reason of the public moneys contributed towards their building and maintenance, they are in the main really parochial schools conducted on behalf of particular denominations.

****

SIZE OF CLASS

317. Where statements of evidence received by us referred to this question, they practically all agreed that 30 is the maximum number of pupils which should constitute a class. The majority of the Council members are of opinion that 30 is an optimum figure. Such a figure would satisfactorily guard against financial wastage and at the same time prevent all but the minimum educational loss. The figure also refers to the primary school only, and takes account of the fact that practical

instruction requiring a great deal of individual attention is not included in the curriculum.

****

DENOMINATIONAL CHARACTERISTICS

331. In the introductory chapter on the history of primary education in Ireland, it was shown that the difficulties encountered by the Commissioners of National Education were, for the greater part, due to their failure to recognise the demands for denominational education. These demands did not come merely from members of one religious faith but from all those who objected to the principle of "mixed" education and who favoured private (i.e., non-state) ownership and control of the schools. In actual fact to-day the overwhelming majority of the National Schools are denominational in the sense that the trustees, manager, teachers and pupils of each school are of the same religious persuasion; less than 3% of the total are "mixed" schools, i.e., attended by children of different religious affiliations, and the State, in fact, assists children of religious minorities to enable them to attend schools of their parents' choice. Hence we consider that the theoretical object of the "system of National Education," which is "to afford *Combined* literary and moral, and *Separate* Religious Instruction to Children of all persuasions, as far as possible, in the same school......," is at variance with the principles of all religious denominations and with the realities in the primary schools, and consequently that it needs restatement. We suggest that it be amended in accordance with Article 44.2.4. of the Constitution, and that the fullness of denominational education may be legally sanctioned in those schools which are attended exclusively by children of the same religious faith.

II.10 Primary Education Proposed Changes, December 1956. (Response of the Minister for Education to the Report of the Council of Education).

The Council of Education submitted its report on Primary Education to the Minister for Education, Richard Mulcahy, on 12th June 1954. On receipt of this report the Minister set up a departmental committee to consider the recommendations of the Council and two years later, in December 1956, he issued a statement which contained a summary of the recommendations which, with the approval of Government, he proposed to accept. The statement made it clear, however, that before these recommendations could be carried into effect, it would be necessary for them to be discussed with the various interested bodies — "ecclesiastical authorities, school managers, teachers — with a view to making the necessary arrangements and adjustments." But the Inter-Party government fell soon afterwards and none of the changes proposed by the Minister in December 1956 were implemented before he left office in March, 1957. The following is the text of the Minister's statement of December 1956:

The whole position has now been carefully reviewed by the Minister and, with the approval of the Government, he proposes that certain recommendations be accepted as an indication of policy in regard to the First Report of the Council of Education.

****

The main recommendations may be summarised as follows:-

1. The "National School" to continue to operate, under the same title as at present, as a school for children between four and eighteen years of age; "Primary education," however, to be defined as meaning, in relation to secular instruction, education up to the end of Standard VI in the programme prescribed or approved for National Schools.
   (Recommendations 2,3,4).

2. The object of the system of National Education to be stated, in the Rules and Regulations for National Schools, so as to give explicit recognition to the denominational character of the schools and, in accordance with Article 44.2.40 of the Constitution, to provide that the Rules shall not discriminate between schools under the management of different religious denominations or be such as to affect prejudicially the right of any child to attend a National School without attending religious instruction at that school. (Recommendation No.1).

3. Adoption of a standard curriculum in all schools other than Infant Schools and Infant Departments or classes. (Recommendations 6, 7, 8 and 14).

4. Broadening of the curriculum by the introduction of Physical Training, Drawing and Nature Study as follows:

(a) One-teacher schools:
Physical Training in all classes — 1/2 hour per week.

(b) Two-teacher schools:
Physical Training in all classes — 1/2 hour per week
Drawing in standards I and II — 1 hour per week
Nature Study or Drawing in Standards III and higher — 1 hour per week

(c) Three-teacher and multiple-teacher schools:
Physical Training in all classes — 1/2 hour per week
Drawing in all classes 1 hour per week
Nature Study in Standard III and higher — 1 hour per week.
(Recommendation No.5).

5. Domestic Economy may be taken in lieu of Nature Study or Drawing in Standard V and above. In urban schools, Elementary Science may be taken in lieu of Nature Study. Managers in all schools to be permitted, subject to the approval of the Minister, to substitute for Drawing or Nature Study another subject of satisfactory practical and educational value.
(Recommendations 5, 6, 9 and 10).

6. The time at present allotted to *written work* in both Irish and English to be reduced, and the time thus made available, together with time taken from other subjects at the manager's discretion, to be devoted to the teaching of the additional subjects. Formal teaching of grammar in the higher standards to be limited to the rudiments which give the broad principles on which correct speech is based.
(Recommendations 16, 17, 23 and 25).

7. Oral expression to take precedence over all other sections of the Irish programme, the main effort to be directed towards giving the pupils fluency in the use of Irish as a medium of ordinary intercourse.
(Recommendation No.15).

8. The attainment, as soon as financial circumstances permit, of a basis of staffing for National Schools more in accord with the recommendations of the Council of Education than is the present basis. Consideration to be given, as soon as the financial situation permits, to the further expansion of Training College facilities in order to provide additional teachers. The new basis of staffing to be introduced gradually as the additional teachers become available and having special regard to the needs of those schools in which the staffing problem is most

pressing and also to such further provision as may be necessary for the education in National Schools of children over 12 year of age.
(Recommendations 26, 27).

9. That a special research and advisory section be set up within the Department of Education, working in co-operation with managers and teachers and educational bodies, to assemble and prepare for application to the teaching of the curriculum, the results of research and experience at home and abroad, with special reference to the advancement of the Irish language in the schools.
(Recommendation No.28).

Other recommendations deal with the teaching of Civics in association with other subjects; the preparation of an Irish language dictionary with word explanations in simple Irish; and refresher and basic courses in drawing for teachers.
(Recommendations 11, 19 and 24).

Before the recommendations can be carried into effect, it will be necessary for them to be discussed with the various interested bodies — ecclesiastical authorities, school managers, teachers — with a view to making the necessary arrangements and adjustments. The Minister proposes to enter into consultation at once with the bodies concerned.

It will not be possible to carry out all these recommendations in full immediately — for example, much preparatory work will be necessary before the Primary Curriculum can be broadened to the extent proposed. The Minister has decided, however, that the recommendations should be published as a whole with a view to securing general agreement, without undue delay, for the initiation of the measures necessary to bring them into effect as soon as possible. He is confident that the most generous co-operation which has marked the consideration of these matters will be continued in bringing about the desired changes.

II.11 Removal of the requirement to teach through the medium of Irish, Circular 11/60 to Managers and Teachers, January 1960.

From the foundation of the Free State in 1922, the keystone of the language revival policy of successive governments was the requirement that subjects in the National School should be taught through the medium of Irish. This policy had caused difficulties over the years and had been criticized by the I.N.T.O in 1941 and again in their report of 1947. In spite of this policy, the Irish language had not been revived to the extent aspired to by the leaders of the new Free State and while census figures showed that the proportion of the population who could speak Irish was growing, this growth was very slow. Many people believed that the policy of teaching through Irish was counter-productive, especially for weaker pupils.

In November 1959, Dr. Patrick Hillery, Minister for Education was asked in the Dáil whether he was satisfied that teaching all subjects through Irish in the schools was educationally sound and was the best way to advance the teaching of Irish. In his reply, he indicated that he had recently been examining the matter and that he was inclined to the view that concentrating on teaching Irish well rather than teaching through Irish would achieve more. In January 1960, a circular (11/60) was issued to schools informing teachers that they were free to transfer the emphasis "from teaching through Irish to the teaching of Irish Conversation" if they felt that the pupils were more likely to make progress in Oral Irish from this approach. It was subsequently argued that this circular marked the first step in the dismantling of the policy of teaching through Irish and in subsequent years the numbers of schools in which all subjects were taught through Irish decreased dramatically.

The following is the full text of the circular:

With reference to the attached copy of Circular No.16/59 relating to inspection, the Minister for Education desires to call special attention to the fact that in future a teacher's work in the teaching of Irish will be assessed as a whole and that there will not be separate assessments of Oral Irish and Written Irish. It should be understood, however, that the Inspector, when making his assessment of the work as a whole, will attach greater importance to Oral Irish than to Written Irish. In this connection the Minister wishes to stress his desire that the teachers should make every effort to advance as far as possible and as quickly as possible the speaking of Irish amongst their pupils. If, with this in view, a teacher is satisfied in relation to pupils whom he may have in a junior class in any year that, having regard to the level of their intelligence etc., he would be likely to make more progress with them in Oral Irish by transferring the emphasis from teaching through Irish to the teaching of Irish Conversation, then such teacher will be free to act accordingly. That of course will be on the understanding that his work in the case of Irish will be assessed principally from the point of view of the advance made by the pupils in the spoken tongue.

II.12 Investment in Education, 1965 (Primary Education)

The Investment in Education survey has been referred to in an earlier section of this book (I.10). The report was published in 1965. While its main influence was in the area of post-primary education, its findings in the area of primary education were also significant. It analysed the resource implications of a system of national education which was dominated by a large number of small schools — almost 85% of national schools employed three teachers or less. It established that small schools were more expensive, both in terms of current and capital costs, than larger schools and attempted to examine the extent to which pupils benefitted from attending small schools. The findings of the report highlighted the financial implications of "the multiplication of small schools" — an issue which had been raised by the British Treasury as far back as the

1880s and which had led to confrontation between the interest groups in national education in the decades before independence. Following the publication of Investment in Education, the government decided to initiate and pursue a policy of closure of small schools — a policy which led to a decline in the number of one and two teacher schools from 3,194 to 1,168 in the period from 1962 to 1979. The following extracts are from Chapter Twelve of the report:

EFFICIENCY

12.60 The data of chapters 9 and 10 indicated that there was scope for achieving an improved use of resources in both first-level (national) schools and second-level (secondary and vocational) schools. Looked at in financial terms it may be said that there are substantial differences in costs as between different types of school and generally it was the smaller schools which were the more expensive. Looked at in terms of the participation problem it was seen that it was the pupils of smaller schools who made the slower progress at primary level, while at the post-primary level the smaller schools had a more restricted range of subjects available. Hence on both "efficiency" and participation grounds there are reasons for examining whether an alternative distribution of schools would be more satisfactory.

12.61 NATIONAL SCHOOLS

From many points of view the parish would appear to be a suitable unit on which to base a reorganization of school size. This would not entail the promotion of unduly large schools. Parishes vary greatly as regards the number of pupils in them, as the following table shows. Some parishes have less than 100 pupils — some of these have only one school and one teacher — while the largest parishes have over 1,000 pupils : the overall average is just under 500 pupils per parish. (This discussion refers only to Catholic parishes and pupils in Catholic schools). It will be seen however, that more than half of the parishes have less than 300 pupils, so that even if all the pupils in a parish were in the one school the enrolment would still be less than that required, on present regulations, for seven or eight teachers which would give one teacher for each grade. Of course one of the effects of re-organization would be to enable say seven or eight teachers to be made available for a smaller number of pupils — hypothetically, if the overall pupil/teacher ratio of 34.3 (Table 9.2) were to apply uniformly throughout, seven teachers would be available for 240 pupils. A re-organization of school size would of course make it easier to supply all schools with the necessary physical facilities and educational aids, as well as making it easier to give remedial attention to "delayed" pupils.

****

12.64 It may also be observed that a movement towards larger schools would give some prospect of being able to implement the Council of Education target of a maximum class size of 40 pupils, in the not too distant future. This possibility would arise because the smaller schools are the ones with the lowest pupil/teacher ratios, hence the amalgamation of these small schools would make it possible to re-allocate teachers among schools so that the class sizes in the existing larger schools would be lowered.

12.65 The larger schools in rural areas might be introduced gradually as existing schools become obsolete. Alternatively, if this question were to be regarded as more urgent, steps somewhat along the following lines might be taken, where agreement could be reached among the parties concerned.

****

12.70 It would in addition, be consistent with the evidence of earlier chapters that larger schools would have a favourable effect on the benefits derived by pupils. The arguments we have put forward for seeking a re-organization of school size are mainly on economic grounds. It seems to us not unlikely, however, that the weight of argument on the educational side will be such as to complement our arguments.

II.13 Rules for National Schools under the Department of Education — 1965.

Since the setting up of the National School system under the terms of the Stanley letter in 1831, the Rules for National Schools had stated that "the system of national education affords combined secular and separate religious instruction to children of all religions and no attempt is made to interfere with the religious tenets of any pupils." The standard Lease for vested National Schools prior to 1965 asserted that the object of the system was "to afford Combined literary and moral and Separate religious instruction to children of all persuasions, as far as possible, in the same school." Despite this stated objective, from the mid 1830s onwards the Commissioners of National Education had recognised national schools which were under the Patronage and management of individual Churches. On many occasions in the nineteenth and twentieth centuries, the Churches had called on the government to give formal recognition to the denominational reality of so many of the national schools and to change the Rules for National Schools to take this reality into account. The Report of the Council of Education in 1953 pointed out that less than 3% of all national schools were mixed schools, i.e. attended by children of different religious affiliations. The Council suggested that the theoretical object of the system should be changed "in accordance with Article 44.2.4 of the Constitution and that the fullness of denominational education may be legally sanctioned in those schools which are attended exclusively by children of the same religious faith."

In 1965, a revised version of the Rules for National Schools was issued by the Minister for Education, P. Hillery. These Rules introduced a number of fundamental changes as far as denominational recognition was concerned. A new Preface was introduced (reproduced in full below), which stated that the State "gives explicit recognition to the denominational character of these schools." Rules which had previously been included to safeguard the rights of parents to send their children to a national school without attending religious instruction were modified in such a way that the safeguards would no longer be as effective. For example, the Rule requiring Religious Instruction to be offered either at the beginning or the end of the school day was modified to read "The periods of formal religious instruction shall be fixed so as to facilitate the withdrawal of pupils to whom paragraph (a) of this section applies." The section of the Rules which had previously exhorted teachers to be "careful in the presence of children of different religious beliefs not to touch on matters of controversy" was deleted.

By recognising the denominational reality of national schools, the State, in effect, authorized school management authorities to give first preference to children of their own religious persuasion in allocating places in a school, where a choice had to be made. This was subsequently to result in the emergence of a demand from parents in some parts of the country for schools where children of all religious, social and cultural backgrounds had equal right of access and led to the setting up of a number of multi-denominational national schools in the subsequent decades.

PREFACE

The rights and duties of citizens of the State in the matter of Education are set forth in Articles 42 and 44.2.4 of the Constitution of Ireland (Bunreacht na hÉireann) as follows:-

ARTICLE 42.

1. The State acknowledges that the primary and natural educator of the child is the family and guarantees to respect the inalienable right and duty of parents to provide, according to their means, for the religious and moral, intellectual, physical and social education of their children.

2. Parents shall be free to provide this education in their homes or in private schools or in schools recognised or established by the State.

3.(1) The State shall not oblige parents in violation of their conscience and lawful preference to send their children to schools established by the State, or to any particular type of school designated by the State.

(2) The State shall, however, as guardian of the common good, require in view of actual conditions that the children receive a certain minimum education, moral, intellectual and social.

4. The State shall provide for free primary education and shall endeavour to supplement and give reasonable aid to private and corporate educational initiative, and, when the public good requires it, provide other educational facilities or institutions with due regard, however, for the rights of parents, especially in the matter of religious and moral formation.

5. In exceptional cases, where the parents for physical or moral reasons fail in their duty towards their children, the State as guardian of the common good, by appropriate means shall endeavour to supply the place of the parents, but always with due regard for the natural and imprescriptible rights of the child.

ARTICLE 44.2.4

Legislation providing State aid for schools shall not discriminate between schools under the management of different religious denominations, nor be such as to affect prejudicially the right of any child to attend a school receiving public money without attending religious instruction at that school.

In pursuance of the provisions of these Articles the State provides for free primary education for children in national schools, and gives explicit recognition to the denominational character of these schools.

CHAPTER I

THE SYSTEM OF NATIONAL EDUCATION

1. Provision for education in prescribed or approved programmes for children between the ages of four and eighteen years is made in schools recognised by the Minister as national schools. Subject to the terms of rule 67 such education shall be free.

2. These Rules do not discriminate between schools under the management of different religious denominations nor may they be construed so as to affect prejudicially the right of any child to attend a national school without attending religious instruction at that school.

3. State aid for the establishment of a new national school may be granted on application by the representatives of a religious denomination where the number of pupils of that denomination in a particular area is sufficient to warrant the establishment and continuance of such school.

4. As an alternative to the establishment of a national school, aid may be granted towards defraying the cost of conveying children to a suitable national school.

II.14 Abolition of the Primary Certificate Examination and Introduction of School Record Card System, March 1968.

The Primary Certificate Examination had been introduced on an optional basis in 1929 and became compulsory in 1943. From the start, the I.N.T.O had opposed the examination and after it became compulsory, had refused to co-operate in its implementation. There had been many meetings between the I.N.T.O and the Department of Education over the years in relation to the examination but it was not until 1967, in the context of the introduction of free post-primary education that the Department agreed to abolish the Primary Certificate.

At a meeting between the management bodies, the I.N.T.O. and the Department in June 1967 it was agreed that a School Record Card System would replace the Primary Certificate and this was notified to schools in October 1967. In March 1968, details of the new system were circulated to managers and principal teachers of all National Schools. The following is the text of the letter and the general instructions relating to the School Record Card System as notified to schools:

DEPARTMENT OF EDUCATION
PRIMARY BRANCH
SCHOOL RECORD CARD SYSTEM
NOTICE TO MANAGERS AND PRINCIPAL TEACHERS

As already announced a decision has been taken to discontinue the Primary Certificate Examination and to replace it by a system of School Record Cards which will chronicle each pupil's background and attainments in the 5th and 6th standards of the primary school. On completion of the primary education course by the pupil the Record Card should be sent to the head of the post-primary school to which the pupil has transferred.

A supply of Record Cards in metal containers will be sent to each national school in the month of April 1968. Should any school not receive the Cards before 10th May, 1968 the principal teacher should notify the Department immediately.

The Inspectors will confer with the Principal Teachers of the schools in their districts in regard to the tests to be carried out for the purpose of assessing the attainments of the pupils in the various subjects. Each principal teacher will be informed in due course of the date and place of the particular conference he will be required to attend.

More detailed instructions in regard to these tests will be sent to managers and to principal teachers at a later date.

A copy of the general instructions to be followed in filling the Record Cards is enclosed for your information.

S. MAC GEARAILT,
Leas-Rúnaí

An Roinn Oideachais,
Márta, 1968.

SCHOOL RECORD CARD — GENERAL INSTRUCTIONS

The principal teacher should ensure:

(i) that a school record card is kept for each pupil in 5th and 6th Standards;
(ii) that the entries on the cards are kept up to date;
(iii) that the cards for each standard are kept in alphabetical order.

The cards should be stored safely in the container supplied by the Department and made available at all times for inspection by the Manager and the Department's Officers.

The card with all the necessary details entered thereon should be forwarded to the principal teacher of the school (post-primary or otherwise) to which the pupil has transferred.

The following instructions should be followed in filling the card:

Pupil

The surname should be entered in block letters.

Family

The purpose of this section is to obtain information about the pupil's family which has relevance to his/her progress at school.

Home Environment

Matters to be adverted to if relevant are:

attitude of family to education; unemployment of breadwinner; father and/or mother dead; ill-health in family, etc.

General

The purpose of this section is to obtain information about the pupil which has relevance to his/her progress at school.

Application

Terms such as — keen, indifferent, thorough, erratic, etc., may be used.

Interests

Special aptitudes, interest in reading, strong and weak subjects, etc.

Health

Where any physical defect in hearing, sight or speech is evident or if general health is not good, a suitable entry should be made. In such cases it is advisable to get, if possible, the opinion of the school medical officer or other doctor.

Remarks

State here any additional information that would be of help to the principal of the post-primary school.

Attendance
This should be entered as soon as possible after the end of the school year. Should a pupil transfer to another school during the course of a school year, the record of the pupil's attendance for the part year should be forwarded to the principal of the school to which the pupil has transferred.

Attainments
The principal should, in cooperation with the class teacher, assess as accurately as possible through tests, written and oral, the attainment of each pupil in the various subjects. The standard reached by the pupil should be indicated by one of the following terms: *very good, good, fair, weak.* The Department relies on the teacher to give an impartial assessment in each case.

II.15 Primary School Curriculum — Teachers' Handbook, 1971.

Following the introduction of free post-primary education in 1967, the government planned to publish a White Paper on Education and in this context a number of sub-groups were set up within the Department of Education to draft the different sections of a White Paper. The primary inspectors involved in this exercise used the opportunity to reappraise and review the primary school curriculum. The educational climate was ripe for reform in this area. Twenty years had elapsed since the I.N.T.O. had published its Plan of Education which called for a radical reform of the primary school curriculum. Since 1951, infant teachers in national schools had based their work on the principles that "individual differences should be recognised and catered for" (II.8) and these principles had begun to percolate beyond the infant classroom.

Although the White Paper was not proceeded with, the first draft of a new Primary School Curriculum was ready in 1968 and the Department invited responses to the draft from various interest groups at primary level. At the same time, individual schools throughout the country were invited to pilot various aspects of the proposed new curriculum. Some small changes were made in the draft programme before its publication in a definitive form in 1971 and the "New Curriculum" by which it has been known for the past twenty years, became the official national school curriculum in 1971. The curriculum was published in the form of a two volume Teachers' Handbook comprising more than 700 pages.

The 1971 curriculum allowed a wide measure of freedom to the teacher and the pupil. It was based on a child-centred ideology and was designed "to enable the child to live a full life as a child and to equip him to avail of further education so that he may go on to live a full and useful life as an adult in society." The curriculum covered a wide range of subjects and teachers were encouraged to adapt the programme to suit the needs and educational environment of the district in which the school was situated. Although the Handbook stated that the curriculum was to be regarded as "an integrated entity, involving linguistic, mathematical and artistic organisation of the child's knowledge and experience," for the purpose of convenience its various aspects were arranged under seven headings as follows: Religion; Language (i.e. Irish and English); Mathematics; Social and Environmental Studies; Art and Craft Activities; Music; Physical Education.

The following extracts from the first volume of the Handbook indicate the basic philosophy underlying the new curriculum:

CHAPTER I
PRIMARY EDUCATION : AIMS AND FUNCTION

General statements concerning the purpose of education have a tendency to lose their impact, not because they are false but because they are by their very nature incomplete. The theory they enshrine may be flawless in itself but its actual influence on practice in schools may at the same time be minimal. Yet the course of education cannot be allowed to become an empiric development. There are certain guidelines which it ought to follow and certain dangers which it ought to avoid.

An outline of the purpose of education should reflect the philosophy of a society. The scale of values in a society will inevitably determine its educational aims and priorities. We in Ireland have our own scale of values.

Each human being is created in God's image. He has a life to lead and a soul to be saved. Education is, therefore, concerned not only with life but with the purpose of life. And, since all men are equal in the eyes of God, each is entitled to an equal chance of obtaining optimum personal fulfillment.

When a child is born into the world he bears the stamp of his heredity, but his development is influenced not merely by his natural endowments, but also and to a very great extent by his environment. How he will develop will depend largely on the success or failure of the combined efforts of his home, his Church and his school to see that his all-round growth is healthy and harmonious.

A child born in this country inherits certain privileges. Its civilisation, which is based on an ancient spiritual and cultural tradition, is part of his birthright: its democratic institutions, which were designed to protect his rights as a free man, are another part. An appreciation of the value of these privileges should foster in the growing child a realisation of his duties towards society and of his responsibility to contribute in a critical but positive manner towards its proper evolution.

AIMS

The aims of primary education may, therefore, briefly be stated as follows:

1. To enable the child to live a full life as a child.
2. To equip him to avail himself of further education so that he may go on to live a full and useful life as an adult in society.

In order that the first of these aims may be achieved, two relevant factors must be taken into account:

(a) All children are complex human beings with physical, emotional, intellectual and spiritual needs and potentialities;

(b) Because each child is an individual, he deserves to be valued for himself and to be provided with the kind and variety of opportunities towards stimulation and fulfillment which will enable him to develop his natural powers at his own rate to his fullest capacity.

A curriculum which is designed to achieve this aim must, therefore, endeavour to cater for the full and harmonious development of each child and must, at the same time, be sufficiently flexible to meet the needs of children of widely varying natural endowment and cultural background. The full development of the child cannot take place in isolation. If he is to know and value himself and form objective standards of judgement and behaviour, he must learn through experience to live and co-operate with other children and with adults and gradually to become familiar with the complex and evolutionary nature of the society of which he is part.

****

THE CHANGING ROLE OF THE PRIMARY SCHOOL

Before the advent of second level education for all, primary education had to serve as the sole basis of formal instruction for a considerable proportion of our people. It was thought desirable, therefore, that children should be as fully equipped as possible, on completion of their primary school course, to meet the demands of the world. Success or failure in after life was thought to depend to a large extent on whether the child had mastered such basic skills as reading, writing and computation. It was, however, realised from the earliest years of the National School system that literacy and numeracy were not synonymous with education, and efforts were made from time to time to widen the programme of instruction and to define the methods of teaching each subject.

Nevertheless, the imparting of knowledge by the teacher to his pupils continued to be accepted as one of the main functions of the school. In order to maintain a general standard of efficiency and to create an objective yardstick of assessment, the central authority took upon itself the duty of defining a syllabus of instruction in each subject for each class. This may have led to a certain uniformity of standards: it certainly resulted in a general uniformity of practice. Education was "curriculum-centred" rather than "child-centred," and the teacher's function, in many cases, was that of a medium through whom knowledge was merely transferred to his pupils.

The changing role of the primary school in recent years, however, has demanded a corresponding change in practice within the classroom.

****

Until a few years ago two major obstacles still remained: the rigid compulsory programme of instruction for all schools and the examination based on it which all children were obliged to take on completion of their primary course. The abolition of the Primary Certificate Examination in 1967 has removed one of these obstacles and it is to be hoped that the new curriculum, which allows a very wide measure of freedom to both the individual child and the individual teacher, will further advance educational development.

****

Chapter II
The Structure of the Curriculum

The traditional method of dealing with the curriculum was to divide it into compartments which were called subjects, to allot fixed periods of time during the day to the teaching of each one of them and to attempt, when the opportunity occurred, to correlate some of these subjects.

This approach is logical rather than psychological and places emphasis on what the child ought to be taught rather than on how he learns at the different stages of his development. Recent research, conducted in many countries, into the learning processes and development of children has shown, however, that knowledge acquired through the child's personal experience and discovery is likely to be more meaningful and purposeful to him than information acquired at second hand. The child is now seen to be the most active agent in his own education. At times, when he tackles problems as an individual, he develops self-reliance and independence; at other times, when he works as a member of a group or of a class he learns the value of co-operation and his social development is fostered.

The teacher is no longer regarded as one who merely imparts information but rather as one who provides suitable learning situations and who guides and stimulates the child in his pursuit of knowledge. Indeed, the words of Pearse appear to have anticipated this development:

> What the teacher should bring to his pupil is not a set of readymade opinions, or a stock of cut-and-dry information but an inspiration and an example; and his main qualification should be, not such an overmastering will as shall impose

> itself at all hazards upon all weaker wills that
> come under its influence, but rather so infectious
> an enthusiasm as shall kindle new enthusiasm.

The role of the teacher while thus seen in a new and different light is in no way diminished in importance.

PSYCHOLOGICAL RESEARCH AND THE TEACHER

Where modern psychology can help the teacher is in its discovery that in child development there are definite stages which follow in a sequence which may be advanced or delayed but not altered. Each person must experience each stage in order to be ready to advance to the next and when experience in one stage is not adequate the over-all development tends to be distorted. Although the sequence is fixed, the rate of progress for individuals is not uniform. Some will pass quickly through one stage and will soon indicate readiness and eagerness for the next, whereas others will need much greater consolidation in the earlier stages in order to advance further. Factors such as social and cultural background as well as natural endowment will clearly affect the individual's rate of progress. The implication, therefore, is that the curriculum should be sufficiently flexible to allow each child to progress at an appropriate pace and to achieve satisfaction and success at his own level.

Furthermore, the young child is not conscious of subject barriers; he views knowledge as a key to life and his questions concerning the world around him range over the whole field of knowledge. The curriculum should reflect this attitude of the child and be seen more as an integral whole rather than as a logical structure containing conveniently differentiated parts.

The decision to construct an integrated curriculum rather than to graft some additional subjects on to the existing one is based on the following theses:

(a) That as the child is one, however complex his nature, so also must his education be one, however complex its nature;

(b) That the separation of religious and secular instruction into differentiated subject compartments serves only to throw the whole educational function out of focus;

(c) That although curricular "subjects" differ somewhat from each other in the areas of knowledge they are said to embrace, some, because of their very nature, defy all barriers to contain them;

(d) That the child's education must take place in a meaningful and relevant context.

The integration of the curriculum may be seen:

(i) in the religious and civic spirit which animates all its parts;

(ii) in its recognition of language, mathematics and artistic expression, not merely as specific areas of knowledge and activity but even more essentially as the means by which all knowledge and experiences are organised and made meaningful;

(iii) in its emphasis on the fact that the child's environment provides the most congenial ground in which the seeds of knowledge may be sown and its organic growth fostered;

(iv) in its acknowledgment of the fact that "school education" and "parallel education" must be clearly seen to complement each other if the child is to live a full life as a child and, later, a full and useful life as an adult in society.

Although the curriculum is to be regarded essentially as an integrated entity, involving linguistic, mathematical and artistic organisation of the child's knowledge and experience, for the purpose of convenience its various aspects are arranged under the following heads:

1. *Religion.*

2. *Language* (i.e. Irish and English. The suggestion made concerning the teaching of Language should be viewed at all times in the context of the two languages being taught and practiced).

3. *Mathematics.*
4. *Social and Environmental Studies.*
5. *Art and Craft Activities.*
6. *Music.*
7. *Physical Education.*

The various syllabuses have been so drafted as to allow the greatest degree of flexibility in selecting the programmes most suitable and feasible for each school, and, perhaps, for each pupil. The school and its environment, its facilities and the particular aptitudes and interests of pupils and teachers, will all be relevant considerations when making this selection.

EVALUATION

It is obvious that the new curriculum points to radical changes not only in content but in methods of teaching. The proposed changes, however, are not to be regarded as being in any way final or definitive. Research and regular evaluation will be necessary if the curriculum is to continue to keep pace with changing conditions.

II.16 Boards of Management of National Schools, 1975, 1980 and 1986

Since the setting up of the national school system in Ireland in 1831, each individual school was run by a manager who was nominated by the school's Patron. By the mid twentieth century virtually all schools were under denominational Patronage, i.e. under the patronage of the Bishop of the diocese in which the school was situated, and the manager was almost invariably the local clergyman — either Catholic or Protestant. As far back as 1868, the Powis Commission had suggested that a greater degree of local involvement would be desirable in the management of national schools. In the early years of the twentieth century, the Resident Commissioner of National Education, W.J.M. Starkie had antagonised the Catholic hierarchy by calling for greater lay involvement in the management of national schools. It was not until after the Second Vatican Council in the 1960s, that the Catholic Church became more responsive to this suggestion and in 1975, a scheme for the setting up of boards of management in all national schools in the country was finally agreed between the main partners in primary education, i.e. Churches, I.N.T.O. and the Department. of Education. All schools which set up a board would be eligible for a new and increased capitation grant and with the incentive of this grant, national schools throughout the country set up boards of management within a very short time.

The constitution and rules under which boards operate are set down in a document entitled — *Boards of Management of National Schools — Constitution of Boards and Rules of Procedure.* This document contains details of the procedures to be followed in electing and nominating board members; procedures for board meetings; duties of the officers of the board and procedures for the selection and appointment of teachers. The duties of the boards are administrative in character and do not impinge directly on curricular or formal educational policy. The board is responsible for the day to day running of the school, including insurance, heating, cleaning and maintenance. It is also responsible for teacher appointments and for all correspondence with the Department of Education.

Since 1975, there have been a number of amendments to the *Constitution of Boards and Rules of Procedure*. The I.N.T.O was not happy with the high proportion of patron's nominees on the original boards and in 1978 they withdrew their participation from the scheme pending a more satisfactory restructuring. In 1980, the churches agreed to reduce the number of patron's nominees from six to four in the large schools and from four to three in the small schools, leaving the patron with 50 per cent of the representation on the boards and the parents and the teachers with 25 per cent each. Other changes were also introduced, particularly in relation to the composition of Selection Boards for teacher appointments. The 1986 version of the Constitution of Boards and Rules of Procedure is the most recent one and the Report of the Primary Education Review Body of 1990 did not recommend any changes to this document.

The following extracts are from the 1986 version of the *Constitution of Boards of Management and Rules of Procedure:*

BOARDS OF MANAGEMENT OF NATIONAL SCHOOLS CONSTITUTION OF BOARDS AND RULES OF PROCEDURE

GENERAL

1. National Schools operate under the Rules for National Schools which are made by the Minister for Education with the concurrence of the Minister for Finance. The Rules are printed in book form and copies may be purchased from the Government Publications Sale Office, Sun Alliance House, Molesworth Street, Dublin, 2. Every person or body of persons on first recognition as manager must give an undertaking in writing that the Rules for National Schools shall be complied with.

DEFINITIONS

2. The *Patron* is the person or body of persons recognised as such by the Minister for Education. The Patron may manage the school personally or may nominate a suitable person or body of persons to act as manager.

Subject to the approval of the Minister, the Patron may at any time resume the direct management of the school or may nominate another manager.

3. The *Trustees* are the persons nominated by the Patron as trustees of the school. They are parties to the lease of the school premises with the Grantor and the Minister for Education as the other parties. The Trustees undertake that the buildings shall continue to be used as a national school for the term of the lease and guarantee that the premises and contents are insured against fire and tempest.

4. The *Manager* is the person or body of persons nominated by the Patron and recognised as manager by the Minister. The manager is charged with the direct government of the school, with the conducting of the necessary correspondence, with the appointment of the teachers, subject to the Minister's and Patron's approval and, where necessary, teachers' removal, subject to the approval of the Patron. The Rules for National Schools state that managers should visit their schools and satisfy themselves that the Rules are being complied with; this requirement shall be fulfilled by the Chairperson of the Board of Management. The Chairperson is required to certify the correctness of the school returns furnished to the Department. The Minister may withdraw recognition from a Board of Management for failure to observe the Rules or if it should appear that the educational interests of the district require it, but such recognition will not be withdrawn without consultation with the Patron, the Board and other interested parties.

5. CONSTITUTION OF BOARDS OF MANAGEMENT

(a) *For schools having a recognised staff of not more than six teachers:*

   (i) Three members appointed by and representative of the Patron;

   (ii) Two members, parents or legal guardians of children enrolled in the school (one being a mother, the other a father), elected by the general body of parents of children attending the school;

   (iii) The Principal Teacher of the School.

In the case of Convent and Monastery Schools where lay teachers form 50% or more of the recognised staff, a Board of eight members as at (b) below would be recognised.

In the case of schools other than those under Catholic patronage, a Board of eight persons as at (b) below would be recognised where particular difficulties arise in connection with ensuring adequate representation on the Board.

(b) *For schools having a recognised staff of seven teachers or more*

   (i) Four members appointed by and representative of the patron;

   (ii) Two members, parents or legal guardians of children enrolled in the school (one being a mother, the other a father), elected by the general body of parents of children attending the school;

   (iii) The Principal Teacher of the school;

   (iv) One other teacher on the staff of the school, elected by vote of the teaching staff.

> In relation to the two teacher-members on Boards of Management for Convent and Monastery Schools having a recognised staff of seven teachers or more or such schools of a lesser size where lay teachers form 50% or more of the recognised staff, the position shall be that if the Principal Teacher be a Religious, the elected teacher-member shall be a lay person, and if the Principal be a lay person, the elected teacher-member shall be a Religious.

NOTE: For the purpose of this paragraph, a parent or legal guardian is eligible for membership while he/she has a child enrolled in the school, and the teacher is eligible for membership while on the authorised teaching staff of the school.

II.17 White Paper on Educational Development, 1980.

The publication of a White Paper on Educational Development in 1980 has been referred to in an earlier section of this book. (I.16). The following extracts indicate the tenor of the White Paper in relation to primary education:

CH. III - THE CURRICULUM OF THE PRIMARY SCHOOL

3.7 There would be substantial agreement that the new curriculum (1971) offers a richer and more flexible framework within which the education of children can take place. Yet the uncomfortable feeling persists that some of the values of the old system have been lost in the pursuit of more esoteric but less tangible educational objectives. In particular, children are thought to be less proficient in basic scholastic skills such as spelling and computation. In this connection, it may be relevant to state that a significant problem of school failure exists here as elsewhere but there is no evidence to support the contention that achievement levels have dropped as a result of the revised curriculum in primary schools.......

3.8. Nothing in the theory and structure of the curriculum suggests that its proper implementation should result in a decline in scholastic achievement. The opposite is indeed the case - the more an educational system tries to accommodate itself to the children's varying needs and abilities, the better should be the prospect that each child should reach his full potential. Nevertheless, adjustment problems were to be expected.......

The following is a summary of the proposals in relation to curriculum:

1. A series of booklets on local environments will be made available as an aid to the teaching of Environmental Studies.
2. The central principle of integration in the revised curriculum will be an important focus of educational attention. The achievement of a proper balance between the various study areas within the integrated methodology will be pursued in consultation with the relevant professional bodies.
3. The Curriculum Unit will continue the systematic evaluation of the curriculum.
4. The problems inherent in the transfer from primary to post-primary education will be considered in the light of the report of the Transfer Committee.

In Chapter V, the following proposals were made in regard to the Administration of the National School:

1. A review of the Constitution of Board of Management and Rules of Procedure has been carried out with a view to having Boards of Management reconstituted under revised procedures in 1981.
2. The policy of school amalgamation initiated over ten years ago has now largely been completed. However, in

> cases where there is local support for amalgamation it will be facilitated.

Chapter II was devoted entirely to a discussion of Irish. This chapter, written in Irish, was translated in an Appendix and the following points were made in relation to primary education:

2.4. ..... most of the research and evaluation, which has been conducted in recent years, has revealed that a higher standard of Irish could be achieved in a good many schools. Among the main factors militating against progress in the language were a lack of interest in Irish in the life of the child outside school and inadequate utilization of Irish as a medium of instruction and as a means of social interaction within the school. It also appears that the competence in spoken Irish of many teachers as well as their grasp of teaching methods could be improved.

2.5 ....It is necessary, therefore, to stress the importance of correlating Irish with other aspects of the curriculum. Accordingly, some other aspect or part thereof should be taught through the medium of Irish in every school. It is essential also to expand the use of Irish as a means of social interaction in the school and the environment. Furthermore, the spoken language should be pre-eminent and more time should be devoted to formal instruction of the spoken language.

The following is a summary of the proposals made in relation to Irish at primary level:

1. Attempts will be made to have an entire aspect or part thereof of the curriculum taught through Irish in every primary school. The spoken language will be pre-eminent and more time will be devoted to the formal teaching of the spoken language.

2. The number of in-service courses relating to Irish and to language teaching methods will be greatly increased.

6. Additional help with regard to teaching aids and equipment will be given to primary schools who teach a worthwhile amount of the curriculum through Irish.

7. Regular objective evaluation of the standard of Irish in primary and second-level schools will be carried out.

11. The assistance that is at present being provided for the development of all-Irish schools will be continued and planning will be undertaken to satisfy the needs of those pupils whose parents wish them to receive their education entirely in Irish.

II.18 Programme for Action in Education 1984-1987

The publication of the Programme for Action in Education by Minister Hussey has been referred to in an earlier section of this book (I.20).

The following extracts are taken from the Chapter on Primary Education:

3.1 A major issue seen by managers, parents and teachers is the inadequacy of funding for National Schools. The difficult financial position of the Boards of Management is recognised by the Minister. The funding of National Schools will be a major priority of the Minister and the Government in the allocation of the resources available for education. In addition, special funding should be directed to disadvantaged areas........

3.2 A major educational challenge to be met relates to the specific needs of children who fall behind the normal level of development with regard to literacy and numeracy......

3.7 It is recognised that the pupil teacher ratio in National Schools compares unfavourably with that obtaining in other developed countries and the Government remains committed to an improvement in the position as soon as financial circumstances permit..........

3.8 The majority of National Schools in Ireland have been established under the patronage of diocesan authorities and on a denominational basis. In recent years, however, representations have been made by voluntary groups of parents for the establishment of National Schools on a multi-denominational basis and three such schools have been established. Where the government is convinced that the establishment of a multi-denominational school represents the clear wishes of parents in an area and where such schools can be provided on a viable basis, support will be given to such developments on the same terms as those which would be available for the establishment of schools under denominational patronage.

3.12 Many of the Rules for National Schools have been modified since the existing publication was issued. A single publication containing an updated version of the Rules will be prepared within the period of the Programme..........

3.13 Educating children of both sexes together is more in keeping with the concept of equality between the sexes and provides a better basis for developing co-operative but equal roles of men and women in adult life............

3.14 The policy of the amalgamation of small National Schools which in the sixties and seventies resulted in a consolidation of many such schools into more viable and resourceful educational units, still remains. Accordingly, one-teacher and two-teacher schools will not be replaced except in circumstances where no suitable alternative provision can be made for the education of the children.......

II.19 Primary Education — A Curriculum and Examinations Board Discussion Paper, September 1985.

When the Interim Curriculum and Examinations Board was set up in 1984, its terms of reference stated:- "The Board shall report to the Minister on the desirable aims, structure and content of curriculum at first and second levels." The Board welcomed the opportunity to consider the child's experience of school, particularly during the compulsory period from 6 to 15, as a continuum. In this context one of the first committees which was set up by the Board was a Joint Committee which considered the curriculum at primary level and junior cycle post-primary level. The first Consultative Document published by the Board — Issues and Structures — concentrated on the curriculum at post-primary level, and particularly at junior cycle. In September 1985 a Discussion Paper on Primary Education was produced. In the Foreword to the document, it was recognised that the introduction of the primary school curriculum in 1971 had been a major development in Irish education. However, it was pointed out that major changes had taken place in Irish society since the introduction of the new curriculum. The participation rates in the educational system at second and third levels had increased enormously and there had been many developments in educational thinking. It was stated that "these and other factors point to the need for a review of all aspects of the primary curriculum including the principles on which it is based and the effectiveness of its implementation."

The Discussion paper (in Irish and English) was a short document of 50 pages. It included a list of empirical studies of primary education which had been carried out since the introduction of the new curriculum fourteen years earlier. It put forward a number of items for discussion, including issues relating to the infant programme, home-school links, sex-stereotyping, computers and transfer and continuity between primary and post-primary schools. It also suggested that consideration should be given to the question of introducing children at primary level to a modern European language.

The following is a summary of the recommendations contained in the Discussion Paper.

RECOMMENDATIONS

7.1 Government action is necessary to overcome the constraints outlined in Chapter 5. In this section, some recommendations are made in relation to the primary school curriculum itself. These recommendations are not in any order of priority.

7.2 There is a need for an *overall review* of the primary curriculum. This should include a review of curriculum practice and a study of the background and of the principles underlying the primary school curriculum. There might be a number of elements in such a review. It might include an evaluation of the adequacy of the documents on which the work of the school is based. It might also focus on the extent to which the recommendations of the *Teacher's Handbook* are being implemented in schools and on the cognitive and attitudinal outcomes of the primary school curriculum in relation to pupils, teachers and parents. In any such analysis, one should attempt to identify the degree to which the practice in schools is compatible with the guidelines in the *Teacher's Handbook* and ascertain whether the perceived effects or outcomes are a result of the implementation of these guidelines.

7.3 *Objectives* for a developmental programme in the different aspects of the curriculum at primary and post-primary level should be formulated, as suggested in paragraph 3.4.

7.4 *Sex-stereotyping* should be eliminated in all aspects of the curriculum. The issue should be tackled at several levels —

- by identifying, drawing attention to and modifying sex-stereotyping in classroom practices such as choice of or emphasis on different subjects for boys and girls.
- by identifying, drawing attention to and modifying specific areas in the *Handbook* and in material emanating from the Department of Education (e.g. film-strips and support material relating to Gaeilge programmes)
- by alerting teachers to sex-stereotyping in commercially produced materials — this could be done through pre-service and in-service education
- by including in the curriculum affirmative action to overcome the effects of hidden stereotyping.

7.5 *Developmental and pilot projects* which are being carried out in the following areas of the curriculum (referred to in paragraph 1.5) should be monitored and evaluated with a view to assessing their potential for inclusion in the curriculum of all primary schools:

Integrated Local Studies programmes
Elementary Science
Peace Education
Development Education
Computers in primary schools
Modern languages in primary schools.

7.6 Separate discussion papers relating to Arts, Language and Science and Technology which contain issues and recommendations relating to those areas of the curriculum at both primary and post-primary levels are being published by the Board in conjunction with this paper.

7.7 The appropriateness of the *mathematics* programme should be examined. In doing this, account should be taken of the role of computers and calculators as aids to mathematics learning and instruction. More attention should be paid to mathematical language and to the treatment of problem-solving.

7.8 An acceptable and effective programme of *sex education* appropriate to the stages of development of primary school children should be developed.

7.9 Pre-service and in-service courses for teachers should take account of ongoing developments in the *theory and practice* of education. In view of the increasing role being played by principals and teachers in developing School Plans and in devising and implementing suitable and relevant programmes for their pupils, courses in Curriculum Studies (Theory and Practice) should play a more important part in the pre-service and in-service education of teachers.

7.10 Pre-service and in-service courses should help teachers to develop skills and expertise in the identification and management of *learning difficulties*. Courses for teachers should also provide the necessary expertise in evaluation and assessment procedures and techniques as outlined in paragraphs 6.21 and 6.22.

7.11 A *policy on in-service education* needs to be formulated and implemented in order to provide opportunities, formal and informal, for continuing teacher development. Teachers should also be enabled to keep abreast of developments both in the content of subjects and in teaching methodology. Gaining access to this new knowledge is time-consuming even when it is available. In-service provision should facilitate and support school-based curriculum development and evaluation. Demands on teacher time, implicit in such development, will have to be taken into account.

7.12 Adequate *resources* including remedial facilities and educational psychological services should be made available, so that children with learning difficulties can be adequately supported within the school

7.13 Schools should be enabled to provide *special support* for children from disadvantaged backgrounds including the children of travelling people.

II.20 Report of the Review Body on the Primary Curriculum, 1990.

The Fianna Fáil election manifesto of 1986 included a commitment to carry out a review of the Primary School Curriculum. In September 1987, Mary O'Rourke, T.D., Minister for Education, disbanded the Curriculum and Examinations Board and in early October she set up the Review Body on the Primary Curriculum. The terms of reference of the Review Body were very specific and were unrelated to the issues which had been put forward in the Discussion Paper on Primary Education which had been issued by the Curriculum and Examinations Board in 1985. The terms of reference, which seemed to suggest a renewed emphasis on Irish, English and Mathematics, and on assessment and evaluation, were as follows:

(a) To analyse the aims and objectives of the present primary curriculum. To identify how effectively these aims and objectives are being achieved with specific reference to Irish, English and Mathematics. Specific attention should also be paid to the last two years of primary school and their alignment to the post-primary curriculum.

(b) To examine what structures could be adopted which would ensure that the objectives outlined for the curriculum could be evaluated as the students progress through school.

(c) The review will also identify priorities for future developments within the curriculum and will recommend strategies for such developments. All existing research data will be made available to the Review Body and will be drawn on as appropriate.

The report was published in May 1990 and broadly endorsed the underlying philosophy and principles of the 1971 curriculum. Although its recommendations were not radical in their import, the Report concluded that "the curriculum requires revision and reformulation in its aims, scope and content, in the manner in which it is implemented and in the way in which pupil progress is assessed and recorded and the way the overall effectiveness of the system is evaluated." The following extracts are from the Summary of Findings and Recommendations:

SUMMARY OF FINDINGS AND RECOMMENDATIONS

The Review Body was asked to examine the aims and objectives of the 1971 curriculum, and the effectiveness of its implementation in relation to these aims and objectives. It was also asked to examine how pupil progress in relation to the objectives of the curriculum might be assessed and what structures could be adopted for this purpose. Finally, the Review Body was asked to make recommendations for future developments in the curriculum.

The Review Body concluded that the curriculum requires revision and re-formulation in its aims, scope and content, in the manner in which it is implemented and in the way in which pupil progress is assessed and recorded and the way the overall effectiveness of the system is evaluated.

The Review Body has identified the resource implications of such a revision if it is to be effective in improving the quality of the curriculum offered, the quality and effectiveness of its implementation and the level of pupils' attainment.

- *Aims of education*
  The aims of education as stated in the Teacher's Handbook are accepted subject to minor amendments in their formulation.

- *Aims and objectives of the curriculum*
  Recommendations are made for the specification of the aims and objectives of the curriculum under four main headings:

  — general aims of the curriculum
  — specific aims of the curriculum
  — general objectives of the curriculum
  — specific objectives of the curriculum

Recommendations regarding the specific aims and general objectives of the curriculum are to be found on pp.10-12.

The Review Body sees the determining of specific objectives of the curriculum as being outside its brief but it considers that such clearly specified objectives are of vital importance in the education of children.

- *Principles of the curriculum*
  The five major principles which have underpinned the curriculum find general acceptance, but the Review Body feels they need to be revised.

- *English in the curriculum*
  A revision of the English programme should be carried out to provide a more detailed specification of aims and objectives and to update the content in the sections dealing with oracy, reading and writing.

- *Irish in the curriculum*
  The development of a new curriculum for Irish with an emphasis on communication skills at appropriate levels is recommended.

  Specific recommendations for the Irish curriculum in Galltacht and Gaeltacht schools are to be found on pp.33-34 (Irish version) and pp.39-41 (English version).

- *Mathematics in the curriculum*
  General objectives for a revised Mathematics curriculum are given.

- *Social and Environmental Studies/Science in the curriculum*
  Recommendations for the development of this aspect of the curriculum overall are on pp.55-56.

****

It is recommended that the existing Nature Study and Elementary Science programme should be integrated to form a new Science programme.

****

- *The arts in the curriculum*
  In revising the programme for the various areas in the expressive arts, there should be a greater emphasis on art appreciation, to ensure a better balance between appreciation of art and expressive activities. There is a need for teachers with specific subject-competence in Music, PE and Drama. Educational drama should have an important place in the curriculum and should be a focus for integrating various aspects of the curriculum.

****

In summary the Review Body recommends

— Health Education should be treated on a cross-curricular basis.

— Modern European Languages should not be introduced into the curriculum in primary schools.

— The introduction of Information Technology is regarded as a valuable and cost-effective way of attaining a variety of curricular objectives.

— Additional resources should be provided to address the needs of disadvantaged pupils.

- *Assessment and evaluation of the curriculum*
  The Review Body has recommended that pupil progress should be assessed through a combination of formal standardised tests and informal teacher assessments. Appropriate standardised tests should be developed and these should be updated regularly.

  The Review Body felt, however, that pupils should not be subjected to over-intensive testing to determine the efficacy of teaching and learning. It has recommended that greater resources be provided for school inspection.

It has also recommended that the principal teacher be responsible for the co-ordination of the internal evaluation of the work of the school. There should also be a more prominent role for the school staff in evaluating the progress of school curriculum planning.

The Review Body has recommended the development of a Department of Education profile card on which a pupil profile would be entered including results obtained in formal and informal assessments. Relevant information from this profile card should be made available to parents, post-primary schools and other appropriate persons and agencies.

- *Implementing and resourcing the recommendations of the Review Body*

  The recommendations of the report fall into six categories. Each category has its own requirements for resources and funding.

  — Those related to the revision of the curriculum and those related to the need for a greater emphasis on particular areas of the curriculum e.g. arts education and language education
  — Those related to staffing in the schools
  — Those related to educational equipment and materials
  — Those related to pupil assessment
  — Those related to teacher and school evaluation
  — Those related to in-service education.

Specific recommendations for an improvement in the overall funding of primary education and for specified needs in each of the above categories are set out.

II.21 Report of the Primary Education Review Body 1990.

Following a decision by the Government, the Primary Education Review Body was set up by the Minister for Education, Mary O'Rourke T.D., on 18th February 1988. Its terms of reference were "to review the primary sector of education and to report to the Government." The Review Body was advised to take account of work already in progress by the Review Body on the Primary Curriculum which had been set up by the Minister in October 1987, and also to take into account such other studies of the primary sector as were already in progress. The areas to be encompassed were to include the structure of primary education, demographic trends and their implications, the quality of primary education and school organisation. The curriculum and matters relating to teachers' salaries were not within the remit of the Review Body.

The report of the Review Body was published in December 1990. It was 145 pages long and it contained 43 sections, including sections on Legal Issues relating to the Primary Education system; Demographic Trends and Their Implications; Inservice Training of Teachers; Staffing in the Department of Education; Educational Research in Ireland and the Financing of Primary Education. It made a total of 107 recommendations. These included a recommendation that the Minister issue a discussion document or Green Paper to initiate a debate on the introduction of an Education Act and that a general review and where necessary, revision of the Rules for National Schools be undertaken by the Department of Education in consultation with the recognised partners in education. It also recommended an immediate reduction in the pupil/teacher ratio to 25.0:1 and an increase in the capitation grant from £28 per annum to not less than £80.

The Review Body recognised that many of its recommendations would have substantial financial implications and that they would only be achieved over time. In this context, the following statement regarding Priorities was made:

PRIORITIES

As regards the allocation of resources, the Review Body is mindful of the ethical dimension which seeks absolute priority for the minimizing of avoidable suffering.

Since the implementation of many of the recommendations contained in this Report will have substantial financial implications they can only be achieved over time. As resources become available priorities must be established. It is the stated intention of the Government to make better provision for the disadvantaged and to reduce further the pupil/teacher ratio. We recommend that the pupil/teacher ratio be reduced immediately to 25.0:1. In addition there is an urgent need to improve the capitation grant and to make better provision for inservice education.

As the economy improves the pupil/teacher ratio should be further adjusted. Such improvements will allow for a reduction in class size and additional staffing for remedial teaching, for the disadvantaged, for children with special needs and a more favourable staffing schedule for infant classes. The provision of extra teachers would also allow for the introduction of a more favourable staffing schedule for schools of four or fewer teachers and for the appointment of administrative Principal Teachers at a lower point on the staffing schedule.

It is difficult to choose extracts from a report which is as wide-ranging in its coverage as the Report of the Primary Education Review Body. The full summary of recommendations takes up ten pages and some extracts from the summary are included here. Also included are extracts on Parents as Partners in education; All-Irish National Schools and Multi-denominational schools. These issues are highlighted here as they indicate an increasing involvement of parents in education in Ireland in the 1970s and 1980s:

SUMMARY OF RECOMMENDATIONS

We recommend that:

1. following consultation with the various interests involved, the Minister issue a discussion document or Green Paper to initiate debate on the introduction of an Education Act;
2. the Minister initiate a formal process of consultation with all interested parties before making changes in rules, regulations or issuing circulars which govern the operation of the primary school system;
10. an advisory committee representing all relevant interests be set up by the Minister to undertake the essential task of formulating a clearly defined policy for inservice courses;
14. a substantial increase be made in the financial provision for Teachers' Centres;
18. a general review and, where necessary, revision of the *Rules for National Schools under the Department of Education* be undertaken by the Department of Education in consultation with the recognised partners in education;
21. the functions of Boards of Management be re-appraised and strengthened;
22. Boards of Management be given much greater autonomy in relation to many matters which at the moment require Departmental approval, and have allocated to them the finance needed to enable them to carry out delegated functions;
25. the inspector (a) hold a formal meeting with the Board of Management on the occasion of a School Report, (b) be available within reason for advice and guidance in connection with such appropriate matters as the Board may require, (c) include a minute in the School Report on the quality of the management being exercised by the Board;

28. the Board play a meaningful role in areas such as the aims and objectives of the school, the School Plan, discipline, the School Report and inservice education suited to the particular needs of the school;
37. a secretary and a caretaker/maintenance person be appointed to all schools on a full or part-time basis depending on the size of the school;
38. the appointment of a Principal Teacher be preceded by a careful analysis of the requirements of the job, with particular reference to the school's individual circumstances;
66. a structured psychological service for primary schools be established;
69. examinations for the purpose of pupil assessment as part of the process of transfer to the post-primary system be not carried out while the pupil is still attending primary school;
86. the inspectorate become involved in the publication of discussion papers, reports or pamphlets as part of the national educational debate about standards, quality of schools, accountability and other matters of interest to the public;
87. immediate consideration be given to the publication of a new-style annual report in which *inter alia* the professional views of the inspectorate can be incorporated.
88. there be much closer co-operation between the primary and post-primary branches of the inspectorate;
89. the standard grant for major building works be raised to 85%;
90. a priority list of major reconstruction or replacement of school buildings be drawn up, made available and adhered to;
99. the inadequate provision for equipment in the primary school, not only in relation to new buildings and extensions, but also in relation to existing schools, be redressed;

100. much better financial provision be made available for educational research, with special emphasis on the co-ordination of research and on the evaluation of existing services;

103. as an interim measure, the proposed Educational Broadcasting Section of the Department of Education be established and enter into consultation with RTE and other broadcasting agencies with a view to providing a schools broadcasting service with particular emphasis on the production of taped audio-visual materials for Irish schools;

104. the Department of Education promote the maximum possible use of information technology in primary schools;

105. in order to make adequate provision for the operating costs of national schools, including the employment of caretakers and secretaries, either on a part-time or whole-time basis, the capitation grant be increased to not less than £80 per pupil;

106. guidelines be issued by the Department of Education to Boards of Management on the preparation of school budgets and audited accounts which would show that the monies were spent for the purposes for which they were intended;

107. the pupil/teacher ratio be reduced immediately to 25.0:1.

Parents as Partners in Education

Article 42 of the Constitution of Ireland states that *the State acknowledges that the primary and natural educator of the child is the family.....* This would imply that parents play a major role in Irish education. However, parents individually or collectively have not become significantly involved until recent years with the schools as partners in the education of their children.

Although in most cases there were good informal relations between schools and parents, it was not until the mid-seventies with the establishment of Boards of Management, that parents became eligible for participation in the management of primary schools. Parents have now moved away from a peripheral role and are becoming more actively involved with teachers and clergy in management structures and policy making. Parents are also active in setting up parents' associations through which collective involvement can be channeled. The National Parents Council (Primary) was established in 1985. Since then a national network has been set up, which is school-based, administered at county level and served by an elected national executive. In addition, parents' representatives have served on a number of bodies established by the Minister for Education to consider and report on aspects of the education system.

A policy for parental partnership in education should be approached from two main viewpoints. First, parents should not be seen merely as consumers who demand a service but rather as interested partners in the education process. Second, parents should be consulted, as other recognised interests are, and have a significant influence on national educational policy and on its local implementation.

****

We recommend that schools be encouraged, subject at all times to the professional autonomy of the teacher, to involve parents in support roles within the classroom.

In addition to the involvement of parents in planning, decision making and management through their membership of Boards of Management, we recommend that schools establish direct communication with the general body of parents through regular meetings with parents and parent associations. Since parent associations do not exist in all schools, we recommend that the Department of Education reiterate its advice in relation to the establishment of such associations.

Parents have a right to know what goes on in the schools their children attend. There should be a free flow of information between teachers and parents. Letters, newsletters, pamphlets and reports should be written in clear, simple language. We recommend that parents be given the right of access to records relating to their own children and that school record cards be designed for that purpose.

****

Financial support has been given by the Department of Education on an *ad hoc* basis to the National Parents Council (Primary) to enable them to extend their activities on a national level. We recommend that financial support continue to be made available until such time as the Council becomes a viable, self-supporting body.

SCOILEANNA LÁN-GHAEILGE (ALL-IRISH NATIONAL SCHOOLS)

Apart from the All-Irish model schools, only three All-Irish schools had been established up to 1971 in English-speaking areas. Since then considerable developments have taken place and there are at present, outside the Gaeltacht areas, sixty-one national schools in operation in which all subjects other than English are taught through the medium of Irish.

An All-Irish school can be established where the Department of Education is satisfied that there is a sufficient demand to indicate that the school will be viable. Initial recognition of such schools is provisional and is reviewed in the light of enrolment trends. For this reason schools are normally first established in temporary accommodation and the Department contributes towards any rental costs incurred. For permanent buildings the cost of the site and the building is borne by the State which means that the State owns the school, although it is managed on the same basis as other national schools.

In addition to the more favourable provisions in regard to site purchase and building, All-Irish schools also have more favourable conditions in relation to pupil/teacher ratios, staff allowances, capitation grants and school transport.

The Review Body recognizes the substantial contribution made by the All-Irish schools in promoting State policy in relation to the Irish Language. It has been represented to us, however, that the more favourable treatment afforded to All-Irish Schools has had an unfavourable impact on enrolment in surrounding schools. We recommend that the implications of this be examined further in the light of an overall policy for the promotion of Irish throughout the primary school system.

Multi-denominational Schools

When the national school system was set up in 1831 the intention was to provide secular and religious instruction for children of different religious persuasions. This would be achieved through combined secular instruction and separate religious instruction. It is a historical fact, however, that most schools were established on the initiative of a particular religious denomination for children of that denomination. The system thus became one of denominational schools, and it is against this background that the demand for multi-denominational schools has grown over the last twenty years.

The policy in relation to multi-denominational education has been defined in the *Programme for Action 1983-1987*, which states:

> Where the Government is convinced that the establishment of a multi-denominational school represents the clear wishes of parents in an area and where such schools can be provided on a viable basis, support will be given to such developments on the same terms as those which would be available for the establishment of schools under denominational patronage.

Multi-denominational schools, therefore, are established in response to parental demand, where the Department of Education is satisfied that there is a need for the school and that the demand is sufficient to indicate that the school will be educationally viable. Initial recognition is provisional and is reviewed in the light of enrolment trends.

Unlike most national schools, where the Patron is usually the Bishop of the particular religious denomination concerned, multi-denominational schools have a group of people or a limited company as their Patron.

****

The Review Body supports the statement of policy in relation to multi-denominational education already quoted from the *Programme for Action 1983-1987* and acknowledges the developments that have already taken place.

III

POST-PRIMARY EDUCATION

III.1 Dáil Éireann — Commission on Secondary Education; September 1921 - December 1922.

The administration of education was taken over by the Provisional Government of the Irish Free State on 1st February 1922. It was not until June 1923 that the Board of Commissioners of Intermediate Education was dissolved and replaced by two Intermediate Education Commissioners, Seosamh Ó Néill and Proinsias Ó Dubhthaigh. In the meantime, the Junior, Middle and Senior Grade examinations continued to be set and marked by the Intermediate Board. On 1st August 1924 a new programme for secondary schools came into operation. This programme was based on the recommendations of a Commission on Secondary Education which had been set up by Dáil Éireann in August 1921.

On 22 August 1921 a conference on intermediate education was held under the authority of Dáil Éireann and made a number of recommendations relating to the secondary school examinations. It recommended that examination papers in all subjects except English, Mathematics and Science be made available bilingually; that the history and geography papers should be such as to allow a student to obtain full marks on questions relating to Ireland; and that Irish should be a compulsory subject and English an optional one. A commission was then set up by Dáil Éireann which held its first meeting on 24 September 1921. Its terms of reference were "to draft a programme which would meet the national requirements, while allotting its due place to the Irish language." The Chairman of this commission was Michael Hayes and its secretary was Proinsias Ó Fathaigh.

At the first meeting, six committees were appointed to deal with various subject areas. A draft programme was prepared within a short period for circulation to "headmasters and teachers" for "criticisms and suggestions'." The final report of the commission was never published but following the last meeting of the commission on 7 December 1922 a series of subject committee reports were sent to the Minister of the Dáil and these formed the basis of the revised subject syllabi and the revised programme which came into effect in August 1924.

The following extract is taken from a letter (undated) which was addressed by the Commission to Headmasters and Teachers of Intermediate schools. It is likely that this document was printed in the final months of 1921 as respondents to the draft were asked to send their communications to the Mansion House not later than 15th January 1922:

DAIL ÉIREANN
COMMISSION ON SECONDARY EDUCATION.

TO HEADMASTERS AND TEACHERS,
Herewith we enclose draft programme for Secondary School subjects which we ask you to carefully consider. We should be glad if Headmasters would consult teachers of the particular subjects before sending us criticisms or suggestions.

Further copies of programmes can be obtained by teachers on application.

The following resumé of the work of the Commission is necessary for a proper understanding of the Reports. The Commission held its first meeting on Saturday, September 24th, 1921, at University College, Dublin. The terms of reference were: "To draft a programme which would meet the national requirements, while allotting its due place to the Irish language."

It will be seen that the business of the Commission was merely to draft a programme. No other matters have been considered.

At the first meeting the following decisions were arrived at:-

(1) That six committees be appointed dealing, respectively, with (1) Irish, English, and other Modern languages; (2) Mathematics, Science, and Manual Training, Agriculture; (3) Classics; (4) History and Geography, Economics and Sociology; (5) Art; (6) Music.

(2) That there be a standing committee, consisting of seven members of the Commission, with power to co-opt.

(3) That each committee make a case for the subject or subjects which should, in their opinion, be obligatory on the programme.

(4) That the programme of the full course be reckoned as a six years course, 12-18.

(5) That there be at least two written and oral examinations, one at 15-16, at which age the great majority leave for business, etc., and one at 18 for those proceeding to the University.

(6) That a good rounded course be provided for those leaving at 16.

(7) That Irish be at least on a level with English on the programme in the groups, etc.

(8) That the fixing of minimum compulsory programme be deferred until the committees shall have furnished reports.

(9) That the greatest possible freedom be given to the school and to the teacher.

(10) That it is educationally unsound to prescribe set uniform texts.

(11) That grants should not be dependent on written examinations.

(12) That in the case of schools where a a majority of the parents of the children object to have either Irish or English taught as an obligatory subject, their wishes should be complied with.

Subsequently the standing committee pointed out that the programmes in preparation are intended to be put into immediate operation over a transition period, and that in this connection the various committees should bear in mind existing conditions with regard to personnel, etc.

In considering the claims of such subjects as Commerce, Agriculture, etc., it should be remembered that the object of the present Commission is to draft a well-balanced programme of Secondary studies which cannot be given a strong vocational bias. The establishment of vocational types of schools is desirable, but does not come within the scope of the present Commission.

It is the opinion of the Standing Committee that detailed programmes should not be imposed on the teachers, provided that the final aim is attained in the various subjects.

The detailed programmes drawn up by some committees are intended to be merely helpful and suggestive. Each school should be free to draw up the details of its own programme, subject to the approval of the Educational Authority.

In the light of the foregoing information we should be glad to have, from teachers, headmasters, and others interested in education, written opinions on the proposed schemes. Further draft reports will be forwarded as soon as they come in.

Communications, giving clear references to particular programmes, should reach the Mansion House not later than January 15th, 1922.

Aided by the criticisms and suggestions which we hope to obtain, the Committees will then further consider their programmes and present final reports for the approval of meetings of the whole Commission.

It should be clearly borne in mind that the recommendations sent herewith are not final, and have not been adopted by the Education Ministry.

Michael Hayes, M.A.,
Chairman.
Proinsias Ó Fathaigh, B.A., H.Dip.Ed.
Hon. Secretary.

III.2 Intermediate Education (Amendment) Act, 1924

Since Intermediate education in Ireland was subject to legislation — i.e. the Intermediate Education (Ireland) Act of 1878 and the Local Taxation (Customs and Excise Act) of 1890 — amending legislation had to be introduced before a change could be made in the method of payment of grants to schools. The government chose to make only minimal amendments to the existing legislation and this consisted of the deletion of a short clause from each of the two acts. In June 1924 the Intermediate Education (Amendment) Act was passed and this cleared the way for the introduction of a revised method of payment of grants to secondary schools. The following is the full text of the Act:

INTERMEDIATE EDUCATION (AMENDMENT) ACT, 1924

(Number 47 of 1924)

AN ACT TO AMEND THE INTERMEDIATE EDUCATION (IRELAND) ACT, 1878, AND THE LOCAL TAXATION (CUSTOMS AND EXCISE) ACT, 1890.

(5th August, 1924)

BE IT ENACTED BY THE OIREACHTAS OF SAORSTÁT ÉIREANN AS FOLLOWS:

1. The several enactments specified in the Schedule to this Act are hereby repealed to the extent mentioned in the third column of the said Schedule.

Repeal of enactments in Schedule

2. (1) This Act may be cited as the Intermediate Education (Amendment) Act, 1924.
(2) This Act and the Intermediate Education (Ireland) Acts, 1878 to 1914, may be cited collectively as the Intermediate Education (Ireland) Acts, 1878 to 1924.

Short title and collective citation

SCHEDULE ENACTMENTS REPEALED

Session and Chapter	Short Title	Extent of Repeal
41 & 42 Vic. c.66.	The Intermediate Education (Ireland) Act, 1878.	In paragraph 3 of section 5 the words "dependent on the results of the public examinations of students."
53 & 54 Vic. c. 60.	The Local Taxation (Customs and Excise) Act, 1890.	Paragraph (ii) of sub-section 3, from the words "amongst schools" to the end of the paragraph

III.3 The Report of the Department of Education for the School Year 1924/25 and the financial and administrative years 1924/5/6. Changes in Secondary Education.

The Report of the Dáil Commission on Secondary Education and the passing of the Intermediate Education (Ireland) Amendment Act in 1924 and of the Ministers and Secretaries Act, 1924, all contributed to major changes in the secondary school system from the beginning of the school year 1924. These changes related to (1) the secondary school programme; (2) grants payable to schools; (3) teachers' salaries; and (4) the introduction of entrance examinations. The changes are clearly and succinctly described in the following extract from the annual report of the Department of Education for the school year 1924/25:

The recent reforms are, as has been said, of a sweeping nature, and include

(a) a revision of the educational basis of the system;
(b) a complete reform of the Secondary programme; and
(c) the introduction of a new system of determining the amount of State financial assistance payable to a school.

The reform of the educational basis of the system was affected by making a course of study over a definite number of years the educational unit instead of an isolated year's work. Hence the old system of grades, each with its year's rigid curriculum, has been abolished, and Junior and Senior Courses substituted. The Junior Course is of three or four years' duration, according to a pupil's age and attainments on entering the school, and leads to the Intermediate Certificate examination, which a pupil nominally takes at the age of sixteen years. The Senior Course is intended to be of two years' duration, and leads to the Leaving Certificate examination, which marks the conclusion of the Secondary stage in education. During the Junior Course the pupil is expected to follow such a curriculum as will give a sound general education. Hence, in order to obtain the Intermediate Certificate which marks the end of this course, the pupil has to pass five subjects, which must include

(1) Irish or English,
(2) Mathematics,
(3) a second language, and
(4) either History and Geography, or Science, or Latin, or Greek.

In the Senior Course, on the other hand, the pupil is allowed to specialise. Hence schools are free to select any five subjects of the programme for their pupils for this latter course, the only restriction being that one of these subjects must be Irish, or English.

As regards programmes, the reform has been similarly fundamental. Under the old system the programme has been, with few exceptions, rigid and narrow, and had to be carried out through the study of prescribed texts on which the examinations were based. Under the new system the programmes are of the widest and most elastic types, prescribed texts have been abolished in all subjects, and the schools now enjoy the maximum of freedom both as regards the range of their programmes and the choice of books to suit their particular needs. In order to ensure that all work may be of a proper standard, teachers are required to submit at the beginning of the year the programmes which are proposed for each class for the year, and the Department's inspectors see that these are suitable in quality and extent, and that the teaching of them reaches a proper standard; otherwise the teachers are entirely free in their choice. At the same time the schools have been to a large extent freed from the incubus of an over-rigid examination system, for although examinations are retained they have not the cramping effect of the examinations of the old system, since (1) they are not based on prescribed texts, and (2) they are no longer the methods by which the income of each school is determined.

As already mentioned, the method of determining the amount of the State financial assistance given to a Secondary School has been completely changed. The principal grant now payable to Secondary Schools is reckoned on a capitation basis, and is normally payable automatically in respect of all pupils between twelve and twenty years of age who follow an approved course of study and make 130 attendances during the school year. In other words, an efficient school can in future calculate on an assured and calculable income each year instead of being dependent on the fluctuating and incalculable chances of the results of individual passes or failures at written examinations. The rate of capitation grant payable for pupils following the lower or Intermediate Certificate Course is £7; that for the pupils following the higher or Leaving Certificate Course is £10.

The grant replaces the following grants formerly distributed to schools under different sets of rules:

"School Grant" (given on results of examination).
"Inspection Grant."
"Teachers' Salaries Grant."
"Additional (Duke) Grant."

The amount of capitation grant distributed to schools in respect of the school year 1924-25 was £149,518 18s. 2d., which exceeded by £51,471 1s. 5d. the total of these four grants distributed to schools in respect of the preceding year (1923-24).

A special bonus grant is also payable to schools in which the Irish Language is used as a medium of instruction. This bonus takes the form of a percentage increase in the capitation grant. In the case of schools in which Irish is used as the ordinary medium of instruction for all subjects the increase is 25 per cent., and in schools in which Irish was used for at least one-half the instruction given during the school year 1924-25 an increase of 10 per cent was made. During the past year the number of schools in the former class was two and in the latter nineteen. In addition to this, Irish was taught as an ordinary subject in all except twelve Secondary Schools during the past year.

Exhibitions, prizes and medals which were formerly competed for at the annual examinations have now been abolished. Instead a number of scholarships are now awarded on the results of the Intermediate Certificate examination. These scholarships are of the annual value of £40, and are tenable for two years in order to enable the holder to complete the secondary course up to the Leaving Certificate examination. The number of these scholarships awarded in 1925 was 75.

As already mentioned in Chapter VI, there are also in Secondary Schools pupils who hold scholarships provided from the local rates by various County Councils. The annual renewal of these scholarships, which are tenable for periods varying from four to six years, is subject to a satisfactory report from the Department's inspectors. Table H gives details of the numbers of scholarship-holders from the various counties attending Secondary Schools. The total number for the Free State during the past year was 471.

One of the weaknesses of the Secondary system under the Board of Intermediate Education was that there was no general system of entrance tests which might ensure that only suitable pupils should enter the Secondary Schools.

In order to ensure that pupils will in future have reached a sufficient standard of education to profit by instruction in a Secondary School, managers of schools are, under the new system, required to hold an entrance examination for all pupils at the beginning of each year, and capitation grant is not payable in respect of any pupil who has not reached a satisfactory standard at this examination.

In addition to the educational and financial reforms mentioned above, a considerable development has also been made in the raising of the status of the Secondary teachers by the introduction of a system of scales of salaries with increments, according to the length of teaching service. The radical nature of this reform arises from the fact that Secondary teachers had never previously been paid by the State. The new system proposes that a Secondary School be required to employ a number of registered teachers in proportion to the number of its pupils, and each of these teachers is entitled to receive a salary of not less than £200 in the case of men, and £180 in the case of women (reductions of £50 and £40 respectively being permitted when the salary includes board and lodging). In addition to these basic or minimum salaries paid by the schools, teachers receive from the State increments, based on the length of their approved teaching service. This incremental portion of the salary is paid direct to the teacher by the Department at the conclusion of each quarter of the school year.

****

As has been noted in the first chapter, an educational co-ordination has been effected between the Primary and Secondary systems by the arrangement of a common programme for the higher classes of the Primary Schools and the lower classes of the Secondary Schools. In addition to this, certain Primary Schools have been accustomed to follow the programme of the secondary branch in their higher standards and to present pupils for the annual Intermediate examinations. Provision has been made for the recognition as Secondary courses of such advanced classes of Primary Schools as follow the approved Secondary School programme, and for the admission of pupils from these classes to the Secondary Certificate examinations on the same conditions as pupils from Secondary Schools. In the past school year Secondary courses were recognised in certain Primary Schools, and 156 pupils from these schools were admitted to the Secondary Certificate examinations in June, 1925.

III.4 The introduction of Irish as an essential subject for the Intermediate and Leaving Certificate Examinations, 1928 and 1934.

When the Intermediate and Leaving Certificate examinations were first introduced in 1924, Irish was not an obligatory subject. Initially in order to obtain a pass in either the Intermediate or the Leaving Certificate examination, a pupil had to pass five subjects which had to include either Irish or English (see Document III.3). From 1928 onwards, Irish became an essential subject for the Intermediate Certificate examination and it became essential for the Leaving Certificate from 1934 onwards. This requirement remained in force until 1973 when it was removed by Richard Burke, Minister for Education.

The following extracts from the Regulations regarding curricula, certificates, examinations and scholarships for the years 1925/6 and 1932/3 include a statement of intent by the Department to introduce the "essential Irish" requirement:

DEPARTMENT OF EDUCATION — SECONDARY BRANCH
PROGRAMME & REGULATIONS FOR THE YEAR 1925-26.

REGULATIONS AS TO THE INTERMEDIATE CERTIFICATE EXAMINATION

11. The purpose of the Intermediate Certificate is to testify to the completion of a well-balanced course of general education

suitable for pupils who leave school at about 16 years of age, and, alternatively, to the fitness of the pupils for entry on more advanced courses of study in a Secondary or Technical school.

12. Recognised pupils who (a) are over 14 years of age on the first day of the school year in which the examination is held, and have followed for three years an approved course, or (b) who are over 15 years of age on the first day of the school year in which the examination is held, and have followed for two years an approved course, are eligible for admission to the Intermediate Certificate Examination.

13. The Intermediate Certificate will be awarded to recognised pupils who satisfy regulation 12 and pass the examination in the same year in not less than five subjects, which must include a subject from each of the following sections:

(a)* Irish or English.
(b) A language other than that taken under (a).
(c) Mathematics; or (for girls only) Arithmetic with any one of the following subjects:- Science, Domestic Science, Drawing or Music.
(d) History and Geography; or Science; or Latin; or Greek; provided no subject taken under this section is presented under any other section.

The subjects of examination will be:- Irish, English, Latin, Greek, French, German, Italian, Spanish, History and Geography, Commerce, Mathematics, Science, Domestic Science (for girls only), Drawing, Music.

14. A recognised pupil who fails in one of five essential subjects will, however, be awarded a Certificate provided that

* It is intended that Irish be an essential subject for the Intermediate Certificate Examination in 1928 and afterwards; and that Science be an essential subject in the year 1930 and afterwards.

his marks in that subject do not fall below the standard required for a pass by more than 10 per cent of the marks assigned to the subject, and that his answering on the examination generally is satisfactory.

15. In each subject there will be one paper, or set of papers, a Pass with Honours being secured by reaching a certain standard.

(a) The standard for Pass shall be 30 per cent., and for Honours 50 per cent.
(b) Alternative papers or alternative questions will be set, if necessary, in Mathematics for pupils following Programme B in place of Programme A.

16. The Intermediate Honours Certificate will be awarded to recognised pupils who satisfy the conditions above, and pass with honours in at least three subjects at the Intermediate Certificate Examination.

DEPARTMENT OF EDUCATION — SECONDARY BRANCH
PROGRAMME & REGULATIONS FOR THE YEAR 1932-33

THE LEAVING CERTIFICATE EXAMINATION

32. The aim of the Leaving Certificate is to testify to the completion of a good secondary education and the fitness of a pupil to enter on a course of study at a University or an educational institution of similar standing.

33. Recognised pupils who have pursued an approved course as recognised senior pupils for two years are eligible for admission to the Leaving Certificate Examination in those subjects which have been included in their course of study during those years. (For special admission of candidates who do not satisfy the conditions of this rule, see Appendices).

34. The Leaving Certificate will be awarded† to pupils who satisfy regulations 12 (3) and 33 above and in the same year (a) pass the Leaving Certificate Examination in five subjects, or (b) pass in four subjects in at least two of which they pass with honours, subject to the limitation in each case that a candidate must pass in the Full Course in either Irish or English.

III.5 Changes in the Secondary Schools Programme 1939/40

One of the welcome innovations of the new Intermediate and Leaving Certificate programmes of 1924, was the freedom given to schools to draw up their own courses and to choose their own textbooks, subject to the approval of the Department of Education. The motivation behind this was to give to schools "the maximum of freedom both as regards the range of their programmes and the choice of books to suit their particular needs." However, this freedom was curtailed fifteen years later when a new programme was introduced in 1939/40.

In July 1937, the Taoiseach, Éamon de Valera took the initiative in calling a conference of the Minister for Education, the Secretary of the Department and the secondary school inspectors. He felt that the secondary school programmes existing at that time were "too narrow and too vague" and he argued that the range of examination subjects should be reduced to allow more time for the teaching of Irish. This latter suggestion was not supported by other members of the conference but it was agreed that "definite texts will be prescribed as part of the Courses in English, Latin, Greek and Modern Continental Languages for both the Intermediate and Leaving Certificate Examinations," thus returning to the practice that had existed before1924. In addition, a new non-experimental lower course in Science "which does not require individual experimental work" was introduced for Intermediate Certificate pupils and pupils taking the Pass Science course for the Leaving Certificate would not be required to take a qualifying practical examination.

† Notice is given that Irish will be an essential subject at the Leaving Certificate Examination of 1934, and subsequent years, and that candidates from schools in which Irish is used as the principal medium of instruction (Class A and Class B 1 Schools) must take the Full Course in Irish.

These and other changes which were introduced in 1939/40 are described in the following extract from a circular which was sent to all schools:

SECONDARY SCHOOLS PROGRAMME FOR 1939/40

It is proposed to make the following revisions in the Secondary Schools' Programme as from the beginning of the school year 1939/40.

1. Abolition of Lower Courses

(a) Lower Courses will be abolished in all subjects except Irish and English. Courses on the lines of the present Full and Lower Courses in these two languages will be retained, but the designations "Full Courses" and "Lower Courses" will be no longer used.

In the Intermediate Certificate Course the Irish courses hitherto known as "An Gearr-Chúrsa" and "An Lán Chúrsa" will be henceforth known as "Gaedhilg" and "Litridheacht na Gaedhilge," respectively; in English the Lower Course will be called "English Language" and the Full Course "English Literature."

In the Leaving Certificate Course the present Full and Lower Courses in these two languages will in future be called the "Honours" and "Pass" Courses, respectively.

"Elementary Mathematics" (for girls only) will be retained in the Intermediate Certificate Course.

Honours will not be obtainable in the following subjects: "Gaedhilg," "English Language," and "Elementary Mathematics."

(b) Instead of the present Lower Courses in Science a non-experimental course (Course E), which does not require individual experimental work, is offered for Intermediate Certificate pupils.

The Syllabus of this course is given on page 15. 300 marks will be assigned to the subject for examination purposes.

(c) In the case of the Leaving Certificate, separate Pass and Honours papers will be set in Science.

The provision relating to a qualifying practical examination will not apply to candidates taking the Pass papers.

In addition to the present separate courses in Physics and in Chemistry a new joint course in these subjects will be provided. The syllabus of this course is given on pages 15 and 16.

2. Prescribed Texts in Languages
Definite texts will be prescribed as part of the Course in English, Latin, Greek and Modern Continental Languages for both the Intermediate and Leaving Certificate Examinations.

Texts will be prescribed for the examination years only and will be changed annually (the names of the texts will be announced between 1st April and 1st June of the preceding school year).

The names of the texts for the 1940 Examinations are given in the latter part of this memorandum.

3. Mathematics
(a) Mathematics will be essential for Boys in both the Approved Course of Study and the Examination for the Intermediate Certificate.

In the case of Girls, Mathematics or Elementary Mathematics will be essential in the Approved Course of Study for the Intermediate Certificate.

(b) The examination papers in Mathematics will contain a larger proportion of straightforward questions.

4. History and Geography

History and Geography will continue to form one subject as at present.

The examination in 1940 will be based on the Courses in this subject in the Programme for 1938/39; the Courses for subsequent examinations are given in the latter part of this memorandum.

5. Approved Courses (Rule 12 at present)

(a) The approved course for recognised junior pupils must consist of not less than six subjects; these must include Irish,* a second language,* History and Geography and Mathematics or (in the case of Girls) Elementary Mathematics.

(b) The approved course for recognised senior pupils must consist of not less than five subjects, of which one shall be Irish.

6. Conditions for passing the Intermediate Certificate Examination

(a) The subjects of examination will be:-

(1) Gaedhilg
(2) Litridheacht na Gaedhilge
(3) English Language
(4) English Literature
(5) Latin
(6) Greek
(7) French
(8) German
(9) Italian
(10) Spanish
(11) History and Geography

* References to a language include, in the case of Irish and English, either of the courses mentioned in paragraph (1) (a) above.

(12) Mathematics
(13) Elementary Mathematics (Girls only)
(14) Science
(15) Domestic Science
(16) Music
(17) Drawing
(18) Manual Instruction
(19) Commerce.

(b) Candidates must pass in not less than five of the above subjects. A candidate, however, whose marks in one of the subjects are less than the Pass Standard (40 per cent) but not less than 30 per cent, and whose average marks in the five subjects reach the Pass Standard, shall be deemed to have passed the examination.

(c) The five subjects mentioned in the preceding paragraph must include —

(i) Irish*;
(ii) at least two subjects from the following: Latin, Greek, English, French, German, Italian, Spanish, History and Geography, Mathematics (boys must take this subject), Science, Elementary Mathematics (girls only), Domestic Science (girls only).

Candidates may not take at the same examination both "Gaedhilg" and "Litridheacht na Gaedhilge," or both "English Language" and "English Literature."

(d) Only one Examination Paper will be set in each subject, and the standards for Pass and Honours will remain as at present, viz : 40 per cent and 60 per cent respectively.

7. Conditions for Passing Leaving Certificate Examination

(a) Candidates must pass in Irish and in four other subjects.

---

* References to a language include, in the case of Irish and English, either of the courses mentioned in paragraph (1) (a) above.

(b) Separate Pass and Honours papers will be set in the various subjects, and the standard for a pass in a subject will remain as at present, viz:— 40 per cent on the Pass paper or 30 per cent on the Honours Paper, and for Honours 50 per cent on the Honours Paper.

(c) The subjects of examination will be

(1) Irish	(12) Applied Mathematics
(2) English	(13) Physics
(3) Latin	(14) Chemistry
(4) Greek	(15) Physics and Chemistry
(5) French	(16) General Science
(6) German	(17) Botany
(7) Italian	(18) Physiology and Hygiene
(8) Spanish	(19) Domestic Economy
(9) History	(20) Drawing
(10) Geography	(21) Music
(11) Mathematics	(22) Commerce

8. Marks for Scholarships

(a) The following will be the marks assigned to the various subjects for Scholarship purposes —

Gaedhilg	300
Litridheacht na Gaedhilge	600
English Language	200
English Literature	400
Mathematics	600
Elementary Mathematics	300
Latin and Greek	400 each
French, German, Italian, Spanish	300 each
History and Geography	400
Science	300
Domestic Science	400
Commerce	300
Music	300
Drawing	200
Manual Instruction	200

(b) The latter part of rule 44(1) providing for a reduction in the marks obtained on Lower Course subjects will be omitted, and the maximum mark will be reduced from 2,400 to 2,200 in the case of girls.

III.6 Report of the Council of Education on the Curriculum of the Secondary School, 1962.

The background to the setting up of the Council of Education in 1950 is described in an earlier section (I.8) The Council's report on the function and curriculum of the primary school was published in 1954. On 12th November 1954, General Risteárd Ua Maolchatha, Minister for Education, in the course of an address to the council, made the following request:

> *That the Council of Education would advise without prejudice to the consideration of the general pattern for primary and post-primary education as to the curriculum which should be followed in recognised secondary schools as a condition for the payment of State grants to these schools.*

The report of the council on this matter was not completed until 1960, when it was submitted to the Minister, and was not published until 1962. The report of almost 300 pages — in Irish and English — dealt with the general conditions governing the curriculum of the recognised secondary school, and the syllabus content for each subject of the curriculum. It did not discuss the broader issue of the system of secondary education nor topics such as the financing of secondary education, the qualifications, conditions of service or remuneration of teachers, or the relationship between vocational and secondary education. In this regard, the council took the point of view that "these and other live questions are simply outside our present terms of reference." Since the council felt that it was important that the curriculum of the secondary school should be considered against the background of the history of secondary education in Ireland, over 60 pages of the report dealt with the historical context. Over 100 pages related to the syllabus of individual subjects at both Intermediate and Leaving Certificate levels. A relatively short section on examinations supported the practice of public examinations at Intermediate and Leaving Certificate levels but recommended that some subjects at Intermediate Certificate be offered at both pass and honours level. The general tenor of the report was conservative and disappointing to those who had hoped that it would provide a blueprint for reform in secondary education. For example, it refuted any suggestions that there was a lack of co-ordination between the curriculum of the primary and secondary schools, stating: "We cannot admit that (this allegation) has any substance with regard to the curriculum of the primary and secondary school....... We cannot see that any greater co-ordination is possible." The report also dismissed the suggestion that free secondary education for all should be introduced, describing such a scheme as "utopian."

The following extracts from the report give an indication of the approach taken to the various issues which were considered:

THE NATURE AND AIM OF SECONDARY EDUCATION

****

164. The school is the instrument which society uses for the preservation and transmission of the culture of the past and for the organised development of the younger generation towards certain ends or ideals. If one were asked to specify these ends or ideals, the answer would have to be sought in the philosophy of education or religious outlook of those responsible for the school. The essential quality, the animating principle of any school, is determined by the ultimate values recognised by the agencies which found and direct it. In Ireland, fortunately, there is no need to dwell at length on the importance of such values. Our schools are the heirs of a great tradition and it is universally recognised that their purpose is, in short, to prepare their pupils to be God-fearing and responsible citizens. The school itself is seen as a

social institution, of its very nature subsidiary and complementary to the family and the Church. In our educational theory a fundamental position is taken up on the spiritual nature and destiny of man. There is no controversy as to the sacredness, responsibility and ultimate worth of the individual person. The purpose of school education, then is the organised development and equipment of all the powers of the individual person — religious, moral, intellectual, physical — so that, by making the fullest use of his talents, he may responsibly discharge his duties to God and to his fellow-men in society.

****

170. Consequently, if it be asked what is intended to be conveyed by a "well-balanced" course of general education our interpretation is that it must have a basic core of humanist and other subjects but that the balance should be in favour of the humanist group.

171. Accepting this view of the nature and aim of secondary education we do not consider it incumbent on us to plan an ideal course or series of courses for compulsory adoption by the schools. It would be temerarious, to say the least, on the part of a body such as ours to dictate to institutions which, for the most part, have grown and developed with the minimum of State patronage to meet urgent needs of our people, particularly in the nineteenth and twentieth centuries, and which have established their own traditions. Wisely, we think, the State has provided approved courses in a variety of subjects, leaving each school a certain degree of choice in the subjects of instruction according to its traditions, circumstances and particular objectives. The recommendations which we make in succeeding chapters are such, we hope, as may be of assistance to the schools without impairing their legitimate freedom.

THE DESIRABLE AGE OF ENTRY ON SECONDARY EDUCATION

182. The question naturally arises: what is the desirable age of entry? If all pupils were to enter the secondary schools at the age of twelve years, it would be possible to ensure a wider range and a greater balance of subjects. However, while recognising the advantages that an earlier general age of entry would give, the Council hesitates to recommend that earlier entry should be insisted on. Attendance at secondary schools is entirely voluntary, and to insist that children commence the secondary course at a particular age might deter many from going to secondary schools who under existing conditions receive the benefits of secondary education. There is also the well-known fact that in some children intellectual development is slow: if the age of entry were twelve such children might be debarred altogether from receiving secondary education, or might give up in disgust after a short time. Further, there is the economic reason — perhaps the strongest of all — for the postponement by parents of their children's entry to secondary schools: in general, fees must be paid, and this expense may be a deterrent, especially where there are a number of children in a family. School books and requisites are also costly. It is quite understandable, therefore, that many parents because of this factor prefer to keep their children as long as possible in national schools, where instruction is free and books and equipment are less expensive.

183. For all these reasons, therefore, the Council does not feel justified in recommending that pupils be obliged to enter secondary schools at a fixed age. In view, however, of the wider curriculum of the secondary school and of the number of new subjects and branches of study which the new entrant must take, or which it is desirable for him to take, the Council strongly favours entry to the secondary school at about the age of twelve years.

****

THE JUNIOR CURRICULUM A DISTINCT EDUCATIONAL UNIT

186. Mention must also be made of the fact that many young people conclude their secondary schooling on completion of the junior course. This is illustrated by the comparative numbers taking the Certificate Examinations. The number of boys who were examined for the Intermediate Certificate in 1955 was 5,677, and the number of girls was 6,634. The corresponding figures for those taking the Leaving Certificate Examination in 1957 were: boys — 3,492; girls — 3,173. From these figures it can be concluded that approximately sixty per cent of the boys who take the Intermediate Certificate Examination proceed to the Leaving Certificate, whereas slightly less than fifty per cent of the girls do so.

187. What becomes of those who do not continue their secondary schooling to the conclusion of the senior course? We have no precise information, but it is possible to conjecture with a degree of probability. Some may go to vocational schools. Others may take a University matriculation examination without presenting themselves for the Leaving Certificate at all. A proportion of the girls who leave after taking the Intermediate Certificate train for office occupations in special commercial schools. It is probable that many of those who leave school on completion of the junior secondary course find employment in commercial and other careers without further formal schooling.

188. It is important, therefore, to note that the curriculum of the secondary school should not be framed to meet the requirements only of those pupils who intend to proceed to a University or similar institution. The junior curriculum must be planned as a unit in itself, since it completes the general education of a considerable number of those who attend secondary schools.

EXAMINATIONS

368. The problem is to preserve the undoubted value of examinations and, at the same time, to eliminate possible abuses. In proposing pass and honours syllabuses in each subject of the junior curriculum, we feel we have gone a long way towards the solution of this problem. Tests set at pass level should be such that any well-taught pupil who has studied with reasonable application and diligence can contemplate with composure the terminal examination of the junior course. At the same time, it is but right that the pupil who is capable of covering without undue strain a wider syllabus in any subject than that set for pass standards should have the opportunity of doing so, and of submitting himself for examination on that wider syllabus at the conclusion of his course. We therefore contemplate an examination paper for honours candidates which would be composed of questions of a more difficult type, and covering a more extended field, than that for pass students. Apart from this proposal to provide pass and honours courses, which applies to all subjects, we have suggested changes in the character of the examinations in individual subjects. We believe that these will enable teachers to deal with the courses in a more liberal manner.

****

INTERMEDIATE SCHOLARSHIPS

****

388. The first question to which the Council addressed itself was whether any system of scholarships should be retained at all. Various arguments are used from time to time against the very principle of scholarships : for example, that the principle is radically evil, appealing to the motives of cupidity and desire for praise; that scholarships disturb the even tenor and

leisurely progress which should be the hallmark of a true school; that preparation for scholarships leads to cramming rather than education of pupils, while school authorities tend to concentrate on prospective scholarship winners to the neglect of the average pupils.

389. While not unaware of possible dangers in scholarship systems, the Council is satisfied that the principle of awarding scholarships for outstanding achievement is sound. Stimulus and incentive are of value in every sphere of human activity and have always been prominent in sane educational theory and practice. Writing in the First Century A.D. the great Roman rhetorician and teacher Quintilian stressed the advantages of competitive effort among students, and in medieval times the element of competition was always present at the elaborately prepared disputations. The *Radio Studiorum,* drawn up in the era of Renaissance studies, prescribed the system of management, methods of study, curriculum and class organisation to be followed in Jesuit Schools. The system included provision for such incentives towards study as the public presentation of prizes for academic merit, and *honesta aemulatio* in the acquisition of learning was encouraged of set purpose. And so down the ages to the present time the principle of awarding prizes, exhibitions, scholarships or other distinctions in recognition of superior merit has been a feature of the generality of educational systems. The Council sees no valid reason for departing from this well-established tradition.

Secondary education for all

428. Finally, we would advert to the frequently reiterated demand that our education system should allow of free secondary education for all. Even a superficial examination of this demand will show that in this unqualified form it is untenable. While the problem is not directly pertinent to the

charge laid on us by the Minister, it would be unrealistic not to face up to it, especially in view of the fact that "secondary education for all" is often urged as a requirement of genuine democracy. In most democratic countries, however, the slogan is usually qualified by the addition "for all able and willing to profit by it." The realisation of this qualified ideal could be accelerated considerably by the greater provision of scholarships, on which we have already animadverted in our first Report (pars.391-394). But the unqualified scheme of "secondary education for all" is utopian : if only for financial reasons. The financial burden would have to be assumed by the State, or by the local authorities, or by both working together as in the provision of vocational education. The cost of maintaining pupils in the few Preparatory Colleges does not warrant the hope that the State could or would be prepared to assume financial responsibility for secondary education on a national scale, especially as the State is already heavily committed in the provision of vocational education.

429. There are also objections on educational grounds. One of these is that only a minority of pupils would be capable of profiting by secondary (grammar school) education, as is attested by the experience of many countries. Furthermore, if secondary education were universally available free for all, the incentives to profit by it would diminish and standards would inevitably fall. The Council is satisfied that, taking into consideration the resources of this small country and the proved merits of voluntary initiative, remarkable progress has been made in the provision and extension of secondary education by voluntary agencies. To illustrate this it is necessary merely to observe that in the school year 1924-25 there were 278 recognised schools catering for 22,897 pupils, whereas in the 1956-57 year the number of schools had risen to 480, and the number of pupils was 62,429.

III.7 Commission on Technical Education, 1927

At the establishment of the Irish Free State (1922) the new government began to address itself to the task of industrial and economic reform. The creation of an educational infra-structure suitably designed to meet these requirements was a challenge to which the government addressed itself. In October 1926 a commission was set up under the chairmanship of John Ingram, Senior Inspector of Technical Instruction "to enquire into and advise upon the system of Technical Education in Saorstát Éireann in relation to the requirements of Trade and Industry." The report was completed and presented to the Minister a year later. Finding that technical education was in need of substantial reform the commission made a wide-ranging and varied set of proposals. The more significant of these included a school leaving certificate for primary school pupils, a greater emphasis on practical subjects at primary school, the introduction of continuation school to provide the link between primary and technical education and teacher education. The following extracts are from the report of the commission:

— *Primary Education in relation to Technical Education*

1. All sixth standard pupils of primary schools should be tested in an examination prescribed by the Department, and that success in this examination should entitle the pupil to the award of a School-leaving certificate.
3. Drawing should be reinstated as portion of the obligatory curriculum for all pupils in primary schools up to and including sixth standard.
4. Arrangements should be made in urban areas to send groups of the more mature pupils of primary schools to the local technical schools for instruction in Domestic Science and Woodwork, and that the technical schools should be authorised to conduct special classes to meet their requirements.

Chapter IV. — *Continuation Education*

6. A system of practical continuation schools and classes should be established to educate young people between the ages of 14 and 16.
7. The programme for continuation schools and classes should be distinct from the programme for technical schools and classes and should be set out in two main groups for rural and urban areas.
10. Pending the provision of new schools continuation classes should be held in technical school or primary school buildings.
14. The curricula of many secondary schools should be altered to meet the special needs of young people entering employment at the age of 16 and should include as *obligatory* subjects : science, drawing, manual instruction and domestic economy.
18. As soon as the necessary accommodation and staff are provided, attendance at continuation classes should be made compulsory in any locality in the following manner:

    (a) *whole-time attendance in urban areas* for all young people between 14 and 16 who are not in employment, only those in approved employment to be exempted.
    (b) *part-time attendance in urban areas* for a minimum of 180 hours in each year of the period for all young people between 14 and 16 in approved employment.
    (c) *part-time attendance in rural areas* for a minimum of 180 hours in each year of the period for all young people between 14 and 16.

Chapter VIII — *Higher Technical Education*

51. There is a necessity for the continuance and wide development of the technological work that has been in the past the function of the Royal College of Science, and that if such technological courses are not to be developed in the future at the Universities, the re-establishment of a separate institute for the purpose will have to be seriously considered.

52. The schemes of technical education in Dublin, Cork and Limerick should be extended to include full-time courses of secondary technical character.

53. The schemes of education in Cork and Rathmines should be extended to include commercial courses of a secondary character on the same plan as proposed for the technical courses.

Chapter XII — *The Training of Teachers required for Continuation and Technical Schools*

79. The proposed new schemes of continuation and technical education should be preceded by intensive training of teachers and that a sum be set apart in the annual estimates of the Department of Education for the expense of their training.

80-90 The State should establish scholarships for the training of teachers as enumerated in paragraphs 309 to 324.

Chapter XIII — *Salaries and Conditions of Service of whole-time Continuation and Technical Teachers.*

91. Definite scales of salaries and of travelling and subsistence expenses should be drawn up by the Department of Education and prescribed as obligatory on local committees employing whole-time teachers.

III.8 Speech by the Minister for Education, John Marcus O'Sullivan, at the Second Stage of the Vocational Education Bill 14 May 1930

In response to the findings and recommendations of the Commission on Technical Education a new Vocational Education Bill was drafted and introduced to the Dáil in the spring of 1930.

Acknowledging the achievements of the Department of Agriculture and Technical Instruction, the minister pointed to the need for the further development of industrially related education. Under the provisions of the bill, all local authorities were required to strike a rate in aid of vocational education and the composition of the local committees was streamlined in order to provide for more efficiency. The strategy of appointing sub-committees, so ably employed under the Department of Agriculture and Technical Instruction, to take charge of specific responsibilities was suggested.

The bill envisaged a two-tier system of vocational education — continuation education for 14 to 16 year olds and technical education for 16 to 18 year olds. The minister was anxious to have it understood, however, that neither continuation education or technical education was solely confined to those age categories.

The following extracts are taken from the Minister's speech at the second stage of the bill in May 1930:

Anybody who has followed the course of technical education in this country for the last decade or twenty years will readily appreciate that there are a variety of things which have made this Bill necessary. Even the lapse of time itself would have been a sufficient reason for the introduction of a Bill of this kind. The system under which we are working at present stretches back as far as its legislative foundations are concerned, practically a generation. In the course of that generation new problems have arisen which those who were responsible for the original legislation had, naturally enough, not been able to take into account, and the existing provisions are no longer enough to enable us to keep sufficiently abreast of the times. I need not say, in connection with this Bill and the necessity for it, that I am not decrying in the slightest the amount of solid work that has been done under the old system; nor do I deny that even under the old system considerable advances are still possible, and in the case of the last few years advances have been made. But undoubtedly the present system, from the purely legislative point of view, is cumbersome, and there are many hindrances contained in the existing legislation, and still more perhaps in the lack of proper provisions, that make a new departure necessary. An overhaul, therefore, is due, and we feel that if this Bill in its main provisions receives the approval of the Oireachtas we will be in a much better position to deal with the problems that will face us at least in the course of the next five or ten years.

****

It may be necessary to give the House some idea of the problem that we have to face and that this Bill gives us, to a large extent, the legislative machinery for dealing with. I have on more than one occasion pointed out the great importance to this country of a proper system of training in the struggle for existence,especially since the War, that most nations in Europe — possibly in the world, but certainly in Europe — have to indulge in. A very important factor that may decide the ultimate outcome will be the training that the youth of the different countries receive. This applies not merely to industrialised countries, but to agricultural communities. It applies in this country not merely to the towns, it applies as well to the country districts. There must be a better preparation for farming instruction, and then a certain amount of other useful instruction of a practical kind, useful to the small farmer especially, can be given to the young boy or girl whose life is destined to be spent on the farm. If the Deputies bear in mind the disappearance from the countryside of carpenters, masons and harness-makers, they can grasp the importance that a practical system of continuation education might be, even from that point of view, to the country districts. Still more important is the question of dealing with a boy of fourteen when he leaves — as most of them do leave — the National School and is going to spend his life in the country. Undoubtedly, so far as the boy from fourteen to sixteen is concerned, the needs of a certain percentage of them are already met, under the educational system of the country, in the existing technical classes that are to be found in operation in different portions of the country, and also in the primary and secondary schools. Continuation education itself is not something entirely new so far as the country is concerned. As I say, a considerable amount of it is done even under the existing schemes, done not in the whole-hearted, not in the clear-sighted way in which we would like it done. Owing to the organic way in which the thing has grown, it is mixed up very often in a very confused fashion with technical education, in the narrow sense of the word; it is mixed up in such a way as I am convinced is not to the ultimate advantage of either the continuation education, on the one hand, or technical education on the other.

****

There is a conception abroad due to the concentration on the compulsory clauses in the Bill that continuation education stops automatically at the age of sixteen and then technical education begins. That is not the case, and there is nothing in the Bill to justify that particular interpretation. However, for the purpose merely of indicating to some extent the problem that we have to deal with, take these ages fourteen to sixteen and sixteen to eighteen, from many points of view, I admit, the more important ages when we are considering vocational education, more important than any other year or set of years that we might mention. The number of young people in the country between fourteen and sixteen years of age I should roughly estimate as being 120,000. Of these, anything up to 45,000 would receive education in primary schools or in secondary schools. That leaves altogether about 75,000 boys and girls in the country, roughly speaking, whose education comes to an end, so far as systematic control of it is concerned, at the age of fourteen unless they go into one of the existing technical schools. If you get an attendance ultimately of 75 per cent of that number you will have altogether, therefore, about 55,000 young people for whom provision will have to be made for continuation education, part-time or whole-time. I have on more than one occasion referred to that problem of the boy who has left school at the age of fourteen and who stays about the farm, who is too young to get technical agricultural training and is in danger in the course of a couple of years of forgetting a great deal of what he learned in the national school. I do not intend to dilate on it now. Everybody is familiar with it. To such it is proposed to give the opportunity, by gradually bringing into operation the weapon of compulsion, of at least continuation of formal instruction. It is quite true that the number of hours per week, in the country districts especially, will make no undue demand on their time. That was clearly envisaged by the Commission. Everybody who knows the condition of the country will probably be in agreement on that point of view. It will mean that they will be getting education of a different type, partly cultural, and there will be a more practical agricultural bias to the instruction they will be receiving.

****

I need not dwell on the importance of technical education so far as industries are concerned. I do not share the view, which some people seem to have, that technical education can create industries. It cannot do so. In fact, to do anything effective, technical education must be in close touch with existing industries. Where they are side by side the problem is to get them to help each other, one being now in advance, and the other advancing in turn. In all countries, schools are now asked to undertake tasks which up to the present were undertaken privately, either in the family or by private employers and companies. That is true of practically every country..... As the Commission put it in Paragraph 30, the current tendency in all modern industrial countries is to make the technical school fulfil a more definite function in the training for industry. In Paragraph 125 they state — I do not know whether the House is in sympathy with it, but we had better accept it as a fact — that the employer cannot afford to use the services of a highly-skilled and highly-paid workman for the purpose of training apprentices, and that this duty is devolving more and more on the technical school.

The Committee, and here I agree with them, pointed out that the existing committees are altogether too large. Sometimes you have as many as 70 members in some of them. They do not all turn up when the business of the committee is to be done. There may be an occasional day or two on which you may have a very large attendance, but as a rule the attendance is nothing like as large as it might be. Now I believe in much smaller committees if effective work is to be done. The Commission suggests something like twelve. Ten or twelve might be enough to have present at a meeting, but I thought it would be well to increase it somewhat, because if you are to limit the number to twelve you will not get them all present. If you had a meeting of ten or twelve it can only be if you have a somewhat larger committee, and therefore we have somewhat enlarged the number which the Committee suggested. You want a small committee to do effective work and at the same time you want a committee which with normal attendance will give a sufficiently large number to be representative of the different interests.

III.9 The Vocational Education Act, 1930

The 1930 Act was an immediate response to the findings of the Commission on Technical Education 1927. An uneveness of growth characterised the development of technical education during the period 1900-1922 with the more prosperous and more densely populated areas achieving a faster growth rate than the thinly populated rural areas. The new act, with a more generous injection of state finance attempted to offset the disparity between urban and rural areas as a network of new technical schools was built throughout the country.

The act introduced a more streamlined administrative structure at local level. The former unwieldy technical instruction committees were replaced by fourteen-member vocational education committees (thirty-eight in all). Their term of office was to run concurrently with that of the local government. Each category of local government, borough, urban and county, was required to raise a rate in aid of vocational education.

Vocational education comprised two components — continuation education and technical education. Both terms were defined by the act. The continuation school, according to the Technical Instruction Commission 1927, was to serve as an intermediate stage for pupils between the age of 14 and 16. It was believed that pupils leaving primary school at the age of 14 " are not mature enough to appreciate the realities of employment and the special forms of instruction that relate thereto." The continuation school was, further, to act as a corrective to what the commission saw as "the dislike of industrial work, which is a characteristic common to the youth of today leaving the primary and indeed the secondary school." Appropriate provision was to be made for the introduction of distinctive continuation school programmes in urban and rural areas.

The change in nomenclature to vocational education was an acknowledgement of a wider trend which sought to broaden the base of traditional selected content of technical education, and accommodate the inclusion of a wider range of subjects in a world of ever-changing industrial and social needs.

While allowing for the progressive measures which the 1930 Act introduced, it must nevertheless be stated that the act re-echoed many of the provisions and principles of its predecessor, the 1899 Act. The concept of continuation education was not too dissimilar to the introductory courses and the day trades technical schools first inaugurated by the Department of Agriculture and Technical Instruction. Both were designed to provide a connecting link between primary school and technical school. The school institution under the provisions of both acts was secular and mixed. Local control was a fundamental feature common to both legislative measures. The following extracts are from the Act:

3. — For the purposes of this Act the expression "continuation education" means education to continue and supplement education provided in elementary schools and includes general and practical training in preparation for employment in trades, manufactures, agriculture, commerce, and other industrial pursuits, and also general and practical training for improvement of young persons in the early stages of such employment.

4. — (1) For the purposes of this Act the expression "technical education" means education pertaining to trades, manufactures, commerce, and other industrial pursuits (including the occupations of girls and women connected with the household) and in subjects bearing thereon or relating thereto and includes education in science and art (including, in the county boroughs of Dublin and Cork, music) and also includes physical training.

8. — (1) The vocational education committee for a borough vocational education area shall consist of fourteen members elected by the council of the county borough which is such borough vocational education area, of whom not less than five nor more than eight shall be persons who are members of such council.

(2) The vocational education committee for an urban district vocational education area shall consist of fourteen members elected by the council of the urban district which is such urban district vocational education area, of whom not less than five nor more than eight shall be persons who are members of such council.

(3) The vocational education committee for a county vocational education area shall consist of—

(a) fourteen members elected by the council of the county which is or includes such county vocational education area, of whom not less than five nor more than eight shall be persons who are members of such council; and

(b) where such vocational education area contains one or more urban districts which are not scheduled urban districts —

(i) if the number of such urban districts does not exceed four, two members elected by the council of each of such urban districts, each of whom may at the discretion of such council be a person who is or a person who is not a member of such council, or

(ii)if the number of such urban districts exceeds four, one member elected by the council of each such urban district who in every case may at the discretion of such council be a person who is or a person who is not a member of such council.

CONTINUATION EDUCATION AND TECHNICAL EDUCATION

30. — It shall be the duty of every vocational education committee —

(a) to establish and maintain in accordance with this Act a suitable system of continuation education in its area and to provide for the progressive development of such system; and

(b) to supply or aid the supply in accordance with this Act of technical education in its area.

31. — (1) Every vocational education committee may, and if so required by the Minister shall, from time to time prepare and submit to the Minister a scheme setting forth the general policy of such committee in relation to continuation education and technical education respectively and showing the mode in which it proposes, in pursuance of such policy, to exercise and perform its powers and duties under this Act.

(2) In preparing a scheme under this section a vocational education committee shall consider all such representations as shall be made to it in relation to such scheme by persons resident in its area having interest and experience in educational matters, and by persons concerned in local manufactures, trades and industries, and by persons qualified to represent the views of employers and employees in matters of educational interest relating to such area.

32. — In performance of the duties in relation to continuation education imposed on vocational education committees by this Act every such committee may do all or any of the following things, that is to say:-

(a) establish and maintain continuation schools in its area;

(b) establish and maintain in its area courses of instruction in the nature of continuation education;

(c) assist in maintaining schools in its area in which continuation education is provided.

33. — Where a continuation school or a course of instruction maintained or provided by a vocational education committee is

attended by young persons who have the prospect of employment in a particular trade, business or occupation, it shall be the duty of such vocational education committee to register and classify such young persons and to provide in the curriculum of such school or in the instruction given in such course (as the case may be) for the educational requirements of such young persons having regard to the nature of the said employment.

34. — In performance of the duties in relation to technical education imposed on vocational education committees by this Act, every such committee may do all or any of the following things, that is to say:—

(a) establish and maintain or assist in maintaining technical schools within its area;

(b) establish and maintain or assist in establishing and maintaining in its area courses of instruction in the nature of technical education;

(c) contribute to the expenses incurred by persons resident in its area in obtaining technical education at schools or courses within or outside such area;

(d) with the special sanction of the Minister, aid persons resident in its area in obtaining further education at technical colleges or central technical institutions or technical training colleges, or other centres of advanced technical education within or outside such area.

35. — A vocational education committee, when exercising the powers in relation to technical education conferred on it by this Act, shall have regard to any existing supply of technical education in its area.

36. — Where a vocational education committee exercises or proposes to exercise its powers under this Act for a particular purpose which is a purpose authorised by this Act, and a question arises as to whether such purpose is a purpose relating

to continuation education or is a purpose relating to technical education, such question shall be referred by such committee to the Minister and the decision of the Minister thereon shall be final and conclusive.

38. — (1) A vocational education committee for a borough vocational education area may, subject to compliance with the next following sub-section of this section, establish and maintain in its area a school (in this section referred to as a day technical college) having for its main object the provision of education in the general principles of science, commerce, or art suited to the requirements of persons employed in positions of control or responsibility in trade or industry.

111.10 Letter from the Minister for Education, John Marcus O'Sullivan, to Most Rev. D. Keane, Bishop of Limerick, dated 31st October, 1930.

The Catholic hierarchy was concerned about some aspects of the Vocational Education Act of 1930, particularly the definition, scope and control of continuation education, the question of Religious Instruction and the issue of co-education. The Archbishop of Tuam, the Bishop of Clogher and the Bishop of Limerick representing the Irish Hierarchy, met the Minister for Education, John Marcus O'Sullivan, in October 1930 and following this meeting the Minister wrote to the Bishop of Limerick communicating formally to him, for the information of the hierarchy, his view and the view of the Department on these matters. The following extracts are from the letter:

My Lord,

On Thursday, 16th instant, His Grace the Archbishop of Tuam, His Lordship, the Bishop of Clogher and Your Lordship, representing the Irish Hierarchy, discussed with me certain aspects of the Vocational Education Act, in which the Church was particularly interested. I gathered that it was the sections dealing with Continuation Education for young persons between the ages of fourteen and sixteen that especially claimed attention. On that occasion I indicated that I should take an opportunity of communicating formally with Your Lordship, for the information of the Bishops, my own view and the views of my Department on these matters.

First I should like to deal with the general scope and purpose of the Act, especially in reference to the provision of Continuation Education, for it is here particularly that misconception has arisen in some quarters.

I may say at once that the title of the Act, viz., "Vocational Education Act," is not intended merely for reference purposes — to provide the Act with a name as it were — but is meant to indicate its purpose and to delimit its scope. On many occasions, before the introduction of the Bill as well as subsequently, I have made it clear that Vocational — not General — Education was the subject matter of the Act. It is not, and was never intended to be, in any degree a general education Act.

For the purpose of better organisation and to prevent much of the confusion that had prevailed under our Technical system, I found it advisable to divide Vocational Education into Continuation Education and Technical Education; but both these branches as legislated for by this Act remain essentially Vocational. By their very nature and purpose the schools to be provided under this Act are distinctly not schools for general education. General education, after the age of 14 years, as well as before the age of 14 years, will continue to be given in Primary and in Secondary Schools. When we can afford to make more universal a system of general education for post-primary pupils it cannot be through the medium of these Continuation Schools.

****

All through I was most careful to secure that no new principle of control in education should be introduced by this Act. I stated this very distinctly at the close of my introductory speech already referred to above. I do not pretend that the system established in this country meets all ideals, but I believe that when all practical difficulties are taken into account there is no need to be uneasy about the present Act.

I strove to secure, with success, as I believe, that the Act should not run counter to established Catholic practice in this country, or to the spirit of the Maynooth decrees governing these matters. This was one of the reasons why I insisted so strongly on the vocational character of the instruction to be provided under the Act. The second reason was that I felt there was a great deal in the criticism so often heard that our education system has hitherto been too one-sidedly theoretical and that however excellent the education given in the Primary and Secondary schools may be, it was not sufficiently balanced by a system of a more "practical" type. This is sometimes adduced as one of the reasons why our young people so readily turn their backs on agricultural and industrial pursuits. With more justice it might be urged that for these latter not nearly enough in the way of adequate provision of instruction was being done. That, I confess, is one of the reasons why I am keen that both as to matter and to method and aims there should — right through — in the vocational course be a definite break with the Primary system.

****

Another matter which your Lordships raised is the question of co-education and night schools especially in the country districts. I think that the Committees ought so to fix the hours of their continuation classes in these districts that boys and girls would not attend the same classes and preferably not attend the schools on the same evening and that, as far as possible, night classes should be avoided.

The only matter that now remains on which to make my position clear is the very important one of Religious Instruction. I may point out that, with the exception of a special reference to the schools of Music in Cork and in Dublin, no subject of instruction is mentioned in the Act. The Act does not profess to set out a curriculum. I think, however, that facilities for the giving of Religious Instruction should be provided by the Vocational Committees. I cannot believe that any Committee will fail in this respect. If, however, in any individual case the Committee should fail I see no reason why we should not use our general powers of approval of courses to bring pressure to bear on them to make the necessary provisions.

III.11 Apprenticeship Act, 1931

The Apprenticeship Act of 1931 included a section on the education of apprentices. The act envisaged that vocational education committees would play a significant role in such education, but it did not make it mandatory for committees to provide all courses required for apprentices. The following is the section of the act which deals with the education of apprentices.

26. — (1) An apprenticeship committee may make representations to the Minister for Education with a view to the provision by the vocational education committee whose functional area is co-terminous with or included in or includes the district of such apprenticeship committee of courses of instruction in the nature of technical education of a type suitable for apprentices engaged in the designated trade for which such apprenticeship committee is established, and that the Minister may, if having regard to all the circumstances he considers that effect should be given to such representations or

any part thereof, forward such representations to such vocational education committee for its consideration.

(2) Where a course of instruction in the nature of technical education provided by a vocational education committee is available for any apprentice employed in an apprenticeship district in a designated trade and such course is held within the normal working hours of such apprentice and at a place within a distance of three miles from the premises at which such apprentice is so employed measured according to the shortest way lawfully and conveniently available for him, the apprenticeship committee for such district for the purposes of such trade may, if it considers such course suitable, make an order (in this section referred to as an attendance order) in the prescribed form requiring such apprentice to attend such course.

(3) Whenever an attendance order is duly made in relation to an apprentice and such order is personally served on such apprentice, it shall be the duty of such apprentice to comply with such order and if he fails so to do he shall, unless he satisfies the Court that such failure was due to sickness or other unavoidable cause, be guilty of an offence under this section.

(4) Whenever an attendance order is duly made in relation to an apprentice and such order is personally served on the employer of such apprentice, it shall be the duty of such employer, if such apprentice is attending or desires to attend the course of instruction which he is required by such order to attend, to afford such apprentice time and liberty to attend such course of instruction without any deduction from wages or any addition to the hours of employment or reckoning such time as lost, and if such employer fails or neglects to comply with the requirements of this sub-section he shall be guilty of an offence under this section.

(5) Every person guilty of an offence under this section shall be liable on summary conviction thereof in the case of a first offence to a fine not exceeding twenty shillings and in the case of a second or any subsequent offence to a fine not exceeding forty shillings.

(6) Any fees which may be payable to a vocational education committee by an apprentice in respect of a course of instruction which he is attending in pursuance of an attendance order shall be paid on behalf of such apprentice by the apprenticeship committee by which such order was made.

III.12 Memorandum V.40; Organisation of Whole-time Continuation Courses in Borough, Urban and County Areas, 1942

Memorandum V.40, which was first published in 1942, 12 years after the passing of the 1930 Act, and subsequently reprinted a number of times, set down the principles underlying the work of the vocational schools and in particular the organisation of whole-time continuation courses. The memorandum was intended "not only to place on record what is of permanent value in the experience gained so far, but also to define clearly the fundamental aims of continuation education and to show the relationship between these and the immediate problems which now confront those who are responsible for the education of young persons." The memorandum was 26 pages long and contained useful information on the organisation of continuation education in Borough, Urban and County areas. The extracts reproduced here are from the Introduction; and the sections on Admission to Courses and on General Organisation of Continuation Courses:

Introduction

The educational system set up under the Vocational Education Act of 1930 has now been in operation for twelve years. In this period steady progress has been made in the organisation of courses of instruction and in the building of schools.

During the same time there has been a growing demand for instruction suited to particular needs and corresponding developments have taken place in the training of teachers and the prescription of their qualifications. While this expansion is still in progress, it may be said that the primary and experimental stage of the work has been completed. Certain principles have been established for the working of the Act in both town and country areas, and in particular for the organisation of the whole-time day continuation courses with which this memorandum deals.

The provision of continuation education entails not only the organisation of practical instruction of various types but also the further development of the training which the pupils have received in their homes and in the elementary school. The main principles which should govern this work and determine the lines of future development are set out in this memorandum for the guidance of members of Vocational Education Committees and their officers. They are set out at length and in descriptive fashion for the benefit of those who are approaching the work for the first time. Where the value of certain types of organisation has been tested by experience these are treated as standards to which particular schemes and schools may be referred. The memorandum is intended not only to place on record what is of permanent value in the experience gained so far but also to define clearly the fundamental aims of continuation education and to show the relationship between these and the immediate problems which now confront those who are responsible for the education of young persons.

Continuation education must be in keeping with Irish tradition and should reflect in the schools the loyalty to our Divine Lord which is expressed in the Prologue and Articles of the Constitution. In all schools it is essential that religious instruction be continued and that interest in the Irish language and other distinctive features of the national life be carefully fostered. The integration of these elements with one another and with the body of the curriculum is a task calling for the co-operative efforts of all teachers. In the good home — the model for ordered social life — tradition, faith, work and recreation blend naturally and easily with one another, and it should be the object of those in control of continuation education to secure similar unity within the school, so that pupils may go out well prepared to play their parts as members of society and guardians of the national inheritance.

Organisation of continuation education

The immediate purpose of day continuation education as organised under the Vocational Education Act is to prepare boys and girls, who have to start early in life, for the occupations which are open to them. These occupations, in general, require some sort of manual skill and continuation courses have, therefore, a corresponding practical bias. About half the time of instruction is apportioned to such subjects as Cookery, Drawing, Rural Science, Typewriting and Woodwork. These subjects are taught in a practical way with the tools and other equipment which the pupil is likely to use later in his calling, and they are taught with the immediate object of enabling boys and girls to make themselves useful as soon as possible in the economic and household spheres.

The general purpose of continuation education is to help each pupil to secure his own ultimate good. This purpose is dealt with more fully in the final section on the general organisation of continuation courses.

****

BOROUGH AREAS

It will be clear from what has been said of the purpose of continuation education that the nature of the continuation courses in any centre must be closely related to economic conditions in the neighbourhood. The centres considered in this section are associated with manufacturing, transport, wholesale and retail business administration and generally with service of value not only to the local population but to a large section of the whole community. These activities are carried on as a rule by companies rather than by individuals and the various economic units are large. All this makes for specialisation and the development of a numerous wage earning class engaged on many different types of work. This class is maintained by a constant flow of young people of both sexes who generally enter employment about the age of 16 years.

For the preparation of these young people for practical life the vocational education committee must organise a considerable variety of different types of continuation education. It is, however, neither possible nor desirable to try to fit every young person for some specific occupation. The child's inclinations and hopes are far from fixed when he leaves the elementary school. Neither he nor his parents are certain of what he will want to do when he reaches 16 years of age. Further, his opportunities for finding the work he wants are no more certain; the average period of the continuation course is two years, and it is impossible to tell what positions will be open in this or that occupation two years in advance. Full specialisation is therefore out of the question and the problem is better dealt with by what may be called group specialisation.

DISTRIBUTION OF OCCUPATIONS

The occupations of persons living in Ireland are given in Volume II of the Census of Population, 1936. The following summary has been prepared from details given in that volume and shows the relative distribution of different types of occupation for the four county boroughs. The figures have been arranged in seven groups selected in accordance with the type of occupation followed. The following notes on the general constitution of each group may be found helpful:

Group A — Agriculture: Farmers, farmers' relatives working on the land, farm labourers, nursery men, garden workers, etc. Those engaged in fishing are also included in this group.
Group B — Manufacture and Maintenance: Bakers, textile workers, boot makers, tailors, dressmakers, carpenters, smiths, mechanics, electricians, printers, masons, painters, etc.
Group C — Transport and Communication: Railway workers, motor drivers, dock labourers, messengers of all types, post office workers, etc.
Group D — Personal Service: Domestic servants, waiters, waitresses, laundry workers, charwomen, hotel and boarding-house keepers, etc. Those engaged in Home Duties are also included in this group.
Group E — Commerce and Clerical Work: Shopkeepers, shop assistants, commercial travellers, dealers, agents typists, clerks, etc.
Group F — Professional Work and Administration: Clergymen, nuns, teachers, medical doctors, lawyers, engineers, architects and students for these professions; army, civil service and local government officials, etc.
Group G — Miscellaneous: Mainly undefined labourers.

****

This table shows at a glance the relative numbers of men and women normally following seven different types of occupation. It is a measure, in terms of occupation, of the economic and social life of each borough and forms an excellent basis for the group specialisation of continuation courses referred to above.

It is clear from this table that boys and girls who have to start earning their living early in life are concerned mainly with Groups A, B, C, D and E. The occupations of Group F require, in general, a long period of preparatory study beginning with a full secondary school course. The final Group — Miscellaneous — consists mainly of untrained or partially trained workers; entry to it is not the object of any young person's ambition, and one of the aims of continuation education is to reduce the numbers of this category.

****

ADMISSION TO COURSES —
Pupils must, unless in the exceptional circumstances specified in Circular 18/41, have attained the age of fourteen years before admission to a continuation school. An examination should be held at entrance for purposes of classification. The examination should be simple in character and should be based on the programme for the Sixth Standard of National Schools. Pupils holding the Primary School Leaving Certificate may be exempted from this examination.

As has been stated, the courses of instruction should be generally of two years duration. The curriculum for the first year should be based on the assumption that all pupils have reached the standard of the Primary School Leaving Certificate. At the end of the first course an examination should be held and pupils should not be allowed to advance to the second year course without reaching a qualifying standard. Pupils over fourteen years who have failed to attain the qualifying standard for entrance to the first year course should be catered for by a preparatory course suited to their needs.

It has been suggested that in some schools provision should be made for third year courses. These should as a rule be more highly specialised towards occupation and should, where possible be associated with work for some definite practical qualification obtained through the Department's or other examinations.

****

GENERAL ORGANISATION OF CONTINUATION COURSES

The immediate purpose of continuation education is the preparation of boys and girls who have to start work early in life for the occupations which are open to them. Attention has so far been directed mainly to the practical aspects of this purpose. Three different types of area were considered, and the nature of the work carried on in each analysed in the light of local economic conditions and of information taken from the latest census of occupations. The special circumstances of each type of area were considered in detail; the relationships between the occupations sought and the nature of the instruction required were explained, and various suggestions for the organisation of continuation courses were offered. Throughout this treatment practical and economic factors were necessarily uppermost.

These are, however, not the only factors to be considered by those in control of continuation courses. The bulk of the time must be allotted to practical subjects because of the urgency of the economic end for the young persons for whom the courses are designed, but this makes it all the more necessary to safeguard the general purpose of the education which is to develop, with the assistance of God's grace, the whole man with all his faculties, natural and supernatural, so that he may realise his duties and responsibilities as a member of society, that he may contribute effectively to the welfare of his fellow man, and by so doing attain the end destined for him by his Creator.

Religious Instruction and Social Education

For this development it is essential that all pupils with due regard to the rights of parent should receive instruction in the fundamental truths of the Christian faith. Vocational Education Committees should, therefore, provide facilities for Religious Instruction and incorporate it in the general class time table of all continuation courses. The local ecclesiastical authorities should be approached with regard to the provision of the actual teaching. The teachers appointed should be accorded the same privileges as the other members of the staff, and every effort should be made to collaborate with them in their work. This collaboration is essential to the production of really fruitful results from vocational education. It is necessary not only that Religious Instruction be given at certain times, but also that the teaching of every other subject be permeated with Christian charity, and that the whole organisation of the school, whether in work or recreation be regulated by the same spirit. In the nature of the case all teachers have opportunities each day of showing the practical applications of religious doctrine, and can do much to form the characters of their pupils by inspiring them to acts of supernatural virtue and self-sacrifice.

****

Women in the Home

A special note is required for that branch of continuation education which deals with Domestic Economy. Reference has already been made to the necessity for organising a Day Junior Technical Course for Girls but the full significance of this work may be missed if it is considered as one of many continuation courses designed to prepare young persons to earn their livelihood in the economic sphere. The Technical Course for Girls is before anything else the most practical contribution which the vocational school can make to the social education of the youth of the country.

****

Those in charge of this training, while bearing in mind its practical and monetary aspects, should be even more alive to its relationship to the education of children and general well-being of the family. Women dealing with Home Duties are concerned not only with practical affairs, but with the most intimate of all human relationships and the most capable housekeeping in the world cannot produce good homes unless those at the head of them are inspired by some higher ideal than economic efficiency. The key to this ideal will be found in Article 41 of the Constitution from which the following phrases are taken:

> *The State recognises the family as the natural, primary and fundamental unit group of society.*
>
> *By her life within the home the woman gives to the State a support without which the common good cannot be achieved.*

The spirit behind these phrases should enliven the teaching of all those in charge of instruction in Domestic Economy subjects, and every continuation course for girls should be conducted on the assumption that each pupil may one day be responsible for the care of a home and a family of her own and for the early education of the children who are to carry on our tradition and form the nation of the future.

III.13 Report of the Commission on Vocational Organisation, 1944

Following the adoption of the 1937 Constitution, Senators Michael Tierney and Frank Mac Dermot proposed that a small commission of inquiry into vocational organisation be set up. Despite reservations on the matter, the Taoiseach Eamon de Valera, established a 25 person Commission, chaired by Dr. Michael Browne, Bishop of Galway. The Commission presented its report in November, 1943 and the report was published in 1944. It was a massive document which was critical of many of the structures of the State and which proposed fundamental reform of the method of government and administration. The report was not received sympathetically by the government and its recommendations were not implemented. The section on vocational education, extracts from which are reproduced here, was openly critical of what was seen as the failure of the system to respond to the needs of agriculture and industry, in spite of the provisions of the Vocational Education Act which had been passed 13 years earlier:

351. The most striking feature of vocational education in Ireland is that the two departments of State which have most to do with the vocational interests and needs of the country, Agriculture and Industry and Commerce, have only indirect and restricted functions in regard to this system. The Department of Agriculture has since its establishment in 1899 maintained the position that it alone has the right to organise education or instruction in agriculture. This position was respected by the Vocational Education Act, 1930, and vocational schools are not empowered to teach agriculture or subjects dealing with live stock, soils or tillage. They have been allowed to give courses in horticulture and bee-keeping and also teach rural science. Thus we have the amazing fact that in the small towns of Ireland, where there is no industry worth speaking of, elaborate and expensive buildings have been erected and classes are maintained to teach, not agriculture, but commerce and domestic economy. If the latter

subject included instruction of use to the occupiers of small farmsteads it would be of some value, but too often it means forms of confectionery. One would imagine that the primary purpose of vocational schools in rural Ireland would be to teach the many sciences comprised in agriculture, but because of the competing claims of different Departments that is not so, and in many counties the vocational schools are not even used by the instructors of the County Committees of Agriculture. The conclusion of the 1926 Commission on Technical Education that commercial courses were over-developed, especially in rural centres, has become unfortunately even more true at the present time. The temptation to frame courses in order to secure pupils is one that must be resisted by vocational education authorities if it involves giving commercial courses and thereby accentuating the low esteem for rural as compared with city life and the flight from the land of our young people.

The Department of Industry and Commerce has no direct power in regard to technical education. While it is keenly interested in the supply of skilled labour, especially for the new industries, it cannot provide the necessary instruction. The Minister for Industry and Commerce is the authority under the Apprenticeship Act, 1931, who decides whether technical education should be compulsory for apprentices in certain trades. Apprenticeship Committees can then merely request local authorities to provide it. This Department is in contact with employer and labour organisations; the Department of Education is not. Furthermore, the Department of Industry and Commerce has charge of Employment Exchanges and unemployment relief. It can make a survey of employment openings in each centre, but cannot direct technical education so as to fit students for such openings and divert them from blind alleys. We have not found evidence that such surveys are ever made or that there is any co-ordination to secure that industry receives an adequate supply of trained workers and that trained workers get employment.

352. But even within the sphere of the Department of Education's control there is a lack of co-ordination, e.g., there is no link between the primary and vocational schools, and in many towns there is overlapping between secondary and vocational schools and the higher standards of primary schools. Such co-ordination would secure that primary school reading books contain matter of a practical vocational nature, that subjects which are prerequisites for vocational education, such as rural science and drawing, should find a place in the curriculum of primary schools, and, above all, that pupils leaving primary schools are sufficiently proficient to profit by vocational education. Continuation education has at times been provided at great expense for unsuitable students; the work could possibly be done by lengthening the course at the primary schools or extending the existing secondary schools.

III.14 Introduction of the Day Group Certificate Examination, 1947

Following the passing of the 1930 Vocational Education Act, guidelines were issued by the Department of Education in relation to the courses and subjects to be offered in vocational schools. The continuation courses, which were 2-year courses, were organised in groups as follows:

1. Preparatory course (co-educational for general subjects)
2. Junior technical course (boys)
3. Junior domestic science course (girls)
4. Junior commercial course (girls)
5. Junior commercial course (boys)
6. Junior rural course (boys)
7. Junior rural course (girls).

Initially there was no nationally certified examination for pupils who followed these courses, but a special committee which was appointed by the Technical Instruction Congress in June 1942 recommended the introduction of a national examination. This examination was held for the first time in June 1947 and the following extract from the Annual Report of the Department of Education, 1946-47, gives details of the examination courses and of the general results of the first examination held in 1947:

(A) GROUP CERTIFICATE EXAMINATIONS

In accordance with the Report of the Special Committee appointed by the Technical Instruction Congress in June, 1942, an examination for Group certificates was held for the first time in June, 1947. The examination was intended for students who had completed a two years' course in a whole-time day Vocational School. Examinations were held for five groups as follows:

(i) A General Certificate in Commerce
(ii) A Secretarial Certificate in Commerce
(iii) A Certificate in Domestic Science
(iv) A Certificate in Manual Training
(v) A Certificate in Rural Science.

In Commerce two Certificates were provided to meet the two main divisions into which the day commerce courses are generally divided. For the General Certificate in Commerce candidates had to pass written tests in Book-keeping. Commercial Arithmetic and Commerce and an oral test in Irish. They could also take written tests in one or more of six optional subjects. In the Secretarial Certificate which is intended for those training as Shorthand-Typists, the compulsory subjects are: Shorthand, Typewriting, Commerce, and Oral Irish. Candidates could also select one or more of six optional subjects.

Candidates for the Domestic Science Certificate were required to pass practical tests in Cookery, Needlework, Laundrywork and Household Management, a written test in Tíos, and oral test in Irish. They could also select one or more of six optional subjects.

To qualify for the Certificates in Manual Training candidates were obliged to pass a practical test in Woodwork or Metalwork, a written test in Mechanical Drawing, and an oral test in Irish. They could take both practical subjects and were at liberty to select one or more of six optional subjects.

For the Rural Science Certificate, candidates must pass a practical test in Woodwork or Metalwork, a written test in Rural Science, and an Oral Test in Irish. They may also enter for written tests in one or more of seven optional subjects.

Certificates were awarded to candidates who passed in the Compulsory Subjects. Any successes secured in the optional subjects were endorsed on the Certificates. To pass a candidate had to secure 50 per cent in a written test and 60 per cent in a practical test.

The general results of the first examination are given in the following table:

Group	Number of students who		Pass %
	Entered	Passed	
Commerce Group — General	413	155	37.5
Commerce Group — Secretarial	102	29	28.7
Domestic Science Group	275	168	61.1
Manual Training Group	561	330	58.8
Rural Science Group	124	46	37.0
TOTAL	1,475	728	49.4

Results in the Domestic Science and Manual Training Groups were good. Better results would have been obtained in the other groups but for the fact that the persistent demand from employers had depleted the numbers in the second year classes in advance of the examination. Generally it was the more intelligent students — those who would have done well in the examination — who were selected for employment.

III.15 Apprenticeship Act, 1959

The full title of the Apprenticeship Act of 1959 was as follows:

> AN ACT TO MAKE BETTER PROVISION FOR THE REGULATION OF APPRENTICESHIP IN CERTAIN TRADES AND FOR THAT PURPOSE TO ESTABLISH A BODY TO BE KNOWN AS AN CHEARD-CHOMHAIRLE AND TO DEFINE ITS POWERS AND DUTIES, TO REPEAL THE APPRENTICESHIP ACT, 1931, AND TO PROVIDE FOR OTHER MATTERS CONNECTED WITH THE MATTERS AFORESAID.

The establishment of an Cheard-Chomhairle provided a new structure for the recruitment, education, examination and certification of apprentices.

The following sections from the act refer to the education and examination of apprentices:

39. — (1) An Chomhairle may make arrangements for the provision by a vocational education committee of courses of instruction in the nature of technical education of a type which An Chomhairle and the vocational education committee agree is suitable for persons employed by way of apprenticeship, in a designated trade, in an apprenticeship district for the purposes of the trade.

(2) Where a course of instruction is provided under subsection (1) of this section by a vocational education committee for persons employed by way of apprenticeship, in a designated trade, in an apprenticeship district for the purposes of the trade, the apprenticeship committee for the district and the trade may —

(a) by notice in writing served on a person employed by way of apprenticeship in the trade and in the district require him to attend the whole of the course, and

(b) by notice in writing served on the employer of a person upon whom a notice under paragraph (a) of this subsection has been served require the employer to afford to the person time and liberty to attend the whole of the course and to sit for any examinations held in relation to the course during normal working hours without any deduction from wages or any addition to the hours of employment or reckoning such time as lost.

(3) Where a person upon whom a notice under paragraph (a) of subsection (2) of this section has been served is allowed time and liberty to attend, during normal working hours, an instruction which is part of a course provided under subsection (1) of this section and fails to attend, then, notwithstanding anything contained in his contract with his employer, he shall not be entitled to receive the amount of any pay (being pay which he would otherwise be entitled to receive) which is apportionable to the period of his absence from his employment by way of apprenticeship unless he satisfies his employer that his failure to attend the instruction was due to sickness or other unavoidable cause.

41 — (1) An apprenticeship committee shall from time to time arrange, through An Chomhairle, with the Minister for Education for the holding, for persons employed by way of

apprenticeship in the trade for which the committee is established and in the district of the committee, of—

(a) a junior examination for persons who have completed approximately half their periods of apprenticeship, and
(b) a senior examination for persons who are nearing the completion of, or have completed, those periods.

(2)(a) The subjects to be included in, and the standard for, examinations under this section shall be determined by the Minister for Education after consultation with the apprenticeship committee concerned.
(b) Examinations under this section shall include practical tests.

(3) The conditions governing entry for examinations under this section shall be determined by the apprenticeship committee concerned after consultation with the Minister for Education.

(4) A person who fails an examination under this section may, at the discretion of the apprenticeship committee concerned, be allowed to undergo such examination again.

III.16 Vocational Education (Amendment) Act, 1970

During the 1960s there was a move towards comprehensivisation of post-primary education in Ireland (see III.18 to III.20). The first comprehensive schools had been opened in the mid 1960s and by 1970 there were plans to supersede these by a new type of school, the community school (III.22). To enable the Vocational Education Committees to become involved in the management structures of the proposed community schools, an amendment to the 1930 Act was necessary and this amendment was passed in August 1970. The following is the full text of the Vocational Education (Amendment) Act, 1970:

AN ACT TO AMEND AND EXTEND
THE VOCATIONAL EDUCATION ACTS, 1930 TO 1962.
(5th August 1970)

BE IT ENACTED BY THE OIREACHTAS AS FOLLOWS:

1. — Subject to the consent of the Minister and to such terms and conditions as may be agreed between the parties, a vocational education committee may, jointly with a person maintaining such school as may be recognised by the Minister for the purposes of this section —

(a) establish and maintain in its area in accordance with the Vocational Education Acts, 1930 to 1962, a suitable system of continuation education and provide for the progressive development of that system,

(b) establish and maintain in its area continuation schools and technical schools,

(c) establish and maintain in its area such courses of instruction in the nature of continuation education and technical education as it considers necessary.

2.— Section 108 of the Vocational Education Act, 1930, is hereby amended by the substitution of the following subsection for subsection (4):

(4)(a)The Minister shall by regulations provide for an election (in this subsection referred to as a new election) of members of a vocational education committee (in this subsection referred to as a dissolved committee) which has been dissolved under this section, to take place at any time not later than the end of the second election year after the dissolved committee has been so dissolved, and upon the completion of such new election all the properties, powers and duties of the dissolved committee shall vest in the committee so elected, notwithstanding that the same may have been transferred by the Minister under this section to any other body, persons, or person.

(b) Section 9 (2) of the Principal Act shall not apply to a new election.

(c) Notwithstanding any other provision of this Act, no election other than a new election shall take place in respect of a dissolved committee.

3. — (1) This Act may be cited as the Vocational Education (Amendment) Act, 1970.

(2) The Vocational Education Acts, 1930 to 1962, and this Act may be cited together as the Vocational Education Acts, 1930 to 1970.

(3) The Vocational Education Acts, 1930 to 1962, and this Act shall be construed as one.

III.17 Establishment of Boards of Management of Vocational Schools — Circular letter 73/74 — July 1974

The principle of setting up boards of management to manage post-primary schools had been established in the comprehensive and community schools in the 1960s and early 1970s. By the mid 1970s agreement had also been reached between the Department, the INTO and management bodies in relation to boards of management for national schools. In July 1974, a circular was sent to each V.E.C. suggesting that a board of management be set up for each vocational school. The following extracts from circular 73/74 indicate the composition and functions of such boards:

****

The Minister wishes to suggest that Vocational Education Committees should avail themselves of the powers conferred upon them by Section 21 of the Vocational Education Act to set up a sub-committee in respect of each vocational school in their schemes which would act as a Board of Management of that school.

The composition, procedure and functions which the Minister considers appropriate to these suggested Boards of Management are set out in the attached memorandum.

Boards of Management constituted in accordance with the terms of this circular should come into operation by the 31st October 1974.

COMPOSITION

1. Each Board shall consist of four members of the Vocational Education Committee and two parents (one of whom shall be a mother) of children receiving education in the school, elected by the parents of children receiving education in the school.

2.(a) Subject to his/her remaining a member of the V.E.C., each Committee's representative will continue to be a member of the Board of Management during the term of office of the V.E.C., subject to the right of the Committee to remove him/her at any time or subject to his/her own right to indicate to the Committee that he/she no longer wishes to remain a member of the Board of Management.

(b) Each representative of the parents will continue to be a member of the Board of Management for so long as he/she is a parent of a pupil attending the school or for the term of office of the V.E.C. whichever is the shorter; subject to his/her right to indicate that he/she no longer wishes to serve as a member of the Board of Management.

(c) A vacancy occurring in the membership of the Board, if it occurs among the representatives of the V.E.C., shall be filled by the V.E.C. from its own members. If it occurs among the parents' representatives, it shall be filled on the election by parents entitled to vote of a representative in accordance with the terms of section 1.

(d) The first Board of Management should be constituted without delay. The nomination and election of an incoming Board should normally be made and done not later than 31st October following the first meeting of the incoming V.E.C. and the first meeting of the incoming Board should normally be held not later than two weeks after its constitution by nomination and election.

****

FUNCTIONS

General

6. The Board shall have responsibility for the general management of the school, subject to the Department's regulations. It will ensure, as far as possible, that the school is adequately equipped and maintained and will report any deficiencies to the Committee for remedy. It will ensure that classes are held on time and in accordance with the timetable.

7. The Board shall determine the uses for community purposes of the school building or grounds at times which will not affect school work.

Finance

8. (a) The Board shall submit to the Committee before a day appointed by the Committee in each year an estimate in such form as the Committee may require of the income and expenditure required for the school during the following financial year.

(b) The Board shall arrange for the making of petty cash disbursements in respect of postage and other minor items and may, subject to such conditions as it thinks fit to impose, delegate this responsibility to the Principal.

Staff Council

9. (a) The Board shall set up a Staff Council, consisting of all teachers of the school under the chairmanship of the Principal.

(b) The Staff Council will consider the curricular arrangements of the school and may make recommendations to the Board regarding the extension of the subject range, the arranging of the timetable and the provision of school equipment.

(c) The Staff Council may, on request, advise the Board on any educational problem which the Board may put before it. The Council may, on its own initiative, make submissions to the Board on any educational matter connected with the school

Religion

10.(a) In exercising its general control over the curriculum and conduct of the school, the Board shall ensure that there is religious worship and religious instruction for the pupils in the school except for such pupils whose parents make a request in writing to the Principal that those pupils should be withdrawn from religious worship or religious instruction or both religious worship and religious instruction.

(b) The religious worship attended by any pupil at the school and the religious instruction given to any pupil shall be in accordance with the rites, practice and teaching of the religious denomination to which the pupil belongs. At least 2½ hours religious instruction as aforesaid shall be given to all the pupils in the school [except those who are withdrawn from religious instruction in accordance with the provisions of sub-paragraph (a) above] in each week during which the school is in session.

(c) If any question arises whether the religious worship conducted or the religious instruction given is or is not in accordance with the rites, practice and teaching of a religious denomination, that question shall be determined by the competent religious authority. Such religious worship and religious instruction may be inspected under arrangements made for this purpose by the competent religious authority on such days and at such times and with such notice as may be agreed from time to time by the competent religious authority and the Board.

(d) The Principal shall be immediately responsible for making arrangements for all the religious worship conducted and for the religious instruction given at the school and for the attendance of pupils thereat.

(e) The Board shall endeavour to ensure that there are at all times sufficient teachers in the school who are appointed, with the approval of the competent religious authority, to give religious instruction as aforesaid.

Home/School Association

11.(a) The Board shall arrange for the setting up of a Home/School Association (the officers of which shall be V.E.C. members of the Board) consisting of the Board of Management, the teachers and the parents of children receiving education in the school.

(b) At regular intervals throughout the year the Board shall convene meetings of the Home/School Association to discuss matters relating to the school.

III.18 Statement by the Minister for Education, Dr. P.J. Hillery, in regard to Post-Primary Education, 20 May 1963.

In 1962, the government, in conjunction with the Organisation for Economic Co-Operation and Development, had set up a survey team to carry out an analysis of Irish educational needs. The report of this team, Investment in Education, was not published until 1965 but by 1963 it was already clear that the government was planning significant new initiatives in Irish education (see I.10). The first indications of this were contained in a statement issued by the Minister for Education, Dr. P.J. Hillery, on 20 May 1963. This was a major policy statement which indicated the direction of educational change in the subsequent decade and included notice of the government's intention to set up comprehensive schools; to extend the two year course in vocational schools to three years and to allow pupils in vocational schools to follow the Intermediate Certificate course. In the statement, the Minister gave details of a proposal to introduce a Technical Leaving Certificate and to set up Regional Technical Colleges.

Apart from the specific proposals which it contained, the general tenor of the statement was unprecedented in the history of Irish education. For the first time, the Irish government would be directly involved in setting up post-primary schools. The statement made it clear that the Department of Education would no longer take a back seat in relation to educational provision but that from now on it could be expected to take an active role in educational planning. The following extracts are taken from Dr. Hillery's statement:

12.... As I see it, the equality of educational opportunity towards which it is the duty of the State to strive must nowadays entail the opportunity of some post-primary education for all.

14.... Provision needs to be made for those for whom neither a secondary nor a vocational school will be available and that provision should contain such variety as to offer a choice of curricula.

.... in Dáil Eireann three years ago I stated that I had no use for an eleven plus or a twelve plus or a thirteen plus test. The overwhelming argument against a selection process at those ages is that it is still too early to decide once and for all on the direction which a child's career should take.

15.... I am convinced that the answer to this particular problem must therefore introduce a new principle into Irish education, namely direct State provision of a post-primary school building.

16. The new type of school I have in mind is a comprehensive post-primary day school. It would provide for children of age about 12-13 to about 15-16 a three year course during which observation and tests would show with fair probability in which direction, academic or technical, each pupil's bent would eventually lie. At the end of the three years in the comprehensive section the pupil would take the Intermediate Certificate Examination, which in any case it may be necessary to amend in several ways. If he passed that Examination he could, if he so wished, proceed to the secondary or technical course, in accordance with his previous showing at the Comprehensive school and at the Intermediate Certificate Examination.

****

18. The Schools envisaged would therefore be Comprehensive schools. They would be open to all children within a radius of about 10 miles. Transport services would accordingly have to be provided for, say, all pupils within the prescribed radius living 3 miles or over from the school. Such pupils would be charged for transport a flat rate of so much per day, the remaining cost of fares to fall on the school budget. There would be a reasonable school fee which could be reduced in cases of hardship.

19. The curriculum of the School would entail for all its pupils a common core consisting of Irish, English, Mathematics and some form of hand-and-eye training (e.g. Drawing, Manual Instruction). Other subjects provided for would be History, Geography, Latin, one (or, where possible, more than one) Continental language, Science, Rural Science, Art, Singing and so on. There is no need to specify Religious Instruction, provision for it must be taken for granted.

If then, for example, after a year's observation it were found that a pupil, having chosen a particular optional subject of an academic type had no aptitude for it, he could thereafter drop that subject and be guided towards one of a more "practical" nature. In this regard, while the entire three years would be an "observation period" of the pupil's aptitude, the first year would be particularly such. What I have just said does not of course purport to give more than a general idea of the work envisaged.

20. In the areas concerned the vast majority or perhaps all of the pupils will be Catholics and having regard to the rights of parents, who in relation to the fundamental principles of education are represented by the Church, and in view of the Church's teaching authority, I have had consultation, which is proceeding, with the Catholic hierarchy on the management of these schools. I am satisfied that it will be possible in each case to constitute a committee of management which will be acceptable to all the interested parties. In this regard I would add that a proposal for the provision of a Comprehensive school of this kind for Protestants, if related to a suitable region, would be welcomed by me.

****

22. Generally the school would cater for a minimum of 150 pupils. Anything less than that number would not permit of the wide variety of subjects that should be included in the curriculum of a Comprehensive school of the sort.

23. So much for the Comprehensive three years junior course. The next question to be considered is the catering for the products of that junior course. Some could at the end of the course (or, naturally, if they so desired, even before that) elect to leave for posts of one kind or another. Other pupils leaving at the end of the course would be those who had failed to benefit adequately from the opportunity they had been given. With regard to the remainder, educational opinion nowadays, while insisting on a rounded education, would seem to favour also a reasonable degree of specialisation after fifteen or sixteen years of age. This then, and not eleven or twelve or thirteen plus, would be the moment for a dividing into the academical and technical camps.

Those of an academic bent would present no great difficulty. They would enter on the Secondary Schools Leaving Certificate course and special arrangements by scholarship or otherwise would be made to facilitate their continued education.

In relation to those with a technical or practical bent I visualise some of them leaving to be apprentices and some of them being catered for in a local technical school which would function either as a senior storey of the Comprehensive School or as a separate technical school. The others, particularly the brilliant among them, raise a problem which is part of a much bigger issue.

****

24.... I believe therefore that the time has come to take a firm step forward in technical education. Accordingly, it is my intention shortly to establish a Technical Schools Leaving Certificate and concomitantly with that to arrange with the appropriate Vocational Education Committees for the provision of a limited number of Technological Colleges with regional status in which the course for that Certificate will be provided.

26. Now I come to the general problem. That general problem is the ill effect, already referred to, which arises from the secondary school and the vocational school operating in watertight compartments. The solution contemplated by me for that situation is not unrelated to the idea of the Comprehensive school and may indeed be said to stem from that pattern. What I have in mind is that within a reasonable period the present two years day course in vocational schools should be extended to three years. I then visualise that pupils who should have completed that three years course would sit, in common with secondary school pupils, for examination in the core subjects — Irish, English and Mathematics — of the Intermediate Certificate Examination, together with two or three more subjects from the widened Intermediate Certificate curriculum. That widened curriculum would give greater scope for practical subjects. It would also cater for the distinctive character and function of the secondary and the vocational school. The great advantage of a common examination would be to give parity of standard to the courses in the two types of school. In any case, a three years course in the vocational school is desirable as a foundation for the Technical Schools Leaving Certificate.

27. In summing up, let me claim for the plan which I have just outlined that it is not set in Hy Brasil or Never-Never Land but would solve in a practical way and within a reasonable time

the main problems of our post-primary education. Firstly, it would cater for a sector of our people whose call for education beyond the primary stage for their children has hitherto been largely unanswered. Secondly, the three years vocational school course envisaged, together with the bringing of the vocational stream throughout the country to a parity of standard and evaluation with the present secondary school stream, would in itself be a very important educational and social reform. Thirdly, the superstructure of the Technical Schools Leaving Certificate with as its supporting base the three years vocational school and the secondary school intermediate courses would give the country a systematic supply of youth with a sufficient technical education to become at a later stage the technicians and higher technicians the country is, as we must all hope, going to need. Fourthly, the examination in common for both secondary and vocational school pupils at the Intermediate Certificate stage would ensure a common standard of work in all our post-primary schools. Finally, the whole plan is a move in the direction, not only of a better coordination of our entire educational system but of equality of educational opportunity.

III.19 Investment in Education - 1966.

The appointment of a survey team by the Minister for Education in October 1962 to report on the Irish educational system has been referred to in an earlier section (I.11). The report of the team, published in 1966, was fact-finding and analytic and its findings in relation to second-level education were to lead to major reform in the subsequent decade. The report compared the probable manpower requirements and the probable supply of suitably-qualified personnel for the projected labour force and estimated that there would be serious deficiencies in the number of persons holding educational certificates at different levels of achievement. In relation to pupil participation, it was found that over 55% of an age cohort dropped out of school before obtaining either the Intermediate Certificate or the Group Certificate. The report also produced evidence that participation rates at both second and third level education were closely related to social class and that geographical location was a factor in the inequality of educational participation. As regards curriculum, the team found that the curriculum in a large number of secondary schools was limited; in boys' schools, classical languages were emphasised but very few boys studied a modern continental language. Science teaching suffered from a lack of laboratories and little attention was paid to aesthetic subjects. The report also drew attention to the large number of very small second-level schools, pointing out that 64% of secondary schools and 73% of vocational schools had less than 150 pupils on rolls.

It is interesting to note that while various strategies were suggested for improving and rationalising the situation, the Investment in Education report did not envisage the introduction of free post-primary education. Various approaches to improving post-primary provision throughout the country were discussed and it was suggested that "it might be useful to adopt solutions which make the maximum use of existing facilities rather than seek to impose a uniform pattern on all areas."

The following extracts from Chapter 12 of the Report give examples of the approach taken by the survey team:

12.24 It may be useful to summarise the existing position regarding post-primary facilities. Until recent years at any rate, the Minister for Education did not assume any direct responsibility for providing such facilities. His function was interpreted as being rather to assist private enterprise and local bodies to provide such facilities as they deemed appropriate and practicable. In consequence the existing pattern of facilities is rather diverse as Table 12.1 indicates.

12.25 Given these figures it would seem that on the basis of present organisational arrangements (e.g. separate boys' secondary, girls' secondary and vocational schools) it would be extremely difficult to provide full facilities in all, especially smaller centres. In particular it would seem from the data of chapter 10 that the smaller centres would probably result in schools which were both expensive to operate and likely to lead to incomplete coverage of subjects.

12.26 In theory then, while post-primary education could be provided in national schools (secondary tops), in vocational schools, in secondary schools, or in the recently announced comprehensive schools, in practice it is likely that in most areas local conditions will reduce the number of effective choices. Consequently it might be useful to adopt solutions which make the maximum use of existing facilities rather than seek to impose a uniform pattern on all areas.

****

PARTICIPATION

12.34 The data of chapter 6 showed that there are significant differences in the extent to which various groups participate in education. Such differences are evident both as between socio-economic groups and between geographical areas. We were unable to examine differences in participation as between various income groups since the necessary data on income distribution are not available.

12.35 While there are no doubt wider and more fundamental considerations which would support any case for greater participation in education, it would seem that there are also economic grounds for seeking to promote such a development. Thus the manpower aspects discussed above are to a large extent bound up with the question of participation, since increased numbers of certificants must largely come from those who otherwise would not be participating in the educational system at that level.

12.36 The participation problem affects every level and division of the educational system. The main stages where different rates of performance were found to occur, are:

(1) rate of progress through primary school
(2) rate of entry to post-primary school
(3) rate of continuance in post-primary school
(4) rate of entry to university and other third-level establishments.

Children of parents in certain social groups including those with lowest income, were found to have a higher probability of failing to maintain their position at each of the stages (2) to (4). This is probably true also of the primary stage and also drop-out at third level, which we were not in a position to analyse. Hence it is unlikely that improving the situation at just one of these stages would be sufficient to ensure a wider participation pattern throughout.

12.37 In general it might be taken that within the context of the existing system, the measures which would stimulate participation on the part of under-represented groups would be the same as those suggested above in connection with manpower, namely, an increase in the number of scholarships or grants available, increased provision of educational facilities and wider dissemination of information regarding educational opportunities. If, however, the object is to stimulate participation by those groups with low participation rates, it may be necessary to be more specific in the type of measure used.

****

12.50 From an organisational viewpoint the first step towards dealing with the problem might be to define, even provisionally, post-primary school districts. Such a definition might be based on the concept that (with limited exceptions for whom special provisions would be made) each such district would (1) have available within it a complete range of post-primary facilities whether or not they were available in one school or even one centre, (2) the potential pupils in each such district would be classified into three or four distance categories with respect to the post-primary facilities. These categories might, for example be (i) within a mile of chosen or nearest acceptable facilities, (ii) within 5 miles of chosen or nearest acceptable facilities, (iii) within effective bus distance (e.g. 10 miles) of chosen or nearest acceptable facilities, (iv) outside effective bus distance of chosen or nearest acceptable facilities; (3) that some responsibility for the transport of children in category (iii), and the boarding expenses of children in category (iv), would be accepted by the State, either directly or through authorized local bodies, (4) that adequate space and teacher facilities to cover pupils in that district in categories (i) to (iii) should be available.

****

EFFICIENCY

12.71 *Post-Primary Schools.* Associated with the problem of securing an improved participation pattern, in the sense of adequate access to subjects and facilities, is the problem of the efficient use of scarce resources in post-primary education. This problem will be particularly acute at junior cycle level if several educational divisions (i.e. national, secondary, vocational and comprehensive) are catering for the same age group (12-15). Among the most scarce resources in Irish post-primary education are: (i) certain kinds of teachers, (ii) certain kinds of relatively expensive equipment such as (a) science laboratories, (b) language laboratories, (c) film projectors, teaching machines and similar equipment, (d) metal and woodworking shops, (e) libraries. It would appear that at the present time the kinds of teachers who are scarce are graduate teachers of (a) mathematics, (b) science, (c) rural science, (d) modern languages and (e) metalwork and engineering teachers. Some of these shortages are more acute in the case of women (e.g. mathematics) or men (e.g. modern languages).

12.72 On the other hand where such resources exist they are frequently not effectively utilised. This applies both to teachers and equipment. As regards equipment it is frequently due to the small numbers of pupils who have direct access to it and to a series of conventions and regulations preventing or discouraging wider utilisation of these facilities.

****

12.81 In the case of smaller centres, which account for about two-fifths of the schools and one-quarter of the pupils, it has been shown already that the problem of developing the existing rather fragmentary provision of post-primary facilities is a complex one. Its solution would appear to involve a considerable re-organisation of the existing system going far beyond the type of administrative changes outlined above for the larger centres, which are designed to facilitate improved use of specialist resources (either teachers or equipment) while maintaining the present pattern of separate provision for different groups of pupils on the basis of various criteria. However, pending a full scale review of the necessary organisational changes, and to some extent independently of any such changes, it might be possible to make specialised resources available to pupils in these centres by adopting a flexible approach to the problem. In particular, the use of itinerant teachers (already in use in the vocational system) and mobile equipment might contribute to a solution of the problem. Similarly the use of teaching machines with suitable programmes might be investigated. Such aids would of course need to be tried out in carefully observed experimental conditions and scientifically evaluated before they would be made available generally. The main burden of the solution in these centres, however, would appear to rest on major organisational changes.

****

FINANCE

12.83 There are many other aspects of education which would merit discussion and consideration, whether the primary interest is manpower, participation or efficiency. The above discussions are in no way intended to be comprehensive, but rather to illustrate the type of problem involved. Before concluding this brief examination it may be appropriate to indicate some of the scope for re-organisation in the area of finance. The one factor common to many of the earlier suggestions was that they would each cost a substantial amount, hence financial arrangements are clearly of some importance.

12.84 The brief discussion in chapter 11 suggested that the greatest scope for reviewing financing methods lay in the fields of post-primary and university education. It was noted that existing arrangements confer an automatic subsidy on all aided post-primary and university pupils, while a second subsidy is in effect conferred on pupils whose families are in a position to benefit from income-tax concessions.

12.85 Taking first the case of scholarships for post-primary schools the earlier discussion in chapter 11 suggested that if in fact the aim of such scholarships is to provide some form of equality of opportunity, there may be grounds for altering their form and, in particular allowing their value to vary with the circumstances of each family, along the lines suggested earlier.

12.86 In the case of secondary schools there may be scope for a more extensive re-arrangement of financing. The total number of pupils with scholarships in 1963/64 was just under 5,000 or less than 6 per cent of secondary school pupils while total scholarship expenditure at a maximum of £360,000 annually is of the order of 7 to 8 per cent of state spending on secondary schools. Accordingly, the opportunity might be taken to broaden the scope of scholarship schemes, while at the same time furthering other objectives in this field. For instance, the present system of capitation grants is in effect a scholarship awarded to every pupil, without regard to ability and without any assessment of his needs.

III.20 Letter from George Colley, T.D., Minister for Education to the Authorities of Secondary and Vocational Schools, January 1966.

The report "Investment in Education" was published in 1965. However, from 1963 onwards, various initiatives had been taken which indicated that changes were on the agenda for Irish education, especially at post-primary level. In January 1966, George Colley, T.D., Minister for Education, issued a letter to the authorities of secondary and vocational schools in which he outlined the future policy of his Department. His four page letter called for "equality of educational opportunity" and he commended the authorities of secondary and vocational schools for their "initiative and enterprise," stating that as a result of their efforts there were 600 secondary schools and 300 vocational schools in the country. It was now possible to "envisage as a practical proposition in the near future the provision of post-primary education for all the children of the country; more than that, to envisage the provision of an education suited to the many different aptitudes and abilities of these children."

The following extracts are taken from the Minister's letter:

TO THE AUTHORITIES OF SECONDARY AND VOCATIONAL SCHOOLS

A Cháirde,

In the course of the discussions which I have had recently with various educational bodies, proposals for the improvement of our post-primary system were examined and a very considerable degree of unanimity arrived at. It seems to me that we are now at the stage when the future policy of my Department should be outlined to all concerned in the provision of post-primary education. I write accordingly to you because I look to you to accord me your full cooperation in the effort to provide for every pupil, to the greatest extent which our resources will allow, an education suited to his needs and aptitudes.

****

The Government has already signified its intention to raise the school-leaving age by the end of this decade. This step will create problems of accommodation and teaching power as well as of curriculum content. The solutions to the problems must be found before the raising of the school-leaving age becomes effective and it is my intention to seek them without delay. But the first step must be to consider how the facilities now available can be used to best advantage.

Hitherto, for reasons which it is not necessary to examine here, Secondary schools and Vocational schools pursued their educational endeavours along widely separated paths; indeed they formed two separate systems, each with its own schools, its own curricula and courses of study, its own examinations and its own cadre of teachers. The Secondary system offered courses of an academic nature almost entirely, while those offered by the Vocational system were mainly of a practical nature. The student opting for either system was required to take the courses offered by the system of his choice, regardless of where his abilities lay. Those suited to the system received an excellent educational service; those not suited, in number not inconsiderable, made the best they could of it.

There are two good reasons, at least, for urging that the barriers between the systems be broken down: first, the denial of a suitable education tends towards frustration in the pupil; second, our national survival demands the full use of all the talents of our citizens.

The first steps in this direction have already been taken. It has been decided that from 1969 the Intermediate Certificate Examination will be open to candidates from the Secondary and Vocational schools in common. New courses have been added and the subject syllabuses are being revised. The courses and syllabuses thus revised will be issued during the current school year and will be effective for both Secondary and Vocational schools in September, 1966. Since the courses will require a minimum of three years' study — on which the pupils will generally enter between the ages of 12 and 13 — the present day continuation course in Vocational schools is extended from two to three years.

****

As you are aware, my Department is at present engaged in a survey of the facilities available in all post-primary schools in this country. This survey, when completed, together with the information already available in regard to school population, will enable us to answer in regard to any area in the country such questions as (1) what is the number of pupils for whom post-primary provision is needed? (2) what facilities are needed to provide for these pupils? (3) what facilities are already available in the area? (4) what additional facilities are needed? The processing of the information so collected will take some considerable time. I feel we cannot afford to wait.

While the time has come when the operation of two rigidly separated post-primary systems can no longer be maintained, this is not to say that the Secondary or the Vocational school need lose its distinctive character. What I have in mind is that there should be a pooling of forces so that the shortcomings of one will be met from the resources of the other, thus making available to the student in either school the post-primary education best suited to him. For example, the Vocational school could afford facilities for the teaching of woodwork to pupils of the Secondary school while that school would give facilities for the teaching of Science to the pupils of the Vocational school. The provision of any necessary additions to the existent facilities would be by arrangement with the authorities of both schools.

As you are aware, comprehensive schools are in the course of erection in three localities — Cootehill, Carraroe and Shannon. These schools will provide post-primary education for all pupils in their areas. They will offer a very broad curriculum, comprising both academic and vocational disciplines. The services of psychological as well as teaching personnel will be available to guide the pupils in regard to the courses of study best suited to their abilities. Apart from their local importance these schools are of general significance because they will signpost the way to an integrated post-primary system of education. Let me add that I do not anticipate that the number of public comprehensive schools will be very great. My aim is that Secondary and Vocational schools, by the exchange of facilities and by other forms of collaboration, should make available a curriculum broad enough to serve the individual needs of all their students, and thereby to provide the basis of a comprehensive system in each locality.

****

Problems will arise. Indeed, I am already aware of some of the difficulties in the way of effective cooperation and collaboration. Insofar as these problems concern my Department I do assure you that I will use all the resources available to me to find satisfactory solutions. The welfare of the pupil is our common purpose and I am confident that with mutual good-will and cooperation we cannot fail to improve our educational system and offer better opportunities to all the pupils in our schools.

III.21 Speech made by Donogh O'Malley, Minister for Education, on 10th September 1966 announcing the introduction of free post-primary education:

Donogh O'Malley was appointed Minister for Education in July 1966 to replace George Colley. Only 8 months had passed since Colley had sent a letter to second-level school authorities in which he had said that "it is now possible to envisage as a practical proposition in the near future the provision of post-primary education for all the children of the country" (III.20). However, there was no indication at that time that free post-primary education was being considered.

Consequently, when Donogh O'Malley, in his first major speech as Minister for Education on 10th September 1966, announced to the National Union of Journalists that he proposed to introduce a scheme "whereby up to the completion of the Intermediate Certificate course, the opportunity for free post-primary education will be available for all families," there was widespread enthusiasm and excitement. During the subsequent months considerable activity took place at school and department levels in preparation for the introduction of free post-primary education in September 1967. Arrangements were put in place for providing free transport and additional school accommodation. Negotiations took place between the department and the school authorities about the basis on which schools would provide free education and the scheme, when finalised, went even further than envisaged by O'Malley in his initial announcement. Those schools which participated in the "free" scheme received an additional grant from the department in lieu of fees and this grant applied to pupils at both junior and senior cycle level. Consequently, free education became available for the full second level cycle, not just "up to the completion of the Intermediate Certificate course" as announced by O'Malley.

However, the additional grant in lieu of fees — a maximum of £25 per pupil — was less than the fees charged by Protestant secondary schools. Therefore a special scheme of means-tested grants was devised for pupils attending schools under Protestant management. The Department recognised that the grants could be paid at a higher level to Protestant pupils who had no option but to be boarders if they were to attend a school of their own tradition.

In subsequent years, the cost of "free" second level education increased significantly and the "grant in lieu of fees" paid by the Department to second-level schools failed to keep pace with inflation, thus making it very difficult for schools to make ends meet and requiring them in many cases to look for a voluntary contribution from parents and to engage in fund-raising activities. Nevertheless the "free scheme" was very successful in terms of providing access to second level education. In 1966 Donogh O'Malley made the point that 17,000 pupils finished their education at primary school level. Within a decade this number had fallen to about 4,000. The total numbers attending second level schools doubled within ten years and have trebled since then. In 1991, 60,000 pupils sat the Leaving Certificate examination as compared to less than 10,000 in 1963. The following extracts are taken from O'Malley's speech:

We are not a nation which can deploy substantial financial resources. We must allocate resources as priorities demand. Productive investment must come first. Investment in education must get priority, for it is a form of productive investment which is vital not only to our future economic development but to the entire national fabric of the growing nation....

.... education must move with the times it is meant to serve. The world of to-day and to-morrow will give scant attention to the uneducated and those lacking in qualifications. We will be judged by future generations on what we did for the children of our time....

There is, of course, a lot remaining to be done with our education system. And I am convinced that we must attack the fundamental weaknesses in that system on a full national scale. And we must begin right away.

There is no difficulty in picking out the basic fault in our present educational structure — and that is, the fact that many of our families cannot afford to pay even part of the cost of education for their children....

Every year, some 17,000 of our children finishing their primary school course do not receive any further education. This means that almost one in three of our future citizens are cut off at this stage from the opportunities of learning a skill, and denied the benefits of cultural development that go with further education.

This is a dark stain on the national conscience. For it means that some one-third of our people have been condemned — the great majority through no fault of their own — to be part-educated unskilled labour, always the weaker who go to the wall of unemployment or emigration.

I believe that this is a situation which must be tackled with all speed and determination. And I am glad to be able to announce to-night that I am drawing up a scheme under which, in future, no boy or girl in this State will be deprived of full educational opportunity — from primary to university level — by reason of the fact that the parents cannot afford to pay for it......

I propose, therefore, from the coming school year, beginning in September of next year, to introduce a scheme whereby, up to the completion of the Intermediate Certificate course, the opportunity for free post-primary education will be available to all families.

This free education will be available in the comprehensive and vocational schools, and in the general run of secondary schools. I say the general run of secondary schools because there will still be schools, charging higher fees, who may not opt to take my scheme; and the parent who wants to send his child to one of these schools, and pay the fees, will of course be free to do so.

Going on from there, I intend, also, to make provision whereby no pupil will, for lack of means, be prevented from continuing his or her education up to the end of the Leaving Certificate course.

I propose that assistance towards the cost of books and accessories will be given, through the period of his or her course, to the student on whom it would be a hardship to meet all such costs.

We must, also, face up to the position of making financial aid available to the pupil who, because of the location of his home, can have post-primary education available to him only if he enters a boarding school.

Finally, there is the university level. While I do not at this stage wish to say anything which might cut across the recommendations of the Commission on Higher Education, I cannot let the occasion pass without referring to the plight of the pupil who has reached a good standard in the Leaving Certificate examination but who, due to the inability of his parents to pay, cannot proceed to a university or other such course of higher education. We must, and we will, come to the assistance of such a pupil. I, therefore, propose to put in train shortly the working out of a scheme to cater for such cases.

III.22 Dept. of Education — Community School document — October 1970.

In October 1970, a document entitled "Community School" was issued by the Department of Education. It was initially sent to the Catholic hierarchy and was subsequently more widely circulated. The document indicated that the proposed new community schools were to be seen in the context of government policy which supported the provision of free post-primary education for all children irrespective of ability and without the use of selection procedures. It was hoped that these schools would eliminate the barriers between secondary and vocational schools and would help to eliminate overlapping and duplication in the provision of teachers, buildings and equipment.

The appearance of the document caused quite a stir and the Minister for Education, Pádraig Faulkner, was asked in the Dáil on 18th November 1970 whether the document reflected Government policy. In reply to this question he said:

> .... On numerous occasions in this House and also in An Seanad I have referred to the necessity to secure in every area of the country post-primary educational provision which would be such as to cater for the aptitude and ability of all the pupils in the area. I referred in this respect also to the necessity to establish larger school units as no small school could by itself provide the range of subjects and facilities which would be required. The memorandum (of October 1970) .... was in the nature of a working document, not a circular. It brought together in a form suitable for discussion my ideas as to how what I had in mind could be achieved by the establishment of community schools.

Following discussion with various interested parties, the Minister issued a statement in May 1971 in which he set out the basis on which community schools would be established "in areas where under existing arrangements educationally viable post-primary schools could not be established."

The Minister originally proposed that community schools should have a board of management of six members — four nominated by the secondary school authorities and two by the V.E.C. The site and building would be vested in three trustees nominated by the Catholic bishop of the diocese and one of the trustees would be taken from names submitted by the local V.E.C. This proposal evoked considerable criticism and among those groups which opposed it were the I.V.E.A., the Presbyterian General Assembly and the Church of Ireland Board of Education. The controversy about the control and ownership of community schools continued throughout the 1970s and it was not until 1980 that Deeds of Trust were finally agreed. Under the terms of the Deeds of Trust the Catholic Church authorities could demand and get reserved teaching posts for members of religious orders, agreed conditions regarding religious teaching and paid Catholic chaplains.

The following is the full text of the statement of 13th May 1971 and of the memorandum of October 1970:

STATEMENT OF MINISTER FOR EDUCATION, PADRAIG FAULKNER, DATED 13TH MAY 1971

In connection with the consideration of the working document on community schools (copy herewith) the Minister for Education wishes to announce that following discussions with various interested parties it is his intention that the following proposals should form the basis for the establishment of these schools principally in areas where under existing arrangements educationally viable post-primary schools could not be established:

1. The Board of Management to consist of 6 members, 4 representatives nominated by the authorities of the secondary schools involved and 2 representatives nominated by the local Vocational Education Committee. All the members of the Board to be drawn exclusively from the local community i.e. from amongst persons residing within the catchment area of the school and two of the four representatives nominated by the secondary school authorities to be parents of children in the school. Membership of the Board to be for a period of five years. The Board to elect one of its members to be Chairman. The appointment of Secretary to be a matter for the Board save that in the event of the Principal not being appointed as Secretary to the Board, he be entitled to attend and take part other than in a voting capacity in the meetings of the Board except on certain occasions when the Board may decide otherwise.
2. It is envisaged that the Board would establish an Advisory Committee consisting of the Principal, Vice-Principal, and representatives of the teaching staff to assist in the running of the school.
3. The site and building would be vested in three trustees nominated by the Bishop of the diocese. One of these trustees to be taken from names furnished by the local Vocational Education Committee. The Minister for Education to be a party to the Deed of Trust.
4. The day to day running costs to be met by the Department of Education.

COMMUNITY SCHOOL (Memorandum of October, 1970)

1. The creation of community schools must be viewed against the background of Government policy in relation to post-primary schools and in particular the following aspects of that policy:-

(a) the provision of free post-primary education for all children irrespective of ability and without the use of selection procedures on transfer from primary to post-primary;

(b) the elimination of the barriers between secondary and vocational schools and the creation of a unified post-primary system of education;

(c) the provision of comprehensive facilities in each area of the country so as to cater for the varying aptitudes and abilities of pupils and to provide reasonable equality of educational opportunity for all our children irrespective of the area of the country in which they reside or the means of their parents;

(d) the elimination of overlapping and duplication in the provision of teachers, buildings and equipment so that the available resources in manpower and finance may be utilized to best advantage and so make resources available to improve the level of services in our post-primary schools.

2. The optimum size for a post-primary school is a matter to which a lot of attention has been given both here and elsewhere. The Advisory Councils for Dublin and Cork have recommended the creation of school units of 400 to 800 pupils. O.E.C.D. expressed the view a few years ago that the absolute minimum size was probably around the 450 mark. The Department's experience has been that in terms of the level of facilities which can be provided at a tolerable cost level, the optimum size is around 800 pupils. Generally the Department has accepted the views of the Dublin and Cork Advisory Councils and aims at the creation of school units of 400 to 800 pupils. It is accepted that given the present

distribution of post-primary schools in this country, it will not always be possible, at any rate in the foreseeable future, to create school units of 400 to 800 pupils everywhere but there are a number of small towns throughout the country which at present have two or three post-primary schools with a total enrolment of something between 400 and 800 pupils. It is felt that in such areas a single post-primary school, if it could be achieved, would provide a better level of service to the area while at the same time removing the divisions which at present exist in our post-primary sectors and the difficulties to which these give rise.

3. On another level, there is growing acceptance throughout the world that education is a life-long process and that second chance education must be provided at all levels. It would seem clear, therefore, that there will be very substantial development of adult education facilities over the next decade. Allied with this, there is in all countries a growing community consciousness and an increasing demand for school facilities (halls, gymnasia, meeting rooms, playing fields, swimming pools, etc.) to be made available out-of-school hours to voluntary organizations and the adult community generally.

4. Community schools are seen as resulting from the amalgamation of existing secondary and vocational schools or in city areas from the development of individual single schools instead of the traditional development of separate secondary and vocational schools. These schools would provide a reasonably full range of courses leading to Group Certificate, Intermediate Certificate and Leaving Certificate. The community school would provide adult education

facilities in the area and subject to reasonable safeguards against abuse or damage to buildings, equipment, etc., would make facilities available to voluntary organizations and to the adult community generally.

5. The community school would be governed by a Board of Management consisting of representatives of the secondary school managers and the local Vocational Education Committee with an independent Chairman who might be the Bishop of the Diocese or other agreed Chairman or with the Chairmanship rotating amongst the representative members of the Board. The representation of any particular interest would vary depending on the circumstances of each case and would be a matter for negotiation with the interests involved. It might prove possible to include representatives of parents or industrial/commercial interests but this would be by way of nomination by the educational authorities involved or by some other way which was agreed by them in the course of negotiations. The site and buildings would be vested in trustees nominated by the parties involved.

6. The Board of Management would be responsible for the administration of the school and its educational policy. The Board would be solely responsible for the appointment of staff, including Principals, Vice-Principals and other posts of responsibility, subject to the usual Departmental regulations in regard to qualifications, overall quota of teachers, number, types and rates of pay to non-teaching staff. In the case of amalgamations existing permanent staff in the schools being amalgamated would be offered assimilation on to the staff of the community school if they applied for it. Rates of salary and allowances would be those

applicable to secondary and vocational schools under the latest arrangements.

7. The capital costs involved (site, buildings, equipment, furniture, playing facilities) would be met in full out of public funds subject to an agreed local contribution. This local contribution would be a matter for negotiation in each individual case.

8. The current costs of running the school would be met by the Board of Management which would be funded directly and in full by the Department of Education. This Department favours an arrangement under which a budget would be agreed annually in advance with the Board of Management and within the limits of that budget the Board would be free to decide how best to utilise the funds at its disposal. The Board would be free, if it thought fit, to supplement its receipts by such local contributions as it might be possible for it to raise for general or specific purposes. The Board's accounts would be subject to audit by the Comptroller and Auditor General in so far as expenditure of public funds was concerned.

III.23 Report on the Intermediate Certificate Examination, 1975

The numbers of pupils in post-primary schools increased considerably after the introduction of free post-primary education in 1967. For many of these pupils, the Intermediate Certificate, with its emphasis on written examinations, was not a satisfactory mode of assessment of their achievements and many people believed that it was time to review and revise assessment and certification procedures at junior cycle level. In September 1970, Pádraig Faulkner, Minister for Education, set up a committee under the chairmanship of Rev. Paul Andrews, S.J., "to evaluate the present form and function of the Intermediate Certificate examination and to advise on new types of public examinations." An Interim report was circulated in 1973 and the final report, which was presented to Minister Burke in 1974 and published in 1975, called for radical changes in the Intermediate Certificate examination. It recommended that the existing system of external examination at the end of junior cycle should be replaced by "an on-going service of school-based assessment, supported by external moderation and nationally normed objective tests." It proposed that a new body be established — Moderation and Educational Assessment Service — to carry out these changes and to maintain this service. The recommendations of the committee were radical but were not in fact accepted by the government and no change took place in the assessment of pupils at junior cycle for a further 15 years:

The following is a summary of the committee's proposals:

The Intermediate Certificate Examination Report builds on the Committee's position as stated in its Interim Report, on the responses of the public to that report, and on the study and research done in the meantime. The Committee sees the present Intermediate Certificate Examination as serving some useful purposes, which are however outweighed by its drawbacks. It offers norms of academic achievement to teachers and pupils; it carries out an assessment which would have to be done by teachers in any case; it is impartial in its marking, and it motivates to work. On the other hand it proposes uniform targets to pupils of a great diversity of ability and aspiration, for many of whom it is not suitable. Its certificates are of little practical use to the majority of successful candidates, and most of those who leave school early and need a certificate, fail to win one. It samples a narrow range of skills, and by leaving some important skills unrewarded, it is effectively a disincentive to their cultivation. It is a poor predictor of Senior Cycle schooling, and its reliability of marking and speed of results could be improved considerably. It discourages innovation and curriculum development, and creates a sharp discontinuity with the integrated studies of the new Primary Curriculum. It was designed for a generation of teachers with inadequate training, and by keeping the responsibility for curricula and assessment in central control, it discourages teacher development and initiative, and shifts responsibility for assessment of pupils from the teacher who knows the pupil, to central markers who do not.

The Committee's proposals could be summarized in two statements. Some form of nation-wide assessment at 15+ is needed for the sake of:

(a) feedback of norms to pupils, teachers and parents;
(b) impartiality of an accepted sort;
(c) guidance for further studies;
(d) motivation to learning.

But such assessment needs to be:
(a) more varied in its modes than the Intermediate Certificate Examination, so as to include assessments of oral, practical and project work, and to relate the mode of assessment to the objectives of the course that preceded it;
(b) wider in its scope, reaching both higher and lower ranges of ability than the Intermediate Certificate Examination grades;
(c) broader in its objects, assessing both cognitive and non-cognitive factors;
(d) more flexible, allowing for various forms of curriculum development and innovation;
(e) frequent, occurring on more than a single occasion in Junior Cycle;
(f) school-based, involving the teachers of the students concerned.

The Committee's proposals are for a system of school-based assessment monitored by a central body (M.E.A.S.), which would take responsibility for all aspects of assessing the curriculum, helping teachers to clarify educational objectives, providing external tests, and opportunities for internal (school-based) assessments, and training teachers in the techniques and principles of assessment and curriculum development. All school-leavers would be given a certificate by the school, with information on all assessment, whether by externally set tests or administered by the school itself. The monitoring, or moderating, of school-based assessment would be effected by collaboration between schools in small groupings. In this way the need for public accreditation of certificates could be balanced by the teachers' need for freedom to develop their own courses and assessments to match the diverse requirements of their pupils. The Committee proposes ways of effecting a smooth transition from the present system to one of school-based assessment.

III.24 White Paper on Educational Development, 1980

The White Paper on Educational Development has been referred to in an earlier section (I.16). The following extracts from Chapters VI and IX provide a summary of the proposals relating to school curriculum at second level and administration of the second-level system:

CHAPTER VI — SCHOOL CURRICULUM AT SECOND LEVEL

1. The Necessary steps will be taken to allow for the introduction of Religious Studies as a subject in the Leaving Certificate Examination.
2. A Curriculum Council will be established to advise the Minister on curriculum and syllabi at second level.
3. Career-orientated courses in senior cycle will be introduced on a pilot basis and pre-employment type courses will be made more widely available.

4. Oral tests in Modern Languages will be introduced in 1985.
5. Courses in Computer Studies will be introduced.
6. The syllabi in Mathematics and the structure of the courses offered will be re-examined.
7. A scheme for giving credit for experimental work in the sciences will be introduced on a pilot basis in Physics at the leaving Certificate Examination, 1983.

CHAPTER IX — ADMINISTRATION OF THE SECOND-LEVEL SYSTEM

1. In addition to comprehensive and community schools already in existence further community schools will be provided. This will bring the number of such schools to about 70 by the end of the decade.
2. Co-operation between secondary and vocational schools in relation to the sharing of accommodation and facilities will be pressed.
3. The policy of providing community schools will not preclude sanction for the establishment, where suitable, of a secondary school and/or a vocational school.
4. The replacement of inadequate prefabricated accommodation will be undertaken at an accelerated pace.

III.25 Community Colleges, 1980

The setting up of community schools has been referred to earlier (III.22). During the 1970s a number of community schools had opened and the White Paper of 1980 suggested that there could be as many as 70 such schools by the end of the 1980s. The vocational school bodies (i.e. the Irish Vocational Education Association, the Chief Executive Officers and the Teachers' Union of Ireland) became increasingly concerned in the late 1970s that the vocational sector would lose out to community schools. The Minister's circular of 1974 (III.17) had reminded V.E.Cs of the provisions of Section 21 of the 1930 Act in relation to the devolved management of individual schools. While these provisions were not initially envisaged as providing for a new type of school, by the early 1980s a new type of school — the community college — had in fact emerged. The early community colleges were simply a renaming of vocational schools but by 1980 a new management structure for these schools was agreed in a number of areas. There is no single model for the control and management of community colleges but the sample model agreement between the Co. Dublin V.E.C. and the Catholic Archbishop of Dublin dating from about 1980 indicates the type of management structure of many community colleges around the country. The following extracts are from the model agreement:

MODEL AGREEMENT FOR COMMUNITY COLLEGES
As agreed between the County Dublin vocational educational committee and archbishop of Dublin.

****

2. The Board shall be responsible for the government and direction of the College subject to the provisions of the First and Second Schedules hereof.

3. (a) The Board of the College when constituted shall consist of ten members nominated or elected as follows:

   (i) Three members shall be nominated by the appropriate Religious Authority these three nominees being hereinafter referred to as "The Archbishop's Nominees."
   (ii) Three members shall be nominated by the Vocational Education Committee hereinafter referred to as "the Committee's Nominees."
   (iii) Two parents of children who are enrolled in the College shall be elected to membership of the Board by the parents of the aforementioned pupils.

One of the Parents' nominees shall be a mother. The parents so elected are hereinafter referred to as "the Parents' Nominees."

(iv) Two members of the teaching staff shall be elected by all the permanent wholetime teachers serving in the school at the time and acting as one body for the purpose of such election. The teachers so elected are hereinafter referred to as "the Teachers' Nominees."

(v) Minority religious representation on Boards of Management will be considered by the Vocational Education Committee where requests for representation are received.
A person nominated to represent a minority religious group(s) will fill an additional place.

(vi) The Principal of the College or in his/her absence the Vice-Principal shall be entitled to attend and speak at meetings of the Board but shall not have a vote nor be entitled to vote.
The Principal shall be the permanent Secretary of the Board and in his/her absence the Vice-Principal shall act as Secretary.

ARTICLES OF MANAGEMENT (EXCERPTS)

****

SELECTION AND APPOINTMENT OF STAFF

6.1(a) The decision of the Board in relation to the assignment of teachers to the College shall be subject to the prior approval of the Committee.

(b) The qualifications for appointments to the teaching staff shall be such as are stipulated from time to time by the Minister.

6.2. The appointment of teaching staff shall conform to the following procedure:

(i) Vacancies for teaching posts to be notified to the Chief Executive Officer.

(ii) Applications for a vacant post shall be sought by the Committee by way of advertisement in the public press.

(iii) The applications received for the vacant post(s) shall be considered by the Chief Executive officer who shall forward them to the Selection Board of five persons constituted from time to time and comprising two representatives of the appropriate Religious Authority, two representatives of the Vocational Education Committee, an inspector of the Department nominated by the Minster. The Chief Executive Officer or his nominee to assist the Board in an advisory capacity. In the case of initial appointments the Principal may also assist the Board in an advisory capacity. The aforesaid members shall constitute the full composition of the Selection Board. The minimum composition of the Selection Board shall be three members; one representative of the Religious Authority, one representative of the V.E.C. and an Inspector of the Department of Education. The Chairman shall be agreed by persons aforesaid from among their own number and shall have a casting vote in the event of a tie. All remaining members of the Vocational Education Committee shall be eligible to act as substitutes if the two named members of the Selection Board are unable to attend.

****

ORGANISATION AND CURRICULUM

9. Subject to the provisions of the Minister as to the general educational character of the College and its place in the educational system the Board shall have the general direction of the conduct and curriculum of the College. The Board shall arrange for the setting up of a Staff Council consisting of all wholetime teachers of the College under the Chairmanship of the Principal.

****

12.(i) In exercising its general control over the curriculum and conduct of the College the Board shall ensure that there is religious worship and religious instruction for the pupils in the College except for such pupils whose parents make a request in writing to the Principal that those pupils should be withdrawn from religious worship or religious instruction or both religious worship and religious instruction.

****

(x) The Committee will appoint a Chaplain nominated by the competent Religious Authority who shall be employed outside the normal quota of the school. He shall be a full-time member of the staff and shall be paid a salary equivalent to that of a teacher in the school.

Suitable arrangements will be made for members of other religions in consultation with the appropriate authorities.

III.26 Programme for Action in Education 1984 - 1987.

The background to the publication of the Programme for Action in Education is given earlier in this volume (I.20). In relation to second level education, no radical reforms were envisaged, rather it was proposed during the period of the Programme, "to ensure the rational and complementary development of the secondary, vocational and community/comprehensive school sectors." It was confirmed that "fundamental change in the nature of these systems is not envisaged," but it would be necessary to ensure that there would be no unnecessary duplication of scarce resources.

The following is a summary of the main proposals in relation to second-level education:

SECOND LEVEL EDUCATION

The Programme will support the complementary development of Secondary, Vocational and Community/Comprehensive Schools.

Greater flexibility will be given to schools to introduce alternative curricula.

Special emphasis will be given to pupils who are likely to drop out before they complete compulsory education or to terminate schooling at the end of the compulsory cycle.

A discussion paper will be prepared on the number of years to be spent in Post-Primary Schools and on the question of the possible restructuring of post-primary courses.

Guidance teachers will be allocated in future on the basis of school needs and taking account of the range of programmes available in the schools.

The level of grants to Secondary Schools will be reviewed on a continuing basis and improved as resources permit.

The grant in lieu of school fees and the capitation grant will be combined to form one "per capita" grant for schools within the free education scheme and from the school year 1984/85 will be based on enrolment of pupils rather than on attendance as heretofore.

Secondary Schools will be empowered to appoint part-time teachers, within the quota of whole-time posts, in lieu of the equivalent number of whole-time teachers.

Consultations will be held to ensure the maximum amount of co-ordination and integration in the provision and use of Post-Primary School facilities.

The co-operation of industry and business will be sought in providing opportunities for Post-Primary School pupils to familiarise themselves with new developments in technology.

Oral examinations in modern continental languages will be introduced in 1986 as part of the Leaving Certificate examination. Funds will be made available for the provision of cassette recorders.

Micro computer facilities will be supplied in 1984 and 1985 for those schools which have not as yet benefited under the scheme.

Urgent consideration will be given to a review of the place of participative citizenship in the school curriculum.

The introduction of Religious Studies as a subject in the Leaving Certificate examination will be facilitated.

The question of the provision of expanded training courses under the E.E.C. Social Fund is being investigated.

Suitable structures will be introduced between the Department of Education and the various State agencies involved in vocational training with a view to avoiding unnecessary duplication of scarce resources.

III.27 Vocational Preparation and Training Programmes, 1984

The introduction of free post-primary education in 1967 resulted in a rapid increase in the numbers of young people attending post-primary schools. However during the 1970s it became apparent that access to free post-primary education did not solve the problem of those who left school early with no formal qualification. In 1977, pre-employment courses aimed at non-academic, post-compulsory pupils were introduced in vocational, community and comprehensive schools. In 1983, the E.E.C. Council of Ministers adopted a resolution providing for the development of vocational training policies in the member states during the 1980s. The aim of the resolution was to provide a full-time, one or two year programme involving basic training and/or work experience to prepare early school leavers who had no qualifications for entry to an occupation. This was to be achieved by increased finance from the European Social Fund. On 2nd May 1984 a circular was sent by the Department of Education to all second-level schools in Ireland inviting them to participate in the new programme. The following extracts are from the circular.

1. INTRODUCTION

1.1 The problem of early school leavers, and in particular those who leave school with no formal qualifications, has been a source of concern both in this country and in Europe generally since the expansion of second-level educational provision in the 1960s. Rising youth unemployment in the mid-seventies brought about a demand for preparation for work programmes and one response to this in 1977 was the establishment of the Pre-Employment Programme in vocational and in community and comprehensive schools.

1.2 Due to the economics crisis in the 1970s and early 1980s and the deterioration in the employment situation in Europe generally and the consequent adverse effects on employment opportunities for young people there has been concern that many young people, on completion of compulsory schooling, are inadequately prepared for the world of work. This applies particularly to those with minimal or no qualifications. The E.E.C. Council of Ministers in 1983 adopted a resolution providing for the development of vocational training policies in the member states in the 1980s. One of the principal provisions in this resolution is that, during the next five years, member states would—

> do their utmost to ensure that all young people who so wish, and particularly those without educational or vocational qualifications, could benefit over a period of six months and if possible one year following full-time compulsory education from a full-time programme involving basic training and/or an initial work experience to prepare them for an occupation.

Since then proposals based on a programme of Vocational Preparation and Training have been included in the Department of Educations application for fund aid from the European Social Fund in Brussels. The Fund is designed to assist in meeting the challenges posed by unemployment in the European Community. A principal instrument in that task is the provision of vocational training.

The European Commission views a lack of appropriate training as a factor in unemployment either, because an inadequate level of training inhibits economic activity and thus depresses employment, or because there is often a mismatch between training and available jobs.

2. The Need for Vocational Preparation Programmes in the Educational System

2.1 The trends in recent Department of Economic Status of School Leavers surveys indicate the following general percentages for unemployment of school leavers one year after leaving school:

Those with no qualifications	45%-50% unemployed
Junior/Inter/Group Certificates	20-25% unemployed
Leaving Certificate	up to 17% unemployed

2.2 There are broadly two groups of young people needing special attention. Firstly, there are those who drop out of school on completion of compulsory schooling and who have inadequate or no qualifications. Secondly, there are those who continue at school but whose programme of study does not contain adequate vocational preparation.

2.3 In the light of the difficult employment situation of young people and the increasing impact of the new information technologies on particular types of work it is necessary to undertake a continual review of preparation for work programmes.

****

4. Aims and Objectives of Vocational Preparation Programme

4.1 Vocational Preparation Courses are intended for young

people of 15-18 years who, having completed their compulsory education, desire to prepare and equip themselves for employment (including especially the two groups described in paragraph 2.2 above).

4.2 The general aim of vocational preparation courses is that of bridging the gap between the values and experiences normally part of traditional education and those current in the adult world of work. Increasingly modern society demands individuals with personal resources and flexibility to cope with the complexities of the labour market and the rapid change of work roles. In the service sector, the most rapidly growing economic sector, personal and interpersonal skills are particularly important and all young workers must have the ability to plan and make life and career decisions if they are to be successful in working life.

III.28 Partners in Education — Serving Community Needs. A Green Paper (November 1985)

National and secondary education in Ireland have been centrally administered for over 150 years. Before 1922 the central administrative bodies were the National and Intermediate Boards and these Boards were replaced in 1924 by the Department of Education in Dublin. This is in contrast to the situation in Great Britain and Northern Ireland where local education structures (e.g. Local Education Authorities in England and the Education and Library Boards in Northern Ireland) have been in existence since 1902 and 1922 respectively. Efforts were made in 1919 to introduce a local administrative structure in Ireland, but these efforts were not successful.

In the Republic, the only regional administrative structures for education are the Vocational Education Committees (V.E.Cs), which were set up under the 1930 Vocational Education Act (IV.3) and which replaced the Technical Education committees set up under the 1899 Agricultural and Technical Instruction (Ireland) Act. No moves were made between 1922 and the late 1960s to regionalise educational administration, although both Labour and Fine Gael party policy documents on education during the period supported such regionalisation. It was not until 1973 that the question of regionalisation was raised by the then Minister for Education, Richard Burke, but the proposal was dropped and was not raised again until 1983. The Programme for Government drawn up between the Coalition Partners that year made a commitment that "administrative structures within the educational system will be reformed so as to make it more decentralised and democratic." During the subsequent two years, a number of official reports highlighted the need for a local co-ordinating structure for aspects of education, e.g. the Report of the Adult Education Commission (1983), and the Report of the National Youth Policy Committee (1984).

In November 1985, Gemma Hussey, T.D., Minister for Education, issued a Green Paper — Partners in Education — in which it was proposed that thirteen Local Education Councils be set up throughout the country. These Councils would have wide-ranging functions in relation to the provision, planning and development of second-level education. The Green Paper also made proposals for new structures for the nine Regional Technical Colleges, the Dublin Institute of Technology, the Limerick College of Art, Commerce and Technology and the Cork Schools of Music and Art.

The Green Paper received a mixed reception from the various educational interest groups throughout the country. The Council of Managers of Catholic Secondary Schools were "disappointed and disenchanted with the proposals" and they described the timing as "particularly inopportune." Representatives of the Vocational Education Committees broadly supported the concept of regionalisation but urged a county-based rather than a regional structure. The issuing of the Paper coincided with a series of financial cutbacks in education and the majority of bodies who responded, reacted negatively to the proposals of the Green Paper. No action was taken to implement these proposals during the remainder of the term of office of the Coalition government, or subsequently.

The following extracts are taken from the Green Paper:

PROPOSED STRUCTURE AND ROLE OF LECs

1. The basic structure would be a Local Education Council for a specified geographical area and an individual Board of Management for each post-primary school.

2. There would be thirteen LECs based roughly on a combination of Local Authority areas. Proposals in this regard are set out in the Appendix.

3. The LECs would consist of, say, 30-32* Members nominated as follows:-

 10-12 from Local Authorities, depending on the number of authorities involved,

 (5) 1 representative each of the following: Youth Services, Training/Manpower Agencies, Adult Education Agencies and economic interests including the social partners.

 5 representatives of the authorities of voluntary secondary schools.
 3 representatives of the authorities of vocational, community and comprehensive schools.
 2 Parents of post-primary pupils.
 2 post-primary Teachers.
 3 primary school representatives (one parent, one teacher, one manager)

*Note: Actual membership might be determined by Order of the Minister to allow some variation as between LECs. In the case of a Council with part of the Gaeltacht included in its area membership of the LEC would include at least one member from the Gaeltacht.

2 post-primary Teachers.
3 primary school representatives (one parent, one teacher, one manager)

5. The following are the suggested functions to be undertaken by the LECs.
   A. The provision, planning and development of second-level education, including technical education, in its region; the provision of a general advisory and educational welfare service (including psychological service and school attendance); the payment of teachers; the maintenance of second-level schools, other than minor works; the payment of capitation and other grants to second-level schools; the promotion of liaison and co-ordination between the primary and post-primary sectors and providing advice in relation to the provision of new primary schools.
   B. The provision and co-ordination of youth services; the provision and co-ordination of training schemes for young persons in conjunction with other appropriate agencies including AnCO, the Youth Employment Agency, CERT and the National Manpower Service; the promotion of industry/school links; the provision and co-ordination of Adult Education in its region.
   C. Consideration might also be given to the transfer of responsibility for the Public Library Service to the LECs.

Note: The employment and dismissal of teachers would be a function for the individual Boards of Management. In the event of a scheme relating to the redeployment of teachers being agreed the scheme might be operated by the LEC in its region.

While the work at present undertaken by the Department's Building Unit would continue to be undertaken by the Department, it is envisaged that the LECs would have an advisory function in relation to the provision of building capital and in determining the priorities for investment. They would also be empowered to make decisions in relation to the provision of an annual budget for equipment within the confines of their financial allocations. Subject to policy guidelines being laid down by the Department, the responsibility for school transport at both primary and post-primary levels might also be a matter for the LECs.

III.29 Curriculum and Examinations Board publications
(a) Issues and Structures in Education, Sep. 1984
(b) In Our Schools, March 1986.

The setting up of the Interim Curriculum and Examinations Board has been referred to in an earlier section (II.19). During the life of the interim Board, its deliberations were mainly concerned with curriculum and assessment at post-primary level. The specific terms of reference set down by the Minister for Education, Gemma Hussey, asked the Board to "make recommendations regarding a new unified assessment system for the junior cycle of second level schooling to replace the present Intermediate and Group Certificate examinations." The aim of such an assessment system would be "to ensure that all pupils will have available to them some certification of their achievements on reaching the end of the period of compulsory school attendance." The Board was also asked to consider the implications of a new approach at junior cycle for the senior cycle as well as initiating a review of the Leaving Certificate as a measure of general education.

The interim Board was in existence from January 1984 to September 1987. During its term of office it published a total of 13 consultative documents, discussion papers and reports as well as regular newsletters.

(a) Issues and Structures in Education

The Board's first publication, a consultative document entitled *Issues and Structures in Education,* was published in September 1984 and in the introduction to the document it was stated that the Board was "anxious to share its initial thinking with those who may wish to contribute to the search for a curriculum and examinations system better suited to current and evolving Irish needs." The document was a short and concise document of less than 40 pages and was presented in sections as follows : Policy Issues; Aims of Education; Second-level education — junior cycle; Second-level education — senior cycle; Assessment and certification; Some operational issues for the Board.

The following extracts from the chapter entitled *The Aims of Education,* indicate the context in which the reform of curriculum and assessment was perceived:

In view of the social, cultural and economic changes affecting Irish society today, the Board believes that an explicit statement of educational aims is needed as a rationale and as a criterion for policy. The Board invites the public to join it in a discussion leading to the formulation of such a statement.

The statement should offer a framework within which the educational requirements of society in general, of the individual and of interested groups could be met and could interact creatively.

It should thus be sufficiently comprehensive to accommodate the many demands — public and private, vocational and cultural, progressive and traditionalist — that are made upon education today, and to relate these to one another in a positive and balanced manner.

The statement should derive from a coherent and acceptable educational philosophy. It should acknowledge the intrinsic value of education for the individual and for society. Finally, it should be capable of translation into practical and effective programmes of teaching and learning.

The Board acknowledges that a general consensus on the aims of education has long existed in Ireland. This has been reflected, for instance, in formal and informal statements by professional educationists, community leaders and Ministers for Education, in educational publications and in official documents (such as *Curaclaim na Bunscoile,* Department of Education 1971; *Rules and Programme for Secondary Schools,* Department of Education; the *White Paper on Educational Development,* 1980; the *Programme for Action in Education,* Government Publication, 1984).

The consensus tends to centre on a small number of broad aspirations, notably

- the realisation of equality of educational opportunity;
- the transmission to each new generation of the developing spiritual and cultural heritage;
- the development of the potential of the individual;
- education for vocational and economic competence.

It is suggested that those aspirations — and perhaps others that might be identified — would, if all their implications were teased out, yield a range of valid educational aims that could be organised into a powerful and cohesive statement.

The first of the aspirations — equality of opportunity — has come to be accepted as public policy in most developed countries since 1945. The others, it might be argued, have always been the concern of education. But the context in which the aspirations must be examined today is radically different from the relatively static context of a few decades ago.

The demands made on educational systems have thus become more complex, extensive and diverse than hitherto. It is no longer easy, for instance, to demarcate particular areas of educational competence proper only to the home, or to the community, or to the school: education is now seen as a continuous, shared process, in which all three participate and must co-operate. Nor is it possible today — if ever it really was possible — to identify a terminal point at which a person's education, even in a more or less formal sense, is "complete": the various levels in a system are now seen as related stages in recurrent, and indeed permanent, lifelong education. Any adequate statement of aims will therefore reflect the growing complexity of education's responsibilities and the growing lateral and vertical continuity of its structure.

If a statement of aims is to become a practical programme for which the public will be prepared to pay, it must take into account the constraints imposed upon education by the realities of time, human capacities and material resources. At the same time, part of the function of an educational system is to help society to generate the cultural and material wealth that will reduce the constraints upon education and permit its further development.

Finally, it must be recognised that in a world of change any statement of educational aims cannot be other than tentative and will be subject to continuous reconsideration and possible revision.

In the section on junior cycle, the document proposed that all pupils at this level should have access to a broad and balanced curriculum encompassing eight categories. The following extracts indicate the thrust of these proposals:

NEEDS:

4.3 An examination of the existing situation leads to an identification of the need for

— a broader and more balanced core curriculum with an increased emphasis on skills and processes;

— a curricular structure that is sufficiently flexible to recognise and accommodate curriculum initiatives at school and regional levels;

— assessment procedures that are determined by the aims and objectives of the curriculum.

PROPOSED CURRICULAR FRAMEWORK

4.4. The curricular framework which is proposed is a response to these needs, and takes account of the existing situation. The framework consists of a Core, which would be obligatory for pupils, and a series of options described as Additional Contributions.....

4.5 In presenting this framework the Board would emphasise that content is only one element of curriculum. Learning processes and methodologies are at least as important.

4.6 The proposed framework divides the junior-cycle curriculum into a number of Categories.

These categories are:

Communication, Language and Literature
Creative and Aesthetic Studies
Guidance and Counselling
Mathematical Studies
Physical Education
Religious Education
Science and the New Technologies
Social and Political Studies

4.8 Within each category, subjects or courses are located either in the Core... or in Additional Contributions....

4.9 Although subjects are identified by their traditional titles, e.g. English, Mathematics, the Board envisages that the objectives, content and methodologies of many of these subjects will be altered significantly and that many subjects will be offered at a number of levels. An interdisciplinary approach to syllabus construction is possible and desirable....

4.10 Since the curriculum should be seen as a continuum from the beginning of formal schooling, the Board believes that

— diagnosis and identification of learning difficulties should take place from the early years of primary education and continue until the end of second level education;
— there should be close alignment between primary school and the junior cycle of post-primary school in curriculum, learning processes and teaching methods;
— there should be no examination for entry to post-primary schools.

(b) In Our Schools, 1986

Early in 1985, a consultative document on Assessment and Certification was issued and this was followed later in the year by discussion papers on Primary Education, the Arts in Education and Language in the Curriculum. Consultations and discussions on the broad framework of junior and senior cycle curriculum took place during 1985, and in March 1986 the Board published its recommendations to the Minister, Patrick Cooney T.D., who had replaced Gemma Hussey as Minister for Education the previous month. These recommendations were contained in a report entitled *In Our Schools — a framework for curriculum and assessment*. This report was short and concise — about 60 pages — and contained 7 sections, including chapters on The School and Education; The Curriculum; The Curriculum at Primary level, at junior cycle and at senior cycle; Assessment and Certification and Strategy for Development. The following extracts are from Section 1 of the Report which sets the context for the recommendations and from Chapters 4 and 5:

EDUCATION FOR CREATIVITY

The Board recognises the need to re-assess our educational goals in the context of the late twentieth century. Schools must ensure that they contribute to the development of those attitudes and attributes which will enable young people to avail of the opportunities of life in the twenty-first century.

Many of the certainties of previous generations will not apply in the future. This is due to changing patterns of enterprise and employment, changing interpretations of work and job, increasingly diverse and expanding opportunities for leisure, changing perceptions of gender roles and rapid developments in technology and information processing. All these factors demand an imaginative response from the education system.

There is a need, therefore, to foster confidence in young people. School programmes which consciously challenge students and reward achievement across the educational spectrum help to develop this confidence. Overcoming the fear of failure is one of the most significant contributions schools can make in preparing young people for adult life. They must be encouraged to think in terms of identifying problems and considering solutions rather than always seeking absolute right or wrong answers to problems. An imaginative failure can be more educationally worth while than a correct, but poorly understood, response.

A necessary pre-condition for student confidence and creativity is the involvement of young people in certain decisions within the school. This is particularly important at senior cycle. Young people should be challenged to accept the responsibilities that this entails.

The Board wishes to ensure that the encouragement of creativity becomes a feature of all courses in our schools. Opportunities for creativity are often best found by linking the experience of school to that of wider community and local environment. Links between schools and local economic and social activities — agriculture, fisheries, forestry, for example, or manufacturing and service industries — have been established in many areas, but the opportunities so presented have not always been exploited to the full. Transition Year options and Vocational Preparation and Training courses will offer many post-primary schools an opportunity to investigate further the potential of the local environment, as a learning resource and as a stimulus to individual thought or action. Creativity in this context can manifest itself in a number of ways: a commercial enterprise, an organised recreational activity, a musical or theatrical event are examples of possible outcomes of individual or group initiative.

The Board recognises that the alienation of youth is an important issue, particularly in areas with severe social and economic problems. Radical curricular alternatives, incorporating the creative potential of out-of-school activities and community-based experience have proved successful for schools in such areas.

School programmes should be framed within a cultural context which emphasises creativity, enterprise and innovation more than conformity and passive learning. The Board is aware that much work is already being carried out in schools in fostering the creative and innovative energies of young people. It wishes to deepen and extend this experience. The Board has proposed the following as a general aim of education:

> To contribute towards the development of all aspects of the individual, including aesthetic, creative, critical, cultural, emotional, intellectual, moral, physical, political, social and spiritual development, for personal and family life, for working life, for living in the community and for leisure.

In seeking to translate this general and long-term aim into short-term goals, the Board has been conscious of the wider educational issues and the fact that different philosophies of education and sociologies of knowledge influence one's concept of the curriculum. It has also been aware that theory and practice in education should not be separate but should influence and reinforce each other through the process of clarifying aims, refining methods and evaluating outcomes.

****

JUNIOR CYCLE — FRAMEWORK FOR DEVELOPMENT

In *Issues and Structures* a suggested curricular framework for the junior cycle was presented. This framework was represented in diagrammatic form, as a circle or wheel consisting of eight segments or categories. These segments represented eight areas of experience which it was felt each child should come in contact with during the three years of junior cycle. Within each category, a distinction was made between core and additional contributions. In the light of the subsequent consultative process, the Board has further developed its thinking on this matter.

The Board now presents the overall curricular framework from two essential and complementary perspectives: first, areas of experience; and second, elements of learning. These perspectives are not in conflict with each other or with the ways in which schools commonly organise teaching and learning. The Board has also modified its position with regard to the relative status of certain subjects and the distinctions between core and additional contributions.

AREAS OF EXPERIENCE

The Board recommends that the junior cycle curriculum of all schools should involve pupils in each of the following areas of experience:

1. Arts education (creative and aesthetic studies)
2. Guidance and counselling
3. Language and literature (a) Irish and English
   (b) Other languages
4. Mathematical studies
5. Physical education
6. Religious education
7. Science and technology
8. Social, political and environmental studies

These are not suggested as discrete elements to be taught entirely separately and in isolation from one another. They constitute a planning and analytical tool. Nor are they exclusively equated with particular subjects (for example, pupils may gain creative and aesthetic experience from language and literature) though inevitably individual subjects contribute more to some areas than to others. Topics such as media studies or moral education might be a feature of all or several of the areas of experience although the emphasis on such topics will differ from area to area.

The categorisation of areas of experience in this way provides a challenge for those involved in syllabus construction to develop to the fullest the potential of each subject area. It also provides an administrative basis for co-ordination between different subjects of the curriculum at junior cycle and for continuity between the primary and the post-primary curriculum. In suggesting that every pupil at junior cycle should experience the above areas the Board is aware that schools have to take into account their existing resources, both human and material. The Board reiterates the point that not only the content but also the form of such experience will vary according to levels of ability and stages of development of students, and that any specific subject may contribute to more than one area of experience.

In post-primary schools, subjects are well established as a convenient and familiar way of organising learning. Therefore it is to be expected that schools will wish to begin at this point, since one of their strengths lies in subjects well taught by staff with specialist training and experience.

****

IMPLEMENTATION

In order to provide guidelines for schools to enable them to develop and co-ordinate programmes and courses within this framework, minimum and maximum time allocations are suggested. These allocations are shown in terms of the total time spent in junior cycle by pupils following a three-year course. The following is the recommended minimum and maximum time which pupils should spend on the different areas of experience.

Where, for example, a school operates a twenty-eight-hour class-contact week over thirty-six weeks, a total of about 3030 instruction hours would be available in that school in a three-year period.

TABLE 1

Recommended minimum and maximum time allocations
in terms of number of hours which should be spent by pupils
in junior cycle on the different areas of experience

Area of Experience	Min.	Max.
1. Arts education (creative and aesthetic studies)	225	750
2. Guidance and counselling	75	150
3. (a) Vernacular languages & Literature	600	750
3. (b) Other languages & Literature	225	750
4. Mathematical studies	300	375
5. Physical education	150	375
6. Religious education	75	375
7. Science and technology	375	1050
8. Social, political and environmental studies	300	750
(Discretionary time)	(700)	
Total hours	3030	

****

RECOMMENDATIONS TO THE MINISTER (Junior Cycle)

4.1 The curriculum at junior cycle should involve pupils in each of the areas of experience listed.

4.2 Course committees should construct syllabuses and courses with reference to their contribution to the different areas of experience.

4.3 Subjects and courses should be offered at up to three levels — Foundation, General and Advanced.

4.4 Schools should decide how they can provide students with the areas of experience by developing the full potential of individual subjects offered by them: a matrix is provided to help in such an exercise.

4.5 Schools should operate within the timetabling guidelines offered by the Board.
4.6 Course committees should specify the particular knowledge, concepts, skills and attitudes to be developed in syllabuses and courses at different levels.
4.7 Short courses may be provided in some subjects.
4.8 Firm foundations in the basic skills of literacy, numeracy and oral communication should be established by the end of junior cycle.
4.9 Diagnosis and identification of learning difficulties should be maintained throughout junior cycle.
4.10 The outcomes of pilot projects in curriculum and assessment at junior cycle should be examined and incorporated as appropriate by the Board.
4.11 The Board, through its validation procedures, should promote the development of courses at junior cycle by schools, networks of schools or other agencies and authorities.

****

RECOMMENDATIONS TO THE MINISTER (Senior Cycle)

5.1 Senior cycle policy should be developed so as to promote consistency of approach across the range of courses both within schools and between the formal school system and the various training agencies, thereby increasing the flexibility of provision for the fifteen—to eighteen—year age group.

5.2 Senior cycle provision should be distinguished by:

— Diversity of provision and approach to meet the differing needs of students
— equality of access for all

- — the centrality of the personal and social development of each individual student
- — the promotion of student creativity, enterprise and innovation
- — responsiveness to employment and further education prospects for students
- — maintenance of standards
- — location of courses in the context of the broad cultural heritage and the social and economic profile of the community
- — facilities for recurrent education (for previous under-achievers or those coming back into mainstream education).

5.3 The Leaving Certificate programme should be adapted to cater for the increasingly diverse needs of students.

5.4 Transition Year programmes and VPT courses should be developed as a means of exploring the flexibility promises to schools in *Ages for Learning: Decisions of Government.*

5.5 The Board, through its validation procedures, should promote the development of courses at senior cycle by schools, networks of schools or other agencies and authorities.

5.6 Validation and certification procedures should be developed for such programmes at senior cycle as are recommended by the Board for the approval of the Minister.

5.7 Programmes at senior cycle should build upon the experiences of and provide continuity from junior cycle.

5.8 Existing and new courses at senior cycle may be expressed in units of study to facilitate flexibility in courses and mobility of students.

5.9 Assessment procedures should be developed in order to recognise and support as many as possible of those areas of the curriculum not presently examined and to encourage the further exploration of the potential of existing subjects.

III.30 Transition Year Programmes — guidelines for schools, January 1986

The idea of a Transition Year Programme for students in the senior cycle of post-primary education was first introduced by Richard Burke, T.D., Minister for Education in the early 1970s. A small number of schools was authorised by the Department of Education to introduce a Transition Year Programme on a pilot basis at that time. It was not however until 1985, following the publication of *Ages for Learning — Decisions of Government,* that a decision was taken by the then Minister, Gemma Hussey, T.D., to permit more schools to offer a Transition Year. The Curriculum and Examinations Board (C.E.B.) was asked to produce guidelines for Transition Year Programmes and these guidelines were published in January 1986. A short time later the government reversed the decision contained in *Ages for Learning* that all pupils would have access to six years of second level education and a further five years were to elapse before Mary O'Rourke, T.D., Minister for Education, announced that all pupils entering post-primary education from 1991 onwards would have the option of following a six year programme. Many schools would offer the Transition Year as an option within the senior cycle.

The following extracts from the C.E.B. guidelines of 1986 explain the thinking behind the Transition Year option and the rationale for the programme:

ESSENCE OF TRANSITION YEAR OPTIONS

Transition Year programmes should be consciously designed to act as a bridge for students to move from a state of dependence to a more autonomous and participative role with regard to their own future. The voluntary nature of a student's enrolment in a Transition Year programme (s/he might have left school at 15 years of age) should be positively exploited.

Guiding young people to become more aware of the decision to remain in school, enabling them to examine consciously the role of being a student and developing a "contract of learning" approach will be time well spent for all concerned. Transition programmes, although catering for students who may wish at the end of their programme to enter the world of work, should not have a narrow vocational focus or job-placement thrust. Career education should, however, play an important role. Neither should such programmes be geared to any specific educational route, though much emphasis should be given to transferable study skills and self-directed learning.

TYO may be said to differ from other educational programmes (e.g. Leaving Certificate) in that, freed from the constraints of a particular kind of assessment and certification, schools have the flexibility to realise in their own way the overall aims of senior cycle with a particular emphasis on the intellectual, social and personal development of the student.

They differ from vocationally oriented programmes in that they do not have training for jobs as a principal aim, nor do they channel students towards any particular career cluster.

Rationale for TYOs

Transition year programmes are intended to facilitate the integrated development of the intellectual, emotional, spiritual, physical, social and vocational capacities of each individual student through structured learning experiences. The general aim of TYO is the preparation of young people for their role as autonomous, participative and responsible members of society. In particular, Transition Year programmes aim to provide young people with the skills and support necessary to

- discover their own individual talents, aptitudes and abilities with regard to future educational and/or vocational participation

- understand their own particular educational and/or vocational needs
- develop those skills and competences necessary to cope successfully with their particular stages of development.

The courses are therefore intended to cater for the needs and capacities of young people within a framework of a broad general education which would include and integrate academic study and careers education. In catering for the varying needs of students, such a broad general education should:

- provide opportunities for students who have been under-achieving to improve their performance
- assist students to take responsibility for their own learning and decision-making
- give due regard to students' previous educational experience and likely future educational vocational requirements
- provide practical opportunities for learning experiences which are based in the local community.

Decisions on the specific curriculum to be followed in TYO will be largely school-based. Programmes offered will vary from school to school. They will reflect the educational ethos of the schools and their traditions, the needs of the students and the nature of the teaching and administrative support available.

III.31 (a) National Council for Curriculum and Assessment — A Guide to the Junior Certificate, 1989

The Curriculum and Examinations Board was disbanded in September 1987 and two months later a new body, the National Council for Curriculum and Assessment was set up by Mary O'Rourke, T.D., Minister for Education. The new Council was an advisory one, whose role was

— to advise the Minister on the curriculum at first and second levels

— to advise the Minister on appropriate modes and techniques of assessment

— to coordinate research and development

— to report on standards of student performance, including performance in the public examinations.

The priority brief given to the council was to draw up plans for the implementation of a new unified system of assessment and certification at junior cycle, to be called the Junior Certificate.

By September 1988, the first drafts of a new syllabus in seven subjects — Gaeilge, English, History, Geography, Business Studies, Science and Art, Craft and Design were ready and were circulated to schools. The Minister announced her intention to introduce the new Junior Certificate examination in 1992 and all pupils entering second level schools in 1989 would embark on the new Junior Certificate courses. There was some initial disappointment that the changes were announced in the form of syllabus revision rather than in the context of a new curriculum framework, but in 1989, with the publication of a Guide to the Junior Certificate, the context of the reform became clearer and it was evident that the council had based much of its work on that of the interim Curriculum and Examinations Board.

The following extracts are from the Guide to the Junior Certificate:

The Junior Certificate : Aims and Principles

The Aim of Education

The general aim of education is to contribute towards the development of all aspects of the individual, including aesthetic, creative, critical, cultural, emotional, intellectual, moral, physical, political, social and spiritual development, for personal and family life, for working life, for living in the community and for leisure.

AIMS OF THE JUNIOR CERTIFICATE PROGRAMME

The Junior Certificate programme aims to:

- reinforce and further develop in the young person the knowledge, understanding, skills and competencies acquired at primary level;
- extend and deepen the range and quality of the young person's educational experience in terms of knowledge, understanding, skills and competencies;
- develop the young person's personal and social confidence, initiative and competence through a broad, well-balanced, general education;
- prepare the young person for the requirements of further programmes of study, of employment or of life outside full-time education;
- contribute to the moral and spiritual development of the young person and to develop a tolerance and respect for the values and beliefs of others;
- prepare the young person for the responsibilities of citizenship in the national context and in the context of the wider European community.

CURRICULUM PRINCIPLES

The Junior Certificate programme is based on the following curriculum principles:

- *breadth and balance:* in the final phase of compulsory schooling, every young person should have a wide range of educational experiences. Particular attention must be given to reinforcing and developing the skills of numeracy, literacy and oracy. Particular emphasis should be given to social and environmental education, science and technology and modern languages.

- *relevance:* curriculum provision should address the immediate and prospective needs of the young person, in the context of the cultural, economic and social environment.
- *quality:* every young person should be challenged to achieve the highest possible standards of excellence, with due regard to different aptitudes and abilities and to international comparisons.

The curriculum should provide a wide range of educational experiences within a supportive and formative environment. It should draw on the aesthetic and creative, the ethical, the linguistic, the mathematical, the physical, the scientific and technological, the social, environmental and political and the spiritual domains.

Features of the Junior certificate Programme

COHERENCE

The Junior Certificate programme provides a coherent and consistent educational experience for young people through a broad, balanced programme while encouraging young people to make connections between the different areas of educational experience.

A conscious attempt is made in the Junior Certificate programme to identify areas of linkage between different subjects. Common themes and issues are often treated in different but complementary ways. For instance:

- *health education:* opportunities arise in different subjects such as Science, Religious Education, Home Economics and Physical Education.
- *media education:* while the new English syllabus explicitly treats of media studies, many other subjects can also contribute to this area, e.g. Business Studies

and Home Economics re Advertising; History, Geography and Business Studies re Current Affairs reporting; Art, Craft and Designing re Graphic and Visual Display and Film.

- *Civic and political education:* all subjects have as a crucial objective the development in young people of positive attitudes towards themselves and their community. The new syllabuses in subjects such as History and Geography, Business Studies and English offer particularly rich opportunities for the development of such attitudes. The Council is putting in place a committee to review the role of Civics in the curriculum.

CONTINUITY

Close attention is given to the primary school curriculum which young people have experienced and to senior cycle programmes which they may wish to enter. The first year of post-primary education should be used to ensure that all students have made a successful transition to a more subject-focussed curriculum.

PROGRESSION

A stated aim of the Junior Certificate programme is to reinforce and further develop in the young person the knowledge, understanding, skills and competencies acquired at primary level. Teaching and learning experiences should be ordered so as to facilitate a pupil's progress, with each succeeding element making appropriate demands and leading to a better performance. It is recognised that a young person's development does not proceed uniformly or at an even pace.

EQUITY OF TREATMENT

In terms of curriculum and assessment, the Junior Certificate offers equity of treatment to all young people. A dual-system of certification at junior cycle has, in the past, created differences of status and esteem as applying to different certificates. These distinctions no longer exist: all young people are seen to be treated equally and their educational achievements validated within the same national framework.

Differentiation

Within the general principle of breadth and balance, it is recognised that the curriculum must allow for differences in the abilities and aptitudes of young people. Accordingly, within the Junior Certificate programme, courses are offered at two (or in some cases three) levels for certification.

The availability of different levels within the Junior Certificate is designed to enable every young person to achieve the highest possible standards of excellence.

The grouping of pupils in classes remains a matter of school policy.

Flexibility

While retaining the practice of centrally defined syllabuses in subjects for the Junior Certificate, a great degree of flexibility is offered to schools and teachers. The use of the local community and environment, as a teaching/learning resource, is encouraged in all subject areas. Treatment of topics, issues and themes in a syllabus may differ from teacher to teacher, from school to school and from region to region; however, the essential knowledge, understanding, skills and competencies set out for each syllabus must be achieved by all. This ensures a better balance between local autonomy and national requirements.

Pilot projects or experimental courses will continue to be undertaken as part of the development of the Junior Certificate programme. The revised syllabuses already issued owe much to the experience gained through such experimental work.

THE EUROPEAN DIMENSION

Ireland's membership of the European Community serves as a backdrop to the Junior Certificate and provides a wider context for its implementation. Teachers are encouraged to highlight the economic, social and cultural implications of this for all our people and to stress the challenges and opportunities which this provides. Subjects such as Modern European Languages, Technology and other technical subjects, Irish, Business Studies and History and Geography are particularly important in this sense but all subject-teaching should incorporate this European dimension.

III.31 (b) N.C.C.A. The Junior Certificate Examination — Recommendations to the Minister for Education, 1990

The new Junior Certificate Examination had been announced by the Minister for Education, Mary O'Rourke, in 1988 and this new examination would supersede the Intermediate and Group Certificate examinations from 1992. The new syllabi were introduced in September 1989 and in January 1990 the National Council for Curriculum and Assessment published its recommendations to the Minister on the Junior Certificate examination. The report was short and concise and included sections on Areas of Assessment; Methods of Assessment; the Structure of Examinations; Reporting of Performance and Special Provisions.

The following extract relates to areas and methods of assessment:

1. AREAS OF ASSESSMENT

1.1 Examinations should be congruent with and reflect the aims and objectives of syllabuses. Thus, for example, in some subject areas, the main focus of assessment should be in the cognitive area (e.g. examining students' ability to remember, judge, imagine and reason); in others, it should be in the psychomotor area (e.g. examining students' knowledge and skills in working with materials such as wood, metal and plastic). Oral and aural competence should be assessed where appropriate.

1.2 Students' feelings, attitudes and motivation should be assessed only insofar as they are relevant to the cognitive and psychomotor areas being assessed. For example, initiative and perseverance would be relevant in the assessment of project work.

2. METHODS OF ASSESSMENT

2.1 The existing range of provisions for examining (written, practical, project, oral, aural), which includes school-based, external and terminal assessments, should be maintained and, where feasible and desirable, should be extended.

2.2 Course Committees (sub-committees charged with drafting syllabuses and associated assessment procedures) should state the methods of examining which they consider desirable, the objective or set of objectives for which each method is to be used, and the weighting to be assigned to information obtained by each method. Actual provision, however, will depend on the availability of financial and other resources.

2.3 In extending the range of methods in examinations, preference should be given to the use of non-written techniques of assessment in languages.

2.4 Steps should be taken to extend the range of assessment techniques used in science.

2.5 In the short-term, oral and aural examinations may have to be conducted as single terminal examinations. More valid and reliable estimates of oral and aural competence might be obtained if assessments were carried out over a longer period of time and in a variety of situations.

2.6 In the short-term also, the examination of practical skills may have to be confined to the assessment of products in a terminal examination. While it is acknowledged that some aspects of practical work (e.g., planning skills, process) cannot be adequately assessed in such a terminal examination, it may be necessary, for practical reasons, to operate within this format.

2.7 Where provision is made for practicals, projects or orals on an optional basis, modifications should be made in the requirements of the terminal examination to take account of this provision.

2.8 A variety of written forms of assessment should be used as appropriate, including objective items, structured and short answer questions, and open-ended or essay questions.

2.9 The inclusion of a folder prepared by the student may be appropriate in the examination of some subjects.

2.10 Care should be taken in the design of examinations to ensure that the language used is appropriate to students' level of linguistic ability.

III.31 (c) N.C.C.A. The Curriculum at Junior Cycle — Curriculum Framework and Junior Certificate Requirements — A Position Paper, June 1991.

In 1986, the Curriculum and Examinations Board had recommended a curriculum framework for junior cycle in its publication In Our Schools (see III.29). However, no decision in relation to this framework had been taken by Patrick Cooney, Minister for Education before the Fine Gael/Labour Coalition fell later that year, nor was any decision taken by his successor Mary O'Rourke, T.D. The new syllabi for the Junior Certificate examination were launched in 1988 without reference to a broader curriculum framework and it was not until June 1991 that the National Council for Curriculum and Assessment recommended such a framework in a Position Paper which was submitted to the Minister and widely circulated. The framework is very similar to that recommended in the 1986 document In Our Schools as can be seen from the following extract:

THE JUNIOR CYCLE CURRICULUM FRAMEWORK

The curriculum comprises all those activities which take place within the organisational framework of the school to promote the development of its pupils. The curriculum should provide a wide range of educational experiences within a supportive and formative environment. It should draw on the aesthetic and creative, the ethical, the linguistic, the mathematical, the physical, the scientific and technological, the social, environmental and political and the spiritual domains.

At primary level five broad aspects of the curriculum are organised around a unifying principle of integration. Towards the end of primary education, curriculum divisions begin, in practice, to correspond more closely to traditional subject divisions. At post-primary level teaching and learning are more formally organised around such subject divisions. The curriculum framework at junior cycle must ensure a smooth transition from one level to the next, recognising that a young person's progress does not proceed uniformly or at an even pace. The junior cycle curriculum must therefore be viewed from a wider perspective than that of subject specification alone.

Over the three years of junior cycle, a broad curriculum framework encompassing the various domains of learning is recommended for all pupils. This framework can be described in general terms as curriculum areas and more specifically in terms of subjects which can relate to one or more areas of the curriculum. The framework provides for appropriate continuity and progression from the primary school curriculum, and for advancement to senior cycle.

Recommended minimum time allocations for the different curriculum areas are calculated on the basis of 28 class-contact hours per week in a school-year of approximately 34 weeks or 168 days. This gives a total of approximately 2820 tuition hours for the three years of junior cycle.

(NOTE: this is based on current requirements of 180 school instruction days of which about 12 days are allocated to state examinations).

The recommended minimum time allocations, in approximate percentage terms, approximate total hours allocation over three years and approximate weekly hours allocation are set out below. The hours allocations over three years are individually rounded up or down for ease of calculation: accordingly the total hours allocated show a slight discrepancy from total hours available; the weekly hours allocation indicates the implications for regular timetabling but it is recognised that implementation need not always depend on uniform timetabling arrangements (see Implementing the Curriculum Framework below).

Curriculum Area	Minimum Time Allocations (approx)		
	%	Hours (per 3 years)	Hours (per week)
Language & Literature			
a. vernacular	20	565	5.6
b. other	10	280	2.8
Mathematical Education	10	280	2.8
Science and Technology	10	280	2.8
Social, Political, Environmental Education	10	280	2.8
Arts Education	7.5	215	2.1
Physical Education	5	140	1.4
Religious Education	5	140	1.4
Guidance, Counselling, Pastoral Care	2.5	70	0.7
Discretionary allocation	20	565	5.6
TOTALS	100	2,815	28

The above framework outlines the parameters of breadth (in its coverage of curricular experiences) and of balance (in the relative time allocations given for the different experiences). This common curriculum framework for all schools will help to ensure equity of treatment for all young people during the period of compulsory schooling. Sufficient flexibility is maintained, however, to allow schools the discretion to interpret these national guidelines in a manner appropriate to their own needs.

****

IMPLEMENTING THE CURRICULUM FRAMEWORK

The curriculum framework which is proposed above is intended for planning and evaluation purposes and as such is not prescriptive.

There are a number of constraints impinging on a school's ability to provide every student with a broad and balanced curriculum, spanning the areas described above. The size of school, the number of teaching staff, the range of curriculum expertise, the resources and facilities available and the curricular tradition of the school can be important factors affecting the capacity of schools to provide such a curriculum. However, the curriculum framework described above is designed to be as flexible as possible to enable schools to maximise their strengths.

The curriculum framework should apply in planning the curriculum for all students, irrespective of such variables as gender, ability, aptitude or geographical location.

There are different ways in which a school may organise the implementation of the Curriculum Framework, including —

- weekly timetable each year, reflecting the overall three-year time proportions for the different curriculum areas;
- blocking areas of curriculum provision in concentrated periods of a half-term or a term;
- weighted provision, varying from year to year, or in exceptional cases, total provision of one area in one school year, with no provision in other years.

III.31 (d) N.C.C.A. The Curriculum at Senior Cycle: Structure, Format and Programmes — A Position Paper, June 1991

The growth in the numbers of young people remaining in school after the compulsory period has been referred to earlier in this book. In 1991, over 60,000 pupils sat the Leaving Certificate examination; of these about 7,000 were repeating the examination. Thus the proportion of the relevant age cohort sitting the Leaving Certificate was almost 80%. The debate on whether senior cycle should continue to offer a general and non-vocationally oriented education, or whether it should develop as a binary system with clearly identified vocational and general tracks, had been going on since the mid 1980s when the Curriculum and Examinations Board had opened up the issue in *Issues and Structures in Education,* and in its subsequent discussion paper on Senior Cycle. Following extensive consultation, the National Council for Curriculum and Assessment indicated to the Minister, in June 1991, that "it recognises and supports the current position whereby the education sector is the dominant provider of programmes for young people in the 15 to 18 year age-group."

The following extract from the Council's Position Paper, which was widely circulated summarises the Council's proposal:

A Proposal for Senior Cycle Curriculum and Certification

1. The provision of a coherent programme of education and training for young people in the post-compulsory schooling period is a matter of concern in most European countries and in other countries. Such provision may include programmes implemented entirely within the education sector, jointly between the education and training sectors or solely within the training sector. In the Irish context, the Council is concerned primarily with programmes within the mainstream school system and to some extent with those

under the auspices of the education authorities in joint action with labour, training or other authorities. The Council recognises and supports the current position whereby the education sector is the dominant provider of programmes for young people in the 15-to-18 year age-group.

2. The Council envisages that the educational needs of young people in the post-compulsory period will be met mainly through the mainstream school programmes, such as the Leaving Certificate. The Council also recognises that other programmes provided in or through schools, should continue to be offered: mainly vocationally oriented programmes (often implemented in conjunction with training bodies, and supported by external funding), aimed at specific target groups. Procedures for the certification of students following such programmes may be the function of a National Certifying Body for vocational training programmes, the establishment of which the Minister for Education has recently announced.

3. The preferred option for Senior Cycle educational provision is an inclusive model i.e. one that will accommodate the greatest number of students with flexibility to cater for a diversity of student needs. The essential feature of the model is the introduction of a CERTIFICATE OF SENIOR CYCLE EDUCATION to be awarded to all students on satisfactory completion of a senior cycle programme or programmes. This certificate would contain a statement of the courses taken and where appropriate the grades obtained in the Leaving Certificate, the Senior Certificate and other appropriate programmes. (In some circumstances Junior Certificate courses and grades might also be recorded).

4. This model is based on current provision, drawing together in a closer relationship the following programmes:

   - Leaving Certificate
   - Senior Certificate (incorporating VPT 1)
   - Transition Year.

   Other programmes including Post-Leaving Certificate and VPTII programmes are not included in this model. They are treated separately.

5. The Council would also wish to consider whether the scope of such an "umbrella" certificate might be expanded to record programmes and qualifications certificated by the National Certifying Body for vocational training. This would offer the advantage of recording all educational achievements of enrolled senior cycle students.

III.32 The National Council for Vocational Awards, 1991

The National Council for Vocational Awards was launched by the Minister for Education, Mary O'Rourke, T.D., on 29th October 1991. The function of the council is to structure courses in vocational/technical education and training on a modular basis and to provide assessment and certification for such courses. The council's remit covers vocational training programmes at pre- and post-Leaving Certificate levels as well as adult education programmes. At the launch of the council the Minister indicated that the setting up of the council would remove any uncertainty regarding course standards and would enable those institutions and bodies conforming to the national standards to obtain accreditation, thereby assisting those seeking employment and informing prospective employers. The new council consists of a chairperson and 14 council members representing various education and labour/employment bodies. There are also 8 regional co-ordinating groups, based on Local

Government Development Regions, and these regional groups will report to the national council.

The following are (a) the terms of reference of the national council; (b) the terms of reference of the regional co-ordinating groups, and (c) a list of courses under the remit of the council:

(A) NATIONAL COUNCIL FOR VOCATIONAL AWARDS
TERMS OF REFERENCE

(a) Subject to the approval of the Minister for Education
 (i) to structure courses in vocational/technical education and training, as provided by the education system, on a modular basis;
 (ii) to develop an appropriate framework of levels of qualification for these courses;
 (iii) to develop modular content for the core modules of such courses to be applied at a national level;
 (iv) to review and approve regional specific modules as proposed by Regional Co-ordinating Groups;
 (v) to establish guidelines, criteria and standards for the assessment of participants' performance by individual course providers;

(b) to monitor compliance with criteria and standards through an on-going review of national returns on performance and the auditing of individual course providers on a targeted/sampling basis;

(c) to certify participants' performance based on the outcome of assessment by course providers, subject to compliance with assessment criteria standards;

(d) to accredit, subject to the approval of the Minister for Education, the awards of a limited number of examining bodies of long standing in the field of vocational/professional education;

(e) to act as a National Agency for the recognition of relevant vocational qualifications obtained in other member states of the European Community and as an Information Centre for authorities in other member states in relation to NCVA qualifications.

(B) Regional Co-ordinating Groups

There will be 8 Regional Co-ordinating Groups based on the new Local Government Development Regions. These Regional Co-ordinating Groups will report to the National Council.

Terms of Reference

(a) to co-ordinate and monitor the provision for technical education and training, as provided by the education system, in its region;

(b) to review and report to the Department of Education on the existing technical education and training provision in the region;

(c) to make recommendations on the suitability of the current provision in relation to labour market needs and on any proposals for change or improvement;

(d) to review proposals from individual programme providers within the education system for new programmes or changes to programmes and submit with recommendations to the National Council;

(e) to make proposals, in consultation with the course provider(s) concerned on region specific modules to be added to the core modules;

(f) to assist the Department of Education in the monitoring of performance;

(g) to provide assistance and support for programme providers in developing and improving region-specific modules, in implementing assessment systems and through the dissemination of information to employers.

In addition, with respect to (a) and (f) the Regional Co-ordinating Groups may report directly to the Department of Education as circumstances require, as well as to the National Council.

(C) COURSES UNDER THE REMIT OF THE NEW COUNCIL

(i) All Vocational Preparation and Training (VPT) programmes in schools other than those included within the Senior Cycle.
(ii) Such vocational training modules in relation to the Leaving Certificate and the Senior Certificate Programmes as may be required by the Department of Education.
(iii) The Vocational Training Opportunities Scheme (VTOS).
(iv) In consultation with the training agencies and other interested bodies it is expected that the following training programmes will be included:

   (a) Youthreach programmes, (First Year)
   (b) Travellers' Workshops,
   (c) Courses in horticulture, amenity horticulture, agriculture, fishing, afforestation in conjunction with the appropriate authorities, Teagasc, Coillte, etc.
   (d) Other adult vocational and technical education courses, as provided by the education system.

IV

TEACHERS — Education, Conditions of service and salaries, 1922-1991

IV.1 Teacher Training Colleges in Saorstát Éireann — (the Irish Free State) — Report of the Department of Education for the School Year 1923/24

The following brief extract from the first published report of the Department of Education describes the situation in relation to primary teacher training in the Irish Free State before and after 1922:

There were thus up to September, 1922, seven Training Colleges receiving grants from the Commissioners of National Education. The number of students for which they were licensed were as follows:

	Men	Women
Marlborough Street	130	165
St. Patrick's	165	—
Our Lady of Mercy	—	200
Church of Ireland	50	85
De La Salle	200	—
St. Mary's	—	100
Mary Immaculate	—	100

The Colleges continued to receive the grants approved in the Balfour Scheme until the high cost of living, occasioned by the European War, necessitated increased capitation grants. In 1917, and again in 1920, the capitation grant was increased and finally the following scales of payment were approved:

Men	Women	Fees paid by students
£78	£65	£12 10 0
£80 10 0	£67 10 0	£15
£83	£70	£17 10 0
£85 10 0	£72 10 0	£20
£88 (max.)	£75 (max.)	£22 10 0 (max.)

Prior to the present scale of payments very few of the students paid any fees, and, in the cases of those who did pay, the amount varied up to £5 per annum. All the students in the Colleges at present pay the maximum fee of £22 10s. per annum.

From 1st September, 1922, Marlborough Street Training College was closed, and from 1st September, 1928, St. Mary's Training College, Belfast, passed under the jurisdiction of the Minister of Education for Northern Ireland.

The Colleges now under the control of this Department are as follows:

	Licensed for	
	Men	Women
St. Patrick's	165	—
Our Lady of Mercy	—	200
Church of Ireland	50	85
De La Salle	200	—
Mary Immaculate	—	100

The full licensed number of students have not, however, been in residence in St. Patrick's, De La Salle, or Church of Ireland Training Colleges, owing to a shortage of candidates for entrance to training in recent years.

An examination on a competitive basis is held each year at Easter for entrance to these Colleges, and, with the exception of University graduates who may be exempted from the examination in whole or in part, all candidates for training are required to qualify in the examination. The candidates are untrained teachers, monitors, pupil teachers, and private students.

IV.2 The National Programme of Primary Instruction, 1922; recommendations with regard to the training of teachers

The background to the publication of this report has been discussed earlier in this book (II.1). The following brief extracts refer to the recommendations of the Conference in relation to (a) the training of teachers and (b) provision to enable existing teachers to acquire a knowledge of Irish.

(A) TRAINING OF TEACHERS

The Conference strongly recommends:

1. That the training of teachers should be conducted directly by the Universities; that the programme for the entrance examination should be equivalent to that for matriculation; that the training course should cover four years and be so arranged as to make provision for all the subjects of the National School Programme; that at the end of the training course a degree should be awarded; and that the Higher Diploma be a post graduate course as at present.

2. That the Universities should, by means of extension lectures, vacation courses, or otherwise, make such provision as will enable existing teachers to qualify for their degree.

(B) PROVISION TO ENABLE EXISTING TEACHERS TO ACQUIRE A KNOWLEDGE OF IRISH

The Conference strongly recommends:

(i) That the Government should take immediate steps to provide facilities whereby existing teachers may at the earliest possible date be fully trained and equipped for the proper carrying out of this programme, especially with regard to the Irish Language.

(ii) That attendance at the classes or courses to be provided should not entail a curtailment of the usual holidays allowed to teachers.

(iii) That the expenses of teachers attending these courses should be defrayed by The Education Authority.

IV.3 Setting up of the Preparatory Colleges — Dáil Debates, 24th February, 1926

In 1926 in an effort to recruit Irish-speaking primary teachers, the government established a network of residential preparatory colleges. There were seven colleges in all — three for Catholic boys, three for Catholic girls and a co-educational one for Protestant boys and girls. Preference was given to candidates from the Gaeltacht. The purpose of the colleges was "to provide a four year secondary school course with the most favourable conditions for young persons who desired to prepare themselves for admission to a training college, to become primary teachers." Irish was not only "the ordinary medium of instruction but also the language of all the domestic and social activities of students." The INTO was critical of the scheme from the outset as it regarded the colleges as offering too narrow an education for prospective teachers who were recruited direct from national schools. T.J. O'Connell, General Secretary of the INTO, spoke at length in the Dáil when the scheme was first outlined in February 1924. The following extracts are from his speech:

With regard to this new scheme of preparatory colleges which it is proposed to substitute for the present arrangements I would like to say a few words. It is proposed to take boys and girls of approximately fourteen or fifteen and put them into institutions or preparatory colleges with a view to training them to be teachers. Such a scheme has its advantages of course, but I am not clear that there is not a disadvantage in segregating boys and girls at that age and having them specialise, giving them the impression that from that age onwards they are to be teachers. I do not know whether that is good or wise. I have my doubts as to its wisdom. I think that if they were left freer up to the age of seventeen or eighteen to decide whether or not they would go in for the profession of teaching it would be better, and I think it would be better also if they carried on the secondary education with other boys and girls who were going for different professions. I think that there would be an advantage in it. I know, of course, that under the present circumstances that is not easy. We may not have the right type of secondary schools to which these boys and girls could be sent. I do see that that is a practical difficulty, but I am not satisfied that the best thing to do is to segregate these boys and girls at such an age as is proposed.

****

It is not made clear in this document, although I think it is the intention from the wording, that children other than those in the Gaeltacht will be eligible for entrance, although the colleges will be situated mainly in the Gaeltacht. I gather in a general way that that is the intention of the Minister, but a superficial reading of this would rather give the impression that entrance to the colleges in the Gaeltacht will be confined to children in the Gaeltacht. I hope that the Minister will make it plain that it is the intention that they will be open to children from all parts of Ireland, provided of course, that they are able to pass the examinations.

IV.4 New Programme for the Training Colleges, 1932

In 1931 the Department of Education ended the Easter scholarship entrance examination to the training colleges and from 1931 onwards candidates were selected on a combination of results from an Easter Preliminary Examination and the Leaving Certificate examination. A training course in the colleges was introduced the following year and this course remained largely unchanged until 1963.

The following extracts from the annual report of the Department of Education for 1932/3 explain the rationale for the change both in the entry requirements and in the training course:

(C) TRAINING COLLEGE ENTRANCE EXAMINATION
OPEN COMPETITION CANDIDATES

In 1931 the new examination system for open competition candidates for entrance to Training Colleges was introduced. Two examinations under this system have been held. The new system consists of an examination at Easter in oral Irish, oral English, Music and for girls a practical examination in Needlework. The candidates who qualify at this Easter Examination are admitted to the Secondary Schools' Leaving Certificate Examination in the following June, and are selected for assignment to the colleges on the combined results of the two examinations.

****

(D) THE COURSES IN THE TRAINING COLLEGES

Up to the school year 1932-33 the scheme of training followed in the Training Colleges was designed to give a course of general education and a course of professional preparation concurrently.

It was designed at a time when the need for supplying general education in the Training Colleges was as great as the need for vocational training.

In other countries similar conditions prevailed, and in these countries likewise the Training College fulfilled the double function.

As facilities for Secondary Education became more general, educational authorities in most countries gradually adopted the view that intending teachers should have had a full course of Secondary Education before they enter the Training College, and that the main concern of the College should be to equip its students with the special knowledge and practical instruction necessary for their future work.

The students now entering the Colleges in Saorstát Éireann have had a course of secondary education, they have passed the Leaving Certificate Examination — many of them with honours. They have acquired in all the principal subjects a proficiency which is adequate to enable them to deal with these subjects in a primary school. Indeed the majority of these students at their entrance to the College would probably have little difficulty in passing the Final Year Training College Examination of ten years ago.

Having regard to all these considerations, the Department reached the conclusion that the general studies of the students should be lessened and their practical studies and exercises augmented. It is estimated that the students in the past devoted three-fourths of their time to general education, and gave only one-fourth to their training proper. It was felt that the ratio might be considerably altered; that in fact the educational work in the Training Colleges could in future be confined to such an amount as might be needed to foster the habit of study in the direction of the student's natural aptitude.

It was also felt that it was desirable to provide for a standard of scholarship that would preserve for the students the advantages which they have so far enjoyed in relation to the University. New programmes for the two years' course in training based on these principles were accordingly drawn up and the students who are doing the first year course in the year 1932/33 are following this programme.

The outstanding features of the new programmes, apart from those indicated above, are the arrangements for the professional training of the students.

The professional course consists of two sections — the first comprising the Principles and Practice of Teaching, and the second those subjects or elements of school work which were not included in the course previously studied by the students or which require a more specific treatment than they have yet received.

The syllabus in Principles proposed for the first year students seeks to include the chief topics of the instruction necessary for them, in order that they may have the right attitude towards their practice in teaching and sufficient knowledge to guide their first attempts in class teaching. The Second Year's course reviews these topics in the light of the experience gained and completes the body of principles and precepts and the practical details of school business that constitute the intital outfit of a teacher.

In addition to the general discussion of educational principles, provision is made for a specific examination of the aims and methods of teaching the different subjects of the school curriculum. This part of the programme will, it is expected, enable the students to lay out practical schemes of instruction, series of lessons suitable for the different standards or groups in a school.

The most important innovation relates to the students' practice of teaching. Hitherto the practice was taken in one school called the Practising School. It is now provided that the students will have opportunities for practice in a number of ordinary national schools approved for the purpose. The Practising School did not give sufficient scope for the fuller practical training which is deemed necessary. The students' work had been done frequently under conditions which are not those obtaining for the class teacher in an ordinary school. Teachers trained in the Practising School have constantly urged that the practice was marred by certain unreal or artificial elements attaching to the conduct of lessons; they felt that they were all the time in touch with a particular type of organisation and dealing with a special class of pupils whose frequent contact with student-teachers rendered them somewhat precocious or sophisticated for normal class-work; they needed, they said, an experience more akin to the actualities of the ordinary school work, and a wider experience. There was the further consideration that if the students were to visit the Practising School sufficiently often and in such large numbers as the need for fuller practical training requires the weakness of such a school as an instrument for the purpose of practice would be emphasised. In fact the school could not cope with the work.

Accordingly the Department has made provision that, while the Practising Schools will still be availed of for the students' practice of teaching, a number of ordinary schools approved for the same purpose will also be utilised.

IV.5 Report of Committee on Teachers' Salaries 1949

All public service salaries, including those of teachers, were cut in 1923 and again in the early 1930s. Teacher dissatisfaction with salary levels grew in the late 1930s and early 1940s, culminating in the national teachers' strike of 1946. The Fianna Fáil Government under De Valera refused to compromise and the strike lasted seven months, the teachers returning to work only following the intervention of Dr. J.C. McQuaid, the Archbishop of Dublin. The appointment of General Mulcahy as Fine Gael Minister for Education in 1948 brought an easing of tension and a Committee on National Teachers' Salaries, under the chairmanship of Judge P.J. Roe, S.C. was appointed "to consider salaries and other grants, including provision on retirement, to be paid to teachers in national schools." The Roe Committee recommended a major change whereby single men and women would be paid on a common salary scale commencing at £150 p.a. and rising in seventeen years to a maximum of £535 p.a. Married men would reach a maximum of £650 p.a. and there would be equal allowances for male and female principals and vice-principals and bonuses for university honour degrees. The five civil servants on the Committee from the Departments of Education and Finance presented a minority report disagreeing with the recommendations on both economic and professional grounds — a common scale would prove too expensive as women now formed the majority of the profession and teachers generally would be receiving salaries higher than those of civil servants. The INTO submitted its own memorandum which was published with the report. The union supported a policy of "equal pay" for men and women and stressed the importance of adequate remuneration for the recruitment of high quality young people into the profession. The union was disappointed when the government, while accepting the principle of the common scale, offered salary rates less than those recommended by the committee: The following extracts are from the report:

At an early stage in our discussions it was agreed by those members of the Committee who sign this Report that in this branch of the teaching profession there existed no sufficient reason for a differentiation between married men and women trained teachers as to the remuneration they should receive in respect of the same work. It was felt by us that in connection with this profession the only justification for this differentiation was the greater responsibility of the male teacher to make adequate provision for the support of a wife and family. We felt that this reason for differentiation could more properly be met by the provision of something in the nature of a marriage gratuity or allowance, and the scales we are recommending have been evolved upon this basis.

The members of the Committee who did not agree to the foregoing decision put before us very forcibly and at considerable length the consideration that, by reason of the grater numbers of women than of men in the profession, the implementation of this decision would result in a considerable increase in the cost of the service. It was suggested that, if the foregoing principle were adopted, the scale recommended by us should be primarily designed as a scale for women rather than for men. We gave the fullest consideration to all these submissions, and decided that, if, as we believed, our decision on the principle was correct, the scale recommended by us should be designed as a scale neither for women nor for men as a class, but should be the scale that we thought would fairly represent proper remuneration for the teacher's work, bearing in mind the various considerations which are later set out in this Report.

We consider that the profession to which our recommendations would apply is one of very great importance to the community as a whole. It is necessary and desirable that the remuneration of the profession should be such as would enable the members of it to have a standard of living which, while not extravagant, would enable them to maintain the status to which they are entitled. All modern states are agreed as to the importance of the teacher's work; the only question is the extent of the burden which should be placed upon the community for the proper remuneration of the teacher. While it may be argued that education is a disinterested profession like medicine and divinity, it is impossible to overlook the fact that we cannot expect high character or intellectual competence without paying the price of qualities like these. There is no sign of backwardness in a nation so unmistakable as this idea that the work of teaching can be performed by well meaning but unintelligent persons. The first step in national progress is to provide that the child shall be taught. The second and more important step is to see that he is well taught, and that those who teach are men and women of knowledge, of ability, and of all the qualities that go to the effective teaching of the young. Only in exceptional circumstances can teachers of this kind be obtained when the profession is badly paid. We consider that payment of salaries which would attract the best possible type of person to the teaching profession would be a sound national investment, that the expenditure involved would be more than repaid in the future, and that the Department of Education could demand a higher standard of educational qualification for recruitment. We have given the fullest consideration to the information and arguments which were put before us as to the increased cost that our recommendations would involve, as to the capacity of the country to bear such increased cost, and as to the necessity for ensuring that National School Teachers were not constituted of a specifically privileged class having regard to the remuneration obtainable by other members of the community. When the status and remuneration of National School Teachers are being considered it must be realised that the system of education in this country is not a system of State education, and that the National School Teachers are not civil servants.

We have not been able to discover any other class of the community whose remuneration would provide a scale to which the remuneration of National School Teachers should be exactly comparable. We have, however, been supplied with information as to the salary scales applicable to various classes of public servants and various employees of semi-public and large business organisations, to all of which we have paid due regard in arriving at the scales which we are recommending. An examination of the scales paid to other classes of the community in state or semi-state employment, whose educational qualifications and positions bear a general comparison to those of the teacher, will go to show that the recommendations could in no circumstances be regarded as excessive.

IV.6 Conciliation and Arbitration Scheme 1951

In 1951 a scheme of conciliation and arbitration for teachers was introduced by the Minister for Education, General Mulcahy. The scheme provided for all claims on salary, allowances and superannuation to come before the Conciliation Council and in the event of non-agreement these claims (with the exception of superannuation) could be referred to an Arbitration Board. The first scheme was temporary and eventually three different schemes were agreed with the INTO (1954), the ASTI (1955), and the VTA (1957). The system of conciliation and arbitration proved an essential and effective mechanism for handling teachers' salaries claims in the coming two decades.

AGREEMENT

Conciliation and Arbitration Machinery in Connection with the salaries and other emoluments of Teachers in National Schools

INTRODUCTION

This scheme is being brought into operation by agreement

between the Minister for Finance and the Minister for Education on the one part and the Irish National Teachers' Organisation on the other part to provide means acceptable to the Government and to the teachers for the determination of claims and proposals relating to the salaries and other emoluments of whole-time pensionable serving teachers in national schools. Matters within the scope of the scheme will in future be dealt with exclusively through the machinery of the scheme, provided, however, that in exceptional circumstances, written or oral approach on such matters to the Minister for Education shall not be excluded.

THE CONCILIATION/COUNCIL

The Council will consist of:

1. a Chairman, who will be a serving civil servant and will be nominated by the Ministers;
2. the official side consisting of two representatives of the Minister for Finance and two representatives of the Minister for Education, all of whom will be serving civil servants;
3. the teachers' side consisting of four representatives of the Irish National Teachers' Organisation, each of whom will be either a serving teacher in a National School or a permanent officer of the Organisation.

The only subjects appropriate for discussion by the Council will be:

1. claims for increase or decrease in the general scales of salary and/or other emoluments payable personally to wholetime pensionable serving teachers in National Schools directly from State funds;
2. claims for increase or decrease in the scale of salary and/or other emoluments payable personally to a category or categories of wholetime pensionable serving teachers in National Schools directly from State funds;

3. principles governing the remuneration payable personally to wholetime pensionable serving teachers in national schools directly from State funds;
4. principles governing the superannuation of serving teachers in national schools.

ARBITRATION

The Arbitration Board will consist of the following members:

1. Chairman;
2. the official side consisting of one member to be nominated by the Minister for Finance and one member to be nominated by the Minister for Education for the hearing of the case;
3. the teachers' side consisting of two members to be nominated by the Irish National Teachers' Organisation for the hearing of the case.

The following matters will, subject to the provisions of sub-paragraph (2) hereunder, be arbitrable, viz.

(a) claims for increase or decrease in the general scales of salary and/or other emoluments payable personally to wholetime pensionable serving teachers in National Schools directly from State funds;

(b) claims for increase or decrease in the scales of salary and/or other emoluments payable personally to a category or categories of wholetime pensionable serving teachers in national schools directly from State funds.

IV.7 Revocation of Rule 72(1) of Department's Rule (i.e. the revocation of the ban on married women teachers) January 1958

Under a new rule introduced by the Department of Education in 1932, all women teachers appointed for the first time to a national school on or after the 1st October 1933 would be required to resign from teaching on marriage. In spite of the opposition of the INTO to this rule, it remained in operation for twenty five years. Its revocation by Jack Lynch, Minister for Education in 1958 has been regarded by some educationalists as the beginning of a new era in Irish education.

The marriage ban was lifted with effect from 1st July 1958 and the terms under which the ban was revoked are contained in the following circular which was sent to managers and teachers by the Department of Education in January 1958:

1. Notice is hereby given to managers and teachers of national schools that Rule 72(1) of the Department's Rules and Regulations, i.e. the rule requiring women teachers in national schools to retire on marriage, will be revoked with effect from 1st July, 1958.

2. Women national school teachers who retired under the terms of Rule 72(1) will be eligible after 30th June, 1958, for recognition in posts in national schools subject to the usual conditions governing the recognition of national school teachers.

3. The following conditions will attach to the re-entry to the teaching service in a recognised capacity, after 30th June, 1958, of women teachers who retired on marriage in accordance with Rule 72(1):

    (a) A woman teacher, on re-entry, will be placed on the salary point corresponding to the point she had reached before retiral on marriage and will be allowed to proceed by normal increments to the maximum of the scale.
    (b) A woman teacher to whom a marriage gratuity was paid will not receive credit for the purpose of pension and retiring gratuity in respect of service

given by her prior to her retiral on marriage unless she refunds to the Minister for Education the equivalent of the amount of the marriage gratuity paid her. To this end, she shall enter into an agreement with the Minister to refund the amount due in such manner and on such conditions as he may specify.

(c) Credit for any purpose will not be given to any teacher in respect of the period intervening between the date of her retiral on marriage and the date of her re-appointment in a recognised capacity in a national school.

4.(a) Women teachers who marry after the 30th June, 1958, are not required to retire on marriage and are not entitled to a marriage gratuity should they opt to retire. However the Minister has decided that teachers at present serving in a substantive capacity (principal, assistant, lay assistant, temporary additional assistant, junior assistant teacher or junior assistant mistress) and to whom Rule 72(1) now applies may, subject to the necessary statutory authority, be paid a marriage gratuity on the usual conditions should they retire on marriage after the 30th June, 1958.

(b) A woman teacher who retires voluntarily from the teaching service after 30th June, 1958, to whom a marriage gratuity has been paid, and who subsequently re-enters the teaching service in a recognised capacity, will, in order to obtain pension and retiring gratuity credit for service prior to her retiral, be required to refund to the Minster the amount of her marriage gratuity plus compound interest calculated at the rate of five per cent per annum from the date of the receipt of the gratuity.

5. Women teachers appointed to a post in a recognised capacity in the teaching service for the first time after 30th June, 1958, will not be eligible for the award of a marriage gratuity.

IV.8 Teachers' Salaries Committee, 1960

The Teachers' Salaries Committee which reported to Dr. P.J. Hillery, Minister for Education, in July, 1960 was asked "to examine and report on principles which might guide the Minister in determining the relationship between the remuneration payable to National Teachers, recognised Secondary Teachers and permanent wholetime Vocational Teachers respectively." The committee which was chaired by Sean O'Broin, made an attempt to establish an acceptable differential scale for the three categories of teachers, but its proceedings were dominated by rivalry between the three teachers' unions who were all represented on the committee. The report recommended the adoption of a "basic school scale" for teachers related to the criteria of qualifications, nature of work and promotion opportunities. It suggested that secondary teachers, therefore, should be paid more than vocational teachers, and vocational teachers more than national teachers. The INTO members of the Committee refused to sign the report and presented a minority report demanding that a "basic personal scale" for teachers should be adopted, and stressing that the work of national teachers had been undervalued.

The following extract indicates the tensions which existed between the INTO and the other members of the committee:

Having studied the material referred to in the preceding paragraphs, the views and proposals of members as they had emerged in discussion, and the submissions made both in writing and orally by the teachers' representatives, we felt that we were sufficiently well briefed to address ourselves to the problem before us. The possibility of an agreed solution being found in the concept of a common scale for all teachers figured largely in our earlier discussions, and it became evident as the field of discussion widened that, while there were opposing views as to the feasibility of adapting such a basis to the conditions obtaining in this country, the implications of that concept would have to be explored very fully before its merits and demerits could be adequately assessed.

We were keenly aware that we had a critical decision to take in choosing between the concept of a "basic personal scale" and that of a "basic school scale," more particularly because of the strong preference of the National Teachers' representatives for a "basic personal scale," a preference which was not shared by the other members of the Committee. The National Teachers' representatives expressed their conviction that a personal scale would lend itself to a more equitable basis of remuneration and, furthermore, that on such a basis regard could readily be had to all the factors to which reference might be made in connection with the concept of a "basic school scale." They claimed that there should be uniformity in the salary structure for the three groups and that teachers with comparable qualifications should be paid the same salaries, irrespective of the type of school in which they taught. All the other members of the Committee were in agreement that, as indicated in paragraph 18 above, the two concepts of a "basic personal scale" and a "basic school scale" should be considered independently of each other and also that, of the two, that of a "basic school scale," taking account of factors additional to the qualification factor, offered the best hope of positive progress in the general circumstances of our educational organisation.

DECISION IN FAVOUR OF A "BASIC SCHOOL SCALE."

After full consideration of the views of all members of the Committee, we decided that our further investigation of the question of relativity principles should be conducted in the light of the general preference, with the exception of the National Teachers' representatives, for a "basic school scale" rather than a "basic personal scale." We would like to emphasise that our decision at this stage in favour of a "basic school scale" did not exclude the possibility of our coming eventually to the conclusion that there should be only one set, or perhaps two sets, of salary scales instead of three as at present. The possibility of further investigating the potentialities of a "basic personal scale" was not excluded either at this stage, but such further investigation was later found to be unnecessary in view of the conclusions to which we came as a result of the investigation of a "basic school scale."

IV.9 Untrained Teachers — Transfer to Trained Scale — proposal of 22nd November 1965

In the early 1960s, there were over 2,500 untrained teachers in the national school system out of a total of 14,000 (about 18%). For a number of years, the position of these teachers, who were on a lower salary scale than trained teachers, had been raised by the INTO in discussions with the Department of Education. In 1965 a proposal was made by the Department that a series of summer courses of training should be made available for untrained teachers. Such courses would take place over three successive summers and could be attended by untrained assistant teachers and junior assistant mistresses. Following satisfactory completion of the summer course an untrained teacher would be deemed "trained" and transferred to the trained salary scale. The INTO initially objected to the scheme but following negotiations about some of the details, the scheme as outlined in the Department's letter of 22nd November 1965 was accepted. The following is the text of the Department's letter.

A Chara,
I am directed to inform you that the Department has had under consideration the establishment of summer courses of training for untrained teachers. It is proposed to offer a twelve-week

summer course — spread over three years, four weeks in each year — and to give concentrated instruction in the principles, theory and methodology of teaching, in child psychology and other allied subjects. Untrained assistants and junior assistant mistresses will be eligible to attend the course. In addition, it is intended to afford those untrained teachers, who have been given special recognition to teach only in small one teacher schools in islands or in remote rural areas, the opportunity of obtaining qualification, provided they had fulfilled the conditions for entrance to training at the Leaving Certificate Examination. The course itself will be exacting; in addition, in the intervals between sessions the trainees will be required to follow a detailed course of reading. All who successfully complete the course will be allowed to enter on the trained teacher scale from 1st July of the year of completion of the course and, subject to the regulations, be eligible for the award of an increment from that date. Those who fail to complete the course will not be eligible for recognition as trained teachers. All applicants must, in the first instance, receive a favourable recommendation from their District Inspector before being permitted to attend the course.

The proposal envisages two courses, each catering for about 50 teachers, being conducted in July, 1966, in Mary Immaculate Training College, Limerick, and in Our Lady of Mercy Training College, Dublin. In the following year there would be a build-up of 200 students in all by the intake of two further groups of 50 each. In the third and subsequent years a further intake of 100 students would take place, making a total number of 300 teachers attending courses. It is intended that only those under 53 years of age on 1st July, 1966, will be selected to attend the training courses so that the minimum period of service by any teacher following the completion of the course would be ten years. Teachers in the upper age groups would be given preference in the matter of selection for the earlier courses to be held.

It is proposed that instruction will be given by Inspectors of the Department, Professors of the Training Colleges and experienced Teachers, but the composition of the teaching staff will depend on the final form the curriculum of the courses will take. A senior Inspector of the Department will, however, be in charge of each training course. It is proposed to charge each teacher a fee of £30 per course of which about £24, i.e. £6 per week, would be paid to the Training College Authorities in respect of maintenance.

The Department is prepared to proceed with the courses of training in July, 1966, provided your Organisation accepts the scheme as a full and final settlement of the untrained teacher problem. It will also be a condition of the introduction of the scheme that for those eventually admitted under the scheme to the trained teacher scale, the difference in the quality and duration of training between them and the teachers who have qualified as national teachers following the normal two year course of training, should be marked by restricting the maximum salary of the former untrained teacher to a point two increments below the current maximum of the trained teacher scale. The Department will be glad to receive these assurances from you at an early date.

IV.10 Report of the Commission on Higher Education, 1967

The Commission on Higher Education, established in 1960, took seven years to present its report. It examined evidence on teacher education from Great Britain and Europe, and received both written and oral submissions in Ireland. Among the report's major recommendations was the establishment of a network of "New Colleges" which would have a more vocational orientation than the existing universities, and the commission recommended that these "New Colleges" would play a central role in the development of teacher education. The primary teacher training institutions should become attached to these "New Colleges" and offer a broad three year degree course for primary teachers. Secondary teacher training also should be developed in the "New Colleges" as well as being expanded within the existing university education departments. Degrees should be offered to teachers in manual and vocational subjects.

The following is a summary of the recommendations of the commission in the area of teacher education:

TEACHER TRAINING AND EDUCATIONAL RESEARCH

The course for national teacher-training should be extended from two to three years.

The national teacher-training colleges should be associated with the New Colleges; the training colleges would form the education departments of the New Colleges and would look to the New Colleges for teaching in special and general subjects.

National teachers during training should be enabled to take a degree of a New College and, subsequently, a university degree.

The general preparation and pedagogical training of teachers for secondary schools should continue to be provided in the universities, but later recommendations regarding university courses may necessitate a reconsideration of the present organisation of teacher-training in the universities.

The New Colleges could reasonably take part in the general preparation and pedagogical training of teachers for secondary schools.

Specialist teachers are necessary throughout the secondary school system to raise the standard both of teaching and of entry to higher education; secondary school teachers should be required to teach only subjects studied during their course of higher education.

A new approach to the preparation and training of teachers for vocational schools could be achieved by the association of the New Colleges with institutions of higher vocational education and the teacher-training colleges.

The universities, the National College of Agricultural and Veterinary Sciences, and the Technological Authority would also participate in the general preparation of teachers for the vocational education service and in their pedagogical training.

Pedagogical training for all categories of vocational teachers is generally recommended. The training of part-time teachers presents special problems, which should be decided on their merits. The lengthening of training courses for teachers of manual instruction should be considered with a view to broadening the content of their training.

Teachers for the new comprehensive schools could suitably be trained in the New Colleges and associated institutions.

Education should be regarded as an essential subject of university study, and university education departments should be appropriately staffed and financed. Steps should be taken to stimulate and promote research in problems of Irish education. The initial need is for a voluntary association of experts to define the problems and to formulate research programmes.

IV.11 Ryan Tribunal on Teachers' Salaries, 1968

The Tribunal on Teachers' Salaries was set up by Donogh O'Malley, Minister for Education in December 1967, and was chaired by Professor Louden Ryan of Trinity College, Dublin. Its terms of reference were "to recommend a common basic scale of salary for teachers in national, secondary and vocational schools" and to suggest "what appropriate additions might be made to the basic scale in respect of qualifications, length of training, nature of duties, etc." The tribunal worked quickly and reported to the new Minister for Education, Mr. Brian Lenihan, in April 1968. It recommended along with the common basic salary scale a scheme of allowances for qualifications and eight graded posts of special responsibility. A single scheme of conciliation and arbitration was to be introduced for all branches of teachers. The report which was meant to be a major move towards a unified teaching profession resulted instead in bitter conflict, and in 1969 all three teachers' unions took strike action. It was not until 1973 that the ASTI finally agreed to a common salary scale and a common system of conciliation and arbitration. The following extracts are taken from the report of the tribunal:

RECOMMENDATIONS ON COMMON SCALE ALLOWANCES, ETC.

.......In the evidence presented to us, the need to improve the status of teachers, and to establish a proper relationship between their emoluments and those in other occupations, was repeatedly emphasised. The status of a profession is not determined by economic considerations alone. In so far as such considerations are relevant, we have had them in mind in reaching our recommendations relating to allowances. In fixing the common scale we have had regard to such general increases in salaries as may occur during 1968-69.

PROBATIONARY SERVICE

We recommend that the period of probation in all schools should be one year, that a teacher on probation should in future receive a salary equal to the minimum of the common scale plus the appropriate allowances for length of training and qualifications, and that the first increment should become payable on completion of one year's satisfactory service from the date of commencement of duty. The decision as to whether or not the year's probationary service is satisfactory should be made by the Department of Education on the recommendation of the appropriate branch of its inspectorate.

SUPERANNUATION:
We recommend that there should be a common, contributory superannuation scheme which should apply to all teachers. (The Department should have discretion to waive the 5% superannuation deduction in the case of secondary teachers who are not members of the existing superannuation scheme for secondary teachers. The Department should also consider how vocational teachers who entered the service before 31 March, 1948, can be assimilated into the new common superannuation scheme). Pensionable salary should consist of scale salary plus all allowances with the exception of children's allowances, and it should be subject to a deduction of 5 per cent. Pensions and lump sum payments should be calculated in the manner now prescribed for national and vocational teachers.

Conflicting evidence was presented on whether or not an allowance should be paid for a pass primary degree. On the one hand, it was argued that a pass degree was the minimum qualification for a teaching post in a post-primary school and in general the minimum status of those who had successfully completed three years or more of training : to pay an allowance for it and also compensate for the period of training in excess of two years would therefore in a sense constitute double compensation for one and the same qualification. On the other hand, it was argued that an allowance is now paid to national teachers for a pass degree, and that length of training and pass degrees are separately rewarded in both Northern Ireland and Britain. To remove the allowance now paid to national teachers for a pass degree would make it extremely difficult to fit existing national teachers into the new framework. We have therefore recommended that all teachers should be eligible for the pass degree allowance.

****

OTHER RECOMMENDATIONS

In our view, the development of a single profession of teaching in large measure depends on a common scale and a common system of superannuation and of allowances for training, qualifications, posts of responsibility and principals and vice-principals, being applied to all schools. We are therefore concerned that our recommendations should have a durable effect in this direction, and that steps should be taken to minimise strains within and upon the new system. There must be careful planning to ensure that shortages of teachers do not develop in any category of school. A single scheme of conciliation and arbitration should replace the present separate schemes for national, vocational and secondary teachers. The development of a single profession of teaching might be further assisted if there were a common course of professional training for all entrants, and the possibilities in this direction might be explored by the Department of Education. If a single profession of teaching is to emerge and endure, no recognised secondary school should have any discretion to supplement or augment the common scale or the common system of allowances.

IV.12 H.E.A. Report on Teacher Education 1970

The Higher Education Authority, established in 1968 following the report of the Commission on Higher Education, considered teacher education as one of its important briefs. A Working Party was set up in 1969 and as the training of teachers was seen as a "wide national issue" the HEA stated: "We feel that we must concern ourselves with the problem generally rather than in relation to any particular group of teachers or any particular region." The 1970 report reiterated the demand for a degree for primary teachers and for the expansion of the teaching and research facilities of the university education departments. It advised that there would be a much increased demand for teachers in the coming decade as the school system expanded, and that inservice education was a priority. The establishment of a teachers' professional council "An Foras Oideachais" was seen as an important step in providing an overall co-ordinating and planning authority.

The following extracts are taken from the report:

AWARD OF DEGREE

A degree is the qualification for most professions and the view is held more and more widely that primary teachers, who form the very base of the educational system, should by way of their training course be enabled to attain this qualification.

****

In the re-structured three years course the syllabus of academic and pedagogical (practical and theoretical) content pursued should be so designed when successfully completed, as to merit the award of a degree. We suggest that the degree concerned be a Bachelorship in Educational Science (B.Ed.Sc.).

This arrangement would have many advantages over the present system. It would enhance the status of the primary teacher and the teaching profession in general, it would bring the aim of a unified teaching profession a step nearer, and it would help to counterbalance any possible drift of students from the Training Colleges to the Universities. On the other hand, if no degree were to be had from the Training College course, then with grants available to students attending the Universities, but not to those at Training Colleges, many potential students may be attracted away from the Training Colleges, with a consequent shortage of suitable teachers at primary level. This issue arises particularly with regard to men teachers. It is felt that under the present university grants scheme men will tend to opt for the university, thus rendering the teaching profession at primary level a predominantly female one. This, we believe, would on educational, social and economic grounds be undesirable.

If the standard of candidates for primary teacher training in other countries is examined, it will be seen that in Ireland we have been more than fortunate in the calibre of such students. While it might be argued that less well qualified people could become just as competent teachers as any, we feel that no effort should be spared to retain the high quality which has hitherto obtained here. With an extended and better training course and with the award of a degree, we think that a sufficient supply of teachers of the present high quality will be forthcoming for our primary schools. As to the actual award of the degree to student-teachers who successfully complete the three year course, we consider that it should come from the proposed Council for National Awards, subject to the conditions and requirements of that body and consultation on its part with the proposed Foras Oideachais. We are convinced that the standards of qualifications awarded by the Council for National Awards must be judged on the inherent quality of the courses leading to these qualifications and on the success of these courses in catering for a diversity of professional needs. Thus the present arrangements for the adoption of courses and the setting of examinations involving the Department of Education, the Universities and the Training Colleges would no longer carry the normal possibility of obtaining various levels of Honours therein and that appropriate financial allowances for Honours would be additional to the normal salary scales.

The question of the registration of teachers after a suitable probationary period would be a matter for An Foras Oideachais.

POST-GRADUATE COURSE FOR PRIMARY TEACHERS

We would also favour the provision for primary teachers of a special optional post-graduate course in one of the academic subjects taken by the student-teacher for his degree or in some branch of Education, including educational administration or planning. The course would lead to an M.Ed. Sc. degree, and the holder of this qualification should have the option of teaching at primary or post-primary level the subjects in which he is academically qualified.

INTERCHANGEABILITY OF TEACHERS BETWEEN THE PRIMARY AND POST-PRIMARY SECTORS

At present the graduates of the Training Colleges may teach only in Primary Schools. They are not permitted to teach at post-primary level without acquiring the further qualifications at present required. We may add that post-primary teachers are also debarred from teaching at primary level except in the case of graduates who take a one-year course in the Training Colleges. Consequently our primary and post-primary system is highly compartmentalised. It takes no cognisance of the possibility that a University graduate might prefer to teach at primary level or that a Training College graduate might show a preference for post-primary teaching. We think that it would be highly desirable, from an educational point of view, to have the rigidity of the present system relaxed. With the recommended upgrading of the courses in the Training Colleges and the award of a degree (together with the facilities for post-graduate study) we think that An Foras Oideachais should give immediate attention to the question of interchangeability of teachers between the primary and post-primary sectors.

EDUCATION OF POST-PRIMARY TEACHERS

The Higher Diploma in Education course to be a full-time one year course.

At present a student-teacher taking the Higher Diploma course may be engaged in full-time teaching from 9 a.m. to 4 p.m.

His teaching duties are usually fairly onerous and include correction and preparation work. This leaves him little time or energy for private study and in addition denies him the use of the library during the day. Moreover, it has been represented to us that since the lectures cannot begin till late afternoon, their content may be compressed. Furthermore, because of the shortage of experienced staff and equipment in the University Departments of Education, the course as such has been stated to have certain limitations. It has been represented to us that it needs some broadening and deepening in the application of modern educational theories, that its pedagogical content should receive greater emphasis and that a new recognition should be accorded to the importance of the technology of teaching. We have been further told that, as a result of the various pressures of the course, good Honours graduates in Science and in Arts are coming increasingly to choose immediate employment outside teaching rather than face the present rigours of the additional year's training. We were also informed that the present arrangements for teaching practice in the schools are often defective. Again, the complaint was made that candidates for the Higher Diploma have often to go from school to school in search of opportunity for their practical work.

****

Having considered the evidence very fully we recommend that from the earliest possible date the Higher Diploma course should be of one year's duration on a full-time basis and that lectures should start not later than 2 p.m. daily.

IV.13 Setting up of Teachers' Centres, 1972

The setting up of teachers' centres in 1972 was a recognition of the importance of in-service education for teachers. From the outset it was envisaged that the centres would provide meeting places for teachers at all levels. They would also act as resource centres and locations for "in-service studies and educational experimentation." The decision of government to set up and fund the centres was announced by Pádraig Faulkner, T.D., Minister for Education in the course of the Education Estimates speech in February 1972. A little more than a year later the Drumcondra Teachers' Centre was formally opened by Richard Burke, T.D., then Minister for Education, who mentioned in the course of his speech that there were thirteen centres around the country "with several more in the pipeline."

The following extract is from Pádraig Faulkner's Dáil speech of 17 February 1972:

An lárionad seo do mhúinteoirí, is smaoineamh nua i gcúrsaí oideachais é. Go hachomair, sé is feidhm dó:

(a) ionad cruinnithe a chur ar fáil a dtiocfaidh múinteoirí le chéile ann chun fadhbanna a gcuid oibre a phlé;
(b) a bheith ina lárionad gléasraí agus treallaimh a ndéanfaidh múinteoirí ábhar a ullmhú ann le haghaidh na scoileanna;
(c) áit tionóil a sholáthar le haghaidh chúrsaí staidéir i gclár na scoile;
(d) a bheith ina ionad teaspáintis do shaothar oidí agus daltaí, téacsleabhair, etc.

Is iomaí gasra staidéir atá ann ar fud na tíre mar a dtig múinteoirí i gcionn a chéile ag beachtú a gciall dá ngairm, ag plé ghnéithe dá gcuid oibre agus ag malartú smaoineamh. Faoi láthair cuirtear as go mór dóibh cionnas gan buan-áit fhóirstineach tionóil, gléasraí nó ábhair thagartha a bheith ar fáil acu. Agus rogha-áiteanna a chur ar fáil ar fud na tíre do na daoine dúthrachtacha seo, sé mo mhian go gcuirfinn ar a gcumas dóibh a dtuigse a neartú, a ndeacrachtaí a réiteach agus a gciall dá n-acmhainn féin a ghéarú le gur fearr a gcuirfí in éifeacht é. Is faoi na múinteoirí féin a d'fhágfaí stiúrú na lárionad seo le tacaíocht na Roinne agus chuirfí fáilte iontu roimh gach aicme oidí, eadar bhunoidí agus iarbhunoidí, mar is cóir do ghairm chomhtáite aon-chuspóra.

IV.14 Report of the Planning Committee on the Establishment of An Chomhairle Mhúinteoireachta, 1974

The planning committee which had been suggested by the HEA 1970 report, was set up by the Minister for Education, Richard Burke, and reported in April 1974. Its terms of reference were "to examine the function proposed by the HEA for an Foras Oiliúna in the light of present and future educational needs and attitudes," and "to consider, in that context, how best its powers and responsibilities should be defined, to enable it to achieve its purposes." The report outlined the powers of the proposed council which would include acting as a registration body and validating authority for teachers' preservice and inservice courses, as well as being an advisory agency on teacher supply and a disciplinary body for professional conduct. The Teachers' Union of Ireland strongly objected to the proposed disciplinary powers of the council and no action was taken on the report. The following extracts describe the functions of the proposed council:

GENERAL FUNCTION

Excluding matters of salary, emoluments and conditions of service, to consider how best to educate teachers; how best to foster, encourage and promote the educational and professional interests of teachers; to advise the Minister for Education and the other relevant authorities on all these matters; and to act as a registration council for teachers.

PARTICULAR FUNCTIONS

(a) To determine, in conjunction with the appropriate authorities, the minimum standards of education necessary for entry to teacher education courses.

(b) To investigate and to keep under continuous review the standards of education, the training and the fitness to teach of persons entering the teaching profession and, when appropriate, to make recommendations about these matters to the Minister for Education and the institutions conducting teacher education courses.

(c) To keep under continuous review such other matters relating to teacher education as an Chomhairle Mhúinteoireachta thinks fit, and to advise the Minister for Education, the Higher Education Authority, the National Council for Educational Awards, the institutions conducting teacher education courses and other relevant agencies thereon.

(d) To recognise, subject to confirmation by the Minister for Education, pre-service teacher education courses.

(e) To review at regular intervals, in co-operation with the educational authorities concerned, the organisation and quality of the instruction and content of the courses given in institutions conducting courses recognised by An Chomhairle Mhúinteoireachta for the purpose of teacher education; and to undertake such other functions in relation to such institutions as may be referred to it by the Minister for Education in agreement with the institutions concerned.

(f) To appoint, in consultation with the institutions concerned, persons to visit these institutions and to report to An Chomhairle on the content and arrangement of courses and the general facilities available in connection therewith.

(g) To withhold, subject to confirmation by the Minister for Education, recognition of a teacher education course or courses where in the opinion of An Chomhairle the course or courses in question fail to reach an adequate standard either as to entry, content or staffing, or where it considers the general facilities of the institutions concerned to be inadequate.

(h) To consider all matters relating to the supply of teachers.

(i) To issue certificates of registration to qualified teachers and to make regulations governing the conditions (including the registration fee) under which registration should be accorded, withheld, suspended or withdrawn.

(j) To establish and keep a register containing professional particulars of (i) teachers who are already recognised, and (ii) teachers who are eligible for registration and apply to be registered. Registration will be for a particular level and function, in accordance with the qualification(s) obtained, and, in the case of teachers in category (ii), will be provisional pending the fulfilment of prescribed conditions.

(k) To make arrangements for the setting up of a Professional Conduct Committee, a majority of whose members shall be serving teachers. The function of this Committee shall be to investigate alleged misconduct or grave professional default on the part of a registered teacher. When the Committee deems it necessary to recommend the removal of a teacher's name from the register, An Chomhairle shall refer the recommendation to the High Court for a decision.

(l) To organise, arrange and advise on in-service courses for teachers; to organise, arrange and advise on courses for serving teachers leading to the acquisition of specialist skills or additional qualifications which would be recognised by the Department of Education; and to approve and arrange for such other courses as it deems appropriate.

(m) To foster, encourage and assist relevant educational innovation.

(n) To recommend and commission research projects on relevant educational matters and, as appropriate, to publish reports thereon.

(o) To promote inquiries and studies on teacher education and related matters and, where appropriate, to publish reports thereon.

(p) To function as an information centre on all matters pertaining to teacher education.

IV.15 Announcement of University Degrees for Primary Teachers, 1973

From the foundation of the state in 1922, the issue of degree status for national school teachers had been on the agenda. The First National Programme Conference in 1922 had recommended that a degree should be awarded at the end of the period of training of primary teachers. The Commission on Higher Education in 1967 and the H.E.A. report of 1970 had also urged a degree for national teachers. When Brian Lenihan, T.D. was Minister for Education he had indicated his government's intention to introduce such a provision, but it was not until 1973 that Richard Burke, T.D. as Minister for Education, formally announced that all students entering the training colleges in Autumn 1974 would embark on a three year course leading to a B.Ed. degree. He made this announcement at the INTO Congress at Easter 1973 and reiterated it during the Dáil debate on the education estimates in October 1973.

The first B.Ed. degrees were conferred in 1977. The three larger Catholic colleges — Carysfort College; St. Patrick's College, Drumcondra; and Mary Immaculate College, Limerick became recognised colleges of the N.U.I. and the Church of Ireland College; Froebel College, Sion Hill; and St. Mary's College, Marino became affiliated to the University of Dublin (Trinity College).

The following extracts are from Minister Burke's estimates speech in the Dáil on 23 October 1973:

For quite a long time now the inadequacy of a two-year course of training for primary teachers has been acknowledged by all, and the contention of the Irish National Teachers' Association and others that the teachers' training course should be crowned with a university degree has been considered reasonable. That there would be difficulties in bringing about these changes no one doubted, but it seemed to me that sufficiently long time had passed on contemplating those difficulties and that the time had come for positive action.

In addressing the annual congress of the INTO, therefore, at Easter of this year, I announced that the course of training for primary teachers would be extended to one of three years as from next year, 1974. One of the consequences of extending the course by a year is that for one year — the second year following the extension of the course; that is, on the basis of my announcement, 1976 — there would be no new teachers entering the service other than those who had already been graduates when entering on training and those who, having been trained on recognised courses in the United Kingdom, had passed the supplementary tests which made them eligible for recognition as national teachers under my Department.

IV.16 Thomond College of Education, Limerick, Act, 1980

The introduction of the B.Ed. degree for primary teachers in the mid 1970s was a major step towards the achievement of an all graduate teaching profession. Another step in that direction was the establishment of Thomond College in Limerick in 1970 as a national college of physical education to train P.E. teachers for post-primary schools. In 1979 the role of Thomond College was expanded to include the training of woodwork, metalwork and rural science teachers. There were initial difficulties in relation to the validation of the B.A. degree and the first graduates of Thomond College had their degrees validated by the National University of Ireland. However, graduates of the second and subsequent years had their degrees validated by the N.C.E.A. and that remained the case until 1991 when Thomond College was dissolved and its students and staff became members of the University of Limerick.

Thomond College had been established on a statutory basis in 1980 and the following extracts are from the Thomond College of Education, Limerick, Act of 1980.

THOMOND COLLEGE OF EDUCATION, LIMERICK, ACT, 1980

AN ACT TO ESTABLISH AN INSTITUTE OF HIGHER EDUCATION TO BE KNOWN IN THE IRISH LANGUAGE AS COLAISTE OIDEACHAIS THUAMHUMHAN, LUIMNEACH, OR, IN THE ENGLISH LANGUAGE, THOMOND COLLEGE OF EDUCATION, LIMERICK, TO DEFINE ITS FUNCTIONS AND TO PROVIDE FOR OTHER MATTERS CONNECTED WITH THE FOREGOING.

[10TH DECEMBER, 1980].

4.—(1) The functions of the College shall be —

(a) to provide suitable degree level courses for the purpose of the training of teachers for service in such schools and institutions as may be determined by the Minister;

(b) to provide courses for teachers already serving in such schools and institutions as may be determined by the Minister;

(c) to provide such other courses as the Minister may from time to time determine;

(d) to engage in research in such fields as the Governing Body may deem appropriate;

(e) subject to the approval of the Minister, after consultation with an tÚdarás —

  (i) to buy and acquire lands or buildings,

  (ii) to institute and, if thought fit, to award scholarships, prizes and other awards.

****

5.—(1) There shall be a Governing Body of the College which, save as otherwise provided by this Act, shall perform all the functions conferred on the College by this Act.

(2) The members of the Governing Body shall be a chairman, the Director and 23 ordinary members.
(3) The first members of the Governing Body shall be appointed by the Government, on the recommendation of the Minister, and shall hold office for a period of one year from the date of their appointment.

****

(3) Without prejudice to the generality of subsection (1) of this section, the Academic Council shall have the following particular functions, that is to say —

(a) to design, develop and implement appropriate programmes of study,
(b) to make recommendations to the Governing Body for the establishment of appropriate structures to implement the programmes of study referred to in paragraph (a) of this subsection,
(c) to make recommendations to the Governing Body on programmes for the development of research,
(d) to make recommendations to the Governing Body for the selection, admission, retention and exclusion of students generally,
(e) to make, subject to the approval of the Governing Body, and to implement the academic regulations of the College,
(f) to propose to the Governing Body the form of regulations to be made by the Governing Body for the conduct of examinations, and for the evaluation of academic progress.
(g) to make recommendations to the Governing Body for the award of fellowships, scholarships, bursaries, prizes or other awards,
(h) to make general arrangements for tutorial or other academic counselling.

IV.17 Review Body on Teachers' Pay — Interim Report, 1980

The teachers' unions continued to press for increased salaries to keep their remuneration in line with other professions. In January 1980 representatives of the three unions met with the Minister for Education, Mr. John Wilson, and asked for the establishment of a Review Body. Faced with the threat of industrial action, the Department of Education agreed and a Review Body, set up under the chairmanship of Mr. Noel Ryan, was asked to present an interim report by September, 1980 and a final report by January, 1981. Its terms of reference were "to examine and report on the level of salary and allowances of teachers on the common basic scale, taking cognisance of the circumstances of other groups with comparable professional qualifications and responsibilities," and secondly "to have regard to the overall assessment of salary levels, allowances and promotion opportunities, to the nature and conditions of their work, including hours of work and length of the school year, and the role and value of the teacher in society."

When the Review Body's Interim Report was published in September, 1980 the teachers' unions were bitterly disappointed as the suggested new basic salary scale and scheme of allowances fell far short of what had been expected. The Review Body itself resigned when the Minister for Education entered into direct negotiations with the unions who achieved a much higher salary award than had been recommended. No final report of the Review Body was published.

The following extracts are from the interim report of the review body:

COMMON BASIC SCALE

Before making our recommendations in regard to the common basic scale we consider it desirable to indicate, in outline at least, the rationale of these recommendations.

Teaching is a profession, and it is to be assumed that a person enters the teaching profession not merely for the purpose of earning a living, or because it happens to be the only gainful occupation available at a particular time, but because that person wishes to teach.

The salary scale should therefore be such as to attract and hold persons of the quality and dedication which the profession needs and the public desires. It must be an adequate reward for the teacher who remains a teacher. It must be such at its commencement as to attract persons of the quality required and thereafter be such as to be an adequate reward for teaching with all that the term "teaching" implies of actual tuition, personal interest in, and care for, the pupil and personal conduct and example on the part of the teacher.

The relative lack of promotional outlets in the profession was consistently stressed in evidence. Promotions, when they occur, seem to us to involve taking the teacher, in greater or lesser measure, away from teaching. Believing as we do that an aptitude for or even an inclination towards school administration is not necessarily to be found in conjunction with the qualities which make a good teacher, we have attempted in our recommendations to remedy what appears to us to be a defect in the present structure of the scale. It is inherent in the teaching profession that the majority of teachers will remain full time teachers throughout their careers but it will, we believe, be seen that our recommendations provide an adequate response to the career aspirations of teachers as well as reflecting an adequate acknowledgement of professional expertise in the care, education and character formation of future generations.

The nature of the teaching profession is such that it cannot be compared precisely with other employments for salary purposes. We have not attempted to place the profession within a specific relativity structure and we do not see the existing relativity with the Civil Service Executive Officer as an appropriate determinant of teachers' salary. We therefore recommend that this relativity cease forthwith. We have had regard to the salaries of those groups with comparable professional qualifications and in a broad sense to those employments which require a roughly comparable period of post Leaving Certificate training. We have taken account of the element of job security in the teaching profession which we believe is of considerable importance by contrast with the inherent insecurity of employment in business or industry in the private sector.

Proposals have been made, *inter alia,* for a new common basic scale based on percentage increases on the existing scale. While we are satisfied that increases are justified we take the view that the inadequacies of the present scale, as we see them, would not be corrected by the application of either a uniform or a varying rate of increase to that scale. The salary we recommend will, we believe, correct those inadequacies but we would emphasise that the salary so recommended is justifiable only if it is overtly recognised that supervision, substitution, parent contact and pastoral care are integral parts of the teaching function and essential to the proper running of a school. The response we would wish to see generated from the teachers is that these requirements will be met by them generously in the part they play in the moulding and development of their pupils. From the evidence presented to us we are concerned that the quality of school service is not being fully maintained at present. The essential good, a basic entitlement of pupils and parents, can only be met when the school has available to it highly trained teachers who will ensure that the teaching, caring and management needs are comprehensively covered. Management/Staff contracts when reviewed, must, we feel, meet the needs of the day. We believe that our salary proposals recognise the value and inherent worth of the profession and we feel it our duty to state that the prerequisite of any such contracts should be the meeting in full of school requirements of teaching, caring and management. Management/Staff contracts should, we believe, incorporate these fundamental requirements and should as a consequence cover the hours of work and length of the school year needed to meet these requirements.

Salary proposals presented to us have, in almost all cases, included a recommendation that the incremental span be shortened. We have considered these proposals in the context of our overall assessment and have had regard to the fact that the vast majority of teachers enter the scale at the second point or higher. We feel, however, that in keeping with current trends in professional employments in the public and private sector, the existing incremental span should be reduced by two points and our recommended salary scale incorporates this provision in addition to providing five special and long phased increments to reflect our view of the importance of senior teachers and of the commitment required of them.

IV.18 White Paper on Educational Development 1980

The White Paper on Educational Development, published in December, 1980, (see I.15), contained specific recommendations regarding inservice provision for teachers, advising that this should be "a matter of priority" in certain areas of new developments — Irish and modern languages, computers and the management role of the school. The network of Teachers' Centres which had been established by the Department of Education in 1972, were to be supported and the forthcoming report on The Inservice Education of Teachers used as a basis for future development.

The following extracts are from the White Paper:

INSERVICE COURSES FOR TEACHERS

Pre-service education provides a foundation or starting point in the professional development of the teacher. Implicit, then, in any such programme of pre-service education and training is the assumption that subsequently, throughout their careers, teachers will have regular, on-going and substantial opportunities for further education, training and renewal. It is, accordingly, heartening to record that the last decade or so has seen a creditable degree of development in the profession of inservice training for teachers, whether by the Department of Education, the Colleges of Education or other educational agencies.

Possible shortcomings in the inservice facilities provided need to be identified and adjusted. It may be, for instance, that duplication on the one hand leads to omission on the other or that certain curricular areas or teaching techniques get undue attention while others receive little or none. Or, indeed, it may be that the courses fail to attract those teachers who might derive the most significant and immediate benefit from them. Further research into the professional needs of teachers is indicated as a first step towards preparing a comprehensive programme of inservice education.

TEACHER CENTRES

The Teacher Centres of which there are twenty-one at present, play an important part in inservice training. They are funded by the Department of Education and cater for first and second level teachers and, in some places, for third-level teachers. Various courses are put on at these centres — some short ones and also courses spread over many weeks to meet the needs of the teachers in the locality. Lectures and demonstrations are given throughout the school year. Experienced teachers and experts in a particular field give lectures and conduct courses. The Department will continue to support the work of the Teacher Centres.

COMMITTEE ON INSERVICE TRAINING OF TEACHERS
In view of the importance which the Department attaches to inservice courses and of the complexity involved, the Department has set up a committee "to identify priority areas of inservice training of teachers and to make recommendations to the Department." The committee is representative of teaching organisations and teacher-training institutions.

IV.19 Report of Committee on Inservice Education 1984

The Committee on Inservice Education was set up in June 1980 and reported in April, 1984. It recommended the establishment of a national council to co-ordinate a comprehensive plan for inservice education. The report stressed the concept of teachers as "lifelong learners" with both personal and professional needs and stated: "This function of inservice education should be viewed as an end in itself and is not to be confused with the professional development curricula and methodology." The report had little effect and was not accepted in the government's *Programme for Action 1984-87.*

The following extracts are from the report:

The aspiration here is to bring about lifelong professional learning as a reality for each teacher. Of course teachers have always needed to be learners and indeed there always have been those who continued to develop professionally throughout their career. But as this could rarely be achieved without overcoming considerable obstacles, it was destined to remain limited in all too many cases. Thus an aspiration which may frequently have been heard and assented to during initial training has commonly failed to reach fruition in the vicissitudes of one's professional life, because of the absence of appropriate facilitating structures. Experience may be educative, but it is not necessarily so. The day-to-day demands of class teaching stimulates the desire to keep abreast of developments in both the content of subjects and teaching methodology, but gaining access to this new knowledge is time-consuming even when it is available. Besides, the teacher today faces problems that reach so far beyond these that a grasp of a whole new area of Educational Theory would be necessary as a conceptual framework for a solution.

****

The explicit support of the teaching profession, of the training institutions and of the Department of Education for the principle of lifelong learning would serve a number of important purposes. Besides treating initial training, rightly, as a foundation, and not as a completed structure, thus recasting its purpose and relieving its overburdened curricula, it would provide teachers with a new model of learning itself, one which would be in closer harmony with our understanding of how adults learn. By breaking down the existing distinction in teachers' own minds between the preservice, the probationary and the professional stages of one's career, it would seek to underpin the integration of learning experiences, whether arising from theory, research or practice, at any and all of these stages, and thereby emphasise the continuity of all three. Thus for the creatively learning teacher, professional growth and personal satisfaction will result from a continuing process in which learning and teaching are fused to the point of being virtually indistinguishable.

When we seek then to design a system of inservice training and education best suited to the cultivation of lifelong learning, the stress must be on the personal and professional autonomy of teachers. In the final analysis the quality and depth of the learning experiences provided, with the incalculable enrichment of education that can result, must ultimately outweigh in importance all considerations of the political or economic concomitants of their provision. Inservice study should, on occasion, be capable of bringing the teacher far beyond the mere acquisition of new knowledge and skills, to demand a widening of interests and a conversion to new values and attitudes. This challenge to lifelong assumptions and the need to unlearn cherished routines — with all the personal trauma involved, demands psychological preparedness as well as time and effort, and relative freedom from other anxieties. As regards provision, it is essential that it be entrusted to the most skilled and sensitive training personnel, and rest on a secure institutional base, as well as attracting commensurate professional recognition. Much important inservice provision in the past has been compromised by erratic and inadequate financing, by planning and implementation inappropriate to professionally experienced adults, or by an understandable reluctance to impose heavy intellectual demands on teachers exhausted after a day in school. As a result of these constraints inservice courses have all too frequently tended to confine their scope more to matters of practice than to questions of underlying principle. In such cases the teachers, for their part, found themselves being invited to alter time-honoured practices but without being personally convinced of the advantages of, or even the need for such changes.

In summary if the essential principle of voluntary participation is to be maintained, and if the notion of lifelong learning for all teachers is accepted as a legitimate aspiration, then three conditions should be fulfilled:

1. It should be recognised that the initial training of teachers provides a foundation rather than a completed structure, on which a strong edifice will subsequently be built.
2. Inservice opportunities, formal and informal, for teacher learning should be provided, maximized and enhanced at all possible points, to ensure that this edifice will be built by every teacher throughout his career.

3. Certain inservice opportunities should be of such a quality and on such a scale as to make possible radical self-appraisal, and the continuous integration of learning experiences by the individual teacher at any stage of his professional development.

IV.20 Programme for Action in Education, 1984-87

The *Programme for Action* (see I.19) stressed the need to curtail the numbers entering the teaching profession, and therefore the numbers of students in both primary and secondary teacher training. The surplus capacity in the training institutions should be utilized to provide inservice courses and the government's new Curriculum and Examinations Board would play a major role in initiating inservice provision in both curriculum and assessment.

The following extracts are taken from the sections on Teacher Training in the *Programme for Action:*

TEACHER TRAINING

****

The future requirement of teachers for National Schools is determined by the wastage rate in the profession, by growth in the number of pupils and by policy measures affecting the pupil teacher ratio or requiring the services of teachers for special interventions. The wastage rate in the profession is particularly low at present and it appears that it will remain so beyond the end of the decade. This is because of small numbers falling due to retire on reaching the age limit during the period in question, combined with a marked decline in the number of posts which become available due to teachers leaving the service for reasons other than reaching retirement age. Under the existing pupil teacher ratios additional teachers will be required to service growth in the number of pupils in National Schools. A number of teaching posts will also be needed for the interventions in areas of disadvantage and improvements in special education provision envisaged in the plan from within the available complement of teaching personnel.

The present policy of restricting the intake to the Colleges of Education so that the output relates more closely to the number of teaching posts likely to be available in National Schools will be continued. This is necessitated by the specific nature of the Bachelor of Education degree which was designed as a qualification for teaching in primary schools and not as a third-level qualification of general application.

The overall reduction in student numbers in Colleges of Education will have to be accompanied by corresponding operational savings in the Colleges and by a restriction in staff recruitment and replacement. It is apparent that some degree of rationalisation and flexibility in the use of resources will be required in the medium term if the academic quality of the courses is to be maintained. Discussions on this matter will be undertaken with the appropriate authorities without delay. In the course of these discussions the question of alternative usage of any surplus capacity within the Colleges will be pursued.

The Department will consult with the appropriate interests concerning the recognition and professional training and development of Post-Primary Teachers. In this respect such consultation should lead to a review of the initial training programmes and induction of Post-Primary Teachers.

Post-Primary Teachers in general are required before appointment, as are all Primary teachers, to have undergone training as teachers, either as part of their degree course or subsequent to it. This requirement does not apply to certain categories of Post-Primary teachers, in particular to some graduates who teach in vocational schools. It is proposed to consult the appropriate interests with a view to amending Memorandum V7 in order to ensure that such teachers will in future be required to have had pedagogic training before appointment to whole-time posts.

The number of students taking the Higher Diploma in Education course will be controlled, taking account of the likely demand for second-level teachers and the recommendation in the preceding paragraph.

There is currently a shortage of metalwork and woodwork teachers caused, in part, by the change-over from two-year training courses to a four-year degree programme in Thomond College. The first output from the new programme has come on stream in 1983. The College is in this year increasing its annual intake of students for these courses and will maintain this increased intake until the supply position has eased. The categories of teachers to be trained in the College will be kept under review in the light of possible curricular developments. The use of Thomond College in the provision of in-service training for Post-Primary teachers will be encouraged.

****

It is recognised that provision made in the past of inservice education has been inadequate and during the period of the plan it is intended to afford a much greater priority to this need in the allocation of available resources. It is not envisaged, however, that such improvement can cover additional payroll costs.

A representative committee has recently reported to the Minister for Education regarding the priority needs to be met for inservice training for teachers. Given the current economic constraints it is not seen that proposals of the dimensions indicated in the report can be contemplated during the period covered by the four year plan. Its principal recommendation of setting up an independent Council should await the experience arising from the establishment of the Curriculum and Examinations Board.

****

A significant portion of the increase now contemplated in inservice training will be by way of strengthening the network of Teachers' Centres and thus making it possible for teachers to avail themselves of inservice provision on a localised basis. The question of utilisation of spare capacity in Colleges of Education for the purposes of inservice education is also being considered. Proposals for inservice courses would also be welcomed from the faculties of Education in the universities.

IV.21 Announcement of the closure of Carysfort College, February 1986

The 1970s and 1980s had been marked by growth and development of third-level education, including teacher training. Demand for third level places had reached a hitherto unprecedented level by the mid 1980s and this growth in demand was projected to continue for a further decade at least. Consequently the decision of government in 1986 to close the country's biggest college of education, Our Lady of Mercy College, Carysfort, came as a shock and a surprise to the educational community generally.

The Programme for Action 1984-87 had stressed the need to curtail the numbers entering the teaching profession, particularly at primary level, in view of the fall in the fertility rate since the mid 1970s and in the number of births from 1981 onwards. The colleges of education anticipated that a move away from their traditional emphasis on preservice education would occur and that they would play a major role in inservice education for primary and post-primary teachers. Carysfort College had submitted a development plan to the Department of Education in 1984 proposing a new role for the college in inservice education and in other educational areas, including postgraduate courses. The Department refused to allow the college to become involved in a joint Master's degree course in education with University College Dublin, and did not respond to the other proposals.

On 4th February 1986, without previous warning, the government announced its intention to withdraw grants from Carysfort College. In spite of opposition from the college authorities, staff and students, and groups and individuals outside the college, and a change of government within a year, grants were withdrawn and the college was closed in June 1988 as a college of education.

During the weeks following Minister Hussey's announcement of the proposed closure there was a Cabinet reshuffle and Patrick Cooney became Minister for Education. On 4th March, 1986 Mary O'Rourke, T.D., Fianna Fáil spokesperson on education proposed a private member's motion in the Dáil that —

> "Dáil Éireann condemns the arbitrary and precipitate decision of the government to close down Carysfort College and requests that immediate action be taken to ensure that this great and valuable institution be retained as an integral part of our higher education system, with a specific role in teacher education."

The following extracts are taken from Minister Cooney's reply to the motion which was defeated by a small majority:

I will expand on why it is not possible to continue Carysfort as a teacher training single purpose institution. The numbers are not required. There is excess capacity in the system which nobody can deny. All our training colleges since their foundation have operated as single purpose institutions to educate and train teachers and they have done their job outstandingly well. In 1974-75 the training course was lengthened to three years. At that stage the colleges took advantage of that to strengthen and enrich their courses and form associations with the universities and this led to the award of the degree of Bachelor of Education to the graduates of the colleges. We have had a core of professional teachers second to none in Europe. That statement would stand objective examination.

One must remember that all those outstanding people were the products of single purpose colleges devoted exclusively to the training of national teachers. Two colleges will continue to be so exclusively devoted, but I put this slight emphasis on the question of single purpose institutions to indicate that what might be in some people's minds, the hope that some people might have for the continuance of teacher training as we know it on a reduced scale in Carysfort with the implication that along with it other activities will be taking place, would be totally out of line with the traditional way in which teachers have been trained. The traditional way has been outstandingly successful, and to have an educational regime in Carysfort that would try to marry the traditional way and some new developments is *a priori* risky and should not be embarked on when there is no need to embark on it because already we have the two other colleges to continue the outstandingly successful training methods that have served us so well for so long. I make that point lest anybody be unwittingly misled after our discussions here this evening as to what precisely my view on that issue is. That is not to say that some facets, some elements, some specialised areas of primary teacher training could not continue to be dealt with in Carysfort, but even saying that I am getting into an area from which I have excluded myself, speculation on what might be the eventual use to be made of Carysfort. I want to get away from that; I do not want to get into it because that is best done within the structures we will set up by the people best qualified to contribute to those structures and, above all, away from controversy and publicity. I have no doubt that when we finish our discussions — there is adequate time for them to take place in a comprehensive and detailed way because the college will be busy with the present student body until they graduate, albeit reducing — we will be able to put together an interesting package.

IV.22 Report of the Primary Education Review Body, 1990

The report of the Primary Education Review Body which was published in December 1990 contained sections on teacher education, inservice training of teachers, teachers' centres and other issues relating to the conditions of service of teachers. In the section on teacher education it was recognised that because of government decisions during the second half of the 1980s to reduce the number of trainee teachers, the facilities of the colleges of education were under-utilised and were likely to remain so for some years ahead. The report recommended that the colleges should be allowed to extend their degree options into areas other than education thus providing additional third-level places for students wishing to follow degree courses in the arts/humanities areas. The report also recommended the development of a comprehensive system of inservice education at primary level and a strengthening of the role of the Teachers' Centres.

The following extracts are from the report:

TEACHER EDUCATION

****

The quality of training in all of the colleges of education is high. However, their facilities are now under-utilised and are likely to remain so for some years ahead. This raises the question of either closing one or more of the colleges or widening their range of options. There was considerable disquiet following the Government decision in 1985 to discontinue teacher training in Our Lady of Mercy College of Education, Carysfort. The loss to the country of such a large and prestigious educational institution has been regretted by many individuals and educational authorities. Although it could be argued that, for the next few years, all teacher requirements could be met by one of the larger colleges, factors other than the immediate requirements for teachers must be taken into consideration when matters of such importance to education are being decided.

Apart from considerations which may arise from an improved financial climate in the country and leaving aside arguments relating to such matters as improved teacher/pupil ratios an increasing demand for teachers will automatically occur towards the end of the 1990s as more and more teachers from the current teaching force reach retiring age. It is much easier to close a college than to open a new one. Therefore the retention of the capacity of the colleges to cope with on-going teacher education requirements is desirable and the ability of the colleges to cope with increased demands later on ought to be safeguarded. We recommend that the existing five colleges of education remain in use.

The resources of the colleges, however, should not be left under-utilised. As regards the wider educational context, it is the stated intention of the Government to provide additional resources to enable a larger number of students to enter third-level education. The universities are already filled to capacity; the colleges of education are under-utilised and will remain so for many years ahead. We recommend that, as all the colleges of education and their lecturers are recognised by the universities for the purpose of B.Ed. degrees, a further extension of current arrangements to enable the colleges to extend their degree options into other areas should now be examined as a possible way forward.

Two new universities were established in 1989 — Dublin City University and the University of Limerick. We recommend that degree options between the Colleges of Education and these universities might also be explored.

IV.23 University of Limerick (Dissolution of Thomond College) Act, October, 1991

Thomond College and the NIHEL had been established on the same campus in Limerick in the early 1970s but operated largely in isolation from each other. The legislation of 1980 (IV.16 and V.19) seemed to copperfasten their individuality. However, with the establishment of the University of Limerick in 1989 and the new thinking on teacher education and the maximum use of resources for larger numbers of students, the government decided to introduce new legislation whereby Thomond College would be absorbed into the University of Limerick. The approach taken in the legislation was to repeal the Thomond College Act of 1980, to transfer the functions, staff, property, rights and liabilities of Thomond College to the University of Limerick and to make some amendments to the University of Limerick Act and the National Council for Educational Awards Act, 1979 (V.14). Thus, to gain a comprehensive view of the changes, the N.C.E.A. legislation of 1979, the legislation on Thomond College and NIHEL of 1980, the University of Limerick Act 1989 and the Act under discussion of 1991, need to be read in relation to each other.

The following extracts include key features of the short University of Limerick (Dissolution of Thomond College) Act of 1991:

An Act to provide for the dissolution of Thomond College of Education, Limerick, and the transfer of its property and staff to the University of Limerick, to amend and extend the University of Limerick Acts, 1980 and 1989, to amend the National Council for Educational Awards Act, 1979, and to provide for connected matters. *(26th June, 1991)*

****

2.— The College is hereby dissolved

3.— The functions of the College under paragraphs (a) and (b) of section 4(1) of the Thomond College of Education, Limerick, Act, 1980, are hereby transferred to the University and shall be performed by the University in accordance with such terms and conditions as the Minister, after consultation with the Governing Body, directs.

4.— Section 4 (as amended by Section 3 of the University of Limerick Act, 1989) of the Act of 1980 is hereby amended by the insertion in subsection (2) of the following paragraph after paragraph (a):

> (aa) The Minister may, after consultation with the Governing Body, by order assign to the University such additional functions in relation to the education and training of teachers in accordance with such terms and conditions as may be determined from time to time by the Minister.

5.— Section 5 of the Act of 1980 is hereby amended by —
(a) the substitution in subsection (2) for "23" of "20,"
(b) the substitution in subsection (4) for "23" of "20," and
(c) the deletion in subsection (4) of paragraph (e).

6.— The National Council for Educational Awards Act, 1979, is hereby amended by —
(a) the deletion in section 1(1) of paragraphs (b), (c) and (d),
(b) the substitution in section 4 for "twenty-three" of "21, and
(c) the deletion in section 5 (1) of paragraph (d).

7.—(1) A person who, immediately before the commencement of this Act, was an officer or servant of the College shall on that commencement become and be an officer or servant of the University on terms and conditions not less favourable than those applicable to that person immediately before that commencement.

****

10.— The University in relation to the performance of its functions shall have due regard to the preservation, promotion and use of the Irish language and to the preservation and development of the national culture and in the training of teachers it shall have due regard to the teaching of the Irish language.

11.— The Thomond College of Education, Limerick, Act, 1980, is hereby repealed.

12.—(1) This Act may be cited as the University of Limerick (Dissolution of Thomond College) Act, 1991.

(2) The University of Limerick Acts, 1980 and 1989, and this Act shall be construed together as one and may be cited together as the University of Limerick Acts, 1980 to 1991.

(3) This Act shall come into operation on such day as the Minster may by order appoint.

IV.24 OECD Review of National Policies for Education in Ireland

This report has been referred to in an earlier section (I.26). Two chapters of the report focused specifically on teachers — their training, professional support, incentives, supply and demand etc. The high quality of Irish teachers was recognised by the OECD examiners and the first of the extracts below refers to this aspect.

Chapter 6 contained a comprehensive discussion on different possible approaches to teacher education in the context of the short-term need to restrict the numbers of trainee teachers. The report pointed out that "there is a teacher surplus mainly because the demand for teachers is being circumstantially choked by the combination of a high PTR and the deferment of measures to faster school improvement" and argued that policy decisions in relation to restructuring teacher education should take account of the longer-term needs as well as the short-term restrictions.

The following extracts relate to (a) the quality of Irish teachers, (b) the approach recommended in relation to preservice teacher education and (c) career-long education and training:

(a) The response given in Ireland to the query "what teachers" is likely to be an emphatic "teachers of high quality." Other countries may be lamenting a lack of good teachers and a concomitant decline in the overall status of the teaching profession, but not Ireland. The following extracts from two of the submissions to this review accurately reflect popular opinion:

> Education for the Irish has always been held in high esteem. It has traditional values in that, when the Irish had nothing else, they had the hedge school. The local teacher was a person of consequence in local society, acting as teacher but also as counsellor and peacemaker when necessary. These values still exist and it is true to say the teaching profession is one that is looked up to and is a popular choice of career for many school-leavers.
>
> It can hardly be gainsaid that this country is fortunate in the quality of its teaching personnel.

The evidence certainly endorses the thrust of that statement. Recruits to the colleges of education responsible for the training of primary school teachers have always been of particularly outstanding academic quality year after year. The colleges have received far more applications than there were places available, and all report that those selected for admission have obtained marks in their final school examination that would have comfortably guaranteed them a university place. The overall quality of the intake to the university departments of education that prepare secondary school teachers has varied somewhat over time according to the number of places available, but is said to have been consistently good, although a teaching career has not been the first choice of many candidates. It is undoubtedly of high academic quality at the present time when the competition for places in most subjects is intense.

(b) Preservice Teacher Education

......the examiners advise against a short-term economic strategy while also dismissing maintenance of the status quo. Instead, they wish to propose an alternative option viewed within a long-term perspective. Their advice is rooted in two major considerations:

(i) if some or most of the present capacity for the initial preparation of primary and secondary teachers is removed, the process of recreating it in order to match the essential qualitative needs of the national education system in the years ahead will be both costly and difficult;

(ii) It is urgently necessary to expand and rationalise the provision of inservice training.

The option proposed by the examiners is that of merger and consolidation. All initial training courses now lead to the award of a degree validated by a university and the students of some Colleges of Education already have access to university courses and general facilities. In short, there is already close collaboration between the monotechnic institutions and the universities. The examiners suggest that this collaboration could be formalised by merging each of the colleges with a university department of education so as to constitute a school or faculty of education. Such a measure has been adopted recently in several OECD countries and in Ireland could have the following advantages:

(i) it could reinforce those practical aspects of training and help disseminate those pedagogical values that have been traditionally associated with the highly-regarded Colleges of Education;
(ii) it could enrich the two types of training by offering a common core of studies and common professional preparation for those who will teach at the lower secondary as well as at the primary level. This would fit in with the general desire to see compulsory schooling designed as a continuum;
(iii) it could strengthen overall educational research and development capacity;
(iv) all the staff of the Colleges and departments of education could be retained but redeployed, where appropriate, according to their qualifications and major professional interests;
(v) all the existing physical facilities and resources such as libraries could be shared on the model of a decentralised campus.

****

(C) THE RATIONALE OF CAREER-LONG EDUCATION AND TRAINING

The challenge that now faces the authorities and indeed the whole teaching profession is how to address in a comprehensive way the needs and aspirations of talented and well-educated young teachers as they make their first full-time professional encounters with the school (induction) and as they progress through their careers (continuing inservice education and training). We believe that the best returns from further investment in teacher education will come from the careful planning and construction of a nationwide induction and inservice system using the concept of *the teaching career* as the foundation. We say "teaching" to emphasise the point that steps must be taken to ensure that Ireland's excellent teachers stay in the classroom and gain satisfaction from doing so. At the same time, the model we propose includes inservice education for principals and other persons concerned with the education service in addition to the classroom teacher.

There is no dearth of potential expertise for induction and inservice purposes within the system, whether in the universities and colleges, the inspectorate, the professional associations and unions and in the schools themselves; nor is there any lack of willingness or enthusiasm to apply it. Ireland undoubtedly has the human capability to build up an outstanding continuing education and training system for all its teachers. We were struck by the widespread agreement about the need to set long-term targets apparent in a very large number of submissions and in our discussions around the country.

The main difficulty is not the lack of personnel but of structures on an appropriate scale and with the required scope of provision and access. The structures are lacking, partly because of the ever-present constraint of limited resources, and partly because the detailed policy planning required to establish them nationally has yet to be undertaken. The 1984 Report of the Committee on *Inservice Education* went some way towards indicating how such plans might be prepared through a new national body but this has not been established and there is a lack of co-ordination at the levels of both policy and provision. There is, moreover, no agreement on whether inservice education shall remain voluntary (as the *Inservice Report* recommended) or become a requirement. We take the latter view and would support the linking of the credential to teach to the meeting of specific inservice demands. It is this pattern that we believe will become widely established in many professions in the future.

IV.25 Memorandum of Understanding between Mary Immaculate College and the University of Limerick, November 1991.

The report of the Primary Education Review Body and the OECD Review of Irish educational policy had recommended that closer linkages be developed between the colleges of education and the universities with a view to more effective utilisation of the resources of the colleges. Following the granting of university status to the University of Limerick and Dublin City University in 1990 there were indicators that the government would welcome links between the two major Catholic colleges and the two new universities. In November 1991 a memorandum of understanding was issued by Mary Immaculate College, Limerick and the University of Limerick about a future linkage. This memorandum is reproduced in full below. No comparable agreement or understanding has yet been issued by St. Patrick's College, Drumcondra at the time of going to press:

MEMORANDUM OF UNDERSTANDING

Memorandum of Understanding related to institutional linkages between Mary Immaculate College of Education Limerick (MIC) and University of Limerick (UL).

1. Institutional linkages will be in accordance with the structure set out in the attached chart. (Not reproduced here but described below).

2. The Governing Body of UL will have not less than one member from the Governing Body of MIC. UL will have reciprocal representation on the Governing Body of MIC.
3. The President of UL would appoint the President of MIC to the Executive Board of the University in accordance with custom and practice.
4. The Faculty Board for Education would comprise the full-time academic staff of the Department of Education of UL and MIC.
   The Faculty Board for Arts/Humanities would comprise the full-time academic staff of the Departments of Arts/Humanities of UL and MIC.
5. The constituent Education Departments would be constituted as a Faculty of Education.
   The constituent Arts/Humanities Departments would be constituted as a faculty of Arts/Humanities.
6. The terms in the academic year in the 2 institutions would be equalised on a phased basis, starting in respect of the 1992 intake.
7. All programmes would be accredited and all awards would be made by the University.
8. All future appointees in MIC would be selected by a five person selection board of which the University would nominate two. Appointments would be made by An Bord Rialaithe of MIC subject to ratification by the Governing Bord of UL.
   Internal administrative appointments in MIC would continue to be a matter for MIC.
9. The MIC Bord Acadúil would be retained, with 4-7 members nominated by the University.
10. There would be 300 B.Ed students and 600 others, together with post-graduate students at MIC.

11. Funding would be via the HEA to UL with specifically designated funding which would be transferred to MIC for separate accounting in respect of MIC activities.
    MIC would collect fees in respect of students registered for its various programmes. Where there would be a joint input by the staff of the two institutions into an academic programme, costs and income would be designated on a pro rata basis.
12. Appointment as Deans for both Education and Arts/Humanities would be open to staff members from MIC as well as to University staff.
13. Students for courses in MIC would be registered by both institutions by way of registration in MIC and all details transmitted to UL.
14. The arrangements would be reviewed at the end of a three year period.
15. Subject to such requirements as may be stipulated from time to time by the Department related to conditions for the training of teachers, including numbers of trainees, other detailed implementation arrangements to be a matter for resolution between MIC and UL.
16. It is recognised that additional funding would be required to meet transition conditions. Further discussions would take place between the Department of Education, UL and MIC.

V

HIGHER EDUCATION

V. 1 University Education (Agriculture and Dairy Science) Act, 1926

The transfer of powers from the British regime to a native Irish government for the Irish Free State took place on 1st. February, 1922. In educational policy the priority of the new government was to gaelicise the education system, with particular reference to primary and secondary education. It established the vocational education system through the Vocational Education Act of 1930 and also enacted legislation affecting N.U.I. colleges. The Agriculture and Dairy Science Act of 1926 had implications for U.C.D. and U.C.C. The Act led to the transferring of the Royal College of Science in Merrion Street to the control of U.C.D. This led to a significant improvement in the amenities for Science and Engineering. The Albert Agricultural College in Glasnevin was transferred to the control of U.C.D. which led to the establishment of the faculty of Agriculture within the College, funded by the Department of Agriculture. U.C.C. also benefited under the terms of the Act in that the Model Farm was transferred to it and a faculty of Dairy Science was set up in the Cork College. Under the terms of the Act the annual government grant to U.C.D. was raised from £42,000 to £82,000. U.C.Cs. annual grant was raised from £20,000 to £40,000 and it also received a capital grant of £63,000 and an annual grant of £13,000 for its Dairy Science Faculty. The 1926 Act had the effect of boosting the work of the colleges and also involved bringing more coherence to bear in the areas of agriculture and science education and research, incorporating them within university structures.

The following extracts are from the act:

An act to transfer the College of Science and the Albert Agricultural College to University College, Dublin, to make financial and other provision for the establishment and maintenance of a faculty of agriculture in University College, Dublin, and the performance by that college of the functions heretofore fulfilled by the College of Science and the Albert Agricultural College respectively, to make financial and other provision for the establishment of a faculty of dairy science in University College, Cork, to make better provision for the accommodation of the National University of Ireland, and for those and other purposes to amend the Irish Universities Act, 1908. [17th July, 1926].

****

DEMISE OF COLLEGE OF SCIENCE TO UNIVERSITY COLLEGE, DUBLIN.

2.—(1) The Minister for Finance shall as soon as conveniently may be after the passing of this Act demise by deed under the official seal the lands and premises described in the First Schedule to this Act with the exceptions and subject to the reservations specified in that Schedule to University College, Dublin, for the term of ninety-nine years from the appointed day subject to such nominal rent not exceeding five shillings as the said Minister shall think proper and subject to such covenants on the part of University College, Dublin, and conditions as the said Minister shall think proper and in particular subject to a covenant against assignment, subletting, or parting with the possession of the said lands and premises or any part thereof without the consent of the said Minister and such covenant or condition as the said Minister shall think proper for securing the carrying out on the demised premises of scientific experiments and tests for Departments of State by the officers of such Departments or the officers of the said College.

DEMISE OF ALBERT AGRICULTURAL COLLEGE TO UNIVERSITY COLLEGE, DUBLIN

3.—(1) The Department of Agriculture and Technical Instruction for Ireland (hereinafter called the Department) shall as soon as conveniently may be after the passing of this Act demise by one or more leases the several lands and premises described in the Second Schedule to this Act to University College, Dublin for the term of ninety-nine years from the appointed day subject to the rents, covenants, and conditions hereinafter mentioned.

****

GRANTS FOR CAPITAL PURPOSES

9.—(1) On or as soon as may be after the appointed day there shall be paid to University College, Dublin out of moneys to be provided by the Oireachtas the sum of £25,000 (twenty-five thousand pounds) which shall be applied by that College for such capital purposes as the governing body of the College shall think fit.

(2) On or as soon as may be after the appointed day there shall be paid to University College, Cork out of moneys to be provided by the Oireachtas the sum of £15,000 (fifteen thousand pounds) which shall be applied by that College for such capital purposes as the governing body of the College shall think fit.

INCREASE OF ANNUAL GRANT TO UNIVERSITY COLLEGE, DUBLIN

10.—(1) So much of subsection (2) of section 7 of the Irish Universities Act, 1908 and the Third Schedule to that Act as provides for the payment of the annual sum of £32,000 to University College, Dublin, shall cease and be deemed to have ceased to have effect as from the 31st day of March, 1926, and in lieu thereof it is hereby enacted that there shall be paid to

University College, Dublin, out of moneys to be provided by the Oireachtas the sum of £66,000 (sixty-six thousand pounds) in the financial year beginning on the 1st day of April, 1926, and the annual sum of £82,000 (eighty-two thousand pounds) in the financial year beginning on the 1st day of April, 1927, and every subsequent financial year.

INCREASE OF ANNUAL GRANT TO UNIVERSITY COLLEGE, CORK
11.—(1) So much of subsection (2) of section 7 of the Irish Universities Act, 1908, and the Third Schedule to that Act as provides for the payment of the annual sum of £20,000 to University College, Cork shall cease and be deemed to have ceased to have effect as from the 31st day of March, 1926, and in lieu thereof it is hereby enacted that out of moneys to be provided by the Oireachtas there shall be paid to University College, Cork in the financial year beginning on the 1st day of April, 1926, and in every subsequent financial year the annual sum of £40,000 (forty thousand pounds) which shall be applied by the said College for the general purposes of the College.

V.2 University College Galway Act, 1929

University College Galway was the smallest of the university institutions, having only 242 registered students in 1925-26. The government was anxious to boost its numbers and also identified the Galway College as a key institution to promote third-level education through the medium of Irish. Through the University College Galway Act, 1929, the college's annual government grant was doubled from £14,000 to £28,000. Scholarship Schemes were devised for students fluent in Irish who wished to pursue third-level studies through the medium of Irish. The Act also required that as far as possible, competence to teach through Irish be an essential requirement for staff appointments.

AN ACT to make provision for increasing the annual grant payable to university college, Galway, and for securing that persons appointed to offices and situations in that college shall be competent to discharge their duties through the medium of the Irish Language. *[17th December, 1929.]*

WHEREAS under the Irish Universities Act, 1908, an annual grant of twelve thousand pounds is now payable to University College, Galway, out of moneys provided by the Oireachtas:

AND WHEREAS the Governing Body of the said College has lately made provision by statute for securing that certain of the professors and lecturers of the said College shall deliver their lectures in the Irish language, and proposes to take such further steps as circumstances may permit to secure that an increasing proportion of the academic and administrative functions of the said College shall be performed through the medium of the Irish language:

AND WHEREAS the said Governing Body has lately reduced the fees payable in the said College by the students thereat and has also undertaken to establish a scholarship scheme for students at the said College who are native speakers of the Irish language:

AND WHEREAS by reason of the matters hereinbefore recited and the fall in the value of money in recent years the said annual grant of twelve thousand pounds has become inadequate for the needs of the said College:

BE IT THEREFORE ENACTED BY THE OIREACHTAS OF SAORSTAT ÉIREANN AS FOLLOWS:—

DEFINITION

1.— In this Act the expression "the College" means University College, Galway.

INCREASE OF ANNUAL GRANT

2.—(1) So much of sub-section (2) of section 7 of the Irish Universities Act, 1908, and the Third Schedule to that Act as provides the payment of the annual sum of twelve thousand pounds to the College shall cease to have effect as from the 31st day of March, 1930, and in lieu thereof it is hereby enacted that there shall be paid to the College, out of moneys provided by the Oireachtas, the sum of twenty-eight thousand pounds in the financial year beginning on the 1st day of April, 1930, and in every subsequent financial year.

Towards meeting further the cost of such measures as the College may hereafter take with a view to increasing the proportion of instruction given through the medium of the Irish language, or making better provision for the study of the Irish language and literature, the Minister for Finance may, if and when he so thinks fit, by order made on the recommendation of the Minister for Education increase the said sum of twenty-eight thousand pounds by such sum not exceeding two thousand pounds.

OBLIGATION TO APPOINT IRISH SPEAKERS

3.— It shall be the duty of the Senate of the National University of Ireland, the Governing Body of the College, or the President of the College (as the case may be), when making an appointment to any office or situation in the College, to appoint to such office or situation a person who is competent to discharge the duties thereof through the medium of the Irish language: provided a person so competent and also suitable in all other respects is to be found amongst the persons who are candidates or otherwise available for such appointment.

V.3 Bunreacht na hÉireann, 1937

The adoption of a new constitution in 1937, involved changes in the universities' representation in the government. The Dáil seats for university personnel were removed and seats in the second chamber, the Senate, were substituted. Since that time graduates of the University of Dublin and the National University elect three senators each to the Senate.

ARTICLE 18.4.
The elected members of Seanad Éireann shall be elected as follows:

(i) Three shall be elected by the National University of Ireland.
(ii) Three shall be elected by the University of Dublin.
(iii) Forty-three shall be elected from panels of candidates constituted as hereinafter provided.

ARTICLE 18.6.
The members of Seanad Éireann to be elected by the Universities shall be elected on a franchise and in the manner to be provided by law.

V.4 Institute for Advanced Studies Act, 1940

Despite the inadequate funding of university institutions and research, new ground was broken by the establishment of the Institute for Advanced Studies in 1940. This was very much the brainchild of the Taoiseach, Eamon de Valera, although he had support for the idea from the Irish Studies Committee of the Royal Irish Academy. It was considered that Ireland was a particularly appropriate location for scientific work in celtic studies. There was a need for much scholarly work on unpublished and unedited Irish manuscripts. There was a need for dictionaries and standardised grammars. Much work also needed to be done in phonetics, linguistics and dialectology. Both de Valera and the Irish Studies Committee considered that it would be best to establish a scholarly institute independent of existing universities but working in co-operation with them.

To the School of Celtic Studies was added a School of Theoretical Physics, linked to the Dunsink Observatory. A number of internationally distinguished mathematicians were interested in such a development. De Valera, a keen mathematician himself, considered that the School would not be expensive to run but would provide an appropriate environment through which Ireland could be seen to make worthwhile research contributions in the field of mathematics. In 1947, a School of Cosmic Physics was added to the Institute.

The bill to establish the Institute of Advanced studies met with parliamentary opposition from some influential speakers who considered that such an institute was unnecessary and would prove detrimental to the interests of existing universities. De Valera steered the bill through to a successful conclusion and from 1940 Ireland had a new and distinguished research institution which has continued to contribute much to the world of scholarship within its ambit of concern.

An act to make provision for the establishment and maintenance in Dublin of an institute for advanced studies consisting of a school of celtic studies and a school of theoretical physics, to authorise the addition to such institute of schools in other subjects, and to provide for matters incidental or ancillary to the matters aforesaid. *[19th June, 1940]*

ESTABLISHMENT OF THE INSTITUTE

2.—(1) There is hereby established an institute of higher learning which shall be styled and known as Institiúid Ard-Léighinn Bhaile Átha Cliath or (in English) the Dublin Institute for Advanced Studies, to fulfil the functions assigned to it by this Act.

2.—(2) The Institute shall be a body corporate with perpetual succession and a common seal, and power to sue and be sued in its corporate name and to hold and dispose of land.

2.—(3) The seat of the Institute shall be in the County Borough of Dublin.

FUNCTIONS OF THE INSTITUTE

3.—(1) The functions of the Institute shall be to provide facilities for the furtherance of advanced study and the conduct of research in specialised branches of knowledge and for the publication of the results of advanced study and research whether carried on under the auspices of the Institute or otherwise.

3.—(2) The facilities mentioned in the foregoing sub-section of this section shall be provided through and by means of Constituent Schools for different specialised branches of knowledge.

ESTABLISHMENT AND DISESTABLISHMENT OF CONSTITUENT SCHOOLS

4.—(1) As soon as conveniently may be after the passing of this Act, the Government shall establish, either simultaneously or successively, under this Act —

(a) a Constituent school to be known as Scoil an Leighinn Cheiltigh or (in English) the School of Celtic Studies, and
(b) a Constituent School to be known as Scoil na Fisice Teoiriciúla or (in English) the School of Theoretical Physics.

4.—(2) Whenever it appears to the Government that it is in the public interest that a Constituent School (other than the

Constituent Schools mentioned in the foregoing sub-section of this section) should be established for the furtherance of advanced study and the conduct of research in a particular specialised branch of knowledge and each House of the Oireachtas has by resolution approved of the establishment of such Constituent School, the Government may establish under this Act a Constituent School for the purposes aforesaid.

The Act set out the functions of the Celtic Studies and Theoretical Physics School. The following extract gives the flavour of what was envisaged for the former:

5.—(1) The functions and duties of the School of Celtic Studies shall be the promotion of Celtic Studies generally, and, in particular, but without prejudice, to the generality of the foregoing —

(a) the investigation, editing, and publication of extant manuscript material in the Irish language;
(b) the grammatical, lexicographical, and philological study of Old, Middle, and Modern Irish;
(c) the phonetic investigation of existing Irish dialects and the recording of the living Irish speech;
(d) the collection and study of Irish place names;
(e) the study of Irish social history and of all branches of Irish history which require for their investigation a knowledge of the Irish language;
(f) the preparation and the recommendation to the Council for publication of works dealing with any of the subjects mentioned in any of the foregoing paragraphs of this sub-section and of other works calculated to promote a more general knowledge of the Celtic languages and of the literatures of those languages and of the cultural and social background of Celtic civilisation;

(g) the training of advanced students in the methods of research in any of the said subjects;

(h) the organisation of seminars, conferences, and lectures on the Celtic languages and on the literatures of those languages and, in particular, on matters of interest to students of the Irish language and of its literature.

V. 5 Report of Commission on Accommodation Needs of the N.U.I. Colleges, 1959

The significant increase in student numbers in the post 1945 period and the failure to expand and update university accommodation led to very severe problems of over-crowding and unsatisfactory facilities, reaching crisis proportions in U.C.D. which had experienced the greatest increase in numbers.

Eventually, in June 1957, a commission was appointed by the Minister for Education to examine the accommodation needs of the N.U.I. colleges. It was the first commission dealing with university affairs which was set up since independence and it was chaired by Mr. Justice Cearbhall Ó Dálaigh. It issued its first interim report, on U.C.D. within a year, in June 1958. Its second interim report, on U.C.C. was issued in October of that year and its report on U.C.G. was made available in April 1959. Its fourth and general Final Report appeared in May, 1959.

Its final report emphasised that the problem of accommodation within the N.U.I. Colleges was a long standing one which had been neglected. The report was a searing indictment of the general neglect which had taken place but the dilemma of U.C.D. was seen as the most serious. The accommodation there was regarded as "wholly inadequate." It endorsed the submission of U.C.D. for accommodation requirements as "reasonable" but "modest" and in relation to research facilities it was regarded as "not adequate." The only satisfactory solution to its problems was regarded as the "transfer of the entire college to a new site" and the Belfield campus was recommended. The Report also endorsed significant building programmes for U.C.C. and U.C.G. Furthermore, the report made the important proposal that a University Development Committee should be established for the execution of the proposed building programmes, to constitute a useful liaison between the Colleges and the Government and "in time, might also be called upon to advise on long-term plans for development and on problems of co-ordination." This proposal was not implemented but may have been influential in prompting the establishment of a Commission on Higher Education in the following year, 1960.

The following is an extract from the Final Report of the Commission relating to the overall recommended building programme and to the setting up of a University Development Committee:

The building programme which we have recommended will cost in the region of £8,000,000. This, in any circumstances, is a very substantial sum to find and one which might normally be expected to be raised over a considerable period of years. The problem, however, cannot, in our opinion, await a protracted solution. Already breakdown point has almost been reached in the Colleges. Twenty years ago the Colleges were full. Since that time accommodation has remained virtually unaltered but student numbers have been growing and the field of university studies expanding. Today, the situation is that university teachers and students have to work under very trying and, in some cases, almost impossible conditions. The persistence of these conditions over a number of years without amelioration is leading, we have found, to a serious sense of frustration among university staffs. Under such conditions the quality and standards of both the teaching and the work of the university cannot for long go unaffected.

Now, more than ever, we cannot afford to allow university standards to fall. A crisis in these training centres would have the gravest consequences for the national life and economy. Our standards in this age must be international and these standards cannot be achieved throughout our universities unless adequate basic accommodation is first provided. The well-being of university education and of the country are closely linked. The solution of the problem, therefore, is urgent and its place in national planning should be high. We think that the solution must be attempted within the limits of a ten-year plan. Spread over a ten-year period expenditure on buildings would amount to an average annual sum of £800,000. We strongly put forward the claims of the Colleges for consideration on this basis in the National Budget.

The execution of the building programme which we have recommended is, both in size and urgency, a very considerable task. To ensure that the task is tackled energetically and carried forward with drive and unity of direction some special form of organisation is in our opinion clearly necessary. We recommend for this purpose the establishment of a University Development Committee.

The University Development Committee, as we see it, would be composed of persons with wide administrative, business and technical experience, and it would have at its disposal such secretarial and expert assistance as it might from time to time require. The Committee would discharge and, as a single body, expedite those functions normally performed by different Government Departments in relation to grants of public moneys for capital purposes. Not least among its objects, the Committee would assist in co-ordinating the building projects of the several Colleges, and in the public interest ensure economy in their execution. The University Development Committee could constitute a useful liaison between the Colleges and the Government, and in time, might also be called upon to advise on long-term plans for development and on problems of co-ordination.

In the recommendation there is, of course, no question of interfering with the independence of either Colleges or University.

Perhaps, the most significant of the accommodation proposals was the re-location of U.C.D. from a centre city site to a suburban site. As early as 1934 U.C.D. had acquired Belfield House and grounds beyond Donnybrook, a few miles from its existing cramped site in Earlsfort Terrace. The intention was to use these facilities for recreational and playing field activities. Under President Tierney in the fifties several other adjoining properties (to a total of 250 acres) were acquired which provided an option of transferring U.C.D. to this expansive, green field site on the outskirts of the city. When the Commission recommended this move, decisive action could no longer be postponed and in June 1959 the Government decided in principle, subject to the approval of Dáil Èireann, to accept the recommendation of the Commission and to transfer U.C.D. to its new site at Belfield, Stillorgan. The decision to move from a centre city site was by no means approved by all interested parties and lively differences of opinion arose. Nevertheless, the sixties were to witness the gradual re-shaping of U.C.D. in the new campus, putting it in a good position to cope with the even greater expansion of numbers which was in the offing.

V.6 Report of the Board of Visitors on U.C.D. 1960

A particular problem concerning university appointments arose in U.C.D. which led to a visitation to the college by Government appointed visitors. In their report they found fault with the practice in operation there. The criticism was not based on unfair procedures but on the fact that the modes of staff appointment were not in line with existing legislation. In 1949 U.C.D. adopted the practice of appointing "assistant lecturers" and in 1953 the grade of "college lecturers" was introduced. Appointments to these positions were made without reference to the Senate of the N.U.I. These posts were renewable on a yearly basis, were usually not advertised and were regarded as promotion posts within the college. With this system of "internal" appointments there went a policy of leaving some professorships and almost all the University lectureships unfilled when these posts became vacant, so that by 1959 there were ten professorships and thirty four university lectureships vacant. The newly introduced "internal" positions gave more control over staff to the university authorities and security of tenure was diminished but questions were raised about such a policy being in breach of the charter of the university. In 1959 the Government agreed to a petition by Justice Kenny that Visitors should be appointed to investigate the situation. The Visitors found that the appointments to assistant lecturer and college lecturer were invalid and found the Governing Body in breach of duty in not taking proper steps to deal with University lectureships when they became vacant. The Government brought in legislation to deal with the situation and to ratify early appointments.

The following extracts are from the Report of the Visitors:

The Board finds:

1. That the Governing Body did not seek legal advice as to whether it was authorised by the Charter of the College, or otherwise, to appoint College Professors, College Lecturers or Assistant Lecturers.
2. That the Governing Body was aware in the year 1956 that eminent Counsel had advised that "The College has no power to appoint College Professors or College Lecturers."
3. That the Governing Body appointed College Lecturers and Assistant Lecturers at all times aware that it was at least doubtful that it was authorised so to do, and on the basis of a belief that the possibility of legal action being taken to question the regularity of such appointments was remote.
4. That the College has on this Visitation ex post facto and for the first time sought to justify on a legal basis the action of the Governing Body in appointing College Lecturers and Assistant Lecturers.

It is unnecessary to set out in detail the arguments advanced in support of the claim of the College that it has power to appoint not only College Lecturers and Assistant Lecturers but also College Professors, but having given careful consideration to the submissions of Counsel the Board has no doubt but that on the true construction of the College Charter and, in particular, of Clauses III and XII thereof the claim is misconceived.

V.7 Report of the Commission on Higher Education, 1967

The problems revealed by the commission on N.U.I. accommodation needs, the unease about appointment procedures in the universities, as well as the desirability of setting up some Body such as the British U.G.C. to act as an intermediary Body between the individual institutions and government departments on policy and financial matters pointed to the desirability of an in-depth appraisal of all third-level education. In 1958 Ireland adopted its first Economic Programme and increasingly it was realised that investment in education had a crucial relationship with the economic and social development of society. It was also realised that a society embarking on a new phase of economic development needed to bring coherence to its third-level provision and that planning needed to be instituted for an era of expansion in third-level as well as in other forms of educational provision. In 1960 the Government took the significant step of establishing the first major commission on higher education since the foundation of the state, appointing Justice Cearbhaill Ó Dalaigh, who had just recently completed his Chairmanship of the Commission on N.U.I. Accommodation, as its chairman. The appointment of a Commission on Higher Education, with wide ranging representation provided a major opportunity for an in-depth study of all aspects of Irish higher education and of its probable needs in the years ahead.

The 28 member commission, appointed by Minister Hillery held its inaugural meeting on 8th November, 1960. Its terms of reference were very wide and, in effect, involved the surveying of every feature of higher education. This wide brief coupled with the thorough approach taken to examining issues, led to a much greater duration of time than was intended before the report become available. The report was not published until the Spring of 1967.

The report was published in two volumes and a summary. It was well organised with its thirty two chapters grouped into seven divisions. In the first instance, the Commission set out the existing provision for higher education and made an assessment of this. Many weaknesses were highlighted as the following extract from the Summary indicates:

AN ASSESSMENT OF THE PRESENT POSITION

The existing system of higher education has developed piecemeal; it is not a unified system but a complex of separate units, involving some unnecessary duplication and leaving areas of higher education unprovided for. Sectional interests play too large a part, and antagonisms between individual institutions have been apparent. There is, as a rule, no planning machinery for the system and too little planning on the part of its component institutions.

Though the State provides the greater part of the income of these institutions, it neither is nor purports to be a planning authority. The financial consultations that annually take place between individual institutions and the State do not serve as a planning process.

The demand for places in the university colleges, especially the N.U.I. constituent colleges, has risen steeply in recent years; at the same time, higher education outside the universities has remained comparatively under-developed.

The standard of entry to the N.U.I. colleges that applied up to 1966/7 was too low for university entrance.

The university colleges have increased their numbers without adding substantially to their accommodation and facilities. On the whole, in relation to student numbers, they are no better staffed now than they were a quarter of a century ago.

Increasing numbers of students, low entry standards, and inadequate staffing and accommodation have produced a highly unsatisfactory situation, in which academic standards are endangered despite the efforts of academic staff to keep them as high as possible.

The university colleges and other institutions deserve credit for the large numbers of well-qualified graduates they have trained, and for keeping the country supplied with professional men and women. Their achievement is less impressive at the level of postgraduate studies and research, where the insufficiency of staff, equipment and accommodation has been especially frustrating.

The system of academic appointments in the National University of Ireland is unsatisfactory, especially because it does not ensure that candidates are assessed by those best qualified to make expert judgments on their merits.

The constitution of the N.U.I. and its constituent colleges, which has remained essentially unchanged since 1908, has become unsuited in several important respects to the needs of a modern university. The constitution of T.C.D. has been more adaptable but it also needs adjustment. The constitutions of the teacher-training colleges, and the higher technical and vocational colleges, which lack any academic self-government, also call for change.

The university, conscious of its obligation to the community, is in a dilemma; it wishes to meet the community's needs and demands and at the same time to fulfil its fundamental obligation to scholarship and learning.

With the exception of U.C.G. the university colleges have failed to develop the use of Irish in their teaching, reflecting the predominant community attitude.

Financial capacity to bear the cost of higher education largely determines the individual's access to higher education and talented students are precluded on this account. Part-time evening degree courses may ease the position for some students, but the difficulties which such courses present to both students and colleges are very great.

In its reflections on the existing situation the Commission feared that the university colleges which were under-financed, under staffed, poorly equipped and, in some cases, poorly housed would be imperilled if they were to take on the very large number of aspiring students. The Commissioners were afraid that irreparable damage could be done to academic standards. The Commission also tried to define what should be the nature of a university and it was uneasy at the university following the path of applied and vocational knowledge and training.

The following extract sets out the Commissions view of the nature of a university.

The university is not a professional academy, or congregation of professional academics, existing merely to provide a training for the several professions. The university is not necessarily the universal provider of all forms of higher education. The university is not a mere purveyor of academic labels. The university is a place for the study and communication of basic knowledge. The university is the repository of the highest standards in teaching and scholarship. The university conserves accumulated knowledge and passes it on to successive generations of students. The university re-examines that knowledge and re-states it in the light of new scholarship. The university adds to existing knowledge and advances it beyond its present frontiers. These are the purposes to which the university must relate its functions, and these are the obligations that the university must be permitted to keep uppermost, no matter what other requirements for professional and technical education fall upon it.

When referring to technological education, later in the Report, the Commission further classified its view of the university's relationship to technology:

Technology, as we have indicated above, is concerned with industry and the industrial applications of science. The nature of technological training is such that it cannot easily be organised by the university; it must be closely associated with industry, sometimes using its facilities, always aware of industry's changing needs, flexible enough to meet these changes, and keeping industry's requirements always in mind. These are not obligations which the university should be asked to assume and, indeed, we feel sure that the university would not wish to assume them. Furthermore, it would seem best that responsibility for technological education and training should be linked with the general responsibility for the development and promotion of technology in the country; this wider responsibility must therefore rest elsewhere than in the university.

But if the university is not the appropriate location of responsibility for technological training and development, it does not follow that the university has no part to play in technological training. The university will retain its basic function of preparing the potential technologist in the relevant fundamental and applied sciences.

This dual concern of the Commission — the danger of the universities in their current condition taking on more than they could support without endangering standards, and the unease that in responding to pressure for more technological and applied education, the universities might be led away from what the Commission believed was the role and function of a university — underlay some of the recommendations of the Commission particularly those concerning the "new colleges." The Commission also favoured the establishment of the constituent colleges of the N.U.I. as independent universities.

The following sets out the recommendations of the Commission on Higher Education:

OUR PRINCIPAL RECOMMENDATIONS MAY BE LISTED AS FOLLOWS:

1. U.C.D., U.C.C. and U.C.G. should be established by Act of the Oireachtas as independent universities to replace the N.U.I., with provision for the special position of St. Patrick's College, Maynooth.
2. The constitution of T.C.D. should be restated by Act of the Oireachtas.
3. A council of Irish Universities should be established by Act of the Oireachtas.
4. The constitution of each university should provide for a governing authority of which a majority of the members would be elected by the academic staff and the remainder nominated by the government.
5. The head of each university should be appointed by the governing authority for a limited term.
6. Permanent academic appointments should be made by the governing authority of the university on the nomination of expert committees.
7. There should be a national minimum standard for entry to the universities, which should be equivalent to a pass in the school leaving certificate examination, with honours in two appropriate subjects. Individual

institutions should be free to prescribe higher standards, and the minimum standard should be reviewed periodically by the Council of Irish Universities.

8. The minimum length of a university first-degree course should be four years (in Arts and Science leading to a master's degree).
9. The staff/student ratio in the universities must be progressively and substantially improved to 1 : 12 by 1975.
10. Postgraduate study and research must be given a much larger place in all departments of the universities.
11. The university teacher must have half his working year (as defined) free for study and research.
12. It is the responsibility of the universities to match student numbers with resources of staff, accommodation, equipment and facilities. It is essential that the present inadequate staff/student ratio be amended and overcrowding eliminated before further expansion is undertaken.
13. No additional university should now be established.
14. To meet part of the expanding demand for higher education, to cater for it in new ways, and to provide a focus of intellectual and cultural life in new centres, a new type of institution — the New College — should be established, initially in Dublin and Limerick, and later in other centres. It would award a Bachelor's Degree after a full three-year course or its equivalent, and Diplomas for a variety of courses of shorter duration.
15. Professional training for Agricultural and Veterinary Sciences, following upon studies in basic or fundamental sciences in a university or new college, should be incorporated with the work of An Foras Talúntais in a National College of Agricultural and Veterinary Sciences, which would have power to award its own qualifications.

16. A Technological Authority, which would incorporate the work of the Institute of Industrial Research and Standards, should be established to promote and assist technological training and research.
17. The period of training for national teachers should be extended to three years. The training colleges should have enlarged functions and be associated with the New Colleges in Dublin and Limerick.
18. Education as a subject of study and research should be firmly established and developed in the university.
19. There is no *prima facie* case for closing any of the existing medical schools. The schools should be assisted to provide undergraduate training to a satisfactory standard, and medical studies should be developed to the highest levels in one school.
20. Law as a subject of study and research should be firmly established and developed in the university, and a degree in law should be a prerequisite for entry to both branches of the legal profession.
21. The National College of Art should be given a new constitution.
22. Business, administrative, and social studies in the university should be firmly based on fundamental sciences.
23. The training of military cadets should be associated with university studies in University College, Galway.
24. New research developments should be accommodated in the universities or existing research institutes unless the contrary case can be established.
25. The separate research institutes and the university should establish close relationships with each other.
26. The Dublin Institute of Advanced Studies and its schools should be given a constitution broadly conforming to the university pattern.

27. The training of technicians should be a primary function of the vocational educational system.
28. The two Dublin Colleges of Technology and the College of Commerce, Rathmines, should severally and in combination be given an independent form of government and academic administration, subject to general financial control of the Dublin Vocational Education Committee.
29. Irish studies should be strengthened and expanded in the universities; this is a necessary condition for the development of teaching through Irish.
30. The main effort in developing teaching through Irish should be continued in University College, Galway, and the other university colleges should methodically develop teaching through Irish.
31. To ensure a supply of Irish speaking staff of high academic calibre, there should be instituted under the Council of Irish Universities (a) special schemes of postgraduate scholarships and fellowships, and (b) a residential foundation in University College, Galway, for Irish speaking fellows, and for postgraduate and senior undergraduate students.
32. The Irish Folklore Commission should be established as an Institute within University College, Dublin, and its unique collection of folklore material should be generally accessible.
33. To ensure that higher education should be open as fully and freely as possible to all qualified students there should be, in addition to university scholarships and other special schemes of financial aid, a national scheme comprising scholarships, loans and grants.
34. There should be a quota of undergraduate places for foreign students in our institutions of higher education, and free entry for research students.

35. Student bodies, local and national, should be recognised as having a positive role in the organisation of student life and should be given corresponding functions and responsibilities.
36. A large-scale programme of hostels for students is not practicable until other more pressing needs of higher education have been satisfied, but student amenities should be expanded without delay and immediate interim measures taken to improve and increase residential accommodation.
37. A permanent Commission for Higher Education should be established by Act of the Oireachtas, to be the financial authority of the system, to assist in implementing this report, and to keep the problems of higher education under continuous review. It would consist of nine members appointed by the government and should report directly to the Taoiseach.

V.8 Report of the Steering Committee on Technical Education, 1967

The "New Colleges" proposal was, to some extent, upstaged by the government's decision to establish Regional Technical Colleges, announced by Minister Hillery in May, 1963. While the commission was sitting the government appointed a steering committee to advise it on the proposed regional colleges. The committee presented an interim report in January, 1967 and a final report in April, 1967.

The Steering Committee endorsed the government's plan for regional technical colleges and set out a broad role for the colleges. The first of nine regional colleges opened in 1970 under the auspices of the V.E.Cs. (Legislation in 1992 gave them a large degree of institutional autonomy). The report of 1967 urged the establishment of regional education councils and the setting up of a National Council for Educational Awards, on the lines of the N.C.C.A. in Britain, for non-university courses.

The following extract from the report sets out the role envisaged for the regional colleges as well as other key recommendations.

We believe that the main long-term function of the Colleges will be to educate for trade and industry over a broad spectrum of occupations ranging from craft to professional level, notably in engineering and science but also in commercial, linguistic and other specialities. They will, however, be more immediately concerned with providing courses aimed at filling gaps in the industrial manpower structure, particularly in the technician area. For reasons outlined later, we also consider that the Regional Colleges should cater for certain types of senior cycle post-primary education.

We do not foresee any final fixed pattern of courses in the colleges. If they are to make their most effective contribution to the needs of society and the economy they must be capable of continuing adaptation to social, economic and technological changes. Initiative at local and national levels will largely determine how far this vital characteristic is developed. We are concerned that the progress of these colleges should not be deterred by any artificial limitation of either the scope or the level of their educational achievements.

RECOMMENDATIONS

1. ....the Steering Committee recommends that the Minister proceed with all eight Regional Technical Colleges, including the CERT amplified Galway Regional Technical College, as soon as possible. The Colleges should be designed around the information given in the Preliminary Brief Report modified by further studies being made by the committee with the Department.

****

8. Supervisory staff should be recruited at least one year before the opening of each college so that they could engage in organisation of their college and recruitment of teachers. Other new teachers should be appointed up to six months in advance and given pedagogic training, teaching practice and opportunities for adaptation of their technical knowledge for teaching purposes.

****

9. Regional Education Councils should be set up having accountability, in as much as it would be possible, for all education in each of the Regions, being duly representative of the interests referred to in Section 9. Executive responsibility should be given to an Executive Bureau, with a Regional Education Director who would be responsible for all the services to the Council. Regional Councils would report to a central authority, either in the Department of Education or in a Sub-Commission for Regional Education.

****

10. Each Regional College should have a Principal, Vice-Principal and Heads of Departments. There should be a managing College Council, representative of the various appropriate interests, with ex-officio representatives of the Regional Education Council.

****

12. The Government should establish a National Council for Educational Awards.

****

V.9 Minister O'Malley's University Merger Proposal, 1967

In the same month that the final Report on technical education was published, April, 1967, the Minister for Education, Donagh O'Malley issued a statement to the effect that a government decision had been made to merge Trinity College and U.C.D. into a single university of Dublin. This became an issue of major controversy. It also reflected a rejection of the Commission on Higher Education recommendation which had urged independent university status for the N.U.I. constituent colleges and non-interference with the independent status of Trinity College. Minister O'Malley stated that a single, multi-denominational university would be set up in Dublin, based on the two existing university institutions. The Minister was not unaware of the significance of such a proposal remarking "It marks the end of an era in the long story of university education in Ireland and also, it seems to me, in the history of the country itself." The Minister argued that his proposal made economic, educational and social sense. This perspective was not, however, shared by many interested parties and very divergent views were expressed in what became a celebrated controversy, known popularly as "the merger proposals." The following is an extract from Minister O'Malley's statement:

University Education in Dublin

Statement of Minister for Education 18th April, 1967

Everybody, I think, will agree that the university situation in Dublin is far from being satisfactory. We have here in the capital city of a small country what are to all intents and purposes two separate and very differently constituted university institutions, each endowed in major part by the State, but each ploughing its own furrow with virtually no provision, formal or even informal, for co-ordination of their efforts or the sharing by them of what must always be scarce but very valuable national resources. Those resources comprise knowledge and skills of the highest quality, accommodation, equipment and material generally.

This is for several reasons an opportune moment to call a halt and assess the position. In the first place there is the general prospect, to which I have referred, of a vast increase in student numbers, with a corresponding increase in expenditure on university provision. Secondly, the Commission on Higher Education has just issued a Summary of its Report and Recommendations. Thirdly, the issue has already come to a head this year by way of university building claims to cater for the increasing demand for places.

For the reasons I have given, however, the Government considers that the public interest demands the establishment of a formal relationship between the two Dublin Colleges. The Government has accordingly authorised me to announce that it is their intention to proceed on the lines of my proposals of December last. Those proposals were framed on the basis of there being one University of Dublin, to contain two Colleges, each complementary to the other.

The two Colleges would be founded on the two existing institutions, University College and Trinity College. One University in Dublin would involve one University Authority, statutorily established on a democratic basis, with a subsidiary authority, similarly constituted, for each of the two Colleges. In the matter of the identity of each College the feeling of the existing authorities will be given the utmost weight. I may add that I have this morning informed the President of University College and the Provost of Trinity College of these proposals.

This moment is not without its solemnity. It marks the end of an era in the long story of university education in Ireland and also, it seems to me, in the history of the country itself.

I have treated mostly of the economic side of things and of training for the professions. Let it not be thought that for that reason the purely educational aspect of a university's functions is regarded by me as of little account. Far be it from me to convey that impression. We are all to some extent followers of Newman in the belief that a university has something more to give its students than mere training. If it is true to itself, it should also give them that indefinable thing which might be called quality. I believe firmly that the new University of Dublin will be better able to give its students "quality," in the best sense of the word, than could, under existing conditions, either of the existing Colleges.

Finally, but by no means least in importance, the new University of Dublin will not be "neutral" denominationally, but multi-denominational, with the fullest respect and recognition for all denominations of students and the fullest mutual respect among them for each other. *Neutralism* in relation to what happened two thousand years ago in Palestine would not have been, and is not, a concept that would have any appeal for the vast majority of Irish parents, whatever their denomination. In the future University of Dublin there will be provision for both Catholic and Protestant Schools of Divinity or Theology. This was not permissible to University College under the 1908 Act.

As I have said, we are at the opening of a new era in higher education. This National problem which has been with us for many generations needs only goodwill for it to be solved satisfactorily. I am confident that that goodwill shall be forthcoming and that the present is the ideal moment to evoke it.

V.10 Minister Lenihan's Statement of Government Policy on Higher Education, 1968

On 6th July, 1968, Minister Brian Lenihan announced the Government's proposals on the re-organisation of the universities. The N.U.I. was to be dissolved with U.C.C. and U.C.G. being given independent status. Trinity and U.C.D. were to form a single multi-denominational university based on the two colleges. Its governing body was to have equal representation from both colleges. The statement set out a division of faculties between the colleges. Maynooth College was to become an associated college of the new university. A Conference of Irish Universities was to be set up to deal with academic issues common to all universities. Also, in line with the Commission's Report, a permanent authority to deal with financial and organisational problems of higher education was to be established.

The following is an extract from Minister Lenihan's statement:

STATEMENT ISSUED BY THE MINISTER FOR EDUCATION ON BEHALF OF THE GOVERNMENT ON 6 JULY, 1968

1. The Government have completed their consideration of the future provision for higher education in Dublin arising from their decision to join University College, Dublin and Trinity College in a reconstituted University of Dublin. In that regard they have examined certain of the basic recommendations of the Commission on Higher Education and have decided in principle to accept the recommendations

   (1) that the National University of Ireland be dissolved and that University College, Cork and University College, Galway be constituted as separate Universities;

(2) that a permanent authority be established to deal with the financial and organisational problems of higher education;

(3) that there be established a Conference of Irish Universities, to deal principally with academic problems common to all the university institutions.

The examination of the remaining recommendations of the Commission is proceeding and a further statement on behalf of the Government in relation to other aspects of higher education will be issued shortly.

2. In relation to the specific questions arising from the decision to join University College Dublin and Trinity College in a reconstituted University of Dublin, the Government have examined fully the final proposals of the Governing Bodies of the two Colleges, together with their original proposals and the variations therein which were suggested by the Minister for Education.

They have in addition taken fully into account the views submitted to them by other parties concerned.

This has been done in the context of the national interest and that of higher education in the country generally.

In that context there are a number of matters which the Government consider to be fundamental

These are:

(1) The University of Dublin should be a corporate body forming one indivisible whole, but within that whole each College to retain its identity.

Each College should accordingly be a corporate body in possession of its present property, but with the use of such property available to the entire University as required by it.

(2) The Governing Body of the University, on which each College should have equal representation, but which would also contain representatives of other appropriate interests, should be the paramount authority for the management and conducting of the University and its Colleges, including the appointment of academic and administrative staff. Each College should have a Council which, subject to the over-all authority of the Governing Body, would administer the affairs of the College. The membership of the Council would consist in majority of representatives of the academic personnel of the College but would include representatives of other appropriate interests.

(3) The University and its Colleges will be multi-denominational and should be managed and conducted on christian principles, but without any religious test for the staff or students, save as may be arranged in relation to the teaching of Theology or Divinity and the directing thereof.

(4) Entry should be to the University and no distinction should be made as between the Colleges in relation to conditions and qualifications for entry.

(5) The allocation of Faculties and Departments as between the Colleges should, as far as may be reasonable and possible and consistent with (1) above, be such as to avoid any unnecessary duplication.

V.11 The Higher Education Authority Act, 1971

The proposal of Minister Lenihan for a Higher Education Authority (HEA) was the only one in his statement to become a full reality. The HEA was set up on an ad hoc basis in August, 1968 and at its first meeting on 12 September, 1968, Minister Lenihan included a statement in his speech on his view of university autonomy as follows:

As I see it, university autonomy relates fundamentally to academic freedom in research, the laying down of courses and curricula, the prescribing of examination conditions and standards, generally determining in what manner and under what regulations university qualifications will be awarded, internal administration and such matters. Academic freedom of course carries with it the right of a university professor or lecturer to speak his mind openly. University autonomy should not, however, be interpreted as freedom simply to present an annual bill to the government and say you are to collect that amount from the taxpayers and allow us to spend it as we see fit. That kind of autonomy could not exist. In this day and age there can be no question of absolute autonomy in relation to any institution which to a greater or lesser degree is financed out of public taxation.

****

It is for you to determine your method of operation. This is only in keeping with the fact that you are in no way an executive arm of the Government or of any Department of State. You are an autonomous body and will function as such in the interim period pending the introduction of formal legislation. It will be for you to advise, not in relation to one aspect of that legislation, but in regard to the whole of the legislation on which higher education will in future be based. This will of course include provision for your own autonomous status.

The H.E.A. was established on a statutory basis in 1971. It can be noted that the Authority was to have a dual function. As an advisory body to the Minister it should monitor, review, advise and play its part generally in furthering the development of higher education and in the co-ordination of state investment therein. Secondly, its central statutory power and function as an executive body was to assess in relation to annual or other periods the financial requirements of the institutions of which it was the funding agency; to recommend for State grants the capital and recurrent amounts so assessed; and to allocate to the institutions concerned the State funds provided. The following extract from the act sets out the general and specific functions of the H.E.A.

3.— An tÚdarás (The Authority) shall, in addition to the specific functions given to it by this Act, have the general functions of—

(a) furthering the development of higher education;
(b) assisting in the co-ordination of State investment in higher education and preparing proposals for such investment;
(c) promoting an appreciation of the value of higher education and research;
(d) promoting the attainment of equality of opportunity in higher education;
(e) promoting the democratisation of the structure of higher education.

4.— In performing its functions, An tÚdarás shall bear constantly in mind the national aims of restoring the Irish language and preserving and developing the national culture and shall endeavour to promote the attainment of those aims.

5.— An tÚdarás shall advise the Minister on the need or otherwise for the establishment of new institutions of higher education, on the nature and form of those institutions and on the legislative measures required in relation to their establishment or in relation to any existing institution of higher education.

6.— (1) An tÚdarás shall maintain a continuous review of the demand and need for higher education.

(2) An tÚudarás shall recommend to the Minister the overall provision of student places to be made within the higher education system having regard to the need to maintain a reasonable balance in the distribution of the total number of students between the institutions of higher education.

Its specific powers and functions are as follows:

7.— An tÚdarás may, annually or at such other intervals as it may determine, require any institution of higher education to submit a statement of its financial position to An tÚdarás and it shall be the duty of every institution of higher education to comply with any requirements which are imposed on it under this section.

8.— (1) Any request by an institution of higher education for State subvention shall be submitted by the institution to An tÚdarás in such manner as An tÚdarás may require.

(2) Requests submitted under this section shall be examined by An tÚdarás annually or at such other intervals as it may determine.

9.— An tÚdarás may relate annual or other financial requirements of institutions of higher education to financial planning over such periods as it considers suitable.

10.— (1) An tÚdarás shall assess amounts of State financial provision, both current and capital, which it recommends for higher education and research or for any part thereof, either in relation to current or future periods.

(2) In making assessments under this section in respect of institutions of higher education, An tÚdarás shall have regard to the accommodation capacity for students of each institution and to the maintenance of a reasonable balance in the distribution of the total number of students as between institutions.

11.— An institution of higher education shall supply to An tÚudarás all such information relative to the institution as An tÚdarás may require for the purpose of performing its functions.

12.— (1) There shall be paid to An tÚdarás, out of moneys provided by the Oireachtas, such amounts for institutions of higher education as may be approved by the Minister with the consent of the Minister for Finance.

(2) Any payment to an institution which An tÚdarás makes out of the amounts that it receives under the foregoing subsection shall be made in such manner and subject to such conditions as An tÚdarás thinks fit.

V.12 Some Higher Education Authority Reports

The H.E.A. published a range of special reports on significant policy issues. It also commissioned a number of reports from consultants on specific themes. Among the early reports published were these on Teacher Education; the Ballymun Project; A Council for National Awards; A College of Higher Education in Limerick; Report on University Organisation.

The following extracts are taken from some of these reports:

V.12.1 Council for National Awards (1969)
There is a well-established demand and in some areas a long-felt need on the part of industry and of actual and potential technological students for further and more advanced technological and other specialised third-level courses.

This has been the experience in the first place of the Colleges of Technology, which are immediately and directly involved in the matter. The existence of such a demand and need is confirmed by the Irish-OECD Report, *Investment in Education,* and by the OECD Report, *The Training of Technicians in Ireland,* as also to some extent by the trend of opinion conveyed to us in the course of our examination of the claim for a university at Limerick.

We are satisfied that to meet this demand and need, and in the process to attract to technological courses more students who have successfully completed the post-primary educational cycle, it is essential that there be formal recognition on a national basis for such courses and qualifications.

In our opinion the solution lies in the setting up of a Council for National Awards, with powers and functions on the following lines:

(i) To grant certificates, diplomas and degrees to persons who have successfully pursued courses of study at third-level educational institutions other than universities;
(ii) To determine the conditions governing the grant of such awards;
(iii) To approve courses of study to be pursued by candidates in order to qualify for such awards, including, where appropriate, arrangements for industrial and commercial experience in association with such courses.

We submit accordingly an initial recommendation that a Council for National Awards be established, but find it necessary to defer a definitive recommendation on the nature of the constitution under which it should operate until we shall have had an opportunity of consulting the authorities of the university institutions. We are requesting their views on the matter and in particular on the question of the award of degrees by the Council. It will be necessary to ensure that these degrees will not in any way be inferior to those of the universities.

V.12.2. Higher Education College for Limerick, 1969

In examining the case for a new higher education institution in Limerick the H.E.A. was influenced by the development of the binary pattern of third-level education in England. It opposed the idea of a new university for Limerick but recommended an institution of a polytechnic character.

****

11. It is in the pattern of the above-mentioned development in Britain that we see a solution to the general Irish demand and need, but more especially to the problem of Limerick and its area, which, in agreement with the Commission on Higher Education, we feel has a special claim for a centre of higher education.

12. In our opinion Limerick, with its population of 60,000, its higher than average post-primary school population and its proximity to Shannon Industrial Estate and Airport, is uniquely fitted for the role of leader in meeting this national need and thus justifying the large State expenditure which would be involved. The kind of institution of higher education we have in mind would also, we are convinced, be that which would best answer the interests of the great majority of Limerick's young people.

This is the heart of the matter. In relation to the future of these young people and, indeed, to that of Limerick as a potential centre and focus of high-grade industrial and agricultural development, the essential advantages of what might be called a College of Higher Education are:

(1) that it would combine the prestige of degree-earning courses of various kinds with an extensive provision on a scale and in a manner not open to a university (that is by way of full and complete courses at technical level) for that very large number of its potential students who either would not have satisfied the precise conditions of university entry or for some reason would not desire to pursue a university course but nevertheless would wish to continue their education beyond Leaving Certificate level;

(2) that it would provide sandwich-type courses for persons already in employment who would wish to improve their education or skills or to add to their qualifications;

(3) that its students would thus tend in the main to be Limerick-oriented;

(4) that, providing, as it should, for areas of study not fully covered in existing institutions and thus catering distinctively for national as well as regional needs, it should attract students from all parts of Ireland and thereby enrich the Limerick region both socially and culturally. In this regard we contemplate part of its intake as coming from the Regional Technical Colleges.

Such a distinctively new form of higher education is in effect that contemplated in the Lichfield Report of

February, 1969, save that our recommendations are made in a national rather than an exclusively regional context.

On the basis, therefore, of our initial recommendation, in Memorandum A, that a Council for National Awards be established, we see a College of Higher Education at Limerick as specially suited to the pioneering of courses of the type with which such a Council would be concerned. We recommend accordingly.

V.12.3 Report on University Reorganisation (1972)

In its report on university re-organisation the H.E.A. took a different view from the Government and urged that U.C.D. and Trinity College be regarded as separate independent universities. It considered that circumstances had changed since the government decision of 1968 and that negotiations between U.C.D. and T.C.D. had paved the way for a greater degree of co-ordination between the two institutions. The H.E.A. also favoured independent status for U.C.C. and U.C.G.

****

In the circumstances of that time there was in our opinion no practical alternative to the Government's Plan of a single University. However hallowed were the traditions which that solution might bring to an end, however great the temporary dislocation which might accompany the Plan's implementation, the problem of lack of coordination in university education in Dublin had to be resolved and, in view of the growing demand for university places and the growing cost of university provision, resolved sooner rather than later.

51.2 In the three years which have since elapsed, however, all three aspects of the impasse have in unforeseeable fashion dissolved. The ecclesiastical ban on the entry of Catholic students to Trinity College has been withdrawn: the proportion of non-Irish students allowed entry into that College has been reduced to 10%; and an Agreement for the amalgamation of a number of Faculties of the two Dublin Colleges has been reached.

52. *Our recommendation : two separate Universities in Dublin linked by a statutory Conjoint Board.*

52.1 In these fundamentally altered circumstances we have come to the view that the radical solution of a single University is no longer a compelling necessity and we therefore support the proposal in the NUI/TCD Agreement that there be two separate Universities in Dublin.

52.2 In recommending accordingly, however, we would emphasise that there can never again be a question of each of the two institutions concerned pursuing an absolutely separate path, with at the same time both of them drawing virtually all their capital and the major part of their current incomes from public funds. There must be found a means not only of carrying out to the best effect the projected amalgamations of Schools and Departments, but also of ensuring the continued collaboration and coordination of the two institutions within the national higher education complex. If there is to be no single university comprising both colleges and so no common Governing Body, we believe a statutory Conjoint Board, as adumbrated in chapter IV, to be absolutely essential.

V.13 National College of Art and Design Act December 1971

The National College of Art and Design which had been under the direct control of the Department of Education experienced turbulent times during the late sixties and early seventies. This was partly due to the atmosphere of student unrest which was characteristic of the times but it also reflected the out-dated administrative procedures and inadequate facilities of the institution. Following much debate new legislation was formulated and was passed in 1971.

The following extracts highlight the role of the new College Board. The courses and awards of the college were to be validated by the National Council for Educational Awards, which was set up in 1972.

4.— (1) There shall, by virtue of this section, be established on the establishment day a board to be known as Bord an Choláiste Náisiúnta Elaíne is Deartha to perform the functions given to it by this Act (in this Act referred to as An Bord).

(2) An Bord shall be a body corporate with perpetual succession and power to sue and be sued in its corporate name and to acquire, hold and dispose of land.

5.— (1) On and from the establishment day, An Bord shall carry out the management of the College and the organisation and administration of its affairs, and shall have all such powers as are necessary for or incidental to those purposes.

(2) In particular, and without prejudice to the generality of subsection (1) of this section, An Bord shall have the general functions of —

(a) establishing and carrying on schemes of education of such scope and extent as it may determine in art, crafts and design.

(b) providing courses for the training of persons as teachers of art,

(c) providing courses and lectures for the further training of teachers of art as such teachers.

(d) providing, if it so thinks fit, lectures on art, crafts and design for the public by members of its academic staff and other persons whom it considers suitably qualified for the purpose,

(e) establishing and carrying on schemes (on which the amount of the expenditure by An Bord shall have been approved of by the Minister) for the giving of scholarships, bursaries, prizes and other awards in relation to art, crafts and design,

(f) holding exhibitions of art and crafts of students of the College, exhibitions of art and crafts and exhibitions devoted to any other subject matter relevant to the activities of the College,

****

(f) providing courses of study in art, crafts and design —

(i) that are approved by any body established by the Minister or by Act of the Oireachtas after the passing of this Act for the purpose of granting degrees, diplomas and other similar educational awards, and

(ii) that lead to the grant of such degrees, diplomas or similar educational awards by that body.

V.14 The National Council for Educational Awards

The Steering Committee on Technical Education, 1967, had recommended the establishment of a National Council for non-university awards. This proposal was endorsed by the H.E.A. in its report of 1969. The Government established the National Council for Educational Awards on an ad-hoc basis in 1972 with the following function:

...to promote, facilitate, encourage, co-ordinate and develop technical, industrial, commercial, technological, professional and scientific education and, in association with these, liberal education,

(a) by the granting and conferring of degrees, diplomas and certificates to and on students who shall, to the satisfaction of the Council, have pursued at an educational institution recognised by the Council, courses of study approved by the Council and who shall to the satisfaction of the Council have passed examinations and/or other tests set or prescribed by the Council; and

(b) by all other such means as may be provided for.

It seemed that a binary third-level system was firmly in place. However, changed plans of a new Government announced in 1974 led to the re-organisation of the NCEA. The Minister for Education, Mr. Burke, as part of the new policy of a "comprehensive" third-level system, informed the NCEA at the first meeting of the second ad hoc Council in February 1976 how it fitted in with the new plans.

> The change to a situation where institutions will be inter-related and their activities co-ordinated, while retaining that measure of freedom and flexibility which will enable each institution to make its full and vital contribution to our overall educational provision, without sacrificing its own individual identity or being deprived of the opportunity to make its own unique contribution to that provision, is not being left to chance.

The N.C.E.A. will be reconstituted to —

> plan and co-ordinate courses and to validate and award non-degree third-level qualifications in NIHEs, Dublin and Limerick, and in the RTCs.

This planning and co-ordinating function is calculated to ensure that no institution within the integrated sector of higher education, be it large or small, will be tempted to chart its own course of development independently of other institutions.

A key change for the NCEA was to be the loss of its degree-awarding powers. The return of a Fianna Fáil Government saw this policy over-turned and the NCEA was given statutory status through an Act passed in November, 1979. The following is an extract setting out some key features of the legislation:

An Act to establish a body to be known in the Irish Language as Comhairle Náisiúnta na gCáilÍochtaÍ Oideachais and in the English language as the National Council for Educational Awards, to define its functions and to provide for other matters connected with the foregoing. *[20th November, 1979].*

3.— (1) The functions of the Council shall be generally to encourage, facilitate, promote, co-ordinate and develop technical, industrial, scientific, technological and commercial education, and education in art or design, provided outside the universities, whether professional, vocational or technical, and to encourage and promote liberal education.

(2) Without prejudice to the generality of subsection (1) of this section, the Council may —

(a) confer, grant or give degrees, diplomas, certificates or other educational awards..........

(b) either recognise a degree, diploma, certificate or other educational award conferred, granted or given to persons who successfully complete such courses, or approve of such course of study or instruction............

(c) assess the standard maintained for the time being by any institution to which this Act applies as regards any course of study or instruction approved by the Council;

(d) for the purpose of promoting degrees, diplomas, certificates or other educational awards conferred, granted or given by it —

(i) take such steps as it considers appropriate either within or outside the State;

(ii) co-ordinate, or assist in co-ordinating, in such manner as it considers appropriate, any two or more such courses of study or instruction conducted by, or provided under the supervision of one or more institutions to which this Act applies.

(iii) for the purpose of enabling them to attend or otherwise pursue or follow any such course, assist the transfer of students from one such institution to another such institution;

(e) through an tÚdarás advise the Minister in relation to the cost of providing, or continuing to provide, or the financing of any course of study or instruction approved of by the Council, or the cost of modifying any course of study or instruction to the extent necessary to secure its approval by the Council.

(3) (a) The Minister may, with the concurrence of the Minister for the Public Service and after consultation with such other Minister of the Government (if any) as the Minister considers to be concerned, by order assign to the Council such functions relating to technical, industrial, scientific, technological or commercial education, or education in art or

design, (being functions additional to those assigned by this Act) as the Minister thinks fit.

4.— The members of the Council shall be a chairman, the Director and twenty-three other members.

6.— (1) The Government shall from time to time as occasion requires, appoint in a part-time capacity a person to be chairman of the Council, and an appointment under this subsection shall, if necessary, operate to make the person to whom it relates a member of the Council.

V.15 Coalition Government Plans for a "Comprehensive" Higher-level Sector, 1974

On 16th December, 1974 the Minister for Education, Mr. Burke, announced wide-ranging government proposals for the future of higher education which contrasted significantly with the policy of the previous administration. The statement indicated that the central problem on planning was based "on one major decision, namely, whether to continue and develop the existing binary system or to initiate the establishment of a fully comprehensive system of higher education." The report of a Departmental Committee favoured the binary model but the Government came out in favour of the comprehensive model. The proposals were that there would be three universities in the state — the University of Dublin (T.C.D.), a new university constituted of the existing U.C.D. and a reconstituted N.U.I. embracing U.C.C. and U.C.G. Maynooth College would have the option of becoming a constituent college of any of the three universities. The NIHEs of Limerick and Dublin, as well as Thomond College would become recognised colleges of the universities as would the major colleges of education. The N.C.E.A. would lose its degree-awarding powers and a Conference of Irish Universities would be established to improve inter-university relationships. The policy shared the fate of earlier official statements in being highly controversial, but also in the more important aspect of little implementation of a lasting character. The varying policy statements did, however, give rise to considerable uncertainty in higher education circles during the mid-seventies.

The following extract sets out the main government proposals.

A.— There shall be three universities in the State: a university to be constituted from the present University College, Dublin; the University of Dublin (Trinity College); the National University of Ireland, comprising University College, Cork, and University College, Galway.

B.— St. Patrick's College, Maynooth, shall have the option of becoming a constituent college of any one of the three universities.

C.— The National Institute of Higher Education, Limerick, shall be a recognised college of the National University of Ireland, with the capacity to evolve into a constituent college of the National University of Ireland or to become an autonomous degree-awarding institution.

D.— The National Institute of Higher Education, Dublin, shall be a recognised college of either of the Dublin universities, with the capacity to evolve into a constituent college of one or other of the Dublin universities or to become an autonomous degree-awarding institution.

E.— The Majority of the members of the governing bodies of the NIHEs, Limerick and Dublin, shall be nominated by the Government on the recommendation of the Minister for Education, and shall include representatives from the trade unions, agriculture, business, industry and educational interests.

F.— A Council for Technological Education shall be established to plan and co-ordinate courses, and to validate and award non-degree third-level qualifications in the NIHEs, Dublin and Limerick, and in the RTCs.

G.— The council shall consist of a chairman and 30 members. It shall be constituted as to one-third of its membership from, and by, the governing body of the NIHE, Limerick, as to one third from, and by, the governing body of the NIHE, Dublin, and as to the remaining one-third, of members nominated by the Government on the Recommendation of the Minister for Education.

H.— The regional technical colleges shall be funded, through the vocational education committees, by the Department of Education in consultation with the Council for Technological Education.

I.— A Conjoint Board shall be established to co-ordinate the two Dublin universities, with a view to ensuring rational use of resources and mobility of staff and students between them.

V.16 Co-operative Agreement between the University of Dublin (T.C.D.) and the City of Dublin Vocational Education Committee (CDVEC), 1976

In April 1976 Trinity College and the CDVEC established a Liaison Council, with six representatives from each institution, to co-ordinate and promote academic co-operation between the two bodies. The arrangement was to be on the basis of parity, with each body retaining its separate and independent identity. One of the significant outcomes of this agreement was that students in the CDVEC Colleges could be awarded degrees by Trinity College. With the grouping of the Colleges into the Dublin Institute of Technology in 1978 an impressive expansion took place in the numbers obtaining such degrees.

The following extract from the agreement sets out the main forms of co-operation which were planned:

(a) Each will make available to the other such facilities and staff as may be appropriate so far as their own internal commitments and contractual arrangements make this possible.

(b) Where it is jointly considered useful to do so, both will co-operate in the design and establishment of courses; and both will collaborate in the operation of courses or components of courses to the extent agreed to be desirable from time to time.

(c) Each may make available to students of the other such awards as may be within its power to institute, and as are jointly deemed to be appropriate.

(d) Both will seek to promote the mobility of students and staff and to provide reciprocal access to courses and facilities.

(e) Both will encourage co-operation in research, development and design, and related activities.

V.17 Reorganisation of the City of Dublin Vocational Education Committee's third-level colleges into the Dublin Institute of Technology (DIT), 1978

The six third-level colleges of the City of Dublin Vocational Education Committee (CDVEC) had expanded significantly in their student numbers, diversity of courses and levels of study in the 1960s and 1970s. In 1978 the CDVEC decided to bring the colleges into a unified, institutional framework the Dublin Institute of Technology (DIT). Under the new arrangements the colleges, in their various locations, would continue their separate activities but would be co-ordinated through the Institute. Extracts from the foundation document set out the new government and administrative structure of the Institute. In 1992 legislation established the DIT as a more autonomous institution from the CDVEC.

The following extracts are from a document entitled CDVEC — Unification of the third level colleges:

NAME OF INSTITUTE

The new Institute would be called *The Dublin Institute of Technology.*

GOVERNANCE OF THE INSTITUTE

The Institute would be set up under Section 21 of the Vocational Education Act 1930.

GOVERNING BODY OF THE INSTITUTE

In accordance with Section 21 of the Act the Governing Body of the Institute will consist of 12 people:

6 Committee members
2 members from Industry and Commerce
1 Representative of the Dublin Council of Trade Unions
1 Student
1 Chairman of the Executive Council
1 Staff representative

The number of people who would normally attend the Governing Body meeting would not exceed 25. There would be 12 voting members and 13 members in attendance. The members in attendance would include the CEO, the remaining College Principals, the Academic Registrar, Chairmen of various sub-committees, such as the Academic Council, etc.

TERMS OF REFERENCE OF THE GOVERNING BODY

The Governing Body shall have responsibility for:

(a) the running of the institute
(b) the development of a fully integrated third level institute
(c) the development of a fully integrated apprentice institute.

THE INSTITUTE'S EXECUTIVE
The Institute's Executive shall consist of the College Principals one of whom will be elected Chairman of the Executive Council and Director of the Institute.

****

FUNCTION OF EXISTING COLLEGE COUNCILS
The Existing College Councils would act as Advisory Councils to the various sub-groupings within the Institute and the minutes of the College Council would be passed in the normal way through the Executive Committee to the Governing Body.

V.18 Legislation for NIHEL and NIHED

The return of Fianna Fáil to government in 1977 led to the re-instatement of the binary policy for higher education and preparation began for a sequence of legislative measures which gave statutory status to the N.C.E.A., NIHE Limerick, NIHE Dublin, and Thomond College. An extract from the N.C.E.A. legislation (1979) has been included under V.14.

The following extract reflects key aspects of the act establishing NIHEL (1980). The legislation for NIHED was exactly the same.

NATIONAL INSTITUTE FOR HIGHER EDUCATION LIMERICK, ACT 1980

An act to establish an institute of higher education to be known in the irish language as an Foras Náisiúnta um Ard-oideachas, Luimneach, and in the English language as the National Institute for Higher Education, Limerick, to define its functions and to provide for other matters connected with the foregoing. *[14th July, 1980].*

4.— (1) The functions of the Institute shall be —

(a) to provide degree level courses, diploma level courses and certificate level courses and, subject to such conditions as the Minister may prescribe, such other courses, including post-graduate courses, as may seem appropriate to the Governing Body;

(b) to engage in research in such fields as the Governing Body may deem appropriate:

5.— (1) There shall be a Governing Body of the Institute which, save as otherwise provided by this Act, shall perform all the functions conferred on the Institute by this Act.

(2) The members of the Governing Body shall be a chairman, the Director and 23 ordinary members.

(3) The first members of the Governing Body shall be appointed by the Government, on the recommendation of the Minister, and shall hold office for a period of one year from the date of their appointment.

6.— (1) Save as otherwise provided in this Act, the Governing Body shall manage and control all the affairs and property of the Institute and shall perform all the functions conferred on the Institute by this Act, and shall have all such powers as may be necessary under this Act for this purpose.

(2) The governing Body may from time to time appoint such and so many committees as it thinks proper to assist it in such manner as the Governing Body shall direct, and the Governing Body may assign to any committee so appointed such duties as it thinks fit.

7.— (1) The Governing Body shall, with the approval of the Minister, from time to time appoint in a whole-time capacity a person to be the chief officer of the Institute and such officer is in this Act referred to as "The Director."

(2) The provisions of the Second Schedule to this Act shall apply to the Director.

8.— (1) The Governing Body shall appoint a body of persons which shall be known as and is in this Act referred to as "the Academic Council" to assist the Governing Body in the planning co-ordination, development and overseeing of the educational work of the Institute.

8. — (3) Without prejudice to the generality of subsection (1) of this section, the Academic Council shall have the following particular functions, that is to say —

(a) to design, develop and implement appropriate programmes of study;

(b) to make recommendations to the Governing Body for the establishment of appropriate structures to implement the programmes of study referred to in paragraph (a) of this subsection;

(c) to make recommendations to the Governing Body on programmes for the development of research;

(d) to make recommendations to the Governing Body for the selection, admission, retention and exclusion of students;

(e) to make, subject to the approval of the Governing Body, and to implement the academic regulations of the Institute;

(f) to propose to the Governing Body the form of regulations to be made by the Governing Body for the conduct of examinations, and for the evaluation of academic progress;

(g) to make recommendations to the Governing Body for the award of fellowships, scholarships, bursaries, prizes or other awards;

(h) to make general arrangements for tutorial or other academic counselling.

12. — (1) The Governing Body shall, as soon as may be after the end of each academic year, prepare and submit to the Minister a report of its proceedings during that year.

(2) The Governing Body shall supply the Minister with such information regarding the performance of its functions as he may from time to time require.

V.19 The White Paper on Educational Development, 1980

In 1980 the Government issued a White Paper on Educational Development. Chapter X was devoted to third-level education. The first paragraph of this section indicated that the Government was determined that its priorities for third-level education were going to be the key ones in the allocation of funding and it also reflected an impatience with the H.E.A. as an independent agency between the Government and third-level institutions. The following extract is from the first paragraph.

10.2 Third-level education, a major area of educational expenditure has a very important function in meeting both the demands of the student and that of society for the student. The contribution made by third-level educational institutions in recent years towards meeting the highly qualified manpower required by an expanding economy is readily recognised. Given the constraints on public expenditure it is essential to ensure that where the Government had identified priority objectives for third-level education, available funds will be applied to meet these priorities. The Government will examine the funding arrangements for third-level education, including the relevant provisions of the Higher Education Authority Act, 1971, with a view to ensuring priority of allocation of resources for such identified areas of national development. In the meantime, the Minister for Education will direct the attention of the Higher Education Authority to the need for ensuring that funds made available by the Government for particular projects should be appropriated accordingly.

The White Paper made a range of proposals, some of which were implemented, others such as the dissolution of the N.U.I. and the building of four new R.T.Cs. are still unimplemented. The following is a summary of the proposals in the White Paper for third-level education:

Summary of Proposals —

1. A Bill will be published shortly providing for the dissolution of the National University of Ireland and the establishment of its constituent colleges as independent universities.
2. The Government will examine the funding arrangements for third-level education, including the relevant provisions of the Higher Education Authority Act, 1971, with a view to ensuring priority of allocation of resources for identified areas of national development. In the meantime, the Minister for Education will direct the attention of the Higher Education Authority to the need for ensuring that funds made available by the Government for particular projects should be appropriated accordingly.
3. The National Institutes for Higher Education and Thomond College of Education will be established on a statutory basis.

4. The National Council for Educational Awards will facilitate and encourage the transfer of qualified students from one third-level institution to another for the purpose of pursuing higher courses.
5. A Committee of four will be established to visit Regional Technical Colleges and report to the Minister.
6. All third-level institutions will play complementary and supportive roles in order to make provision for varied community needs.
7. Further emphasis will be placed on technology, with particular regard to Engineering and Manufacturing Technology and Electronics and Computer Technology.
8. Considerable additional provision will be made for Certificate and Diploma level places in the Dublin area. There will be significant expansion of Engineering education in all regions at both graduate and technician levels. The opportunities for Business Studies will be enlarged.
9. Four new Regional Technical Colleges will be provided in the greater Dublin area.

****

V.20 Programme for Action in Education 1984-87

The Programme for Action in Education has been referred to in earlier sections (I.21, II.18 and III.26). Chapter 6 was devoted to third-level education and the following are the main proposals for this level:

The Government will continue to provide third-level education for as many young people as possible.

The rationalisation of courses within and between the various colleges will be undertaken.

Priority in financial support will be given to academic developments which are geared to ensuring that graduates are kept abreast of rapidly changing technology.

A review will be undertaken concerning the extent to which the Regional Technical Colleges have succeeded in achieving the goals originally set out for them.

In order to achieve a greater through-put of students without incurring major capital costs, the feasibility of redesigning courses on the basis of a four-term academic year will be examined.

The question of whether four-year degree courses can be reduced to three years without a lowering of standards will be examined.

The promotion of evening degree courses and modular degree programmes will be examined.

The feasibility of extending the provision of courses in link-Colleges or out-centres of Regional Technical Colleges will be investigated.

An identification of unit costs on a per-student and per-graduate basis will be undertaken. It is proposed that consultants be employed to carry out the necessary studies.

In consultation with the interested parties, the question of reducing staff/student contact hours in the Colleges of Technology and the R.T.Cs will be examined with a view to allowing for increased student numbers to be catered for without corresponding staff increases.

The N.C.E.A., in conjunction with the H.E.A. and the I.V.E.A., will be asked to prepare for submission to the Minister norms and criteria regarding the qualifications of staff employed in courses approved by the Council.

Where feasible, and in order to achieve economies, bulk-buying by third-level institutions will be encouraged.

The question of introducing a loan/grants scheme for students is being considered by the Government.

Links between higher education and industry will be intensified.

Discussions will be initiated relating to the question of bringing forward legislation to establish independent universities.

V.21 Partners in Education — Green Paper, 1985

In 1985 the Minister for Education issued a Green Paper entitled *Partners in Education : Serving Community Needs.* The first part was concerned with the establishment of local education councils, with significant responsibilities for post-primary education (see III.28). The second part set out ministerial proposals for management structures for the R.T.Cs. and the D.I.T. These colleges had proved very successful and had expanded impressively. It was considered that their management structures needed to be reformed and given more autonomy.

The following extracts relate to these proposals.

FUTURE MANAGEMENT STRUCTURE OF RTCs.
The difficulties arising out of the overall statutory limit of twelve on membership of Boards of Management has already been mentioned. It is, accordingly, suggested that the Boards

of Management might be larger and more representative than they are at present. More importantly, the Board ought to be in a position to carry out important functions without the necessity to refer back to a parent body such as a VEC. Such functions would include the recruitment of staff, subject to general guidelines laid down by the VEC/LEC with the approval of the Minister, and the keeping of their own accounts. In short, provision ought to be made to allow RTCs to operate with considerably more autonomy than heretofore while retaining their links with the VEC/LEC system.

SUMMARY OF RECOMMENDATIONS:

The following recommendations are made:-

(i) That the D.I.T. be constituted as an independent institution by legislation. In acknowledgement of the involvement of the City of Dublin VEC in the development of the D.I.T. significant representation on the Governing Body should be given to the City of Dublin VEC or to that LEC representing the Dublin City area. There would be one overall Director of the Institute and there would be six Heads of Colleges (or schools) under and responsible to the Director.

(ii) The RTCs and the Limerick College to be reconstituted so that each would have a much expanded and more independent Board of Management. The Board would be a sub-committee of the appropriate LEC or VEC but its decisions would not be subject to confirmation by the parent body; the College budget would be paid through the VEC/LEC; the institution would maintain its own accounts and recruit its own staff.

(iii) In the case of the Cork RTC, the Schools of Music and Art would be incorporated into the RTC.

(iv) Each RTC would have a College Council as at present.

V.22 Report of the International Study Group on Technological Education, 1987

The International Study Group was set up in 1986 by the Minister for Education "to examine third-level technological education outside the universities and to consider the case for a new Technological University". In this Report the Group emphasised that third-level technological education was firmly rooted within the universities as well as in newer institutions. It considered that there was a need for greater co-ordination of this type of education and that the H.E.A. was the body which should be empowered to bring this about. The Group's most notable recommendation was that the status of the two NIHEs should be raised to that of independent universities, a recommendation which was given legislative effect in 1989. The following extract is taken from the report of the International Study Group on Technological Education:

CO-ORDINATION OF TECHNOLOGICAL EDUCATION

The Higher Education Authority's role in the co-ordination of technological education is hampered in that a substantial section of the higher education system is not designated for the purposes of its Act The Group sees the need for greater overall co-ordination of technological education developments in Ireland and recommends that this task should be carried out by the Higher Education Authority. Increasing specialisation in the individual colleges is inevitable and the Authority should guide this evolution towards specialisation and complementarity. The composition of the Authority's membership may need review to fulfil this role properly.

RECOMMENDATION

The Higher Education Authority should be fully involved in all matters relating to the planning, financing and co-ordination of all third-level activities.

Scholarship at the NIHEs

The Group saw that academic issues were paramount in its consideration of the case for university status for the Institutes. The Group's view is that standards of scholarship at the NIHEs are as high as those of universities: they have reached a stage of development and achievement where they should be self-accrediting.

NIHEs as universities

The Group considers that the NIHEs should have the title and status of universities.

Legislation for new universities

In the Group's view, the present legislation governing the NIHEs needs amendment to change the title of the Institutes, to give them degree awarding powers and to provide statutory Academic Councils with responsibility for the academic affairs of the universities. The composition of the Academic Councils should be stated in the legislation. The Councils should have the power to grant degrees and other awards. Provisions for detailed Ministerial control should be relaxed.

Recommendations

The National Institutes for Higher Education at Dublin and Limerick should be self accrediting, and should be established as independent universities — the NIHE Limerick having the title University of Limerick and the NIHE Dublin having the title Dublin City University or the University of Leinster.

The title "technological university" should not be used.

Governing Bodies of the new universities should have the power to enter into, and carry out, contracts on behalf of the universities, and have the power to form companies. Academic Councils of the new universities should be statutorily established.

V.23 University of Limerick and City of Dublin University Act, 1989

The Government accepted proposals of the International Study Group regarding the conversion of the NIHEL and NIHED into independent universities. This was done by legislation in 1989 and thus the first new universities since the state was founded were established. The approach taken was not through elaborate new legislation but by means of short acts which confined themselves to making necessary amendments to the legislation establishing the NIHEs in 1980 (V.18). Thus, it is necessary to read the legislation of 1989 in association with that of 1980. Indeed, the act itself states in relation to Limerick that —

> "The Act of 1980 and this Act shall be construed together as one and may be cited together as the University of Limerick Acts, 1980 and 1989."

As was the case with the legislation in 1980 the acts were almost identical for Dublin and Limerick. The following extract is taken from the University of Limerick Act 1989.

UNIVERSITY OF LIMERICK ACT, 1989

An Act to provide that the national institute for higher education, Limerick, shall become and be a university, to amend the national council for educational awards act, 1979, and to provide for other matters connected therewith. *(11th June, 1989)*

****

1.—(1) The National Institute for Higher Education, LImerick, shall by virtue of this section become and be a university and shall be known in the Irish language as Ollscoil Luimnigh and in the English language as the University of Limerick and shall perform the functions assigned to it by the Act of 1980 as amended by this Act.

****

3.— Section 4 of the Act of 1980 is hereby amended by —

(a) the substitution of the following paragraph for paragraph (a) of subsection (1):

"(a) the pursuit of learning and the advancement of knowledge through teaching, research and collaboration with educational, business, professional, trade union, cultural and other bodies and, without prejudice to the generality of the aforesaid, the University shall have the following functions —

(i) to provide courses of study or instruction in such fields as the Governing Body may deem appropriate,

(ii) to confer, grant or give degrees, diplomas, certificates or other educational awards, on the recommendation of the Academic Council, to or on persons who satisfy the Academic Council that they have attended or otherwise pursued or followed appropriate courses of study, instruction or research provided by the University, or by such other colleges or institutions as the Governing Body may approve, and have attained an appropriate standard in examinations or other tests of knowledge or ability or have performed other exercises in a manner regarded by the Academic Council as satisfactory.

(iii) to confer honorary degrees on persons in such manner and subject to such conditions as the Governing Body, after consultation with the Academic Council, may deem appropriate, and

(iv) to enter into arrangements with other relevant institutions inside and outside the State for the purposes of offering joint courses and of conducting research and development work and to enter into arrangements, including participation in limited liability companies, for the purpose of exploiting the results of research and development work undertaken by the University either separately or jointly," and

(b) the substitution for paragraph (a) of subsection (2) of the following paragraph:

"(a) The Minister may on the recommendation of the Governing Body after consultation with an tÚdaras by order assign to the Institute such additional functions as the Minister thinks fit."

****

5.— Section 8 of the Act of 1980 is hereby amended by —

(a) the substitution for subsection (2) of the following subsection:

(2)(a) "The Governing Body may by regulations made under this section provide for the membership, of which a majority shall be holders of academic appointments and not less than 3 students of the University, representative of the student body, and terms of office of the Academic Council established pursuant to sub-section (1) of this section.

(b) The members appointed to the Academic Council shall hold office for period of three years and shall be eligible for re-appointment," and

(b) the substitution for paragraph (g) of subsection (3) of the following paragraph:

"(g) to make recommendations to the Governing Body in relation to —

(i) the appointment of external examiners,
(ii) the award of fellowships, scholarships, prizes or other awards,
(iii) the conferment, grant or award of degrees, diplomas, certificates or other educational awards,
(iv) the conferment of honorary degrees."

6.—The National Council for Educational Awards Act, 1979, is hereby amended by —

(a) the deletion of paragraphs (b) and (c) of subsection (1) of section 5.
(b) the deletion of "four" and the insertion of "six" in paragraph (f) of subsection (1) of section 5, and
(c) the deletion of "three" and the insertion of "five" in paragraph (g) of subsection (1) of section 5.

VI

SPECIAL ISSUES

VI.1 Report of the Commission of Inquiry on Mental Handicap 1965

When the Irish Free State was established in 1922 there were very few facilities, educational or otherwise, for people with handicaps. There were schools for blind and deaf children dating back to the nineteenth century but there was only one institution specifically designed to provide for the needs of people with a mental handicap. It was not until the mid 1950s that the issue of educating children with special needs was seriously addressed. A number of voluntary organisations was formed and together with a small number of religious orders, they began to set up special schools which were subsequently recognised by the Department of Education as special schools.

In February 1961 a commission of inquiry on mental handicap was appointed, chaired by Kevin Briscoe. The report of this commission which was published in 1965 was an historic document and provided a framework for subsequent developments in the education and care of the mentally handicapped. The report was detailed and comprehensive, almost 200 pages long, and covered issues such as available services; diagnostic and assessment service; pre-school and school facilities for mildly, moderately and severely handicapped children. There were also chapters on adult care; residential centres; prevention and research; and training of personnel, as well as organisation, finance and legislation.

The following extracts from the report provide:

(a) an overview of the historical situation in relation to law and practice in Ireland concerning the handicapped and

(b) a summary of some of the main conclusions and recommendations.

(a) Developments in Ireland

17. The Brehon Laws, the ancient laws of Ireland, which were codified about the fifth century, made special provision for five categories — idiots, fools, dotards, persons without sense and madmen. These were exempted from the punishments inflicted for certain crimes and were protected from any exploitation which might be attempted on account of their mental condition. In later times, however, there is little evidence that much, if any, provision was made for them. As in Britain, in the eighteenth century, the destitute were dealt with, if at all, under the Poor Law. The provision of workhouses was authorised by law as early as 1703 in Dublin and 1735 in Cork and an Act under which county infirmaries were established as "receptacles for poor who are infirm and diseased" was passed in 1765. In the nineteenth century the mentally handicapped continued to be dealt with under the Poor Law, the main basis of which was the Poor Relief (Ireland) Act, 1838, which was modelled, as to all its main provisions, on an English Act of 1834. The Act of 1838 authorised the provision of workhouses in which it was lawful to relieve such destitute poor persons as by reason of old age, infirmity, or defect might be unable to support themselves, destitute children and such other persons as would be deemed to be destitute poor and unable to support themselves by their own industry or other lawful means. The Act was permissive, but the Poor Relief (Ireland) Act, 1847, made necessary the provision of "due relief for all such destitute poor persons as are permanently disabled from labour by reason of old age, infirmity or bodily or mental defect." In the year 1878 the Poor Afflicted Persons Relief (Ireland) Act, authorised the

sending of idiots and imbeciles to any hospital or institution for the reception of such persons and the payment of a sum not exceeding 5/- weekly for the maintenance and instruction of such persons. In addition to such provision as was made under the Poor Law, some provision was made under the Lunacy Laws. Public provision for lunatics or insane persons was made in the eighteenth century, but it was not until the nineteenth century that any substantial provision was made for them. Under the Lunacy (Ireland) Act, 1821, most of the present district mental hospitals were erected. During the nineteenth century a number of Committees and Commissions examined the position of the insane or lunatic poor in Ireland and it is clear from their reports, and from other reports, that appreciable numbers of the mentally handicapped were maintained in mental hospitals. One special institution, the Stewart Institution for Imbeciles, containing about 100 beds was opened in Dublin in 1870 and was entirely supported by charitable donations. The Lunacy Regulation (Ireland) Act, 1871, which is still in force, made provision for the supervision of the estates of lunatics (any person "found by inquisition idiot, lunatic or of unsound mind, and incapable of managing himself or his affairs"). The Idiots Act of 1866 did not apply to Ireland, nor did the Elementary Education (Defective and Epileptic Children) Act, 1899. The Royal Commission, 1904, examined the position in Ireland, as well as in England, Wales and Scotland; though it made recommendations in regard to Ireland similar to those made in regard to Britain, these recommendations were not implemented. No Acts, corresponding to the Mental Deficiency Act, 1913, or the Education Acts of 1914 and 1921 were enacted in regard to Ireland. On the establishment of the State in 1922, the Stewart Institution was still the only centre dealing specifically with the mentally handicapped. The mentally handicapped continued to be catered for, to a large extent, in mental hospitals and in county homes, which succeeded the institutions provided under the Poor Law. There has, however, been a steady growth of special accommodation. In 1926 the Sisters of Charity of St. Vincent de Paul opened their first School and Home. Other religious orders entered the field at later dates — The Hospitaller Order of St. John of God (1931), the brothers of Charity (1939), the Sisters of Charity of Jesus and Mary (1954), the Congregation of the Daughters of Wisdom (1955). In 1959 the Cork Polio and General Aftercare Association opened its first residential centre. All these bodies cater for all grades of mental handicap. In addition to the bodies concerned with residential accommodation there has been, particularly in the past decade, a large increase in the number of voluntary bodies concerned with the care of the mentally handicapped. In Dublin the Association of Parents and Friends of the Mentally Handicapped opened its first day school in 1956. Various other Associations have been formed in different areas. In 1960 the National Association for the Mentally Handicapped of Ireland was formed. The position reached to-day is that there is now a vastly increased interest in mental handicap, a dissemination of information on the nature and extent of the problem and an earnest desire that active steps should be taken to provide adequate services, medical, social and educational to meet the requirements of the mentally handicapped.

(b) SUMMARY OF CONCLUSIONS AND RECOMMENDATIONS:

1. There should be a clear obligation on each health authority to make available for its area a diagnostic, assessment and advisory service, so that mental handicap can be diagnosed and assessed and that help and advice for the mentally handicapped and their families can be provided from the earliest possible date.

2. To provide a diagnostic, assessment and advisory service:

   (i) school teams should be formed comprising the School Medical Officer, a school psychologist and a social worker;
   (ii) general teams should be formed, comprising a psychiatrist, a psychologist and a social worker.

3. To permit the school teams to operate successfully, a schools psychological service should be developed and an adequate number of psychologists should be employed by the Minister for Education for work in the schools.

4. The school teams should normally deal with the problem of mental handicap as it manifests itself in the school system and they should refer to the general teams cases of doubt or difficulty, cases in need of residential care and cases where the parents or guardians request that the children should be referred for a second opinion.

5. The general teams should be based on the voluntary bodies providing services for the mentally handicapped. They should provide services at their own centres and at such other centres as may be arranged with health authorities. They should deal with all persons not attending day schools and such of those attending day schools as are referred to them by the school teams.

6. Any parent or teacher should be at liberty to seek the help of the School Medical Officer or the school psychologist. Any medical practitioner should be at liberty to refer patients to the general teams.

7. Health authorities should pay, at agreed rates, for the services of the general teams, subject to their recognition by the Minister for Health, as suitable for the provision of services.

8. Every effort should be made to discover mental handicap as early as possible.

9. Guidance should be provided for the family, so that the handicapped child may be helped to develop his limited potential.

10. Nursery units should be established, where feasible, to provide such training and treatment as is required and to relieve parents during part of the day, of the strain arising from the care of the mentally handicapped in the home.

11. The curriculum of special education should extend over a period of at least nine years i.e., from seven to sixteen years of age.

12. The curriculum should consist of two clearly differentiated stages corresponding to the pre-adolescent and adolescent stages in child development.

13. Schools should continue to be given a wide measure of freedom in the elaboration of their programmes in accordance with approved principles and official encouragement should be given to systematic experimentation in relation to content and methods of teaching.

14. In the final year of special schooling provision should be made for a suitable course of pre-vocational training.

15. Where a sufficient number of pupils between the ages of four and six years are enrolled, a suitable programme on nursery school lines should be provided for them.

16. The maximum size of classes for mildly mentally handicapped pupils should be sixteen and when the number of classes exceeds six there should be a teacher for each class in addition to the principal teacher.

17. Special schools and classes should be amply supplied with teaching aids, apparatus and materials to enable teachers to make full use of group and individual methods and to enable their pupils follow a wide range of practical activities.

18. Special education for mildly mentally handicapped pupils should be provided mainly in special schools, both day and residential, but in some cases use should also be made of special classes for slow learners.

19. Schools for 150 to 200 pupils should be regarded as the optimum size; day schools should be established only in those areas where it is expected that there will be a need for not less than four classes when the school is fully established; a minimum of 100 residential pupils should be specified for residential schools.

20. Schools for mildly mentally handicapped pupils should be entirely separate from schools for moderately mentally handicapped pupils.

21. Education suited to the needs of mildly mentally handicapped pupils should be provided for 1 per cent of the school population by 1975.

22. Adequate financial aid should be provided for the transport of pupils to special schools and classes.

23. As late ascertainment is likely to persist for a considerable time, provision should be made in a number of special schools for pupils over eleven years of age who have not previously received special education.

24. The term "mentally handicapped" should not be used in the official designation of special schools and classes.

25. A suitable form of education should be provided for all moderately mentally handicapped pupils who are capable of benefiting from it — in general those who have intelligence quotients from about 35 upwards.

26. While schools for the moderately mentally handicapped should continue to be established within the national school system, they should be entirely separate from schools for mildly mentally handicapped pupils.

27. Day schools for the moderately mentally handicapped should be closely associated with nursery and care units of day centres for the mentally handicapped.

28. The maximum size of a class in a school for the moderately mentally handicapped should be 12 pupils.

29. Special national schools should be attached to all residential centres which cater for moderately mentally handicapped children and day schools for this grade should be established wherever a minimum of 20 pupils can be brought together for the purpose.

30. All schools for the moderately mentally handicapped should be provided with the facilities of a normal school including accommodation and equipment for the teaching of practical subjects.

31. In day schools adequate arrangements should be made for school meals and transport of pupils to and from school as well as for such services of a medical nature as the pupils may require.

32. Schools for the moderately mentally handicapped should be staffed with specially qualified teachers who are personally suited to the task of teaching moderately mentally handicapped children.

33. Care units should be established to provide training and care, on a day basis, for severely handicapped children and for moderately handicapped children who are unable to benefit from the education provided in schools for the moderately handicapped.

VI.2 Special Education in Ireland — an article by T.A. Ó Cuilleanáin, Assistant Chief Inspector, in Oideas, Autumn 1968

The following extracts from an article by T.A. Ó Cuilleanáin, assistant chief inspector in the Department of Education with responsibility for special education at that time, summarise the situation in relation to special education in Ireland in the mid 1960s.

At the end of 1967 there were already in operation 62 special national schools catering for five main categories of handicapped children:

Type of School	Number of schools	Total average enrolment for the year 1967
1. Schools for blind and partially sighted children	2	185
2. Schools for deaf and severely hard-of-hearing children	3	591
3. Schools for mentally handicapped children	32	2,637
4. Schools for physically handicapped children	21	847
5. Schools for emotionally disturbed children	4	164

****

Most of these schools have been established during the past twenty years, a period during which there has been a tremendous growth of public interest throughout the world in the welfare of disabled persons, both children and adults, and a consequential increase in administrative action by public authorities to alleviate their problems. International organisations such as the World Health Organisation and international and national associations concerned with particular handicaps have helped to stimulate and develop public interest through conferences, publications and research. The development of special education in this country owes much to the activities of voluntary organisations, notably those concerned with mental handicap and cerebral palsy, which have helped greatly in recent years to educate public opinion and to stimulate local initiative in the establishment of special schools.

While special education is in large measure of very recent origin in Ireland it should not be overlooked that religious bodies have been active in this field for many years. Schools for deaf mutes were established at Cabra, Dublin, by the Irish Christian Brothers and the Dominican Sisters under the auspices of the Catholic Committee for the Deaf, in the middle of the nineteenth century, but they did not become national schools until 1926 and 1952 respectively. Schools for blind children were opened by the Irish Sisters of Charity and a community of Carmelite Brothers in Dublin shortly after 1870 but they did not enter the national school system until 1918. While no doubt these schools for the blind and deaf were given some concessions from the outset as far as the curriculum of the national schools was concerned they were staffed on the same basis as other national schools. It was not until 1952 when the schools for the blind were given a special teacher-pupil ratio of 1 : 15 and a grant for special equipment that these schools became in any real sense special schools. These changes resulted from recommendations made by a committee which the Department had set up in 1948 to enquire into the education of the blind. This seems to have been the first occasion on which the Department gave official recognition to the special needs of handicapped children.

Special staffing arrangements for the schools for the deaf followed a few years later.

Schools for the mentally handicapped were recognised for the first time in 1955 and they were soon given a pupil teacher ratio of 1 : 20. However three of the pioneers among these schools: St. Michael's, now at Glenmaroon, Dublin: St. Augustine's, Blackrock, Dublin, and Our Lady of Good

Counsel, Lota, Cork, had been in operation on a more limited scale outside the national education system for a long time.

VI.3 Report of a Committee set up to consider the Provision of Educational Facilities for the Children of Itinerants, 1970

Following the publication of the Report of the Commission on Itinerancy in 1968, the Department of Education set up a committee to consider the provision of educational facilities for the children of itinerants. The report of this committee was published in the form of a 7 page memorandum in Oideas 5, in autumn 1970. Although short, the report addressed issues such as pre-school education, voluntary classes, post-primary education, after-school activities, and night classes as well as the provision of primary education for three different categories of itinerant families:- (1) Category A families — those occupying semi-permanent sites, or housed or in the process of being housed; (2) Category B families — those "who move in a certain narrow circuit around cities and towns and whose itinerary is generally unvaried;" (3) Category C families — those "who move in a wider circuit embracing many counties and who break the regular route for particular occasions e.g. Ballinasloe Fair."

In general, the report made it clear that the Department took the point of view that itinerant children should normally attend ordinary national schools and that they should "proceed through school in the normal way." At the same time, this should not preclude their receiving the benefits of any special provision made for itinerant children or for "backward children generally."

The following extracts from the report indicate the general approach recommended for the education of itinerant children:

I. General

1. This memorandum indicates the approach of the Department of Education to the matters raised in the report of the Commission on Itinerancy in relation to the educational provisions to be made for the children of itinerants. The

general aim in regard to itinerants is to integrate them with the community, and the Department accepts that educational policy in regard to their children must envisage their full integration in ordinary classes in ordinary schools. The degree to which such integration can take place will vary with circumstances and time, and implementation of the policy, to some extent at least, may have to keep in step with progress made towards the general integration of itinerants with the community. Nevertheless, realisation of the aim must be sought sooner rather than later, if only for the reason that the provision of better educational facilities will assist in securing the general integration of itinerants with the community. But further than that, the itinerant child has a right to expect the school system to attempt to meet his special needs.

2. For the purpose of determining the kind of educational provision to be made, three categories of itinerant families may be distinguished:

A. Families who occupy quasi-permanent sites and for whom houses are being provided, and families who were recently housed and are in the process of being settled.

B. Families, constituting the majority of itinerants, who move in a certain narrow circuit around cities and towns and whose itinerary is generally unvaried.

C. Families who move in a wider circuit embracing many counties and who break the regular route for particular occasions, e.g., Ballinasloe Fair.

3. The approach to the educational provision to be made for each category must be varied, and regard must be had to the number and ages of the children involved. However, the educational problems of itinerant children are similar in many respects to those of backward children generally, aggravated

by social disabilities and a vagrant way of life. Solution to the educational problems of itinerant children will, therefore, be on the same lines as that for other backward children, modified to suit their special difficulties.

4. In general, the Department favours the placing of itinerant children of an age at which children normally begin to attend school in the ordinary classes for their age-group; they would proceed through school in a normal way. This is already being done in a number of schools and the Department would expect it to continue. Nevertheless, this would not preclude their receiving, where necessary and feasible, the benefits of any special provision made for itinerant children or for backward children generally.

5. The Department is prepared to consider favourably all reasonable proposals along the lines indicated in this memorandum.

II. CATEGORY "A" FAMILIES

6. Families in Category A — those occupying semi-permanent sites, or housed, or in the process of being housed — occur in varying numbers. Where only small numbers are involved, children from such families would be expected to attend local national schools (see pars.9-10 below). Where there would be larger numbers and where their placing in ordinary classes would present particular educational problems, there can be two approaches: the special school and the special class. Either arrangement, the Department considers, should be a prelude or preparation for their integration in classes in ordinary national schools, consonant with their age and progress achieved. However, some of the older children may have to continue in a special school or class; they may have only a few years in which to acquire fluency in conversation

and a good knowledge of the 3Rs, and, as progress is likely to be slow, they may not reach a standard that would fit them for transfer to ordinary classes.

7. The Department does not favour the establishment of small special schools for itinerants. In view of the larger numbers of children involved, and as an experiment, the Department has provided a special school at Ballyfermot, Dublin; the school has a staff of four teachers and a minimum enrolment of 66 pupils is expected. Pending experience of the operation of this school, it is not intended to establish a further special school for itinerants; in any event, it is unlikely that there is a similar large congregation of itinerant families elsewhere.

8. The most fruitful approach to the provision of educational facilities for itinerant children, where their numbers warrant it, lies in the establishment of special classes attached to ordinary national schools. From the beginning the child is introduced to a normal school atmosphere; he gets an awareness of the demands and disciplines of ordinary school life; he sees and hears other children at work and at play and is motivated to join them, and transfer to ordinary classes presents fewer difficulties. Itinerant children who have been placed in a special class should be given the opportunity of integrating with pupils in ordinary classes for as many school and out-of-school activities as possible, with total integration as the ultimate aim. When the children are prepared and ready for placement in ordinary classes they should be encouraged to make the transition and should be assisted in overcoming their initial difficulties; and arrangements for transfer should be made after consultation with the parents and with the teachers and managers involved.

9. Where the number of itinerant children, by itself, would not warrant the establishment of a special class, it may be possible

to establish a class for educationally retarded children, or to provide remedial teaching, which could also serve the needs of itinerant children requiring special assistance.

10. If the number of itinerant children in a school does not warrant the making of any of the provisions indicated in the preceding paragraphs, it will be necessary to deal with the children in ordinary classes, utilising the teaching and organisational techniques that would be feasible and appropriate in the case of children with educational disadvantages. In such cases, favourable consideration would be given to applications for grants towards the cost of additional teaching aids, as envisaged in paragraph 16 below.

VI.4 Report of the Committee on the Education of Children who are Handicapped by Impaired Hearing, February 1972

In May 1967, the Minister for Education, Donogh O'Malley set up a committee with the following terms of reference:

> To review the provision made for the education of deaf and partially deaf children and to make recommendations.

The committee was chaired by T.A. Ó Cuilleanáin, Department of Education. At the request of the Minister, the committee submitted an interim report in October 1967 on a proposal to establish a special day school for deaf pupils in Cork. The final report of the committee which was published in February 1972, was 177 pages long. It covered issues such as the Classification of the Deaf; the Incidence of Deafness; Diagnosis, Assessment and Guidance; The Education of Mildly and Moderately Deaf Children; The Education Needs of the Provision for Severely Hard of Hearing and Profoundly Deaf Children; and The Training and Supply of Teachers and Residential Staff. Each chapter of the report contained a number of recommendations.

The following extracts from the final chapter of the report give a general indication of the tone of the report and its approach to the issues raised:

10.2 Throughout our discussions we have kept in mind the generally accepted views that:

(i) the overriding aim of special education for children with impaired hearing is to minimise the effect of their disability and thereby enable them to achieve their optimum development and adjust successfully to living and working in the community when they leave school;
(ii) handicapped children, especially young children, should not be separated from their families unless this is unavoidable and that where residential education is necessary the period during which children are away from home should be kept as short as possible;
(iii) whenever possible handicapped children should be educated in ordinary schools.

10.3 In this report we have distinguished between hearing disabilities and the extent to which they handicap individual children and we have classified hearing-impaired pupils in accordance with their educational needs rather than by the degree of their hearing defect. We have recommended a variety of measures which can help to reduce the extent to which these defects may handicap the child and thereby make his educational needs less acute. These measures may be expected to ensure not only that less severely handicapped pupils make satisfactory progress in ordinary classes but that a growing number of pupils whose disabilities are more pronounced are enabled to benefit from ordinary schooling. The extent to which this latter aim can be achieved will be greatly influenced by the effectiveness of measures taken to ensure early diagnosis and pre-school guidance, by the establishment of a visiting teacher service, by technical advances in the field of electronics and by improvements in the staffing and equipment of ordinary schools.

****

10.5 Bearing in mind:

(i) that if severely handicapped pupils are to achieve social adequacy in adult life the provision for them of special educational facilities of the highest quality is of paramount importance, and

(ii) that the existing special schools have acquired very valuable experience and skill in this field of education,

we have concluded that the best interest of those hearing-impaired children who cannot make adequate progress in ordinary schools and for whom special day provision could not be made, would be better served by the further development of the existing schools than by the provision of new residential schools at other centres. We have discussed in some detail measures designed to ensure that children attending residential schools are not isolated from their families and from the community and that living conditions in these schools are made as home-like as possible.

****

10.6 Because some of the circumstances which have influenced our recommendations may change radically in the years ahead it will be important to keep developments in this field of education under regular review. We recommend accordingly that the Minister for Education appoint a committee representative of the interests mentioned above to act as an advisory body in matters relating to the education of the deaf. We envisage that it would also be the function of the committee to ensure:

(i) that adequate instruments are developed for the measurement of educational attainment and linguistic progress among hearing-impaired children in Ireland;

(ii) that the Department of Education and bodies engaged in educational research in Ireland are advised of those aspects of the education of the deaf on which research could usefully be carried out;

(iii) that those concerned with the education of the deaf be kept informed of the results of educational research, in this country and elsewhere, which are relevant to their work.

VI.5 Report of the Committee on the Education of Physically Handicapped Children, 1981

In May 1977, John Bruton, T.D., Parliamentary Secretary to the Minister for Education, set up a committee "to review the provision made for the education of the physically handicapped and to make appropriate recommendations having regard to the need to make the best possible use of the resources available." The committee was chaired by Tomás Ó Cuilleanáin, Director of Institiúid Teangeolaíochta Éireann and included among its membership Dr. T.M. Gregg, Medical Director of the National Rehabilitation Board; Miss K. Ryan, Principal of the Central Remedial Clinic School and Mr. T. Kilraine, Principal, Senior Comprehensive School, Ballymun.

During the course of their deliberations, members of the committee visited schools attended by physically handicapped pupils. In addition some members visited the United Kingdom and France to study facilities for the physically handicapped in those countries. The committee also invited oral and written submissions and carried out a number of detailed enquiries regarding physically handicapped children.

The preface to the report referred to the fact that the committee was very conscious of the vital role education can play in mitigating the handicaps which may result from severe physical disabilities. It went on to state:

> Experience in this country and abroad has shown that suitable education in the widest sense of the term can enable many persons severely physically handicapped from birth or childhood to achieve economic independence as adults and enjoy a full social life. Others can be helped to gain the maximum benefits from sheltered employment and enjoy at least a measure of independence in their daily lives. Even in the case of the most severely handicapped who are incapable of engaging in any productive activity the development of their limited potential through education can give purpose to their daily lives and help to reduce its tedium and frustrations.

The following extracts are from a summary of the recommendations relating to existing educational provision:

REVIEW OF EXISTING EDUCATIONAL PROVISION

15. That the needs of the special schools for the physically handicapped be examined individually by the Department of Education with a view to providing additional help to classroom teachers wherever necessary.

16. That (a) all new special school buildings, or extensions to existing ones, should have part of the accommodation designed so as to facilitate co-operative teaching and (b) the grant scheme in operation for the provision of materials and equipment for pre-vocational training in schools for the mentally handicapped be extended to schools for the physically handicapped.

17. That the National Rehabilitation Board provide psychological services to the three special day schools in Dublin.

18. That the team involved communicate their knowledge of children in ordinary schools to their colleagues in the Health Services and in the Department of Education.

****

30. That whenever it is proposed to enrol a disabled pupil in an ordinary school the matter be taken up with the school in advance of the date of enrolment by a professional who is well informed about the child's needs.

31. That where a disabled pupil is attending an ordinary school —

    (a) all matters relating to his medical condition which are relevant to his education be made known to the school with his parents' permission;
    (b) advice be provided by medical personnel on the day to day management of the child in school;
    (c) the Department of Education should ensure that the school receives professional advice in devising and implementing instructional programmes;
    (d) additional tuition be provided if necessary either through the remedial education services or the home tuition scheme;
    (e) if the school is not already accessible the Department of Education allow grants within reasonable limits in order to make it accessible;

(f) if the school, in conjunction with the parents, is not able to arrange for help in dealing with incontinence the Director of Community Care be empowered to recruit a suitable person on a part-time basis for his work.

(g) the Director of Community Care provide medical and therapeutic services as necessary.

32. That all new schools be fully accessible to the disabled.

VI.6 The White Paper on Educational Development, 1980 (Special Provision).

Chapter IV of the White Paper on Educational Development (referred to in Section I.16) related to special educational provision. The following extracts from chapter IV include a summary of the proposals in this regard:

THE HANDICAPPED

4.1 Special educational provision for children who are handicapped by serious disabilities has a long tradition in this country. These children have largely been provided for either in special national schools or in special classes attached to ordinary national schools.

4.2 This policy of separate provision of special educational services has in recent years been questioned on the grounds that it is not necessarily calculated to promote the optimum human development of the children in question and it has been replaced in some countries by a policy of total integration of all children into ordinary schools. The need for special provision is not at issue: what is at issue is whether it should continue to be made on an integrated or on a segregated basis.

4.3 As has been pointed out, the revised curriculum for primary schools is based on the assumption that the quality and rate of learning are dependent on the ability of the learner and that educational programmes must be organised to take account of the wide range of differences between children. The reduction in the pupil-teacher ratio and the increased provision of special remedial programmes are factors which have increased the capacity of ordinary schools to provide an appropriate educational service for children with learning disabilities. Thus the prospect of the integration of the handicapped is not as daunting now as it would have been even ten years ago.

4.4 But it must also be recognised that many of the arguments which favour segregation still retain their cogency. Among these is the quality of the service provided by way of separate provision over the years in Ireland. The issue of integration is a very complex one which cannot be fully discussed in a White Paper. While full integration will be the first option to be considered, other options, including that of complete segregation, are being kept open.

****

SUMMARY OF PROPOSALS

1. The integration of handicapped children with other children will be a first option to be considered in individual cases, while recognising the need for some segregated schooling.

2. The Department will organise inservice courses for teachers of handicapped children in addition to the full-time courses already being provided and will provide a consultancy service to the special schools.

3. Curriculum guidelines for schools for moderately mentally handicapped children are being issued.

4. The twin objectives of curriculum development and teacher education will be pursued so that the educational provision for disadvantaged children will reach the highest standard consistent with available resources.

5. Finance will be made available on a generous scale for the improvement and decoration of inner Dublin City schools and for the provision of teaching aids in these schools. This money is being made available from the Inner City Fund which is administered by the Inner City Group under the overall aegis of the Minister for the Environment.

6. Existing facilities for travelling children will be kept under review and will be extended as the need arises.

7. The provision to be made at second level for the educationally disadvantaged will be examined by a working party.

8. In future first enrolment of children under five years of age will be permitted only on two dates each year, namely, the first day of the school-year and the first school day in January after their fourth birthday.

9. The present policy of assigning remedial teachers to particular schools or groups of schools will be continued.

VI.7 Report of a Working Party on the Education and Training of Severely and Profoundly Mentally Handicapped Children in Ireland, January 1983

A working party was established in 1980 by the Minister for Education and the Minister for Health and Social Welfare, with the following terms of reference:

1. To examine the educational and training needs of children with severe and profound mental handicap.

2. To consider the nature of the personnel necessary to meet these needs.

3. To make appropriate recommendations to the Minister for Education and the Minister for Health and Social Welfare.

The chairman was Seán MacGleannáin, Divisional Inspector, Department of Education. The working party included representatives of the Departments of Education and of Health; the National Association of the Mentally handicapped of Ireland; An Bord Altranais; Irish National Teachers' Organisation; Regional Health Boards; the Psychological Society of Ireland; the National Association of Boards of Management of Special Schools; Special Education Department, St. Patrick's College; the Royal College of Psychiatrists and the Irish Paediatric Association. Questionnaires were sent to all known agencies providing services for severely and profoundly mentally handicapped children and submissions were invited from all interested parties.

In the introduction to the report, the working party stated that

> It is the policy of the Government to integrate as many handicapped children as possible in ordinary schools. Whatever about the merits of integrating less handicapped children in ordinary schools, the working party is of the view that the education and training

> needs of severely and profoundly mentally handicapped children are such that they could not be met, in the foreseeable future, by attendance at ordinary schools.

The following extracts are from the summary of recommendations of the report:

2.4 Each child should have access to an education and training programme designed with his particular learning needs in mind, and subject to review from time to time. A detailed progress record of each child's development should be maintained, and this should be transferred with the child if he moves to any other agency.

****

2.8 Where a school for moderately mentally handicapped children agrees to enrol pupils assessed as severely or profoundly mentally handicapped, additional resources should be made available by the State to satisfy the additional special caring and learning needs of these pupils. A flexible approach should be adopted, and the needs of each school examined on an individual basis, including the teaching duties of the Principal.

****

2.10 In the case of large separate day care units, the present structures should be maintained, but one teacher should be introduced for each 12 children. Such teachers should be eligible for recognition in schools for moderately mentally handicapped children, and should be attached for salary, superannuation and seniority purposes to the nearest school for moderately mentally handicapped children. Such teachers would report to the Principal Teacher of the school to which they were attached but would work as members of the interdisciplinary team within the care unit. They would have special responsibility for educational curriculum planning and implementation, under the general guidance of the Principal Teacher. The head of the care unit would have responsibility for coordinating the work of all the disciplines. Where a number of teachers are assigned to a particular unit, one or more of them should be appointed to posts of responsibility in the care unit, and such post holders would be responsible for the coordination of the educational programme on a day to day basis.

****

2.19 Any centre offering a formal educational programme for a specified time each day to all children in space specially allocated for that purpose should be redesignated a Developmental Education Centre.

****

2.22

(i) Formal induction training should be provided for all teachers who are about to take up duty with severely and profoundly mentally handicapped children.

(ii) Teachers employed in recognised Developmental Education Centres should be eligible for secondment to the Diploma Course in Special Education, and that course should be modified and expanded to meet their special needs.

(iii) All teachers during their basic training should be acquainted with the methodology, theory and practice of teaching children with mental handicap, including severe and profound mental handicap.

VI.8 Programme for Action in Education 1984-87

The Programme for Action issued in 1984 by Gemma Hussey, T.D., Minister for Education, has been referred to in section I.21. The programme contained a chapter on special Education (Chapter 4) and the following extracts are taken from that chapter.

4.1 Educational provision for children diagnosed as mildly mentally handicapped was made originally through the establishment of special schools throughout the country. In recent years there has been a demand to meet the educational needs of these children in ordinary National Schools and a substantial number of special classes has been established for this purpose. Such an arrangement is seen as facilitating the integrating of the children with their peers. While special schools will continue to operate in this field, their role is seen as one which will in future cater for children with more serious learning disabilities in the mild mental handicap range and for children who cannot be catered for through special classes in ordinary National Schools. In addition, the special schools will be encouraged to become resource and reference centres for teachers and pupils in special classes throughout their area. The educational provision in special classes will be closely monitored so as to achieve the maximum possible by way of integration.

4.2 In general provision for children diagnosed as moderately mentally handicapped has been seen as best made through special schools. A number of pilot schemes, where special classes for such children in the younger age groups have been established in ordinary National Schools, are being carefully monitored to assess their progress. As the children get older there would appear at present to be no adequate way of providing for their education and training except through special schools. Consideration will be given to the establishment of further special classes for children in the moderate mental handicap range where a viable demand exists and where it would not be possible to service the needs of the children except on a residential basis. Work will continue on the special curriculum which is being prepared for these children and it is intended that the final part of the four-part curriculum will be published during the period of the plan.

4.3 At present children who are diagnosed as severely mentally handicapped are catered for in a number of residential institutions throughout the country which provide for their care needs. There is no educational input provided by teachers. The Minister has been advised by a special committee that the children concerned would respond to a carefully structured and prepared educational input and that the main requirement to provide for the education of the children concerned would be the appointment and special training of teachers. In accordance with general policy of giving priority to the disadvantaged it is proposed during the period of the plan to appoint and train a cadre of teachers each year with a view to the progressive implementation of an educational programme for the children concerned.

****

4.5 The special schools for the mentally handicapped cater for children up to the age of 18 and provide a suitable educational programme. The post-primary needs of mildly mentally handicapped children who complete their Primary education in special classes in National Schools have been the subject of an investigation by a departmental committee. Provision has already been made for such children at post-primary level in a limited number of centres by the allocation of extra teachers. Such provision will be expanded during the course of this programme to cover progressively the centres involved. While the mildly mentally handicapped will share much of the school's activities with the other pupils, special provision will be prepared for them by way of an appropriate curriculum and inservice programmes for the teachers.

****

4.7 Educational policy in respect of the children of travellers is to integrate them as far as possible in the ordinary schooling provision at both primary and post-primary levels. It is recognised, however, that such children are subject to disadvantage of a kind not shared by their settled peers and, accordingly, a number of special educational measures are adopted. These include aid towards the establishment of pre-school classes, special classes in National Schools, a number of special schools at primary and post-primary level, aid towards school transport and co-operation with AnCO in the operation of training centres for adolescent travellers. A limited visiting teacher service has been established in the larger urban areas with a view to providing special educational support for the children of travellers and to encouraging their attendance at the school facilities provided. This service will be continued.

4.8 Despite considerable progress in this area it is estimated in a recent report that only some 50% of travellers' children of school-going age are in attendance at school. The Government has asked a special committee of Ministers of State to address itself to the recommendations of the Review Body on Travelling People with a view to recommending appropriate action.

4.9 A new remand and assessment centre at Cuan Mhuire, Whitehall, for girls referred by the Courts will be brought into operation during the first year of the plan. The Centre will offer a comprehensive interdisciplinary assessment in a family atmosphere, and the reports furnished should assist the Courts in making meaningful decisions as to each girl's welfare.

****

VI.9 Guidelines on Remedial Education, 1987

In 1987 a booklet entitled "Guidelines on Remedial Education" was issued by the Department of Education. This booklet addressed a number of the issues which were being debated in relation to the underachievement of some pupils at school. The booklet provided an overview of developments and achievements in the area of remedial education during the 1970s and 1980s. It discussed methods of organising special help for pupils with learning difficulties, including identification and record keeping. It referred to the changing role of the remedial teacher and to the importance of liaising with parents. The following extracts indicate the approach suggested in the guidelines:

1.2 REMEDIAL EDUCATION

The assignment of teachers to specialise in remedial work has constituted the main additional resource for dealing with underachievement in primary schools. The limited success of educational systems in the elimination of learning failure has resulted in a reappraisal of the aims, objectives and organisation of remedial education both in Ireland and elsewhere. Remedial teachers themselves have been the first to seek clarification on aims, and to question the effectiveness of the manner in which they are deployed in schools, and to suggest alternatives. Many teachers, including remedial teachers, are convinced that a greater emphasis on prevention would yield better long-term results than the present emphasis on remediation and some are organising their remedial programmes accordingly. There is a growing conviction that the withdrawal model of service delivery, so widespread in our schools, is not necessarily the most effective. There is a feeling also that remedial programmes generally have been too preoccupied with the teaching of basic skills in literacy and numeracy when a wider focus on the total needs of children may be more important. Traditionally remedial education has been concerned with the learning needs of less able children. For some time, however, the special needs of children at the other end of the ability range have been highlighted. In a number of schools the remedial teacher participates in and, sometimes, initiates programmes designed to meet the special needs of such children. While the term "remedial" is used in this document in the interests of clarity and because it has widespread acceptance in the system it is, nevertheless, becoming increasingly inadequate as a description of what many schools and remedial teachers are now doing under the general heading of "remedial" education.

1.3 Integration of Pupils with Special Learning needs

The general international trend to integrate children with handicaps in ordinary schools is also evident in this country. In larger schools special classes have been established for children with mental handicap. Where it is not feasible to establish such classes it is not unusual to find individual children with mild mental handicap attending ordinary classes. There is a growing tendency for children with physical, sensory and other impairments to attend ordinary rather than special schools. This is especially true where attendance at the special school involves travelling long distances and/or residence away from home. It is likely that this trend for pupils with handicaps to attend ordinary schools will continue and probably intensify during the next decade or two. The presence of such children with a wide range of special needs in ordinary classes has implications for the organisation of remedial education in schools.

1.4 The Need for Clarification and Discussion

Changes in the aims, objectives and organisation of remedial education have implications for all teachers and for others who have an influence on the learning environment of children, including parents and educational administrators. These changes raise many practical questions of administration and organisation which need clarification, discussion and agreement if the changing approaches are to be effective.

These guidelines are a contribution to the discussion. They do not provide any detailed consideration of curriculum or methodology, nor are they intended to be prescriptive or directive on the matters which are discussed. Their purpose is to offer general guidelines on the aims and organisation of remedial education and on practical questions which every school faces in seeking to create a learning environment suited to the needs of all its pupils and especially those who are having difficulty at school.

VI.10 Educational Provision for the Children of Travelling Families, 1989

A survey of the educational provision for the children of travelling families was carried out by inspectors from the Department of Education in February and March 1988 to determine (a) the number of travelling children attending national schools; (b) the number attending pre-schools; and (c) the number and location of children of school-going age who are not attending any school. The results of this survey were contained in a brief (unpublished) report which was completed in January 1989.

The following extracts from the report indicate some of the findings of the survey:

****

This survey showed that the greatest number of schools catering for travelling children was in the following counties:

(i) Dublin (62);
(ii) Cork (37);
(iii) Limerick (27);
(iv) Tipperary (20);
(v) Wexford (19);

This reflects the urbanisation of the travelling community which has taken place over the past few decades.

EDUCATIONAL PROVISION IN NATIONAL SCHOOLS

The survey showed that 375 schools cater for the children of travelling families, of which 106 were located in cities, 231 in towns or villages and only 38 in rural areas. The total number of these children enrolled in national schools was 3,953 and their age distribution was as follows:

4 - 8 years	=	40.5%
9 - 12 years	=	43.3%
12 years	=	16.2%

****

NATURE OF EDUCATIONAL PROVISION

Great credit is due to all who have shown such commitment in actively promoting the education of travelling children. Such provision often requires considerable flexibility in teaching methodology and class organisation. An examination of the most prevalent practices shows that 3 strategies are relied upon as illustrated in the following table:

(i)	Number of pupils in special classes (29.8%)	=	1,178
(ii)	Number of pupils partly integrated but given additional assistance on withdrawal basis (35.7%)	=	1,410
(iii)	Number of pupils integrated in ordinary classes (34.5%)	=	1,365

The number of special classes for travelling children in ordinary national schools is now 120 and the special capitation aid in respect of such classes has been increased to the level of that payable in respect of children in special schools.

TRANSPORT

Transport is provided for pupils in the case of 113 of the schools and in all but two of these the transport arrangements are regarded as quite satisfactory.

****

NUMBER OF TRAVELLING CHILDREN NOT ATTENDING PRIMARY SCHOOL

Despite the excellent work which has been done, there are grounds for concern about the number of travelling children of school-going age who are not attending school. The survey showed that 353 between the age of 4 and 12 and 115 over the age of 12 were not attending school. There were also 629 children under school-going age. It is felt that these figures must be treated with some caution due to the difficulties of providing precise information about families whose pattern of movement and residence tends to be very erratic.

****

VI.11 Report of the Primary Education Review Body, 1990 (Special Education)

Section 22 of the report of the primary education review body (II.21) covered special education. The report confirmed that the official policy of the Department of Education in relation to the education of children with handicaps was one of integration where possible "while retaining the option of segregation where necessary." It was indicated, however, that the review body was of the opinion that there are limits to the degree of integration which is possible and that there are considerable financial implications in the implementation of integration. They recommended that a special commission or committee be set up representing all the interests involved to examine and report on the entire problem. Acting on this recommendation, Minister O'Rourke set up a Special Education Review Committee in Autumn 1991. At the time of going to press, this committee had not reported.

The following extract is taken from section 22 of the report of the Primary Education Review Body:

A number of significant developments have occurred in the field of primary education since the Commission of Inquiry on Mental Handicap reported in 1965. For example, the new curriculum for primary schools in 1971 made the ordinary primary school a much more suitable place for children with special needs. The official policy of the Department of Education is now one of integration of children with handicaps, where this is possible, while retaining the option of segregation where necessary. The Minister for Education, in common with other Ministers for Education of the European Community, has subscribed to a declaration to pursue a policy of integration. We are of the opinion, however, that there are limits to the degree of integration which is possible and that in many instances, partial integration may be the only feasible option.

There are considerable financial implications in the implementation of integration whether full or partial. For example, substantial costs will be involved in the adaptation of buildings and in providing suitable equipment, extra staffing and communication aids. Pupils with visual and hearing impairments enrolled in ordinary schools have some access to a visiting teacher service. Integration will involve the extension of this service to children in other categories and in addition the appointment of care personnel for certain groups. For some pupils home tuition may be necessary also. We recommend that all programmes of integration be carefully planned and evaluated.

We are informed that the major review of services for the mentally handicapped, currently under way in the Department of Health, seems to indicate that mild mental handicap should not come within the ambit of mental handicap at all, but rather should be considered as part of the general problem of learning disability. Such a policy, of course, would have considerable implications for the Department of Education.

What is clear to us is that a detailed analysis of the multiplicity of issues relating to handicapped children would be a time-consuming undertaking requiring the co-operation of a wide range of persons with special knowledge of the different categories of handicap. Therefore we recommend that a special committee or commission, representative of all the interests involved, be appointed to examine and report on the entire problem. Among the issues which need particular study are:

(a) the integration of pupils with special needs into the education system generally;

(b) the appointment of additional care personnel where necessary;

(c) the co-ordination of services already provided for the different categories of handicap;
(d) the question of an appropriate visiting teacher service and home tuition for all handicapped children;
(e) the development of remedial education;
(f) the question of schooling for disabled pupils at the post-primary level;
(g) the methods of identification of pupils with special learning needs;
(h) clarification and co-ordination of the role of the various government departments dealing with handicapped persons;
(i) guidance and information for parents, teachers and school authorities on services available;
(j) the use of modern technologies in educating handicapped children;
(k) curricular guidelines;
(l) the preservice and inservice training of teachers for special education;
(m) class size;
(n) the development of a network of ancillary and professional services;
(o) the necessity for a set level of provision for children with particular handicaps;
(p) an independent advisory service for parents on school placement;
(q) an assessment statement for each child with a special need in order to determine the appropriate level of provision necessary in each case.

VI.12 Needs and Abilities — a policy for the intellectually disabled. Report of the Review Group on Mental Handicap Services, July 1990

The review group on mental handicap was established in 1986 following discussions between the Department of Health and representatives of some of the major organisations providing services for people with intellectual disability. As predicted by the Primary Education Review Body (IV.11) the review group on mental handicap made a clear distinction between the educational needs of those who were referred to as "mildly mentally handicapped" and those referred to as "moderately, severely or profoundly mentally handicapped." As regards the former, the review group referred to them throughout the report as "persons with general learning difficulties." The latter group was referred to as having a "moderate, severe or profound degree of intellectual disability." The report did not directly enter the debate on integration versus segregation of children with special needs but welcomed the fact "that increasing numbers of pupils with general learning difficulties are now being provided with educational opportunities in their local environment." The report condemned the current practice of referring children with general learning difficulties to centres for intellectually disabled persons for assessment. Instead it was recommended that a specialist staff of psychologists, social workers and speech therapists should be employed in the educational service.

The following extracts are from the summary of recommendations of the report:

1. The term "mental handicap" should no longer be used. Formal debate should be initiated amongst the interests concerned, with a view to arriving at a consensus on the most appropriate terminology to be used.

2. Children with general learning difficulties should not be referred for assessment to centres for intellectually disabled persons.

3. Multi-disciplinary support services to pupils with general learning difficulties should not be the responsibility of services for intellectually disabled persons.

4. Children and adolescents with general learning difficulties should not be referred for residential services if the only reason for doing so is to facilitate attendance for special education.

5. The Departments of Health and Education should ensure that a higher level of multi-disciplinary support is available to the pupil with general learning difficulties leaving local educational services.

6. The Departments of Eduction and Labour should take action to facilitate those with general learning difficulties in pursuing further education, vocational training and employment placement for school leavers. Second and third level educational establishments operated under the Department of Education should be especially conscious of the need to facilitate the further education of these young people.

****

9. A number of pilot educational and support programmes for parents should be undertaken by health boards in conjunction with the Department of Education to complement services for disadvantaged children.

10. The health board pre-school developmental service should be particularly directed to those children in districts where cultural, social, emotional and material deprivation are evident. General practitioners and other community care personnel should receive special training in the screening and detection of abnormalities.

****

20. Close liaison will be required between the frontline and multi-disciplinary support personnel of the pre-school programmes and their counterparts in the school programmes.

21. Existing inputs to special education programmes by multi-disciplinary support teams funded by the Department of Health should be formally recognised by the Department of Education.

****

29. All pupils who avail of special educational programmes should have access to pre-vocational and vocational training as appropriate. Vocational training should be of at least three years' duration and centres should be locally based and close to ordinary schools and colleges.

VI.13 Report of the Commission of Inquiry into the Reformatory and Industrial School System, 1934-1936

In 1934, a Commission of Inquiry was appointed by the Minister for Education, Tomás Ó Deirig, "to enquire into and report on the Reformatory and Industrial School system in Saorstát Éireann and matters connected therewith including:

1. the existing statutory provisions and other regulations in relation to Reformatories, Industrial Schools, and Places of Detention, and the committal of children and young persons thereto;

2. the care, education and training of children and young persons in Reformatories and Industrial Schools, and their after-care and supervision when discharged from these institutions;

3. the treatment and/or disposal of children committed to Industrial Schools who are found to be suffering from physical or mental defects;

4. the staffing of Reformatory and Industrial Schools, and the qualifications and conditions of service of the teachers employed therein;

5. the arrangements for defraying the expenses of these institutions."

The Commission was chaired by Mr. G.P. Cussen, Senior Justice, Dublin District Court.

The enquiry began in May 1934 and the report was completed and signed in August 1936. Evidence was invited by advertisement as well as by special invitation. Visits were made to the two Reformatories which then existed and to nine Industrial Schools as well as to the place of Detention at Summerhill, Dublin and the Home for Mentally Deficient Children in Cabra. In addition, individual members of the Committee paid visits to upwards of forty

Industrial Schools and to St. Augustines; Colony for Mental Defectives, Obelisk Park, Blackrock.

The final report was 80 pages long and addressed the various issues referred to in the terms of reference. The following extracts are taken from the Summary of Principal Recommendations and Conclusions.

1. The present system of Reformatory and Industrial Schools should be continued subject to the modifications suggested in the Report. The Schools should remain under the management of the Religious Orders who have undertaken the work.

2. Justices should be allowed a greater discretion as to age and period of detention in committing children to both Reformatories and Industrial Schools.

3. In some Industrial Schools children are retained at the sole expense of the school beyond the age of 16 years — the present age for discharge — so as to undergo special courses of training. In such cases the Minister for Education should be given power to authorise retention up to the age of 17 years, subject to payment of an appropriate grant.

4. The committal of young children under the School Attendance Act, 1926, for a short period has often a salutary effect. We recommend its continuance.

****

15. Reasonable contact of pupils with the outside world is desirable and should be permitted to a greater extent than is the case at present.

16. The present period of Home Leave (14 days per annum) should be increased to at least three weeks. Parents and guardians should be informed of the existence of the privilege, and children with no suitable homes or relatives should be sent for a holiday in camp or in another institution conducted by the same Order. An additional grant might be considered where children are sent to camp.

****

20. Although the standard of Primary Education attained in the schools is, according to the reports furnished by the Inspectors of the Department, reasonably satisfactory, we consider that —

(a) the Primary Teachers in these Schools should have the same general training, and qualifications, in Irish as the Teachers in the National Schools.

(b) Where possible, children in Industrial Schools should attend the local National Schools;

(c) a full school day should be spent at literary subjects, and pupils between the ages of 12 and 14 years should receive preliminary occupational training which should be given on Saturdays or on other days outside the ordinary hours of instruction;

(d) facilities for more advanced education for talented and exceptional pupils should be provided, and payment of the grants should continue where this involves attendance at an outside school.

(e) Occupational training (except in cases of children who are considered backward in the literary course) should commence on the 1st July following the completion of the fourteenth year and should include, in addition, two hours' daily literary instruction;

(f) the work of inspection should be under the charge of one Inspector who would thereby acquire special experience of the education given in these institutions.

****

35. The conditions of service of the lay teachers of literary subjects are unsatisfactory, principally for the following reasons:

(a) they are required in many schools outside the ordinary teaching hours to discharge disciplinary and supervisory duties in addition to teaching;
(b) they are not entitled to pensions or gratuities on retirement;
(c) service in these schools by qualified literary teachers who may subsequently receive appointments in National Schools is not recognised for pension purposes; and
(d) their inadequate remuneration.

The conditions of service for lay teachers in these schools call for substantial improvement and we recommend:

(a) that the cost of literary education should be defrayed out of the State grants for Primary Education (apart from the normal grants for maintenance, & c.);
(b) that future appointments of teachers should be on the same conditions as in National Schools, and duties other than teaching should not be assigned to recognised teachers who are not members of a religious community.
(c) that unqualified teachers who have given long and faithful service but whose teaching efficiency is not satisfactory and whose services could be otherwise availed of, should be employed on other duties in the Institutions or, if this is not possible, they should be

retired with compensation or pension, the cost of which should be defrayed by the School Managers;

(d) the possibility of making special arrangements for the admission of the younger teachers to a recognised Training College might be explored departmentally;

(e) that payments as recommended under (a) should not be made until a school has the minimum staff qualified in accordance with the Regulations for National Schools.

VI.14 Report of the Committee on Reformatory and Industrial Schools, 1970

In 1967 the government set up a committee to carry out a survey on Reformatory and Industrial Schools. The terms of reference of the committee were: "To survey the Reformatory and Industrial Schools systems and to make a report and recommendations to the Minister for Education." The Minister subsequently agreed that the committee's inquiries should include all children in care. The committee was chaired by District Justice Eileen Kennedy.

The report of the committee was published in 1970 and was 136 pages long. It consisted of 10 chapters covering topics such as Who Comes into Care?; Residential ; Reformatory Schools; Aftercare; Prevention; Jurisdiction over Children and Young Persons. The report also contained a summary of a survey carried out by the Department of Psychology, U.C.D., on the extent of mental handicap and educational backwardness and of educational problems in Industrial and Reformatory and Industrial Schools.

The report was prefaced by the following statement which set the context for the committee's approach and recommendations:

> All children need love, care and security if they are to develop into full and mature persons. For most children this is provided by a warm, intimate and continuous relationship with their parents, brothers and sisters. Children in institutions have for the most part

> missed this happy relationship. If they are to overcome this deprivation they must, therefore, be given love, affection and security by those in whose care they are placed.
>
> The recommendations made by the Committee in this report are based on the assumption that all those engaged in the field of Child and Family Care agree that this must be their fundamental approach to the work they are undertaking.

The following extracts are from the summary of the major recommendations of the report, followed by the summary of the recommendations on education:

2.1 The whole aim of the Child Care system should be geared towards the prevention of family break-down and the problems consequent on it. The committal or admission of children to Residential Care should be considered only when there is no satisfactory alternative.

2.2 The present institutional system of Residential Care should be abolished and be replaced by group homes which would approximate as closely as possible to the normal family unit. Children from the one family, and children of different ages and sex should be placed in such group homes.

2.3 We find the present Reformatory system completely inadequate. St. Conleth's Reformatory, Daingean, should be closed at the earliest possible opportunity and replaced by modern Special Schools conducted by trained staff.

2.4 The Remand Home and Place of Detention at present housed at Marlborough House, Glasnevin, Dublin, should be closed forthwith and replaced by a more suitable building with trained child care staff.

2.5 The staff engaged in Child Care work, who have responsibility for the care and training of children, their mental and emotional development, should be fully trained in the aspects of Child Care in which they are working.

2.6 We recognise that education is one of the most important formative influences on the children with whom we are concerned, whether they are deprived or delinquent. All children in Residential Care or otherwise in care, should be educated to the ultimate of their capacities. The purpose of the education they receive should be to help them to develop as adequate persons. To achieve this end, they will need facilities over and above those available to children reared in the normal family.

****

SUMMARY OF RECOMMENDATIONS ON EDUCATION

1. All children whether in Residential Homes or in Special Schools or otherwise in care should be educated to the ultimate of their capacities.

2. It will be necessary to provide children in care with more than the normal educational facilities. It will, in other words, be necessary to overcompensate for deprivation.

3. A programme of over-compensation should involve a team approach by those concerned with both the residential and educational aspects of the problem of catering for children in care.

The following recommendations could form part of the educational approach to a programme of over-compensation:

4. Where possible every effort should be made to provide pre-school education and the teachers participating should have special training. Psychological and other advisory services and proper equipment should be provided.

5. Every effort should be made to provide facilities for early diagnosis of all the factors likely to affect a child's progress at school.

6. Schools catering for children from Residential Homes should be enabled to provide special and remedial teaching and psychological services should be provided.

7. Special counselling should be available to help children (a) develop personally (b) make full use of their opportunities (c) make educational, vocational and career choices.

8. Provision should be made to enable Homes to provide general activities which would supplement the education received at school.

Education Outside the Homes

9. Children in Residential Homes should receive their education with other children in schools located outside the Homes. Children in Special Schools should be allowed, if possible, to attend school, or some classes, outside the Special Schools.

Third Level Education

10. Students who are in care should be given every opportunity to avail of third level education. Where they do not succeed in obtaining any of the normal grants, special arrangements should be made to offer them third level opportunities if it is considered to be to their advantage.

Education in Special Schools

11. Children in Special Schools are quite likely to be school dropouts, to suffer from the effects of deprivation and to be educationally backward. Every effort should be made to bring them back into the mainstream of education and to provide them with extra facilities which will help them overcome their backwardness and the effects of deprivation.

12. The curriculum should include a wide range of subjects and activities and should aim at all-round development, while providing opportunities for children to get the usual examination certificates.

13. Because of the special problems posed by children in Special Schools it will be necessary to allow an even more generous pupil/teacher ratio than is allowed in Special National Schools.

14. There is a special need for personal counselling in Special Schools.

15. The chaplains should be carefully selected and should have a full understanding of the problems involved.

16. The Department of Education should pay teachers' salaries and the cost of educational equipment directly.

17. Junior Special Schools should be recognised as Special National Schools and Senior Special Schools should be recognised as Special Post-Primary Schools.

18. All of those teaching in Special Schools should have extra training for their work and should be paid special allowances when they have completed such training.

19. The Minister for Education should retain responsibility for the education of children in care while responsibility for the residential aspect is transferred to the Minister for Health. There should be a more formal link both medical and otherwise between the two Departments to ensure that all the needs of the children are met.

VI.15 Report of the Committee on Adult Education in Ireland, 1973

In May 1969, Brian Lenihan, T.D. Minister for Education, asked Con Murphy assisted by an Advisory Committee, to carry out a survey on the needs and possible structure of Adult Education in Ireland. Following publication of an Interim Report, it was agreed that the work should be completed by the committee as a whole and the Final Report was submitted to Richard Burke, Minister for Education in November 1973.

The report was over 170 pages long and addressed issues such as — What is Adult Education? Resources; Needs; Structure: Research; and Costs. Adult Education was defined as "The provision and utilisation of facilities whereby those who are no longer participants in the full-time school system may learn whatever they need to learn at any period of their lives." The definition did not distinguish between formal and informal adult education but stressed that the process of adult education is geared to "servicing the needs of adults in every sphere of human development."

The following extracts from chapters 3 and 4 refer to the overall needs in adult education and indicate the structures which should be set up to provide for these needs:

GENERAL CONCLUSIONS

3.4 A realistic attempt to service the more urgent needs of adult education in Ireland will require:

- a general acceptance by all of the need, urgency and importance of Adult Education;
- a statement of Government Policy on the objectives of this Report;
- the allocation of finances necessary to provide for:
  - (i) the extension of existing facilities;
  - (ii) technological aids;
  - (iii) the training and remuneration of adult educators;
  - (iv) administrative purposes;

- the greater involvement of University Education Departments, the Institutes of Higher Education and the Regional Technical Colleges in Adult Education for training and research;
- the implementation of preparatory and inservice training for all those engaged as adult educators and in community development;
- the establishment of residential centres for adult education;
- the development of Radio and Television services;
- the development of Correspondence Courses;
- the provision of an effective Information and Counselling Service for adults;
- the annual publication of a Directory of Adult Education agencies;
- the possible establishment of an Institute of Industrial Relations;
- the provision of a non-residential Trade Union College;
- the continuous assessment of the Adult Education provision;
- a re-assessment and co-ordination of all agencies involved in adult education;
- the integration of Youth Education, Adult Education and Community Development services at National and Local levels;
- the establishment of links with other National and International agencies of Adult Education;
- a permanent Structure capable of supplying these needs.

In Chapter 4, we will deal specifically with structure. So far as the other needs are concerned. it is important to note that many voluntary and statutory agencies are servicing some of them to a greater or lesser degree. To improve on their servicing however, the co-operation of all agencies, the pooling of resources and shared responsibility by all members of the community, are vitally necessary.

4.10 Summary of Recommendations

- The establishment of a separate section within the Department of Education with responsibility for Adult Education.
- The allocation of a specific budget for the provision and servicing of adult education.
- The establishment in each county or county borough, of a statutory body — the County Education Committee — with responsibility for the development and servicing of all sections of the educational system.
- The County Education Committee to be serviced by advisory committees, including one specifically for adult education.
- The appointment of a County Director of Education who would be the Chief Officer of the County Education Committee.
- The appointment of additional officers including an officer for adult education to develop and extend the services of the County Education Committee.
- The appointment as an interim measure of the present Chief Executive Officer of the Vocational Education Committee as the County Director of Education.
- The establishment of Regional Education Committees to administer the provision of non-University third level education services in their regions and the appointment of Chief Education Officers to service these Committees.
- The establishment of an inter-departmental committee to afford communication between different Government Departments concerned with adult education.
- The introduction of the necessary legislation to give effect to such of these recommendations which require it.
- The recognition of Aontas as the National Voluntary Advisory Body on Adult Education.
- An annual grant from the Department of Education for Aontas.

VI.16 Lifelong Learning — Report of the Commission on Adult Education, 1983

In September 1981, the Minister for Education, John Boland, announced that he was establishing "an advisory body to prepare a national plan for adult and continuing education." The commission was appointed in October of that year and was chaired by Dr. Ivor Kenny, Director General of the Irish Management Institute. Its terms of reference were as follows:

(i) to clarify and, where necessary, identify needs on a local and national level in association with existing agencies;
(ii) to identify the necessary educational and administrative resources to meet these needs and to have regard to the necessary financial provision, bearing in mind the total resources available to the economy;
(iii) to assess the current status and potential development of what is at present being done by both voluntary and statutory agencies — recognising the unique contribution that each has to make;
(iv) to examine whether a National Council should be established with central planning, co-ordinating and financing functions to plan, co-ordinate and finance the expansion of services and to support the providing agencies;
(v) to present to the Minister for Education not later than 1st October 1982 its report in the above matters.

The commission was asked by the Minister to report within twelve months and this deadline was almost achieved. The report was published in 1983 and was 161 pages long. It included the results of a survey on attitudes to and involvement in adult education, carried out by Irish Marketing Surveys Ltd. In his foreword, the chairman emphasised that the report "is not about night classes. It is about lifelong learning."

The following definition of adult education was put forward in the report:

The definition we have worked with is as follows:

Adult Education includes all systematic learning by adults which contributes to their development as individuals and as members of the community and of society apart from full-time instruction received by persons as part of their uninterrupted initial education and training. It may be formal education which takes place in institutions e.g. training centres, schools, colleges, institutes and universities; or non-formal education, which is any other systematic form of learning, including self-directed learning.

The following extracts are from the recommendations of the report:

ROLE OF THE SOCIAL PARTNERS

2. We look with confidence to the future support of the Social Partners, government, employers and trade unions in the development of adult education. We believe they should keep that development in the forefront of national aims in the years to come.

ENCOURAGEMENT OF CERTAIN FIELDS OF ADULT EDUCATION ACTIVITY

We recognise there are fields in which important work is being done. We wish to endorse that work and recommend further development be encouraged and assisted by the government, employers and trade unions in association with adult education agencies.

These fields are:

— national youth work services
— pre-retirement courses
— education in rural communities
— community education in urban areas

- national cultural education; all those areas of study and exploration of the various strands of our national heritage
- information technology education
- mass media education
- political education, the study of international organisations, including environmental education and peace studies
- women's education, including career development and mobility education
- parental education
- industrial relations
- health education.

THE UNEMPLOYED

3. The Department of Social Welfare should take steps to remove, insofar as is consistent with avoiding abuse, the restrictions in the unemployment benefit system on participation in education by the unemployed. To facilitate it in this, it should study precedents in other countries through which such revision has been achieved.

****

SECOND LEVEL EDUCATION

9. The Department of Education should extend to the Day Vocational and Intermediate Certificate examinations the provisions which enable adults to take subjects at the Leaving Certificate Examination.

10. The Department of Education should revise its rules to allow for the allocation of wholetime teachers so as to facilitate day-time provision for adult groups. Such provision should take into account the need for especially favourable weighting for adult students in the assignment of teaching personnel.

SCHOOL BUILDINGS

11. The utilisation of the substantial resources of voluntary secondary schools for the provision of adult education should be facilitated by School Authorities and Local Adult Education Boards.

12. The Department of Education should ensure the educational briefs for the building and development of all schools includes provision for prospective adult students and should emphasise this aspect in briefing sessions for design teams. In this context the trend towards the organisation of courses for adults during the day time should be noted. We recommend that the Department of Education allow creche facilities to be provided by school authorities for children of parents who are availing of second-chance education.

****

THIRD LEVEL EDUCATION

18. Third Level Institutions should, having regard to regional and national needs, and to their own special areas of expertise, commit themselves to educational provision which will contribute to the development of a comprehensive national programme of Adult and Continuing Education. We believe they have a particular contribution to make in the following areas: provision of part-time undergraduate programmes, extra-mural studies programmes, community and rural development programmes, continuing professional education, training of adult educators and research into adult education.

19. Third Level Institutions should be more flexible in their entry requirements for mature students and should in general facilitate easier access for such students to higher education.

20. Third Level Institutions should adopt new approaches to facilitate greater participation in part-time day and evening courses such as modular credit systems, accreditation for experience and credit transfer between institutions.

****

23. In order to promote a greater appreciation of the concept of lifelong or permanent education we recommend that the subject education be more widely taught at undergraduate and post graduate level in the universities.

24. Again, in the Colleges of Education and other relevant Third Level Institutions, the subject education should include a module designed to give an understanding and appreciation of the lifelong education concept.

****

DISTANCE EDUCATION

34. The Department of Education should expand the steering committee of the National Centre for Distance Education at N.I.H.E. Dublin to reflect its concern with various levels of education and its collaboration with other interests in the field.

35. The Department of Education should make resources available to facilitate the appropriate provision of distance adult education courses.

VI.17 Report of the Educational Broadcasting Committee, October 1982

Under the terms of the First National Understanding for Economic and Social Development (1979), it was stated that "A study will be undertaken of the value of educational broadcasting at all levels from primary to adult education." As a result of this commitment, the Minister for Education, John Wilson, appointed the Educational Broadcasting Committee in December 1980. The committee was chaired by B. Ó Miodhacháin, Assistant Secretary, Department of Education. The inaugural meeting of the committee was addressed by the Secretary of the Department, L. Ó Laidhin, and in his address he asked the committee "to undertake a survey of the present scene in educational broadcasting and evaluate thoroughly its potential for enhancing the education process in all its many fields."

The report of the committee, which was published in October 1982, was 90 pages long. It described the Irish experience in educational broadcasting and included a review of recent studies and reports on the issue. The report also indicated the preparedness of the Irish educational system for educational broadcasting and proposed new structures and a financing system.

The following is the summary of the recommendations of the report:

BROADCASTING LEGISLATION

1. A responsibility for educational broadcasting should be placed on any new agencies which might be granted a licence.

NEW STRUCTURES

2. A National Educational Broadcasting Council should be established, in the long term, on a statutory basis with budgets allocated to it to carry out its responsibilities.

3. In the immediate future the R.T.E. Authority should set up an Educational Broadcasting Council without prejudice to the long-term goal already stated.

4. The Educational Broadcasting Council should be served by two Standing Committees, one of which would relate to pre-school and schools broadcasting while the other would focus on adult and some forms of third-level education. These bodies should have stated functions and be composed mainly on a representative basis, reflecting appropriate interest groups.

5. The Educational Broadcasting Council should have suitable accommodation and the assistance of an administrative executive level of staffing together with requisite support staff commensurate with the developmental responsibility that should properly attach to this initiative.

6. An Educational Broadcasting Section should be established within the Department of Education.

7. The present grants for audio-visual equipment in schools should be significantly increased.

FUNDING

8. The normal sources of funding for education should be used.

9. Some monies must be made available from Exchequer sources in the Vote for the Department of Education and be specially designated to educational broadcasting.

10. The Educational Broadcasting Council should actively explore the possibility of obtaining additional sponsorship of programmes from commercial interests.

11. In the longer term, the Government should plan a minimum annual investment in educational broadcasting of a sum equivalent to 1 per cent of the amount of money paid as teachers salaries.

LEVEL OF OUTPUT

12. Initially the minimum output over a 35 week school year should be five hours of educational material per week on radio and six hours on television, two and a half hours of which would be acquired from abroad.

THE IRISH LANGUAGE

13. Irish language programmes should be provided on radio and television to cater for people with different levels of proficiency in the language.

14. Consideration should be given to subsidising broadcasts in Irish.

TEACHER TRAINING:

15. Satisfactory training and experience in educational broadcasting should be made available for student teachers and inservice teachers.

16. Satisfactory training and experience in educational broadcasting should be made available for adult educators and tutors.

ASPECTS OF DISTRIBUTION

17. The Educational Broadcasting Council should examine the potential of agencies such as the National Film Institute and the local authority library system for the distribution of educational broadcasting material.

NEW TECHNOLOGY AND DEVELOPMENTS

18. The Educational Broadcasting Council should keep itself informed about advances in educational technology and communications and utilise them for the benefit of Irish learners where appropriate.

COPYRIGHT

19. The Government should examine the position with regard to copyright and educational broadcasting material so as to enable flexible use of broadcasting.

GENERAL

20. Special care should be taken to ensure that all new schools and schools being refurbished, be equipped to receive and use educational broadcasts.

VI.18 Action Handbook — how to implement gender equality, 1985

The issue of gender equality in education was one which was not addressed in any real sense in Ireland before the 1980s. Reports such as Investment in Education in 1965 had provided evidence of inequality in participation in third level education as well as gender imbalance in the choice of subjects in second level schools. During the term of office as Minister for Education of Gemma Hussey, T.D., and subsequently of Mary O'Rourke, T.D., gender equality issues were included on the educational agenda. In 1984 during the Irish presidency of the Council of Ministers of the European Community, Minister Hussey highlighted the question of equal opportunities for boys and girls in education and a special conference on the topic was held in Brussels. One of the outcomes of the Conference was the publication of an action handbook — How to Implement Gender Equality — in 1985 and this handbook was issued to Irish schools by the Irish government.

The following is the full text of the introduction to the handbook.

The publication of this handbook is the first in a series of initiatives to be undertaken in the framework of the new Community action programme to promote equal opportunities for girls and boys in education. The programme was adopted by the Council and Ministers of Education on 3 June 1985.

The need for action of this kind was identified at the high level conference on equal opportunities held in Brussels on 27-28 November 1984 at the initiative of the Irish presidency of the Council. The conference brought together Ministry officials, representatives of equal opportunities agencies in Member States, a range of experts including those involved in the Community programme on the transition of young people from education to working life, and also Members of the European Parliament.

Despite general provisions for equal treatment in education and training, girls tend still to make "traditional" educational and vocational choices, opting in greater numbers than boys for general as opposed to technical education, pure science as opposed to applied science, shorter vocational courses as opposed to fully-fledged apprenticeships with on-the-job training. Generally, they restrict themselves to a very narrow range of careers, many of which offer poor employment prospects or are being transformed as a result of the introduction of new technology.

If young women are to play an equal role in a technology-based economy in the future, they will need to be nurtured into a "technological culture" early in their school careers. Positive action for girls and young women needs to be pushed energetically at all levels of education — to change attitudes, to raise the awareness of all those involved in education and to encourage girls to make full use of the opportunities offered to them.

This handbook contains a great many examples and suggestions for action drawn from European experience. It concentrates on the need to improve access to education and training opportunities, as well as the more difficult task of changing attitudes. It is divided into four main chapters, each covering a different part of the education system. The handbook should serve as a guide and a point of reference. Differences in the structure and management of Europe's education systems, as well as their cultural variations, will of course determine how and to what extent the ideas contained in the handbook can best be implemented. However, whether the handbook is used in its present form or in a form adapted and developed to suit national circumstances, I hope that it will make a useful and practical contribution to work in each Member State on improving equal opportunities for girls and boys at school.

P. D. Sutherland,
Member of the Commission of the European Communities.

VI.19 The Place of the Arts in Irish Education — Report of the Arts Council's Working Party on the Arts in Education 1979 (by Ciarán Benson).

In 1976 the Arts Council decided that there was an immediate need for a detailed investigation of the arts in Irish education before the Council could formulate an education policy. The Calouste Gulbenkian foundation agreed to fund the post of Education Officer for two years and Ciarán Benson was appointed to the post in January 1978. Within the space of a year he produced a report which has come to be regarded as a key document in relation to the arts and education in Ireland. The report was wide-ranging in its coverage of the place of the arts in education at all levels as well as extra-curricular, adult and community education in the arts. The following extracts are taken from —

(a) the background to the report, and
(b) the conclusion and summary of recommendations:

(a) The arts have been neglected in Irish education. The Arts Council has been aware that this was one factor hindering the effectiveness of the Council's own work. This judgement was based on experience, but also reflected the conclusions of relevant reports over the last thirty years.

Professor Bodkin in his 1949 Report on the Arts in Ireland wrote,

> "In Irish schools, the subject of art, in either the historical or the practical aspect, is neglected. Few of the principal schools and colleges, for either boys or girls, employ trained teachers to deal with it, or possess the requisite accommodation and equipment for the purpose." (p.31).

The 1961 report by the Scandinavian group on Design in Ireland noted that "......the Irish school child is visually and artistically among the most under-educated in Europe....." (p.49).

The Report of the Council of Design in 1965 stated that "Indifference to the importance of good design in every aspect of the school (often dictated by what is felt to be economy) has been part of an educational tradition in which art as a whole has been gravely undervalued." (p.6).

Again in 1976 the report by J.M. Richards, Provision for the Arts, noted the pressing need to improve the position of the arts in Irish education. For example, the report states that

> "More needs to be done to persuade boys' schools to provide music courses; their neglect of music is an affront to education standards."

****

(b) 8.3 The last decade has seen a very rapid development of the Irish education system. The arts have benefitted from this expansion but not greatly. The peripheral role which the arts have traditionally played in Irish Education has been perpetuated in the recent changes. The reasons for this are complex, and an understanding of the position of the arts at any single level of education can only be reached by considering the inter-relationships of all levels. For example, a knowledge of how primary teachers are trained is necessary before one can understand why the arts are developing so slowly in the primary system. But the problems faced by colleges of education in training students to teach the arts cannot be appreciated until the position of the arts in the post-primary schools is considered. This Report tries to provide the necessary information and perspectives for such an overview.

8.4 In many areas, but particularly in relation to the provisions for the arts in primary and post-primary schools, the picture is unfavourable. Lack of money and, in some cases, lack of official encouragement, are important factors which are hampering development. Among other influences, the Department of Education is a cause of the present neglect of the arts in education. Conversely, the Department is motivated only in so far as it is made aware of, and can respond to, the more readily apparent needs and wishes of society. Within the Department itself there is a need for searching examination of its own provisions for the arts in education. To facilitate this, we have suggested that, as a first and urgent priority, the Minister for Education consider setting up a planning committee for the development of the arts in the primary and post-primary schools. Such a committee must work in the confidence that their suggestions and recommendations will be acted upon.

The Arts Council also has an important contribution to make to the development of the arts in education.

****

8.6 The Report has shown that there is much cause for hope that the arts can develop in education. The level of interest in the different arts and the range of activities which young people engage in outside school time is very encouraging. But interest, goodwill and an increasing number of people within the community enjoying the arts will not alone be sufficient to ensure their proper development in the formal education system. It seems likely that in the future the pressure on Irish educational financing will be greatly increased due to increases in enrolments and other factors. But it is vital that in any planning of future developments in Irish education, the arts must not again be cast to the periphery of considerations, but be seen where they belong, as a central concern of education. The opportunities for ensuring this are more plentiful than ever before and the rewards to the nation, potentially great. Will the challenge be met?

****

SECTION A

Key Recommendations 8.8

1. That the Arts Council should build up a specialist educational arts service. This will require at least one full-time education officer and a satisfactory budget. Some of the duties of this service will be those already carried out by other officers of the Council. For example, community arts, specialist training courses and certain aspects of the existing bursaries scheme could become part of the education section.

2. The Arts Council should seek a meeting with the Minister for Education to consider the possibility of a planning committee for the development of the arts in primary and post-primary education being set up within the Department of Education.

3. The Arts Council should set up a consultative committee to monitor and encourage the development of the arts in education along the lines suggested in this report.

4. This consultative committee should seek liaison with other organisations involved in the arts in education, and particularly with any planning committee that the Minister for Education might establish within his own department.

VI.20 The Arts in Education — a Curriculum and Examinations Board Discussion Paper, 1985

The work of the Curriculum and Examinations Board has been referred to in sections II.19 and III.29. The following extracts are taken from its discussion paper, The Arts in Education, which was published in September 1985:

CONCLUSION

7.1 While many teachers, students, parents and community organisations work in and for the arts with enthusiasm and dedication, and have achieved a great deal, the evidence presented here is unequivocal: existing provision is inadequate and must be improved if the educational needs of our youth are to be met. Previous reports on arts education in Ireland have made recommendations, many of which have been ignored. It is imperative that this should not be allowed to happen again.

7.2 The lack of understanding of the value of the arts in our society is the greatest impediment to change and to better provision for arts education. Until and unless the arts are taken seriously and their unique educational contribution recognised, the present low status of the arts in Ireland will be perpetuated and the indefensible neglect of arts education allowed to continue.

7.3 Arts education must be broad and allow for a wide range of experience in various arts disciplines. A properly conceived rationale is necessary to provide the basis for policy relating to the arts in the curriculum. From an educational point of view the change that is needed can no longer be postponed. The arts are not peripheral but central to the education of every child.

7.4 If there is to be major and significant improvement in the quality of arts education in our schools, greater resources must be allocated. It is clear that ideal and long-term needs involve considerable expenditure. In the interim, however, a start can be made and a certain amount achieved: planning and changes in attitudes to arts education can be effected at a relatively low cost. However, there are financial implications involved in providing:

- school-based assessment
- adequate space and arts materials
- sufficient qualified arts teachers
- more adequate pre-service education for teachers and continuing inservice education.

8. Recommendations

8.1 Recommendations for Immediate Implementation

8.1.1 There must be an overall plan for the development of the arts in education.

8.1.2 A rationale must be developed for each arts discipline with clearly stated aims, objectives and criteria. The involvement of practising teachers is essential in this work.

8.1.3 There must be a complete review of the education of teachers for the various arts areas.

8.1.4 Efforts must be made to develop more favourable attitudes towards the arts in education.

8.1.5 Sexist attitudes towards the arts in education must be removed.

8.1.6 Problems relating to subject-choice at post-primary level must be resolved.

8.1.7 Existing arts syllabuses should be reviewed and where necessary revised.

8.1.8 Links should be encouraged between the arts and other subjects across the curriculum at post-primary level.

8.1.9 Closer relationships should be established between arts education in the school and the community.

****

VI.21 Access and opportunity — a White Paper on the Arts, 1987

In 1982 the coalition government led by Garrett Fitzgerald created the post of Minister of State for Arts and Culture. Four years later during the final days of the coalition government, Ted Nealon, T.D., Minister for State, produced a White Paper on the arts. In the White Paper the government purported "to formulate a comprehensive cultural policy which will meet the needs of culture and the arts, nationally, for the remaining years of this century." The paper addressed a wide range of cultural issues and included a discussion on the cultural dimensions of various government departments and agencies, including the Department of Education.

The following extract is from chapter 5 of the White Paper:

The education system holds the key to future cultural and artistic development in Ireland. The educational process will have considerable influence both on our emerging artists and their potential audiences and therefore the successful implementation of the cultural policies proposed in this White Paper will depend to a considerable extent on the degree to which our education system can respond to the objectives outlined.

In addition, there is an important economic dimension to our provision for creative education. For example, it is recognised that education in art and design is vital to our industry, which needs the services of talented well-qualified designers and technicians, if our products are to be able to compete on international markets. Education in industrial design, communications design, fashion and textiles design, craft design and in other design fields has a very important part to play in our economic development and in our capacity to create employment.

Higher-level education in these areas is dependent on the encouragement of the creativity of our people from the earliest age.

These remarks serve to highlight the importance to our culture of the educational system and of changes being introduced in that system.

However, to give adequate consideration to the position of culture and the arts in our education system would require a separate and substantial study which would not be wholly appropriate to this document.

Major curriculum reform is now underway, with the establishment of the National Board for Curriculum and Assessment, which will shortly become a statutory body.

The report of the Interim Board, presented to the Minister for Education in March 1986 demonstrates the need for greater emphasis on the development of creativity in our educational system and opens the way for a major advance in this area. The Government looks to the Curriculum and Examinations Board to provide leadership in this field and to bring about the changes in our educational system at primary and secondary level necessary for the implementation of this cultural policy.

At third level, there have been notable advances in recent years particularly in the area of visual education.

The National College of Art and Design has been rehoused in a specially converted premises at Thomas Street; its facilities have been developed and its student numbers expanded. Degree-level courses in a number of disciplines at the NCAD have received approval from the NCEA and the College is now planning the introduction of post-graduate courses.

The older Schools of Art at Cork and Limerick have also been revitalised and expanded in recent years, while new Departments of Art and Design have been established at most Regional Technical Colleges. The introduction of courses in design throughout the country has been a significant development.

The Department of the Taoiseach will maintain contact with the Department of Education, the HEA and the NCEA in relation to specialist education in the arts at third level and in particular, in relation to teacher education. It is recognised that substantial changes will be needed in our Colleges of Education, if teachers in our schools and colleges are to be equipped adequately to enable them to play their part in the attainment of a major objective of Government policy contained in this White Paper, which is to develop the creative potential of our young people.

In addition, the Taoiseach's Department will maintain contact with agencies concerned in the field of adult and continuing education with a view to promoting increased provision for creative learning in this sector.

VI.22 The Arts Council and Education 1979-1989

Ten years after the publication of the Benson Report (VI.19) the Arts Council published a review of developments in education during the previous decade. While the review acknowledged and celebrated the many individual educational initiatives in the arts, the overall tone of the review was one of disappointment that the national situation had not changed significantly during the decade. The following extract from the review indicates this disappointment:

The Arts Council has exercised its right of comment regularly in the past ten years. Often its criticisms have been rejected, and indeed deeply resented, by education authorities. Often too, the Council has been accused of being unnecessarily negative. The response of the Arts Council is that to describe a negative state in any realm of life is not to be negative but to be accurate. The Council acknowledges — and seeks to support — those schools and teachers where there are very real achievements in arts eduction. But an education system which allows such achievements is not the same thing as one which provides for them. The fact that a national youth theatre, orchestra or choir exists or that an individual child has lessons in art, dance or music may be a matter of privilege created by parental income, geographical location or fortunate educational opportunity. An educational system, properly speaking, should not depend on such variable factors.

The interest and enthusiasm of individual inspectors, principals, teachers and parents are acknowledged by the Arts Council and have been factors critical to the implementation of the Arts Council's educational policy. Nonetheless, to paraphrase the Arts Council's report on music education Deaf Ears? (1985), enthusiasm is not enough. Our mathematical education does not depend on enthusiasm alone. At all stages of the education system, the arts require and deserve the same attention in terms of time, resources, staffing and syllabus design as do languages, the sciences, history and geography. We cannot profess the educational centrality of the arts and then betray that profession in our provision and practice. We must either change our practice so that it accords with statements of policy or else concede that the arts are not an educational priority and then be prepared to justify that stance.

It is important to record that in 1986, when the Arts Council organised a programme of nineteen public meetings throughout the country, as part of its consultative process to inform its submission to Government at a time when a White Paper on the arts was being prepared, the issue of greatest concern to those attending was the neglect of the arts education of their children.

****

VI. 23 Tuarascáil an Choimisiúin um athbheochan na Gaeilge — achoimre ar an tuarascáil dheireannach, 1963 Report of the Commission on the Restoration of the Irish Language — Summary of the Final Report, 1963

I roinn II den imleabhar seo léiríodh go raibh sé riachtanach go mbeadh ról tábhachtach ag an gcóras oideachais sa Saorstát in athbheochan na teanga mar chéad teanga an náisiúin. Rinne na comhdhálacha den chéad agus den dara clár náisiúnta i 1922 agus 1926 (II.1 agus II.3) focasáil beagnach an t-am ar fad ar an gceist seo agus bhí an Ghaeilge agus an córas oideachais fite fuaite trína chéile i rith na gceithre deichniúr tosaigh den stát nua. D'ainneoin fianaise a léirigh nach raibh ag éirí go sásúil leis an bpolasaí níor athraíodh an polasaí go ceann níos mó ná daichead bliain agus níor cealaíodh an riachtanas foirmeálta chun chuile ábhar sa bhunscoil a mhúineadh trí Ghaeilge go dtí 1960 (II.11).

Ba thréimhse athbhreithnithe agus measúnacht í ar shaol na hÉireann i gcoitinne blianta tosaigh na seascaidí agus sampla amháin an athbhreithnithe seo is ea bunú an Choimisiúin um Athbheochan na Teanga. Sholáthraigh tuarascáil an choimisiúin a foilsíodh i 1964 neart faisnéise ar cheart na teanga ó thaobh cúrsaí staire de agus ó thaobh an scéil mar abhí sé ag an am agus mhúnlaigh an tuarascáil polasaí an Rialtais ar an gceist seo, as sin amach.

Bhí an roinn ar oideachas an chuimsitheach agus an fhadchúrsach. Tugann an gearrshliocht annseo, ón achoimre ar an tuarascáil dheireanach, an pointe tosaigh óna ndearnadh na hiliomad moltaí tábhachtacha le fios dúinn. Déanann an sliocht, ach go háirithe, fócas na tuarascála ar riachtanas d'anailís teangeolaíoch ar structúir na Gaeilge agus an gá chun cúrsa forásach teagaisc atá grádaithe go mion a shuntasú. Cuireadh an anailís seo i gcrích agus foilsíodh a torthaí sa tuarascáil *Buntús Gaeilge* roinnt blianta ina dhiaidh sin. Bunaíodh nuachúrsa Gaeilge do dhaoine fásta, *Buntús Cainte,* ar thorthaí na hanailíse seo agus tionscnaíodh nuachúrsaí Gaeilge do bhunscoileanna a bhí bunaithe ar *Buntús Gaeilge* roimh dheireadh na seascaidí.

In section II of this volume, it has been shown that the educational system of the Irish Free State was required to play a major role in the restoration of the Irish language as the first language of the nation. The first and second national programme conferences of 1922 and 1926 (II.1 and II.3) focussed almost exclusively on this issue and during the first four decades of the new state the Irish language and education were inextricably linked. Despite evidence which suggested that this policy was not achieving a satisfactory level of success, it remained unchanged for over 40 years and it was only in 1960 that the formal requirement to teach all subjects in the national school through the medium of Irish was removed (II.11).

The early years of the 1960s were a period of review and appraisal in Irish life generally and the setting up of the Commission on the Restoration of the Irish language is one example of this review. The report of the Commission, which was published in 1964, provided a wealth of information on the question of the Irish language, both historically and currently, and pointed the way forward for future government policy in this area.

The section on education was comprehensive and far reaching and the short extract reproduced here from the summary of the final report only serves to provide an indication of the starting point from which numerous and significant recommendations were made. In particular the extract highlights the report's focus on the need for a scientific linguistic analysis of the structures of the Irish language and the need to devise "a progressive and carefully graded course of instruction." This analysis was carried out and its findings were published in the report *Buntús Gaeilge* some years later. A new Irish language course for adults *Buntús Cainte* was based on the findings of this analysis and new Irish language courses for primary schools were developed by the end of the 1960s also based on *Buntús Gaeilge:*

SECTION V — THE EDUCATIONAL SYSTEM

(18) General Observations

The schools alone cannot restore Irish as the language of the people. While very noteworthy progress has been made in extending the knowledge of Irish through the educational system over the past forty years, the Commission emphatically states that its restoration as a vernacular will be inevitably retarded until such time as the practical day to day use of the language outside the schools is adequately encouraged and fostered. In this context, it is clear that the work of the schools for Irish must be directed towards giving children from English-speaking homes a functional command of the language to be used in later life rather than towards formal studies of its linguistic structure.

The Commission attaches considerable importance to the advances made in America and in many European countries in recent times in the scientific treatment of languages to be taught as "second languages." It is confident that the principles on which these advances were based can now be applied to the teaching of the Irish language in schools in the non-Gaeltacht areas.

While much of the good work for the language done in the schools has been wasted because of the failure to back it up outside the schools, some of it has also been spoiled by weaknesses within the educational system itself. The greatest of these was undoubtedly the over-emphasis placed on the written as against the spoken language. There has been a tendency to tail off the use of Irish according as the pupil progressed through his educational course — a widespread use of the language at infant's stage followed by a decreasing use up to the higher standards. For pupils who proceeded to post-primary education there was still less use of the language as a spoken tongue, outside the Class A secondary schools and University College, Galway. The impression must have been inevitably conveyed that Irish was something connected with school and especially with the earlier years there, and that every step forward was a step away from the language until the pupil was finally finished with it on leaving school. This illogical situation must be righted and a serious effort made, not only to co-ordinate the use of the language at all levels of education, but to co-ordinate the various Irish courses in a properly graded system so that one will follow naturally from the other.

(19) Primary Education

****

The Commission has made a careful study of all the objections put forward against the use of the primary school for the purpose of giving children a working knowledge of Irish, with special reference to the effects of bilingualism on the normal child and the age when the teaching of a second language should begin. Having gone into each one of these objections and having before it the findings of internationally recognised authorities, the Commission has no hesitation in stating emphatically that

(a) the introduction of Irish to children from English-speaking homes at Infant Standard level is not alone not harmful to them but may be regarded as a positive aid to their intellectual development when it enables them to attain genuine bilingualism at an early age; moreover, the beginning of the learning of a second language from the earliest school years is gradually becoming widely adopted abroad as a method offering the best hope of producing fluent speakers;

(b) apart from the fact that the national aim to restore Irish is being served by making Irish speakers of primary school-children, they would gain a positive *educational* advantage through being enabled to become genuinely bilingual, and the break-through from monolingualism to bilingualism would make the learning of other languages later much easier.

Since the primary school curriculum is a wide one, it is quite clear that only a limited amount of time can be given to the formal teaching of Irish. Therefore, in order to derive the optimum benefit from the available time, it is necessary that a progressive and carefully graded course of instruction be planned and followed. ......The selection and grading of the language structures and vocabulary to be taught at various levels should be regarded as one of the first duties of a special Research Section, which should be set up by the Department of Education. It is to be understood that this type of scientific sifting and grading of languages for the benefit of learners has been done abroad with outstanding success in the case of various other languages.

VI. 24 An Páipéar Bán ar Athbheochan na Gaeilge, 1965 White Paper on the Restoration of the Irish Language, 1965

Foilsíodh tuarascáil dheireanach an Choimisiúin um Athbheochan na Gaeilge i mí Eanáir 1964. Eisíodh Páipéar Bán, bliain ina dhiaidh sin inar leag an Rialtas amach a pholasaí ginearálta i leith na Gaeilge agus a thuairimí ar mholtaí an Choimisiúin. Athluadh sa réamhrá don Pháipéar Bán 'gurb í an aidhm náisiúnta ná an Ghaeilge a athbhunú mar ghnáth chóras cumarsáide'. Tuigeadh go dtógfadh an aidhm seo a lán ama agus sár-iarracht le cur i gcrích agus go mb'éigean do gach aichme den phobal bheith páirteach sa fhreagracht chun an aidhm sin a bhaint amach. Chuimsigh tuarascáil an Choimisiúin mionmholtaí ar Ghaeilge sa chóras oideachais ag gach leibhéal agus léirigh roinn iomlán an Pháipéir Bháin ina raibh níos mó ná 40 leathanach, freagra an Rialtais ar na moltaí. Tógtar na hailt seo a leanas as Caibidil IV den Pháipéar Bhán.

The final report of the commission on the Restoration of the Irish Language was published in January 1964. A year later, a White Paper was issued in which the government set out its general policy on the Irish language and its views on the commission's recommendations. In the introduction to the White Paper it was reiterated that "the national aim is to restore the Irish language as a general medium of communication." It was recognised that this aim would take much time and effort to achieve and that all sections of the community must share the responsibility of working for the realisation of this aim. The report of the Commission had contained detailed recommendations on Irish in the educational system at all levels and a full section of the White Paper, running to more than 40 pages, indicated the government's response to these recommendations. The following paragraphs are taken from Chapter IV of the White Paper:

162. The importance attached to the part which can be played by the educational system in the restoration of the Irish language is underlined by the attention the Commission has given to the services which come within the ambit of the Department of Education. If progress in extending the use of Irish among the public in general has been slower than expected, this is not due to lack of enthusiasm or diligence among those concerned with the teaching of the language in the schools. The Department of Education has constantly endeavoured to ensure that Irish shall have a special place in the curricula of all schools. Most school authorities and teachers have co-operated fully in applying the Department's directives, sometimes in the face of considerable difficulties. It is vital to the success of the language policy that the efforts of everyone concerned with teaching Irish should continue and be made more effective.

163. ....The special position of Irish as a subject should therefore be established even in the pre-school period. The parent or other person who conditions the mind of a child by constantly associating the adjective "compulsory" with Irish is

doing a disservice not only to that individual child but to other children and the nation in general. A positive attitude of goodwill on the part of parents and others in a position to influence children is also necessary if young people are to be encouraged to use Irish in their everyday activities both during their school days and when they enter adult life.

165. As regards the part to be played by the educational system, the various measures outlined in the Second Programme for Economic Expansion for improving the extending educational facilities in general will help to make the teaching of Irish more effective. Further measures to this end will be announced as the various investigations now in progress are completed. As regards university education in particular, decisions on policy measures will be taken when the report of the Commission on Higher Education has been received and considered.

VI. 25 Comhairle na Gaeilge — An Ghaeilge san Oideachas, 1974
Comhairle na Gaeilge — Irish in Education, 1974

Ceapadh Comhairle na Gaeilge ag an Rialtas i mí Mheithimh 1969 chun cabhrú le hathbhreithniú ar pholasaí teanga agus chun comhairle a thabhairt ar fhóras na teanga as sin amach. Thuig an Chomhairle ó thosach go mba ghné thábhachtach dá chuid oibre ná athbhreithniú a dhéanamh ar áit na Gaeilge sa chóras oideachais. I 1971 foilsíodh *Teanga agus Pobal* agus cuireadh moladh faoi bhráid an Údaráis Um Árdoideachas maidir le hoiliúnt múinteoirí agus faoi stádas na Gaeilge sna hOllscoileanna. I mí Meithimh 1970 d'fhoilsigh and Chomhairle tuarascáil den teideal *Ag Feidhmiú Polasaí Teanga* inar moladh go mbunófaí eagras nua reachtúil — Bord na Gaeilge — a mbéadh sé mar aidhm aige úsáid na Gaeilge ar fud na tíre a leathnú. Foilsíodh tuarascáil dar teideal *Chuig Polasaí Teanga na Gaeilge sa Chóras Oideachais* san Earrach 1973 agus foilsíodh doiciméid deireanach na Comhairle — *An Ghaeilge san Oideachas* — i mí Meithimh 1974. Ba thuarascáil chuimsitheach í síud ina raibh mion mholtaí maidir leis an nGaeilge agus an chóras oideachais ag gach leibhéal. I measc na moltaí thuas, bhí ceann amháin a mhol go gcuirfí cúrsa i Staidéir na Gaeilge ar fáil sa chlár iarbhunscoile agus go mbeadh scrúdú cainte agus scrúdú scríofa sa Ghaeilge mar chuid den chúrsa sin. Léiríonn an gearrshliocht anseo thíos an comhthéacs ina bhfuil mionphlé agus moltaí na tuarascála leagtha amach:

Comhairle na Gaeilge was appointed by the government in June 1969 to help review Irish language policy and advise on its future development. An Comhairle recognised from the start that an important feature of its work would be to review the position of Irish in the educational system. In 1971 it published *Language and Community* and made submissions to the H.E.A. on the training of teachers and the position of Irish in the universities. In June 1972 An Comhairle published a report *Implementing a Language Policy* in which it recommended that a new statutory body, Bord na Gaeilge, be set up with responsibility for extending the use of Irish throughout the country. In spring of 1973 a report entitled *Towards an Irish Language Policy in Education* was published and in June 1974 An Comhairle's final document *Irish in Education* was published. This was a wide ranging report containing detailed recommendations regarding the Irish language and education at all levels. Among its recommendations was one which stated that "a course in Irish studies be introduced into the post-primary school curriculum" and that "oral and written communication in Irish should comprise part of the course."

The short extract reproduced here provides the context in which the detailed discussion and recommendations of the report are set:

CHAPTER 1
TOWARDS AN IRISH LANGUAGE POLICY IN EDUCATION

1. Comhairle na Gaeilge in its report *Implementing a Language Policy* has recommended guidelines for a gradual and flexible Irish language policy, based on the concept of diglossia. This approach requires efforts to influence the use of Irish throughout the community and to enhance the role of

Irish within the educational system. While drawing attention to the probable need to make provision for the special circumstances of Northern Ireland, the report has tentatively mentioned the aim of "20% use of Irish on average, by persons outside the Gaeltacht by the end of the century." This envisages that most Irish people would normally carry out some 20% of their daily conversations in Irish by the year 2000. To bring this situation about, a comprehensive community language development programme has been proposed under the aegis of a statutory state board, Bord na Gaeilge. In conjunction with this programme, an integrated supporting programme would have to be developed within the educational system, with the primary object of enabling Irish people in general to understand and use Irish.

2. With this two-pronged strategy in mind the present report makes recommendations for improving the teaching of Irish at the pre-primary, primary, post-primary and higher levels. Many of the proposals have been accepted in principle in the past and, to some extent, implemented — though not always in a coherent or consistent fashion. The present report attempts to co-ordinate the best features of past policy and to suggest some new approaches with a view to ensuring that the educational system will be geared to promote the emergence of a high proportion of active bilinguals in this country within the next generation.

****

5. Comhairle na Gaeilge see the restoration of Irish as fundamentally important not alone in protecting the individuality of thought and feeling which Irish people have inherited but in giving it new dimensions. The development of the potential of each person in a community is influenced to a great extent by the culture which the community inherits and any significant expansion of that culture will influence to a

large degree the development of the potential of all who share it. Properly taught within the educational system, the Irish language opens up for Irish people, through Irish literature and history, some two thousand years of Irish life. It makes them conscious of that network of behaviour, thought and feeling which they share not only with the Irish community of the past, but also with most of the people of Ireland today, both in the Gaeltacht and outside it. For Irish men and women an adequate knowledge of Irish is essential to that awareness of mind and feeling and to that integration with community on which much individual development depends. This could be held to be one of the main objectives of education in its widest sense. The restoration of Irish is probably as crucial to those who wish to develop a special Irish culture or experience mainly through the English language as it is to those who wish to do so mainly through Irish.

6. Any long-term plan for the teaching of Irish must include these objectives as a basic element. As to the short-term, it should be stressed that teaching Irish as a second vernacular could be of minimal educational value, if it is not taught in a manner and to a degree which ensures at least partial realisation of the general objectives. Put at its simplest, teaching some Irish in schools, but not teaching it to the point where most students can gain real-life experience through it — watching television programmes in Irish, conversing with other Irish speakers, understanding or identifying with an Irish song or poem, etc. — would be an educational waste of major proportions. To be educationally valid, then, any general programme for teaching Irish within our educational system should aim at giving all our children the opportunity of learning sufficient Irish before leaving school to enable them to attain minimum targets of the kind indicated above. In turn, the community's attitude to Irish should be such as to ensure that knowledge can be translated into use both during and after school years.

7. Comhairle na Gaeilge believe that a suitable graded plan not only for the teaching of Irish from infancy to school-leaving age, but also for the teaching of some other subject(s) through Irish, for the gradual development of a system of Irish-medium schools, and for promoting Irish in the school environment, is necessary to achieve this situation.

VI. 26 An Páipéar Bán um Fhóras san Oideachais, 1980
The White Paper on Educational Development, 1980

Rinneadh tagairt don Pháipéar Bán in roinnt ranna tosaigh den imleabhar (I.16, II.17, III.24, IV.18, V.19, agus VI.6). Tugadh caibidil den Pháipéar Bán suas go hiomlán don Ghaeilge, caibidil a foilsíodh trí Ghaeilge agus trí Bhéarla. Rinne an Páipéar tagairt don Ghaeilge i ngach leibhéal den chóras oideachais agus rinneadh níos mó ná fiche moladh atá leagtha amach anseo i slí achomair:

The White Paper on Educational Development has been referred to in a number of earlier sections of this volume (I.16, II.17, III.24, IV.18, V.19, and VI.6). A full chapter of the white paper was devoted to the Irish language — a chapter which was published both in Irish and in English. The paper referred to Irish at all levels of the education system and made a total of 20 proposals, all of which are reproduced here in summary form:

Summary of Proposals

1. Attempts will be made to have an entire aspect or part thereof of the curriculum taught through Irish in every primary school. The spoken language will be pre-eminent and more time will be devoted to the formal teaching of the spoken language.
2. The number of inservice courses relating to Irish and to language-teaching methods will be greatly increased.
3. Teachers at first and second level will be assisted to attend courses in the Gaeltacht.

4. A high level of competence particularly in oral Irish will be expected of students seeking admission to Colleges of Education. Information in this regard will be furnished to second-level schools.
5. It will be expected that a significant proportion of the professional course in Colleges of Education will be done through Irish and that every student will have an opportunity of teaching through Irish during his training course.
6. Additional help with regard to teaching aids and equipment will be given to primary schools who teach a worthwhile amount of the curriculum through Irish.
7. Regular objective evaluation of the standard of Irish in primary and second-level schools will be carried out.
8. There will be a continuation and an intensification of the research at present being conducted in relation to language-teaching methods and in particular in relation to the curriculum and methods of teaching Irish. The Linguistics Institute of Ireland will be strengthened in order to extend the range of this work.
9. Continuity from first to second level in relation to conversation classes, reading matter and teaching methods will be ensured.
10. Support will be provided for schemes which enable teachers and senior standard pupils from national schools in Galltacht areas to spend a period of time in the Gaeltacht during the school-year.
11. The assistance that is at present being provided for the development of All-Irish schools will be continued and planning will be undertaken to satisfy the needs of those pupils whose parents wish them to receive their education entirely in Irish.
12. A special committee of inspectors, teachers and other educationalists will be established to study the curriculum in Irish and English for Gaeltacht schools.

The special circumstances that obtain in the case of Gaeltacht schools will be taken into consideration in the context of the appointment or retention of teachers in such schools.

13. A committee will be established to cater for the needs of post-primary students of low ability and to devise an appropriate syllabus for them.

14. (a) Irish courses in second-level schools, especially those in the junior classes, will be revised so as to enable greater emphasis to be placed on conversation and on the basic structures of the language.

(b) The structure and methods of examination will also be altered to correspond with the new emphasis upon the conversational approach. In future $33\frac{1}{3}$ per cent of the total marks in the Leaving Certificate Examination will be reserved for the oral examination.

(c) Every effort will be made to improve the competence of second-level teachers in relation to Irish language teaching methods and in relation to the instruction of other subjects through the medium of Irish.

15. There will be continued provision for schemes to foster teaching through Irish in second-level schools and a special effort will be made to ensure that an adequate supply of suitable textbooks and teaching aids will be made available to support this work.

16. Steps will be taken to ensure that a full second-level course through Irish will be available to every child from either a Gaeltacht or a Galltacht area, who received his/her primary education through Irish and who wishes to avail of such a course.

17. Greater emphasis will be placed upon the role of Irish in Vocational Education and arrangements will be made to conduct courses through Irish in the case of posts where a sound knowledge of the language is a basic requirement.

18. Under the adult education schemes, evening classes in Irish will be established which will be particularly suitable for parents who wish to provide support in the Irish language for their children. The newly appointed organisers will be expected to provide enjoyable activities through the medium of Irish.
19. The Department of Education will continue to support the Irish Colleges and will endeavour in every way possible to strengthen the specifically educational aspects of their work.
20. The Committee on Educational Broadcasting will be asked to make recommendations regarding the provision of suitable Irish programmes, both on radio and television, for young children, for primary and post-primary schoolchildren and for parents.

VI. 27 Bord na Gaeilge — Plean Gníomhaíochta don Ghaeilge, 1983-86 Action Plan for Irish, 1983-86

I 1972 mhol Comhairle na Gaeilge go mbunófaí eagras reachtúil nua — Bord na Gaeilge (VI.25). Ghlac an Rialtas leis an moladh seo agus ó bhunú an eagrais is fórsa an tábhachtach é Bord na Gaeilge maidir le comhairle agus tacaíocht a thabhairt ar an nGaeilge i ngach gné de shaol na tíre. Ní bheadh sé indéanta laistigh de theorannaí imleabhair mar seo omós cóir a thabhairt do mhóréacht Bhord na Gaeilge i leith na Gaeilge agus do shaol na tíre i gcoitinne. Cuireadh na gearrsliochtanna anseo thíos ó Roinn 3 de phlean gníomhaíochta an Bhoird don Ghaeilge 1983-86 san áireamh mar spreagadh do ghoile an léitheora le súil go ndéanfaí taighde níos doimhne ar shaothar Bhord na Gaeilge:

In 1972, Comhairle na Gaeilge had recommended that a new statutory body, Bord na Gaeilge be set up (VI.25). The government accepted its recommendation and since its foundation Bord na Gaeilge has been a very important force in advising on and supporting policy on language in all areas of Irish life. It would not be possible in the limited confines of a volume such as this to pay adequate tribute to the major contribution of Bord na Gaeilge to the language and to Irish life generally. The short extracts provided here from the Bord's Action Plan for Irish 1983-1986 are included merely to whet the appetite of the reader to research in greater depth the work of Bord na Gaeilge.

RÉAMHFHOCAL.

Bheifí níos gaire go mór do staid dhátheangachais ina mbeadh an Ghaeilge slán dá sroichfí an pointe faoi dheireadh an chéid go mbeadh cumas maith labhartha sa Ghaeilge ag trian den phobal ar a laghad, cumas réasúnta i labhairt na teanga ag tuairim is trian eile, agus buntuiscint ar an teanga mar aon le cumas éigin labhartha inti coitianta go maith i measc na coda eile.

Níl sin a bhaint amach i láthair na huaire. Ach ba chuspóir insroichte é.

Is é an bunrud a mholtar go gcuirfí béim breise ar chumas labhartha na Gaeilge a chothú. Chuige sin b'inmholta go soiléireofaí na haidhmeanna teagaisc a bheadh ann ó rang go rang sa tslí is go mbeadh forás leanúnach ag teacht ar chumas labhartha na ndaltaí agus go mbeadh sásamh le fáil acu as an nGaeilge d'úsáid.

Is rud an-tábhachtach faoin gcuid seo den phlean, go bhfuil tacaíocht an Roinn Oideachais go ginearálta leis na bunnithe atá le déanamh.

I gcúrsaí bunscolaíochta, saineofar na siollabais agus na cúrsaí Gaeilge d'fhonn treisiú le cumas labhartha agus cumarsáide na ndaltaí. Féacfaidh an Roinn lena dheimhniú go gcaithfear an t-am is gá leis an nGaeilge i ngach rang chun an teanga a mhúineadh go sásúil. Tabharfar cúnamh do mhúinteoirí chun an Ghaeilge d'úsáid le linn dóibh bheith ag plé le gnéithe eile den churaclam — rud a bhí i gceist ó thús sa Churaclam Nua.

I gcás an iar-bhunoideachais, tiocfaidh ionadaithe ón gcéad agus ón dara leibhéal le chéile, faoi choimirce an Roinn Oideachais, d'fhonn siollabas leanúnach in múineadh na Gaeilge ó aois 4 go dtí 15 a rianadh. Athbhreithneofar freisin agus déanfar sainiú beacht ar spriocanna Shiollabas Gaeilge na hÁrdteistiméireachta.

San athbhreithniú seo cuirfear béim ar leith ar ghnáthchumas cumarsáide, Cuirfear le tábhacht an scrúdú cainte san Árdteistiméireacht agus cuirfear tús le béalscrúdú sa Mheánteistiméireacht.

Chun go bhféadfaí an méid sin a chur á dhéanamh le lánéifeacht níor mór deiseanna áirithe a chur ar fáil d'ábhair múinteoirí a mbeadh an Ghaeilge, nó ábhair trí Ghaeilge, á dteagasc acu níos déanaí. Ba cheart go mbeadh an chaoi acu caighdeán sásúil a bhaint amach sa teanga féin agus cleachtadh a fháil, le linn a dtréimhse traenála, ar í a usáid mar mheán teagaisc in ábhair eile. Ba chóir go bhfaighfidís oiliúint sna modhanna múinte teanga is déanaí agus go mbeidís eolach ar thorthaí an taighde idirnáisiúnta atá déanta ar mhúineadh teangacha.

Beidh an Roinn Oideachais ag plé leis na Coláistí Oideachais agus leis na hOllscoileanna chun a dheimhniú go mbeidh na deiseanna sin ar fáil ag gach ábhar múinteora. Tá cur síos sa phlean ar na hathruithe a mheastar a bheith inmholta.

I gcás na nábhar múinteoirí dara leibhéil, tá Bord na Gaeilge ag moladh do na Coláistí Ollscoile ar fad nach bhfuil a leithéid acu cheana, aonad substaintiúil amháin de Chúrsa an Árd-Teastais san Oideachas a chur ar fáil trí Ghaeilge. Táthar á mholadh freisin go mbeadh Cúrsa Árd-Dioplóma i múineadh na Gaeilge in ngach coláiste ollscoile agus go mbeadh feidhm leis an scrúdú cainte a chuirtear ar ábhair oidí iar-bhunscoile.

Tá Bord na Gaeilge ag moladh don Údaras Árd Oideachais scéim a tharraingt amach i gcomhar leis na Coláistí Ollscoile chun go mbeadh raon fairsing ábhar trí Ghaeilge á dtairiscint de réir a chéile do mhic léinn ollscoile.

Ba thábhachtach an ní é go mbeadh ionad ag an nGaeilge freisin sna coláistí tríú leibhéil sa tréimhse teicneolaíochta. Is í Comhairle Náisiúnta na gCáilíochtaí Oideachais a thugann aitheantas do na cúrsaí in ocht gcinn is fiche de na hInstitiúidí sin agus a bhronnann cáilíochtaí (idir Chéimeanna, Dioplómaí Náisiúnta agus Teastais Náisiúnta) ar a gcuid mac léinn. Tá ráiteas polasaí i dtaobh na Gaeilge agus na Gaeltachta ó Chomhairle Náisiúnta na gCáilíochtaí Oideachais sa phlean seo.

Aithnítear an tábhacht a bhainfeadh le greasán níos fairsinge fós de scoileanna lán-Ghaeilge a bheith ann - chun go neartófar de réir a chéile an bunphobal Gaeilge a bhfuil trácht air sa Réamhrá. Aithnítear freisin na riachtanais oideachais ar leith a bhaineann leis an nGaeltacht.

Beidh a gcion féin á dhéanamh ag an gComhchoiste Réamhscolaíochta, ag Comhar na Múinteoirí Gaeilge agus ag Gaelscoileanna, trí eagras oideachasúla atá ag obair faoi choimirce Bhord na Gaeilge agus a bhfuil torthaí substaintiúla cheana féin ar a gcuid oibre.

Beidh sé ina chuspóir sa phlean gach cúnamh is féidir a thabhairt do mhúinteoirí. Chuige sin an moladh faoi Lárionad Acmhainní, na moltaí faoi Chúrsaí Inseirbhíse, agus na scéimeanna éagsúla chun timpeallacht dhátheangach a chothú in institiúidí oideachais.

VI.28 Programme for Action in Education, 1984-87

Tá tagairt déanta cheana féin san imleabhar seo do Chlár Oideachais 1984-87 (I.21, II.18, III.26, IV.10, V.20 agus VI.8). Baineann an cheithre alt thíos le cheist an Ghaeilge sa chóras oideachais.

The Programme for Action in Education has been referred to in sections I.21, II.18, III.26, IV.20, V.20, and VI.8 of this volume. Four paragraphs in chapter 2 referred to the Irish language in education and these paragraphs are reproduced below:

2.4 The Government is committed to the greater use of the Irish language and the continued strengthening of its position in the educational system. Bord na Gaeilge's Action Plan for Irish, Plean Gníomhaíochta don Ghaeilge 1983-1986, published with Government approval in April last contains many proposals for the advancement of Irish in various areas of Irish life and particularly in education. Those proposals which fall within the competence of the Minister for Education will be implemented subject to the availability of resources. In addition, the feasibility of introducing a course in Irish Studies as a support for the study of Irish will be examined.

2.5 Some of these proposals relating to education have been or are being implemented, particularly those relating to Irish in the Colleges of Education and the holding of day conferences for primary teachers. Other proposals such as the development of more all-Irish schools, the teaching of some aspect of the curriculum through the medium of Irish, improving the monitoring of the Oral Irish examination in the Leaving Certificate and increasing the grant to all-Irish Secondary schools will be implemented in the short term. A Committee representative of Roinn na Gaeltachta, Údarás na

Gaeltachta and the Department of Education is at present examining educational problems peculiar to the Gaeltacht and will be reporting to the Minister. When this report has been furnished its recommendations will be responded to as positively as possible. A pilot programme of action research in the field of Irish language teaching is being developed by the Curriculum Development Centre at Shannon in collaboration with the E.E.C.

2.6 Concerns have been expressed about the position of the Irish language in schools. In the main, these refer to the standards of Irish at primary level, the drop-out in the numbers of pupils taking Irish after the Intermediate Certificate and the lack of text books in Irish. However, the absence of a supportive environment outside of the school which would provide motivation for the children constitutes a major obstacle. Greater use will be made of the conferences between teachers and inspectors at Primary level to identify particular weaknesses and to propose remedial action. Inservice courses on a greater scale will be provided. The question of appropriate training for teachers for all-Irish schools is at present being examined. One of the smaller Training Colleges provides a course of training substantially through the medium of Irish. A proportion of places in the competition for entry to the Colleges of Education is reserved for native speakers of Irish. There is no easy, quick solution to the difficulty of providing text books in Irish. An early examination of the range of text-books and other teaching materials will be undertaken.

2.7 A task force will be set up in the Department to identify areas for action and to monitor progress particularly in relation to the implementation of the recommendations in Bord na Gaeilge's Action Plan for Irish.

VI. 29 Tuarascáil an Chomhchoiste um Oideachas sa Ghaeltacht, 1985.

I 1980 reachtóladh cruinnithe idir oifigigh na Roinne Oideachais agus Údarás na Gaeltachta faoi fhadhbanna oideachais sa Ghaeltacht. Níos déanaí sa bhliain sin, foilsíodh Páipéar Bán um Fhorás san Oideachas agus d'aontaigh an tAire Oideachais go mbunófaí coiste le hionadaithe ón Roinn Oideachais agus ó Roinn na Gaeltachta chun oideachas sa Ghaeltacht a phlé. Foilsíodh tuarascáil chuimsitheach ón gcoiste seo i lár na n-ochtóidí. Rinne an tuarascáil réim mhór moltaí i leith bhunoideachais, iarbhunoideachais, oideachais den tríú leibhéal maraon le printíseachtaí in oideachas teicniúil agus teicneolaíoch. Bhí móriomlán de 62 mholadh sa tuarascáil ach níl ach líon beag díobh san áireamh anseo:

In 1980, meetings were held between senior officials of the Department of Education and Údarás na Gaeltachta about the problems of education in the Gaeltacht. Later that year the White Paper on Education and Development was published and the Minister for Education agreed that a committee should be set up with representatives from the Departments of Education and the Gaeltacht and Údarás na Gaeltachta to discuss education in the Gaeltacht. A comprehensive report on the matter was completed by this committee and published in the mid 1980s. It made wide-ranging recommendations in relation to primary, post-primary and post-secondary education, including apprenticeship, technical and technological education. The report contained a total of 62 recommendations, only a small number of which are included here:

PRIMARY EDUCATION

2. That the averages which operate for the appointment and retention of teachers in all-Irish schools outside the Gaeltacht be extended to Gaeltacht schools.
3. That special arrangements apply in allocating assistant teachers for remedial teaching purposes to Gaeltacht schools, bearing in mind the size of the schools, and that such allocation be permitted to groups of adjacent small schools, in no case more than five to a group, in

accordance with the recommendations of the inspector regarding the remedial education needs in the schools.

****

5. That a series of Irish readers suitable to Gaeltacht schools be prepared which would take into account the environment of the children and working life in the present day Gaeltacht and that the classical books in Irish which originated in the Gaeltacht be made available to the schools.

****

14. That the Special Education Section of the Department of Education investigate the special educational needs of handicapped children whose mother tongue is Irish and recommend suitable arrangements for them.

19. That a working group of educationists which would include teachers from Gaeltacht schools be established for the purpose of preparing a suitable curriculum for the Gaeltacht schools. That such a curriculum be sufficiently flexible to cater for the varying needs of primary schools in the Gaeltacht and that the Department of Education give the necessary support to the implementation of this curriculum.

POST-PRIMARY EDUCATION

21. That any special advantages of the system of classification of schools at present applied to Irish and bilingual secondary schools, be extended to vocational, community and comprehensive schools in the Gaeltacht as appropriate.

22. That at least one class group working through the medium of Irish be established in every school area catering for Gaeltacht children.

****

Addendum

The following report which was prepared by an internal committee in the Department of Education in 1972 has not previously been published. It came to our attention when the typesetting of this volume was virtually completed but due to its significance we decided to include some extracts at this point in the volume.

III.18 (a) Tuarascáil Shealadach ón Choiste a Chuireadh i mbun Scrúdú a Dhéanamh ar Oideachas Iarbhunscoile, 1962

In June 1962 a committee was formed in the Department of Education, on the instructions of the Minister, Dr. P.J. Hillery, "to consider the present position of post-primary education, particularly in its social aspects and to make recommendations." The committee was chaired by Dr. Duggan, deputy chief inspector and its secretary was Dr. F. O'Callaghan, inspector, who drafted the report. It is perhaps relevant to note that in the spring and early summer of 1962 arrangements were being made to recruit the survey team which produced the report *Investment in Education* in 1965 (I.10). It seems likely that at that stage it was expected that the survey team would confine its deliberations to the economic aspects of education and that the internal departmental team would focus on the social aspects of education. The departmental committee had not envisaged producing a report until 1963 and had made arrangements for visiting Northern Ireland and England in January and February, 1963. However, at the end of November 1962 the committee was informed that "an outline blueprint for post-primary education" should be completed by 8th December and the interim report from which the following extracts are taken was completed by that date:

****

4. (i) In concerning ourselves with defects within the present post--primary system of education we are doing more than merely accepting a literal interpretation of portion of our remit. We recognise that our present system of secondary schooling has its roots well established in tradition, and has, in the face of considerable difficulties, provided an important

service, if not to all Irish children, at least to considerable numbers of them. Its expansion in recent years, together with changes both in content and stress in its curricula, might be interpreted as a sincere effort to re-model itself to suit modern needs. That this re-modelling process is hampered to some extent by the very traditions it values so highly we have no doubt, and we feel that the time is not only approaching but has in fact arrived when we can no longer allow traditional patterns to unduly influence educational planning and provision in a world where a social, political, economic, scientific and technological revolution has taken place and is still proceeding. There are, of course, other factors both economic and legislative, over which the schools themselves can have very little control, which also tend to retard modern development

****

4. (iv) ....The haphazard picture, however, which emerges from the figures in paragraph 4 (iii) would indicate that the present provision and consequent incidence of attendance is scarcely beneficial to children, or to the State, if a set period of post-primary education, reasonably planned and adequately provided for is recognised as a national necessity from a social and economic point of view.

5. That such a period of post-primary education is, in fact, a national necessity, is a viewpoint we heartily endorse. This point of view appears to be widely accepted, not only in this country, but in most European countries, in very many of which a period of attendance at post-primary schools is obligatory.

****

6. It is primarily as a result of these consideration that we unhesitatingly recommend a compulsory and free period of

post-primary education for all Irish children. We qualify this recommendation, naturally, by accepting subnormal and mentally-retarded children, whose special problems are being considered by a Government-appointed commission.

12. It now remains in view of our recommendation of a period of free and compulsory post-primary education for all children between the ages of 12 plus at one end, and 15 plus at the other end, to determine what form this period of education should take. It is necessary to state at this stage that we reject entirely the basis on which pupils enter Secondary and Vocational Schools at the present time. This basis is haphazard in its operation and is not rooted in balanced consideration of intelligence, depends on some considerations of finance and social standing and certain other compulsive forces of persuasion and competition. We do not consider that these forces should be operative within education generally and we fail to see how they can in their present application exclude injustice to some children.

13. We had considered firstly the idea of applying some form of selection, by aptitude and intelligence test on entry to the post-primary system, with subsequent streaming into schools of different kinds. We were unanimous in rejecting this possibility. The advantages of any such system would be far outweighed by the almost inescapable injustices in its operation and by the disadvantages inherent in the system itself...............

14. The next step in our examination was the possibility of establishing Comprehensive Schools. While we were attracted by the social and educational desirability of these schools, we consider their establishment impracticable. Comprehensive schools of their very nature need to be large and to give a suitable range and organisation of programme and activities

require an intake of about 200-300 pupils annually. We consider schools of this size impossible, largely because of the low population density in most areas in the country...........

15. As a final possibility, then, we can only consider a comprehensive system. This, to us, means that the distinction at present recognised between vocational schools and secondary schools should disappear, and that a common form of post-primary course, extending over a three-year period, should be available both in existing vocational and existing secondary schools. We believe that this suggestion is workable, that it would of necessity require a drawing together of the curricula of both types of school with considerable advantages to both; would tend to eliminate social barriers currently created by educational cleavages, and would provide for the "missing rung in the educational ladder" which currently prevents pupils of promise in vocational schools from attaining the top of the ladder no matter what talent they may possess, or no matter how assiduously they apply themselves to study................

16. In subsequent paragraphs we shall deal more fully with the educational aspects of this proposed system. For the moment it will suffice to say that the units we envisage following this common course would be termed "Junior Secondary Schools;" that physically they would be housed in existing secondary and vocational schools and that in general they should aim at operating with a minimum of 120 pupils, that is, an annual intake of 40. We recommend that the full cost of these schools should be met out of public funds, local and/or central, and that in addition, wherever necessary, public funds should also bear the costs of a school transport system and subsidise a school meals service even of a limited kind...........

25. The general development of Post-Junior Secondary School education would in outline, consist of a three-year senior secondary course from15 plus to 18 plus which would be divided into three broad streams, the first tending to Liberal Studies, the second to Science and Technology and the third to Business and Management. In addition to this Senior Secondary Course, we propose a service of pre-employment courses, generally lasting for one year and strongly vocational in nature........

26. We are not prepared to recommend that the senior secondary school courses should be available free to all pupils who wish to partake of them. Broadly we would divide the entry to these schools into three categories, not to be confused with divisions of studies mentioned in the previous paragraphs. This division into categories we find convenient as a means whereby public funds might be channeled into a system of education whose buildings will now be in part publicly owned (developed technical institutes) and in part privately owned (developed secondary schools). The current expenditure of each of these institutions might be compiled and divided by the number of student places available to arrive at a costing per student-place. We would then propose a generous scheme whereby full free places would be available to pupils of considerable merit and assisted places to pupils who, while not showing outstanding merit would still in our opinion be capable of benefitting to a worthwhile extent from the senior sdhool programme. Full free places would be assessed on the cost per student place, cost of transport to and from school and cost of school meals where these are necessary, and cost of school books. Assisted places would be assessed on the same basis, but only half their cost would be defrayed out of public funds.........

35. There remains then the vital question of how such a framework of post primary education could be implemented and administered within this country. This question occupied much of our deliberations and discussions. Throughout this report, when financial matters were discussed we have made reference to public funds, both central and local. We are all strongly of the opinion that there should be some local contribution towards the costs of all forms of education within any area, and since, for purposes of local contribution, County and Borough areas are well defined, we naturally tend to recommend these as suitable area units. We do, however, have reservations about the smaller town boroughs, and think that in the interests of good organisation these should be considered in conjunction with the counties in which they lie...........

36. Local statutory committees for post-primary education, with power to raise funds from the rates, and the right of supplementing these funds considerably from the central authority, should be set up. These committees while being nominated principally by the County Councils and Urban District Councils of the areas concerned, just as the vocational committees now are, should have, in addition, nominees of the Bishops whose dioceses form part of these counties, to represent the religious communities providing secondary education and also a nominee to represent the interests of religious minorities. This committee would take over all the present functions of the vocational committees and arrange for the disposal of funds to the post-primary education system in operation in its area. For this and other purposes it would maintain a chief executive officer and administrative staff.

****

APPENDIX I

Ministers for Education, 1919-1991

Government	Term of Office	Parties	Minister for Education	Minister's party
First Dáil	Jan.1919-Aug.1921	Sinn Féin	None	—
Second Dáil	Aug.1921-Sept.1922	Sinn Féin	J.J. O'Kelly/M. Hayes	Sinn Féin
Provisional	Jan.1922-Aug.1922	Pro-Treaty	F. Lynch	Pro-Treaty
	Aug.1922-Sept.1922	Pro-Treaty	E. MacNeill	Pro-Treaty
Cum. na nGael	Sept.1922-Sept.1923	Cum. na nGael	E. MacNeill	Cum. na nGael
Cum. na nGael	Sept.1923-June 1927	Cum. na nGael	E. MacNeill	Cum. na nGael
			J.M. O'Sullivan (from Jan.1926)	Cum. na nGael
Cum. na nGael	June 1927-Oct.1927	Cum. na nGael	J.M. O'Sullivan	Cum. na nGael
Cum. na nGael	Oct.1927-Mar.1932	Cum. na nGael	J.M. O'Sullivan	Cum. na nGael
Fianna Fáil	Mar.1932-Feb.1933	Fianna Fáil	T. Deirg	Fianna Fáil
Fianna Fáil	Feb.1933-July1937	Fianna Fáil	T. Deirg	Fianna Fáil
Fianna Fáil	July 1937-June 1938	Fianna Fáil	T. Deirg	Fianna Fáil
Fianna Fáil	June 1938-July 1943	Fianna Fáil	T. Deirg (to 8.9.39)	Fianna Fáil
Fianna Fáil			S.T.Ó Ceallaigh (to 27/9/39)	Fianna Fáil
Fianna Fáil			E. De Valera (to 18/6/40)	Fianna Fáil
Fianna Fáil			T. Deirg (to July 1943)	Fianna Fáil
Fianna Fáil	July 1943-May 1944	Fianna Fáil	T. Deirg	Fianna Fáil
Fianna Fáil	May 1944-Feb.1948	Fianna Fáil	T. Deirg	Fianna Fáil
Inter-Party	Feb.1948-June 1951	Fine Gael/Labour Clann na Pobl./Clann na Talm.	R. Mulcahy	Fine Gael

APPENDIX I (continued) — MINISTERS FOR EDUCATION, 1919-1991

Government	Term of Office	Parties	Minister for Education	Minister's party
Fianna Fáil	June 1951-June 1954	Fianna Fáil	S. Moylan	Fianna Fáil
Inter-Party	June 1954-March 1957	Fine Gael/Labour	R. Mulcahy	Fine Gael
		Clann na Pobl./Clann na Talm.		
Fianna Fáil	March 1957-June 1959	Fianna Fáil	J. Lynch	Fianna Fáil
Fianna Fáil	June 1959-Oct.1961	Fianna Fáil	P.J. Hillery	Fianna Fáil
Fianna Fáil	Oct.1961-April 1965	Fianna Fáil	P.J. Hillery	Fianna Fáil
Fianna Fáil	April 1965-Nov.1966	Fianna Fáil	G. Colley (to 13/7/66)	Fianna Fáil
Fianna Fáil	July 1966-Nov.1966	Fianna Fáil	D. O'Malley	Fianna Fáil
Fianna Fáil	Nov.1966-Dec.1968	Fianna Fáil	D. O'Malley (to 10/3/68)	Fianna Fáil
		Fianna Fáil	B. Lenihan	Fianna Fáil
Fianna Fáil	Dec.1968-June 1969	Fianna Fáil	B. Lenihan	Fianna Fáil
Fianna Fáil	June 1969-Feb.1973	Fianna Fáil	P. Faulkner	Fianna Fáil
Coalition	Mar.1973-July 1977	Fine Gael/Lab.	R. Burke (to 1/12/76)	Fine Gael
			P. Barry (to July,1977)	Fine Gael
Fianna Fáil	July 1977-June 1981	Fianna Fáil	J. Wilson	Fianna Fáil
Coalition	July 1981-March 1982	Fine Gael/Lab.	J. Boland	Fine Gael
Fianna Fáil	March 1982-Dec.1982	Fianna Fáil	M. O'Donoghue (to Oct.1982)	Fianna Fáil
			C.J. Haughey(6th-27 Oct.1982)	Fianna Fáil
			G. Brady	Fianna Fáil
Coalition	Dec.1982-Feb.1986	Fine Gael/Lab.	Gemma Hussey	Fine Gael
	Feb.1986-Mar.1987	Fine Gael	P. Cooney	Fine Gael
Fianna Fáil	Mar.1987-1991	Fianna Fáil	Mary O'Rourke	Fianna Fáil

APPENDIX 2

SOURCE REFERENCES

(The References are those given in the catalogue to Government Publications)

I General

I.1 The Constitution of the Irish Free State (Saorstát Éireann), 1922. **1/22**

I.2 The Ministers and Secretaries Act 1924. **16/24**

I.3 School Attendance Act, 1926. **17/26**

I.4 Report of the Inter-Departmental Committee on the Raising of the School-Leaving Age, 1935. **R.58/1; P.2086**

I.5 Bunreacht na hÉireann (Constitution of Ireland)1937. **P.P.63/1**

I.6 School Attendance Bill, 1942. **1943, I.R. 334-7**

I.7 Report of the Departmental Committee on Educational Provision, June 1947 (Unpublished).

I.8 Setting up of the Council of Education, 1950. **E.28/1**

I.9 Report of the Commission on Youth Unemployment, 1951. **R.82; Pr.709**

I.10 Investment in Education, inaugural speech, October 1962 (Unpublished).

I.11 Second Programme for Economic Expansion, 1963. **F57/1; Pr.7669**

I.12 Third Programme for Economic and Social Development, 1969 - 1972. **F.57/7**

I.13 Ár nDaltaí Uile — All Our Children 1969.

I.14 School Attendance Act, 1926 (Extension of Application) Order, 1972. **105/72**

I.15 Programme for National Development, 1978-1981. **Y7**

I.16 White Paper on Educational Development, 1980. **E89; Prl.9373**

I.17 Report of the Pupil Transfer Committee, 1981. **E92**

I.18 The Way Forward - National Economic Plan, 1983 - 87. **1982 : Y12 : Pl.1061**

I.19 Programme for Government, December 1982 (Unpublished).

I.20 Building on Reality, 1985 - 1987. **1984 : Y13 : Pl.2648**
I.21 Programme for Action in Education, 1984-1987. **E95 : Pl.2153**
I.22 Ages for Learning — Decisions of Government, May 1985.
I.23 Report of the Committee on Discipline in Schools,1985. **E100; Pl.3437**
I.24 Programme for National Recovery, October 1987. **Y19; Pl.5213**
I.25 Programme for Economic and Social Progress, January 1991.
I.26 O.E.C.D. Review of National Policies — Ireland, 1991

II National Education

II.1 First National Programme of Primary Instruction, 1922.
II.2 Circular to Inspectors, November 1922.
II.3 Second National Programme Conference, 1925-1926.
II.4 Report of the Committee on Inspection of Primary Schools, 1927. **1926-8; E.P.1**
II.5 The Primary Certificate Examination, 1929 - 1967. **Dáil Debates, 1941; Cols.1085-7 and 1097**
II.6 Circular to Managers, Teachers and Inspectors on Teaching through the medium of Irish; July 1931.
II.7 Revised Programme of Primary Instruction, 1934. **E.P.10/4**
II.8 The Infant School - An Naí-Scoil - Notes for Teachers, 1951. **1951-5; E.P.10/5**
II.9 Report of the Council of Education on the Function and the Curriculum of the Primary School, 1954. **E28/2; Pr.2583**
II.10 Primary Education Proposed Changes, December 1956. (Response of the Minister for Education to the Report of the Council of Education) (Unpublished).
II.11 Removal of the requirement to teach through the medium of Irish, Circular 11/60 to Managers and Teachers, January 1960.
II.12 Investment in Education, 1965 (Primary Education). **1966; E56; Pr.8311**
II.13 Rules for National Schools under the Department of Education — 1965. **E.P.8/11**
II.14 Abolition of the Primary Certificate Examination and introduction of the School Record Card System, March 1968.

II.15 Primary School Curriculum, Teachers' Handbook, 1971. **E81 and E81/1**

II.16 Boards of Management of National Schools, 1975, 1980 and 1986. **1986; E102**

II.17 The White Paper on Educational Development, 1980. **E.89; Prl.9373**

II.18 Programme for Action in Education , 1984-1987. **E95:Pl.2153**

II.19 Primary Education - a Curriculum and Examinations Board Discussion Paper, September1985.

II.20 Report of the Review Body on the Primary Curriculum, 1990.

II.21 Report of the Primary Education Review Body, 1990. **Pl.7632**

III Post-Primary Education

Secondary

III.1 Dáil Éireann — Commission on Secondary Education; September 1921 - December 1922.

III.2 Intermediate Education (Amendment) Act, 1924. **47/24**

III.3 The Report of the Department of Education for the School Year 1924/25 and the financial and administrative years 1924/5/6. Changes in Secondary Education. **1926/8; E.6/1**

III.4 The introduction of Irish as an essential subject for the Intermediate and Leaving Certificate Examinations, 1928 and 1934. **1922-5; E.I.53 and 1932-4; E.I.5/10**

III.5 Changes in the Secondary Schools Programme 1939/40. **Circular No.16/39**

III.6 Report of the Council of Education on the Curriculum of the Secondary School, 1962. **E.28/3; Pr.5996**

Vocational/Technical

III.7 Commission on Technical Education, 1927. **R.39**

III.8 Speech by the Minister for Education, John Marcus O'Sullivan, at the Second Stage of the Vocational Education Bill, 14 May 1930. **Dáil Debates, 14/5/1930**

III.9 The Vocational Education Act, 1930. **29/30**

III.10 Letter from the Minister for Education, John Marcus O'Sullivan, to Most Rev. D. Keane, Bishop of Limerick, dated 31st October, 1930 (Unpublished).

III.11 Apprenticeship Act, 1931. **56/31**

III.12 Memorandum V.40; Organisation of Whole-time Continuation Courses in Borough, Urban and County Areas, 1942.
III.13 Report of the Commission on Vocational Organisation, 1944. **R.76/1; P.6743**
III.14 Introduction of the Day Group Certificate Examination, 1947.
III.15 Apprenticeship Act, 1959. **39/59**
III.16 Vocational Education (Amendment) Act, 1970. **15/70**
III.17 Establishment of Boards of Management of Vocational Schools — Circular Letter 73/74 — July 1974.

Post-Primary

III.18 (**a**) Tuarascáil Shealadach ón Choiste a Chuireadh i mbun Scrúdú a Dhéanamh ar Oideachas Iarbhunscoile, 1962 (Unpublished).
III.18 Statement by the Minister for Education, Dr. P.J. Hillery, in regard to Post-Primary Education, 20 May 1963.
III.19 Investment in Education — 1966. **E.56**
III.20 Letter from George Colley, T.D., Minister for Education, to the Authorities of Secondary and Vocational Schools, January 1966.
III.21 Speech made by Donogh O'Malley, T.D., Minister for Education, on 10th September 1966 announcing the introduction of free post-primary education.
III.22 Department of Education — Community School Document — October 1970.
III.23 Report on the Intermediate Certificate Examination, 1975. **R.126; Prl.4429**
III.24 White Paper on Educational Development, 1980. **E.89**
III.25 Community Colleges, 1980.
III.26 Programme for Action in Education, 1984 - 1987. **E.95**
III.27 Vocational Preparation and Training Programmes, 1984.
III.28 Partners in Education — Serving Community Needs. A Green Paper (November 1985). **E101; 3598**
III.29 Curriculum and Examinations Board Publications
(**a**) Issues and Structures in Education September 1984
(**b**) In Our Schools, March 1986.
III.30 Transition Year Programmes — guidelines for schools, January 1986.

III.31 **(a)** The National Council for Curriculum and Assessment — A Guide to the Junior Certificate, 1989.
III.31 **(b)** N.C.C.A. The Junior Certificate Examination — Recommendations to the Minister for Education, 1990.
III.31 **(c)** N.C.C.A. The Curriculum at Junior Cycle — Curriculum Framework and Junior Certificate Requirements —a Position Paper, June 1991.
III.31 **(d)** N.C.C.A. The Curriculum at Senior Cycle: Structure, Format and Programmes — a Position Paper, June 1991.
III.32 The National Council for Vocational Awards, 1991.

IV TEACHERS — Education, Conditions of Service and Salaries, 1922-1991

IV.1 Teacher Training Colleges in Saorstát Éireann, (the Irish Free State) — Report of the Department of Education for the School Year 1923/24. **E.I.53**
IV.2 The National Programme of Primary Instruction, 1922; recommendations with regard to the training of teachers.
IV.3 Setting up of the Preparatory Colleges — Dáil Debates, 24th February, 1926.
IV.4 New Programme for the Training Colleges, 1932. **E.I.5/10**
IV.5 Report of Committee on Teachers' Salaries, 1949. **R.80; Pr.9634**
IV.6 Conciliation and Arbitration Scheme, 1951.
IV.7 Revocation of Rule 72(1) of Department's Rule (i.e. the revocation of the ban on married women teachers) January 1958. **Circular 11/58**
IV.8 Teachers' Salaries Committee, 1960. **R.99; P.5694**
IV.9 Untrained Teachers — Transfer to Trained Scale, proposal of 22 November 1965.
IV.10 Report of the Commission on Higher Education, 1967. **E59; Pr.9326**
IV.11 Ryan Tribunal on Teachers' Salaries, 1968. **E.61; Prl.87**
IV.12 H.E.A. Report on Teacher Education, 1970. **E/67**
IV.13 Setting up of Teachers' Centres, 1972. **Dáil Debates; 17/2/1972**
IV.14 Report of the Planning Committee on the Establishment of An Chomhairle Mhúinteoireachta, 1974 (Unpublished).

IV.15 Announcement of University Degrees for Primary Teachers, 1973. **Dáil Debates; 1973, 380-381**
IV.16 Thomond College of Education, Limerick, Act, 1980. **34/80**
IV.17 Review Body on Teachers' Pay — Interim Report, 1980. **E87; Prl.9232**
IV.18 White Paper on Educational Development, 1980. **E.89**
IV.19 Report of Committee on Inservice Education, 1984. **E.99; Pl.2216**
IV.20 Programme for Action in Education, 1984 - 1987. **E.95; Pr.2153**
IV.21 Announcement of the closure of Carysfort College, February 1986. **Dáil Debates, 4/3/1986**
IV.22 Report of the Primary Education Review Body, 1990. **Pl.7632**
IV.23 University of Limerick (Dissolution of Thomond College) Act, October, 1991. **16/91**
IV.24 O.E.C.D. Review of National Policies for Education in Ireland.
IV.25 Memorandum of Understanding between Mary Immaculate College and the University of Limerick, November 1991.

V Higher Education

V.1 University Education (Agriculture and Dairy Science) Act, 1926. **21/26**
V.2 University College Galway, Act, 1929. **25/29**
V.3 Bunreacht na hÉireann, 1937. **P.P.63/1**
V.4 Institute for Advanced Studies Act, 1940. **13/40**
V.5 Report of Commission on Accommodation Needs of the N.U.I. Colleges, 1959. **R.93**
V.6 Report of the Board of Visitors on U.C.D. 1960.
V.7 Report of the Commission on Higher Education, 1967.
V.8 Report of the Steering Committee on Technical Education, 1967. **Prl.371**
V.9 Minister O'Malley's University Merger Proposals, 1967. **Studies, LVI, Spring 1967**
V.10 Minister Lenihan's Statement of Government Policy on Higher Education, 1968.
V.11 The Higher Education Authority Act, 1971. **22/71**
V.12 Some Higher Education Authority Reports. **E73; P.2276**
V.13 National College of Art and Design Act, December 1971. **28.71**

V.14 The National Council for Educational Awards. **30/79**

V.15 Coalition Government Plans for a "Comprehensive" Higher-Level Sector, 1974.

V.16 Co-operative Agreement between the University of Dublin (T.C.D.) and the City of Dublin Vocational Education Committee (CDVEC), 1976.

V.17 Reorganisation of the C.D.V.E.C's third level colleges into the Dublin Institute of Technology (DIT), 1978.

V.18 Legislation for NIHEL and NIHED. **30/80**

V.19 The White Paper on Educational Development, 1980. **E.89**

V.20 Programme for Action in Education, 1984-87. **E95**

V.21 Partners in Education — Green Paper, 1985. **E101**

V.22 Report of the International Study Group on Technological Education, 1987.

V.23 University of Limerick and City of Dublin University Act, 1989. **89/14**

VI Special Issues

Special Education

VI.1 Report of the Commission of Inquiry on Mental Handicap, 1965. **K.84; Pr.8234**

VI.2 Special Education in Ireland - an article by T.A. ÓCuilleanáin, Assistant Chief Inspector, in Oideas, Autumn 1968.

VI.3 Report of a Committee set up to consider the Provision of Educational Facilities for the Children of Itinerants, 1970. **E70**

VI.4 Report of the Committee on the Education of Children who are Handicapped by Impaired Hearing, February 1972. **E75**

VI.5 Report of the Committee on the Education of Physically Handicapped Children, 1981. **E91; Pl.484**

VI.6 The White Paper on Educational Development, 1980 (Special Provision). **E89; Prl.9373**

VI.7 Report of a Working Party on the Education and Training of Severely and Profoundly Mentally Handicapped Children in Ireland, January 1983. **1984 : E96 : Pl.1969**

VI.8 Programme for Action in Education, 1984-87. **E95**

VI.9 Guidelines on Remedial Education, 1987. **1988; E105**

VI.10 Educational Provision for the Children of Travelling Families, 1989.

VI.11 Report of the Primary Education Review Body, 1990.

VI.12 Needs and Abilities — a policy for the intellectually disabled. Report of the Review Group on Mental Handicap Services, July 1990.

Reformatory Schools

VI.13 Report of the Commission of Inquiry into the Reformatory and Industrial School System, 1934-1936. **R59/1**

VI.14 Report of the Committee on Reformatory and Industrial Schools, 1970. **E68; Prl.1342**

Adult Education

VI.15 Report of the Committee on Adult Education in Ireland 1973. **Prl.3465**

VI.16 Lifelong Learning - Report of the Commission on Adult Education, 1983. **1984 : E97; Pl.2282**

Broadcasting

VI.17 Report of the Educational Broadcasting Committee, October 1982. **1984 : E98; Pl.1571**

General Equality

VI.18 Action Handbook — how to implement gender equality, 1985. **1987 : E104**

The Arts

VI.19 The Place of the Arts in Irish Education — Report of the Arts Council's Working Party on the Arts in Education 1979 (by Ciarán Benson).

VI.20 The Arts in Education — a Curriculum and Examinations Board Discussion Paper, 1985.

VI.21 Access and opportunity — a White Paper on the Arts, 1987. **Y18; Pl.4518**

VI.22 The Arts Council and Education 1979-1989.

The Irish Language

VI.23 Report of the Commission on the Restoration of the Irish Language — Summary of the Final Report, 1963. **R102 : Pr.7256**

VI.24 White Paper on the Restoration of the Irish Language, 1965. **R105; Pr.8061**

VI.25 Comhairle na Gaeilge — Irish in Education, 1974.

VI.26 The White Paper on Educational Development, 1980. **E89**

VI.27 Action Plan for Irish, 1983-1986.

VI.28 Programme for Action in Education, 1984-1987. **E95**

VI.29 Tuarascáil an Chomhchoiste um Oideachas sa Ghaeltacht, 1985.